SKENE'S
ELEMENTS OF
YACHT DESIGN

INTREPID running free.

SKENE'S ELEMENTS OF YACHT DESIGN

THE EIGHTH EDITION OF
NORMAN L. SKENE'S CLASSIC BOOK
ON YACHT DESIGN,
COMPLETELY REVISED AND UPDATED BY

FRANCIS S. KINNEY

DODD, MEAD & COMPANY   **NEW YORK**

ILLUSTRATION CREDITS

The sketch of a launching disaster on page 11 from a photograph in *The Illustrated London News* by my sister, Mrs. Arthur Gengler.

Plans of the SUNFISH on page 12: courtesy of AMF International, 261 Madison Ave., N.Y. 10016.

Photos of INTREPID's model with water pressure contours on page 22 by the author.

The picture of half models of AMERICA's Cup twelve meters on page 23: courtesy of Mr. D. W. Gardner.

The Time Allowance Table on page 28: courtesy of the North American Yacht Racing Union.

Plans of the SOLING on page 39, and the diagram of Gustav Plym's self steerer on page 162: courtesy of *Yachting World*.

Both photographs of INTREPID—frontispiece and in Chapter II—and one of YANKEE GIRL sailing on the wind in Chapter IV: courtesy of Mr. Stanley Rosenfield.

The picture of YANKEE GIRL racing at Cowes in Chapter IV by Beken & Son, Cowes, England.

The photographs of SANTA MARIA on page 50, and of the little SANTA MARIA in Chapter X: courtesy of Mr. Arthur Gengler.

Photo of SANTA MARIA's cockpit table on page 59 by the author.

Pictures of a Coast Guard boat in surf in Chapter XII: courtesy of the U.S. Coast Guard.

The graph on page 122 of optimum prismatic coefficients for narrow boats (used for multihulls) from a 1927 edition of this book: courtesy of Yachting, Inc.

All the photographs and diagrams in Chapter XIV: courtesy of the Davidson Laboratory, Stevens Institute of Technology and Mr. Pierre de Saix.

Plans of the LORCHA, a Chinese junk, on page 164: from C. R. G. Worcester's *Sail and Sweep in China,* published by Eyre and Spottiswoode, Ltd.

Illustrations of an integrator, and a spline with weights in Chapter XVIII: courtesy of Keuffel & Esser Co.

Drawing showing dimensions of the human figure on page 201: by Ernest Irving Freese from *Architectural Record* c/o McGraw-Hill, Inc.

Five drawings in Herreshoff's rules on pages 243-261: courtesy of the New York Yacht Club.

Fiberglass construction details on page 268: from *Marine Design Manual for Fiberglass Reinforced Plastics* by Engineers of Gibbs and Cox, Inc. Copyright 1960 McGraw-Hill, Inc.

The table on electric wire size on page 304: courtesy of the National Fire Protection Association, Boston, Mass.

All the photographs of the PIPE DREAM Cruising Sloop SOUTHERLY used as an example throughout: courtesy of Mr. Ragnar Widen, Kungsor, Sweden.

The Table of Pipe Davits on page 327: courtesy of *The Rudder* and Mr. Robert M. Steward.

CONTENTS

Determine Mast Section — Testing a Model to Destruction — Tangs —
Chain Plate Sizes — SANTA MARIA's Aluminum Mast Details

Section Modulus — Freeboard — Free Surface — Frahm Antirolling Tanks —
Trials — Range — Fuel Consumption — Gasoline — Diesel Oil — Electrical
Loads — Wiring Size — Wire Sizes for Amperes — How to Calculate the
Horsepower Needed to Run an Alternator — SANTA MARIA's
Wiring Diagram

SKENE'S
ELEMENTS OF
YACHT DESIGN

ACKNOWLEDGMENTS

In writing and illustrating the eighth edition of this trusted work, first published in 1904, and for whatever its small contribution to knowledge may be, I should like to thank the following people for their help with it:

Mr. P. de Saix
Mr. F. G. du Pont
Mrs. A. Gengler
Mr. A. A. Gilbert
Mr. R. B. Harris
Mr. A. Mason
Mr. K. Meyer
Mr. J. B. McPherson
Mrs. M. McVeigh
Mr. D. R. Pedrick
Mr. H. J. Pierce
Mr. P. L. Rhodes
Mr. A. Rusich
Miss D. Russell
Mr. O. J. Stephens II
Mr. R. Stephens Jr.
Mr. G. G. Wyland
and my wife, Mary F. Kinney

FRANCIS S. KINNEY

Huntington, New York

Particulars of 19 Designs Shown Here from Shortest to Longest Water-Line Length

Name	L.O.A.	D.W.L.	Beam	Draft	Sail Area in Sq. Ft.	Displacement in Pounds
DORY	12′ 0″	10′ 0″	3′ 6″	4″	Oars	125
SUNFISH	13′ 10″		4′ 0″		75	139
SOLING	26′ 9″	20′ 0″	6′ 3″	4′ 3″	250	2,200
TREMELINO	28′ 7″	21′ 3″	8′ 4″	3′ 0″	367	6,670
FIDELIA	29′ 0″	21′ 3″	8′ 4″	3′ 0″	387	7,000
LORNA DOONE	33′ 0″	25′ 0″	10′ 6″	3′ 0″	613	13,950
SOUTHERLY	36′ 7″	25′ 5″	10′ 6″	5′ 8″	616	13,450
SANTA MARIA	43′ 5″	29′ 0″	11′ 0″	6′ 2″	786	20,200
ENDEAVOUR	42′ 10″	30′ 0″	12′ 0″	2′ 10″	825	21,500
WAUPI	45′ 0″	31′ 3″	12′ 0″	6′ 6″	880	23,400
MISCHIEF	42′ 7″	32′ 0″	13′ 0″	4′ 3″	936	26,600
MALU	41′ 8″	33′ 0″	13′ 11″	4′ 6″	774	33,800
YANKEE GIRL	55′ 8″	40′ 0″	14′ 4″	8′ 4″	1,355	37,150
INTREPID	68′ 0″	45′ 0″	12′ 0″	8′ 1″	1,750	66,357
COLUMBIA	69′ 5″	45′ 6″	11′ 10″	8′ 11″	1,846	56,890
EGRET	56′ 6″	47′ 0″	15′ 3″	4′ 7″	1,361	70,200
TOREA	57′ 6″	47′ 0″	16′ 4″	7′ 0″	1,376	85,950
PALAWAN	67′ 6″	50′ 6″	17′ 6″	6′ 8″	1,926	98,000
RANGER	135′ 2″	87′ 0″	21′ 0″	15′ 0″	7,950	372,990

CHAPTER I

INTRODUCTION

The fascination of designing boats is perfectly summed up by these lines by John Masefield:

> When I saw her masts across the
>   River rising queenly,
> Built out of so much chaos
>   Brought to law,
> I learned the power of knowing
>   How to draw,
> Of beating through into the
>   Perfect line:
> I vowed to make that power of
>   Beauty mine.

There is something about boats which makes one feel they are living creatures—each as different from her sisters as human beings are from each other. The very fact that one refers to a boat as "she" shows that since time began men have loved their boats. What is it that gives a boat such personality?

Is it a series of compromises that combine speed, comfortable accommodations, and seaworthiness in just the right proportion? Or is it more than the attainment of these functional qualities—that certain thing that makes these qualities fall into harmony—that most elusive thing called beauty?

"Eureka! I have found it!" cried Archimedes, about 2200 years ago. It is a happy moment, indeed, when the designer can utter these words himself.

Science is an important aid in designing any kind of a yacht, but the rudiments of naval architecture are not difficult to grasp and are set forth here in their most practical form. It is hoped that this book will be of definite use to yacht designers, both amateur and professional alike.

Since three quarters of the earth's surface is covered by water, the need for boats will always exist. That over eight million boats are registered in the United States alone shows the great wave of interest in boating which has caught the public's fancy.

"The simplest design is usually the best" is a good rule by which to judge a design. It is easy to make things complicated and expensive, but it requires a great deal of thought, combined with experience, to keep a design simple, practical, and inexpensive. The eraser should be the most useful tool used by a designer, and he should never be afraid to use it! "Beating through into the perfect line," as Masefield says, means using the eraser—again, again, and again.

A Skene Chock well-known to yachts-men.

To try and describe how to make a boat look beautiful is just about impossible. One can work one's heart out and make a design look well on paper, only to discover to one's horror that when the boat is first launched, she is an ugly duckling.

Perhaps the one single line that crowns or damns the whole creation is the sheer line. It may look well in plan view on paper, and it may look well in profile view on paper, but be careful—some peculiar effects can happen in the three-dimensional view. To ensure the chances of not producing an ugly duckling, the prudent designer or prospective owner should have a half model made before building his dream boat. In this respect, the old method of starting a design from a model was superior.

"Good design makes use of that which has gone before" is another good motto to go by. In fact, almost every new boat is based on one that has gone before, starting with the cave man's log canoe. Each succeeding design should aim to improve upon its forerunner. Before starting a new design, it is wise for the architect to do some research to discover how others may have handled the same problem. Then try to do it better. There is a happy medium between extreme originality or novelty, which tends to produce a freak design, and direct copying, which no designer worth his salt would even consider. Be conservative! Safety of life is involved. Any boat should be designed to weather that one hard, unexpected squall that may knock her down, swamp her, and sink her, resulting in serious injury or loss of life.

Another important aspect in designing is the effect of waves on the hull. The shape of the sections at the bow and stern are most important in both sail and power boat design. In a sailboat, if the bow sections are a flat U-shape, the bow will pound and slam into the waves, with the spray being thrown well out. On the other hand, if these same sections are a deep V-shape, there will be no pounding, but the spray will be thrown up and blow back over the deck, soaking the crew. There is a happy compromise between these shapes. This shape is very critical and was brought to my attention many years ago when sailing boats of two different designs, both from the board of the same designer, the late Charles D. Mower. One, a Vineyard Sound Interclub sloop, had a beautiful, long overhanging bow which had flat U-sections at the entrance. She had what I would call a wet bow. The other boat was a Katama-class sloop of the same water line length, but not such a long bow. This change in the profile produced sections at the entrance only slightly different from the Vineyard class. The speed of both designs was almost identical when comparing times over triangular courses on the same afternoons. The Katama had the better bow and did not soak her crew with spray every time a wave was encountered. "Seakindly" describes her.

In powerboats the same principle applies. Here the introduction of a spray guard is often helpful to force the spray out and away from the hull. Some of these

Development of sailing yachts over a period of ninety years

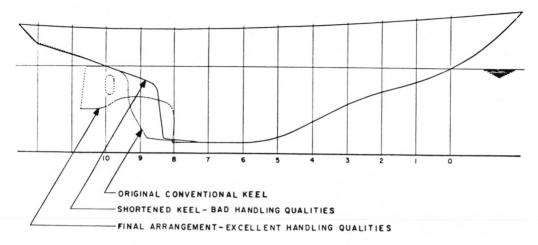

ORIGINAL CONVENTIONAL KEEL

SHORTENED KEEL — BAD HANDLING QUALITIES

FINAL ARRANGEMENT — EXCELLENT HANDLING QUALITIES

The changes made to BAYBEA's underwater configuration increased her speed and improved her steering so much that most competitive sailboats designed today incorporate them.

are even placed below the water line when the boat is at rest, so as to be that much lower when the bow lifts when at full operating speed. An inverted bell shape is excellent for the section of a power boat bow, because it combines the soft-riding and spray-throwing qualities required in order to be seakindly.

As for the stern, the problem here is to avoid sucking up a big stern wave which slows up the boat and makes her squat. Here the sections should be flat; that is, they should have a very shallow angle to the water level to produce a desirable flat wake. When you see a boat going through the water leaving little or no disturbance, there is a good design. Of course, the length of the boat in displacement or nonplaning types determines the speed. The square root of the designed water line times 1.25 equals the speed in knots.

A good illustration of the speed-length ratio is the familiar sight in New York harbor of a large vessel, such as the QUEEN MARY, entering the North River at, say, ten knots (which is about one-third of her full speed), with a group of tugboats and other small craft running alongside at the same speed (full speed for them). The QUEEN MARY will not even show a bow wave, and her wake will be as flat as a pancake, while the tugs and various small craft will seem to be pushing a huge bow wave before them and sucking up the whole harbor behind.

New materials made by man are augmenting nature's best material—wood. Plywood, impregnated fiberglass, and welded aluminum construction, as well as the old standby, welded steel construction, and ferro cement are being used with more and more success. Each has its advantages, whether it be light weight, reduced maintenance, freedom from rot, greater strength, watertightness, or more usable space inside the boat. Each also has its disadvantages: proneness to corrosion, greater initial cost, brittleness, inflammability, greater weight, lack of resistance to abrasion, possibility of metal fatigue, chance of cracking due to vibration, and others. The successful designer will incorporate many of these materials in one boat, and he must know where each can be used to best advantage. For example, a wooden boat may be built with a plywood deck, covered with fiberglass. She may have a weldment of galvanized steel for her mast step, a centerboard and trunk of bronze, aluminum hatches, and aluminum masts. Or a fiberglass boat may have a wooden cockpit coaming, simply to make it friendly to the touch—like a mahogany bar in a saloon. Or again, a steel boat may have a teak deck to take the curse off too much metal as well as to reduce excessive heat and sweating below.

It should be the ambition of every designer to contribute his part to progress in the art, whether it be from knowledge derived at sea, in the building yards, or at the testing tanks. There is always room for improvement.

The English language is full of terms and sayings from our nautical heritage. I can think of many illustrations:

"Learn the ropes" and "Know the ropes" need no explanation.

"I like the 'cut of your jib'" is a compliment to a person just as it is to the shape of that sail, when well made and well set.

Another, almost directly from a boat's structure, is "to keep things on an even keel."

Also, when you are sick, you are "laid up."

There's too much "backing and filling" when a person can't make up her mind (sails aback when the ship is hove to, or filling when getting underway).

Then, when this person has made up her mind, everything's all "squared away" (when a sailing ship runs before the wind her yards are that way).

"Between the devil and the deep" comes from a sailor's job of caulking a difficult seam under the stern called the devil seam. When a sailor had to do this job at sea he was literally hanging on a bosun's chair between the devil and the deep blue sea. This devil seam is now called the garboard seam. "Between the devil and the deep" also referred to the critical moment of a keel hauling—the midpoint in that punishment, when a man was hauled down under the ship and up the other side, barnacles cutting him badly.

"The devil to pay" was properly "the devil to pay and no pitch hot" when the ship was heaved over on the beach and the tide was coming in. Paying a seam was done by covering the caulked oakum or cotton with hot pitch.

"Posh" is another word. It is derived from accommodations when steaming from England to the Far East. The ticket agent selling a steamer passenger a round-trip ticket for the best stateroom each way would mark the ticket "P.O.S.H.," which stood for Port side Out, Starboard side Home, this being the shady side of the ship, hence the coolest and best in each direction.

The term "son of a gun" originated in Elizabethan times, when it was difficult to get men to serve in the British navy. These unfortunates were shanghaied, and once aboard were never allowed ashore when their frigate returned to port for fear that most of them would jump ship, and because of the difficulty of impressing replacements. So to help prevent this from happening plenty of grog was issued, and women were brought aboard by small boats from the local taverns. Suffice it to say the male progeny of these unions on the gun deck were referred to by the term "son of a gun."

"By and large": Few people using this expression realize that it came from sailing by the wind and at large, usually when entering a spacious harbor or roadstead.

"Bitter end" means the anchor chain is all out of the locker. For yachtsmen the bitter ends of halyards must be made fast so they won't travel up the mast when let go.

In this sailor's language there are several dictionaries of nautical words available, some of them running over four hundred pages long with eight thousand words or more defined. These are the words that are, or have been, used by seamen in connection with their work.

Out of this vast nautical vocabulary I should like to list *eight motions of a boat at sea:*
Roll—To incline rhythmically first to one side then the other when in a seaway.
Pitch—To plunge so that the bow and stern rise and fall in the water.

The pitching of a sailboat beating to windward can be, like a hobby horse, so violent as to stop her, when her length coincides and is in tune with the wave length between crests. If you want to come about, she will be "in irons." To get her going again divide your crew and spread them as far forward near the bow and as far aft near the stern as possible. Then ease sheets and sail her "full and by."

Most of the time, on the other hand, the wave length is either shorter or longer than the boat's length. So it pays to keep the weights, including the crew, as near amidships as possible. It slows a boat down, when racing, if a weight such as the anchor is stowed way forward on the bow, because its weight must be lifted by each oncoming wave. There is more resistance in the sailboat so commanded than there is in a sister ship whose skipper stows his anchor amidships.

Heave—The rise and fall of the entire boat at sea.
Yaw—to lurch, or swing, to either side of a course. Rotation about the verticle axis.
Surge—Forward and aft motion due to the swell of the sea. Acceleration and deceleration.
Sway—Broadside motion from side to side.
Broach To—To swing to the wind by accident when running free, through bad steering or by the force of a heavy sea. Dangerous because when a boat is swung across the cresting seas and in a trough, she may be knocked down and founder, or at least lose her masts.
Pitch Poll—A disaster to a boat in which a breaking sea astern casts her stern over bow in a forward half-somersault. Among others who have had this experience

is Sir Francis Chichester in the latitude of the "Roaring Forties," sailing from Australia to Cape Horn. In his case he was running before it under bare poles in steep cresting seas. Although his boat was much too tender, as you can tell by looking at the pictures of her under sail, she righted herself because of her deep lead ballast keel and water-tight integrity. He did not lose his rig, and sailed home to tell about it.

This book is about designing single-hull vessels and does not attempt to cover multi-hull craft, namely catamarans, trimarans and such.

Catamarans are undoubtedly the fastest sailboats. "One mile per hour per foot and more" their enthusiasts say about their craft's speed. Bob Harris' design BEVERLY, a 25-foot catamaran, sailed at a high speed of 21.6 knots on a broad reach. This was officially clocked in the One of a Kind Regatta held by *Yachting* magazine in Miami a few years ago. The wind was blowing 22 knots at the time. Steve Dashew's 32-foot catamaran BEOWULF made the incredible record of 31.7 m.p.h. over a measured mile on a close reach behind the Long Beach break-water this year. The breeze was 26 m.p.h. But just as every rose must have its thorn, so the beauty of sailing so fast has a thorny point, which is an inherent tendency to capsize. When knocked down by a squall, a catamaran will not lie on her side and right herself again, but will flip right over upside down with her mast pointing at the bottom. Granted, small ones do provide great sport speeding close to shore. Although I may be wrong, in my opinion you should never go to sea in one, because it might be a fatal mistake.

Trimarans are probably a little safer, because when the leeward pontoon starts to submerge you have some warning, but the unescapable fact is that all multi-hull craft tend to tear their hulls apart. There is a constant twisting and separating strain as the two or three hulls of such craft meet the waves in a seaway at different moments, and out of cycle. They may sink from leaking badly at strained joints, or just fall apart and sink after capsizing. The old feeling that a sailor acquires in childhood is basically right. That is, the single-hull sailboat with a lot of ballast as low on her keel as possible is the safest.

Some people cannot understand why a steel ship floats. Their thinking is that, since steel cannot float by itself, a ship built of it cannot float. All they have to do is take an empty tin can and try floating it in a sink full of water. As long as air is inside, it will float, but when filled with water it sinks, just as the TITANIC did.

Displacement means the act of displacing. Suppose a bathtub is filled to the brim. In order to take a bath a person gets in the tub, and what happens? The water runs over the top, because he is displacing it with his body.

Now suppose it was a big enough tub, like a small swimming pool, so that he was able to float in it. And suppose also that you could collect every drop of the overflowing water and weigh it. You would discover, just as Archimedes did over 2000 years ago, that the displaced water weighs exactly the same as the person who floated in the tub.

Archimedes' principle in part is applied in determining the displacement of boats. The volume beneath the water surface of a floating boat displaces a certain volume of water. When the weight of this volume of water is determined, it is found to weigh exactly the same as the boat. So when you find the total weight of a boat, you know where on her lines she will float by calculating that submerged volume. (How to do this is explained in Chapter XXIII, A Manual of Calculations.)

But unexpected things happen at first launchings. If she floats deeper than predicted, she is heavier than the designer has estimated. If she floats higher than expected, even when fully loaded, she is lighter than her designer's estimate, perhaps because the builder was able to save weight in her construction.

The weight of a metal ship can be more accurately estimated, because we know exactly what the metal weighs, but wooden ships are built of a material which differs in moisture content, soakage of water and species of tree, not only from country to country, but from plains to mountain forests. So we never really know exactly what wood weighs. It would thus be advisable for a designer to have his track shoes handy for a quick getaway at the first launching of his wooden creation!

I know of three instances in which boat performances badly embarrassed their designers at launching time. One boat, a wooden motorsailer, floated five inches above her designed water line when loaded. She had to have more outside lead ballast to bring her down. Although it was expensive, it actually made her a better boat. Needless to say, her designer reduced his fee.

Another case of bad performance at launching time involved a 48-foot fiberglass yawl. She was 17 inches out of trim, 9 inches down by the bow, and 8 inches high aft. Shoddy construction methods and lack of attention to the plans by her builder were not corrected in time. Unfortunately, most of her lead ballast, which was all inside, was poured too far forward. It all had to be chipped out later with an air hammer at a frightful cost, then repoured exactly as designed.

The worst launching I have ever seen a picture of was a 480-ton steel Italian tanker. Two pictures appeared in the *Illustrated London News* many years ago! First, one of her sliding down the ways stern first with flags flying and spectators waving. Second, a most dramatic picture taken a few moments after she hit the water. She rolled over on her side and was sinking! As the last blocks were taken away, the ship heeled over and went down the slipway listing to starboard. Officials, workmen, women and children, who had been allowed on board for the launching, were thrown into the harbor. A dozen workers who were below were trapped, but all were rescued by harbor craft and firemen. Her name was the PIERO RIEGO GAMBINI, and it happened in Naples.

I sincerely hope that this book in its small way will be used to advantage to

A NAVAL ARCHITECT'S NIGHTMARE
THAT HAPPENED!

help avoid such human errors. It is written in layman's language, not from the point of view of an engineer, which should make it easy to understand for those of us like me with little or no technical training.

In all design work it is most important to check calculations several times, and as a further check to do them another way. For this reason, wherever possible, I have given two or more different methods for calculating the following: displacement, immersion, stability, trim, scantlings, spar sections, rigging loads, horsepower and propellers. All calculations are presented in their simplest short cut form with no attempt made to derive the theory behind each. These short cuts have been added to my notebook over a thirty-year period, and are here presented as a collection of methods, charts, rules and formulae on how to design yachts. In conclusion, let me tell you of that fine feeling shipmates have for their sailing craft.

I noticed when sailing, every time the wind freshens, a sustained lifting of the spirits in which it seems almost at times as if you become the ship, and the ship becomes you. . . . *You*, if you are the helmsman with your hands on the rim of the wheel, feel the ship respond to your commands, but not your commands alone, for she is also obeying the commands of the wind and sea. *You*, if you are one of the crew who winches in a jib sheet and gives the ship an extra quarter of a knot's speed, or just if you ease the mizzen sheet an inch or two, so the ensign flies free at its peak. *You*, even if you are the cook whose accomplishment is cooking a hot meal for all hands, when she is sailing on her ear in a lump of a sea. She is your ship now. And now your shipmates cling to her weather rail affectionately, or nod their heads at each other as proud relatives might, or say warmly, "Feel her go. She's a good ship," or "This is what she wants."

Family fun boat or spirited racer—the SUNFISH is today's most popular one-design sailing class. Simple, easy-to-handle rig makes her the perfect boat for the beginner, yet even the most advanced sailor finds her exciting to sail, challenging. Portability, too, is an important feature.

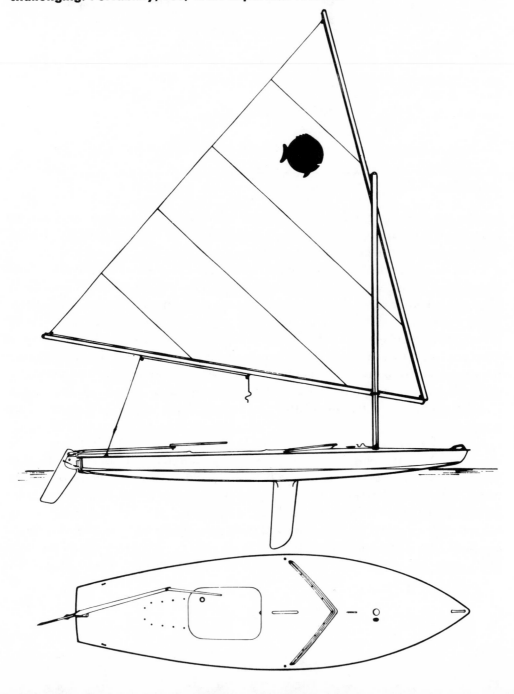

CHAPTER II
UPKEEP

She scorns the man whose heart is faint
And doesn't show him pity.
And like a girl, she needs the paint
To keep her looking pretty.

"It's not the initial cost; it's the upkeep." This is the expense that stops most people from becoming boat owners. Just how much is the upkeep per year? Not many owners will tell you—they don't want their wives to know.

An accurate answer to this question would depend on two basic facts: (a) How much work does the owner do himself, and (b) What type of material is the boat made of. Assuming that the owner is not the "do it yourself" type, we can come up with some fair guesses based on the original cost of the boat:

For wooden and steel boats, say 5 to 12% per year.

For aluminum and fiberglass, say 2 to 5% per year.

It simply is not honest to say that upkeep costs can be eliminated entirely. The bottom of every boat must be painted at least once a year with antifouling paint, no matter what her construction.

A designer should be, and usually is, a boat owner himself. He will thus have firsthand knowledge of maintaining a boat. With this knowledge, acquired as a ship's husband, he should be able to incorporate features, in his new designs, that will reduce upkeep. His clients will be happy owners, instead of being plagued with major repair bills and repeatedly expensive outfitting charges, finally selling their boats in disgust.

Planning ahead can reduce repairs and maintenance to a minimum. Remember always that the simplest design is usually the best. It is not easy to achieve simplicity. The great temptation is to make things complicated. The more equipment and the more gadgets that are added means that there are that many more things to go wrong. Putting them right takes time and money. It should be the responsibility of every designer, therefore, to keep the following practical ideas in mind when designing a new boat:

Keep the bilge clear and clean.

Bilge tanks are a poor idea. They prevent the tightening of keel bolts and hinder cleaning.

Tanks should never be built into a boat so that they cannot be removed. A situation where a tank must be cut in half to be removed is no credit to the designer. Tanks should be heavy and well made. Rivets may tear loose from the force of liquid sloshing about, so an ample number of baffle plates are required. Personally, I like Monel metal for tanks; in the long run it is worth the extra cost.

Flexible lines of hose should be used for tank fills, particularly on fuel tanks. They always seem to come apart and leak at the deck connection, due either to the working of the ship itself or to just plain poor pipe fitting. Usually they don't allow for the crown of the deck when threading the deck plate to its pipe, and so the threads are stripped, causing leaks here. So, by specifying an oil-tight hose in the line at this point, the designer sets up a fool-proof system for minimum maintenance.

Gasoline vents should be located high to the atmosphere, with a flameproof screen covering their enlarged opening.

Flexible oil-tight hose connections between fuel supply lines and engines are a must, to absorb vibration. If copper tubing is used by itself here, it becomes brittle with fatigue, after a year or so of shaking, and will crack and leak. A fire or an explosion can easily be caused by neglect of this requirement.

Keep the engine dry and clean; the same for generators and wiring. Distributors and carburetors must be accessible, as these are the most vital parts of a gasoline engine. It's not a bad idea to locate an engine in a stateroom, with a box over it and air ducts to it. The box is easily removed and forms a good table.

An engine should be installed so that it can be cranked by hand. There should be a proper oil-tight drip pan beneath, to keep grease and oil confined to this one spot.

Ventilation of the entire boat is important, ventilation of engines particularly so. Remember that diesels suck in a tremendous amount of air. Natural ventilation

How to clean a fuel strainer

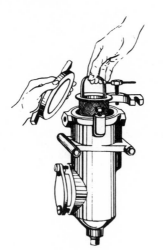

Every boat should have its fuel tank designed like this. It eliminates trouble with water and dirt in the fuel by collecting such matter in its special sump. This water and dirt is easily lifted out in the removable tube shown.

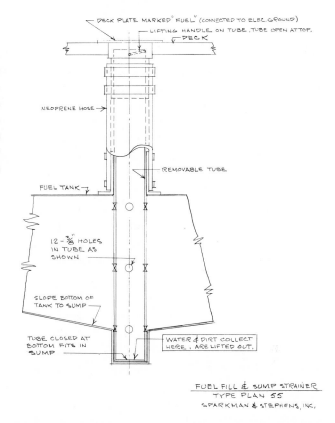

is the best. Blowers require attention, and even the best of them are not sparkproof.

Smoke pipe installations must be laid out so as to draw properly, otherwise, back drafts may asphyxiate those below.

Exhaust lines should be laid out to prevent sea water from entering the engine. Exhaust pipes should be made up in sections, so as to be easily removable. Use a heavy gauge copper, say .109-inch, particularly on water-jacketed exhausts for diesels. As a rule, diesels have higher-capacity pumps on their cooling water systems. Because of this, water flows through the water-jacketed exhaust at a faster rate; it corrodes the tubing in less time. To keep sea water out of the exhaust it is good design to install vertical mufflers, if possible. The gate valve is also good for this purpose. If an engine is idle for very long, there's bound to be some condensation inside the pipe, which can get into the valve chambers in small amounts, enough to cause damage. A T pipe connection with a short, vertical pipe extending downward makes a good trap. Have a plug at the bottom for drainage.

Toilets, unless properly installed, can sink a boat. The discharge line should have a vented loop, high above the water line, so as to prevent back siphoning, and of course, the intake and discharge lines must have sea cocks.

Bilge pumps also, if improperly installed, may produce the reverse of what they are supposed to do, siphoning the water into a boat instead of pumping it out. Check valves are not reliable, so use the vented loop placed high above the water line as a nonsiphoning device.

Rudders must be well reinforced. If it is not possible to put in a generous number of drifts through the wooden blade to the stock, then flat bar straps should be welded to the rudderstock and riveted to the blade. Rudders take more of a beating when the boat is hove to and going backwards. The deep, narrow ones do a better job than the shallow, long ones. Rudder ports should have flange plates with gaskets bolted to the horn timber of wooden boats. Just a pipe, threaded and screwed in the wood, is not enough to take the punishment required of this fitting. If the rudderstock projects far above the horn timber, it should be supported at the top, or trouble will occur.

Electrical wiring should be fastened with insulated clips, so that no mechanical damage will occur to the insulation on the wire. How often one sees a metal staple cutting into the insulation on wiring! In a year or so such wire will be short-circuited. Rewiring is expensive, so a little attention here will save a lot of headaches later.

> "And like a girl, she needs the paint
> To keep her looking pretty."

I have noticed that when an experienced owner orders a new boat, he will specify that there should not be any varnished surfaces. Or perhaps the varnished brightwork will be limited to just a few handrails or moldings. How sensible! Do you remember the wooden station wagon bodies of not so long ago? How quickly the wood turned black, if it was not revarnished often. That's what happens to varnished surfaces on a boat, but faster around salt water.

Where a painted surface will require one new coat every year, a varnished surface will need three coats of varnish in the same length of time. At least five coats of varnish are required for a new surface and then three per year thereafter. So paint the surface, instead of varnishing, and save on upkeep.

It's that varnished mahogany foredeck, sparkling in the lights at the Motor Boat Show, that sells outboard runabouts. The appearance is most attractive, but from a maintenance point of view nothing could be worse. The beating from salt water spray is too much for any varnish. This is why you always see powerboat people washing down their boats with fresh water. Some captains prefer to save the work of revarnishing by covering the forward face of their varnished deck-houses with canvas to keep the spray off. Why not paint it in the beginning? Another bad thing about a varnished wooden foredeck is that it's very slippery, especially when wet. Not only impractical, but dangerous. Boatmen beware!

Powdered pumice when mixed with any paint and applied to a deck will make an excellent nonskid surface. Heavy canvas, say Number 8, makes a good rough surface. But you should be careful not to put too much paint on it, or it can build up to a smooth, slippery surface soon. Teak left bare makes the nicest surface of all, but it is heavy and expensive.

After experimenting with several different wooden boats over a period of 30 years or so, it is my opinion that the number one way to save on upkeep is to leave the boat in the water all year round. Why is that?

Well, in the first place, it's better for the boat because she is in her element. This means she is supported evenly, over her entire bottom, by water. If she were hauled out, as most boats are for half the year, she would be sitting high and dry, supported at only a few points by keel blocks and uprights pushing into her unevenly at each point of support. Every time she is hauled and launched, she suffers the greatest strain, prolonged by staying ashore. In the second place, the drying-out process ashore is not good because it shrinks the planking and opens the seams; so the seams must be filled before painting and launching, requiring time, labor, and money.

Another saving in wet storage is that you can leave the mast in place, instead of taking it out and putting it in, year in, year out.

Paint on a mast should stand up well for two or three years in all weather. It's possible to paint the mast every third year from a bosun's chair and never take the mast out. Of course, if it's an aluminum mast, you can practically forget it.

In Northern ports, boat owners are afraid of ice. However, if the boat is properly laid up and secured in a good location, even the thickest ice can do no damage. One of the ways to avoid ice damage is to tie the boat to floats in a marina, well protected from storms from all directions. The boat, the ice, and the floats will then all rise and fall together with the tide. The danger comes when the ice moves past the hull. This is why a boat should never be left at a mooring in the ice where the slightest current will move ice past it. Thin sheet ice cuts planking like a knife. But thick ice in a well-protected boat basin doesn't hurt the boat a bit.

In the winter of 1961 the ice was 23 inches thick around our boat, and that spring there was not even a scratch on her bottom paint. We walked around the boat on the ice, sprinkling rock salt close to the hull. This melted through and kept her free. Better than rock salt for keeping a boat free of ice are devices now available for blowing air bubbles underneath on each side of the hull. The tiny bubbles seem to prevent ice from forming where they rise. This may be due to the warm water being brought to the surface, or to the motion created by the rising bubbles. These devices consist of a small compressor, electrically driven and automatically controlled by a thermostat, with a hose or pipe having small holes to allow the air to escape.

It's a good idea to have a well-ventilated winter cover, using the boom as a ridge pole. It will keep the snow and ice off the deck and rain water out of the scuppers. This is important if the boat is left in the water, because the rain water will freeze in the scuppers. Of course all through hull connections should have sea cocks. Close the sea cocks. Disconnect their pipes or hoses and drain each system. Then you have eliminated the danger of sinking from frozen bursting pipes.

On our boat it's easy to lay up the engine for the winter. There is a long hose running from the water pump to the intake sea cock. We disconnect this after shutting the sea cock. Then with the engine running, the hose is put in a bucket of fresh water which is sucked in by the water pump, thus flushing out the salt in the system. Next, we mix a solution of antifreeze and fresh water and put the same hose in this bucketful. The engine pumps antifreeze through the whole cooling system, including the water-jacketed exhaust. It remains there all winter. That's all we do, just that. Sounds simple, and it is.

In this way things are well laid up for the winter on our good little ship, and the long winter months pass slowly into spring.

With the spring come the long days of scraping, sanding, painting, more sanding, and painting again. This ''sea fever'' that drives us to such hard work is in our blood and cannot be denied.

INTREPID close hauled on the port tack.

CHAPTER III

TWELVE METERS

Today perhaps the most specialized branch of yacht designing lies in the field of designing a 12-meter yacht for the America's Cup competition.

A lot of time, effort and money ($1,000,000 to design, tank-test many models, build and campaign one boat for one season) are spent every few years in the attempt to defend this cup by members of the New York Yacht Club, or to win it by individuals from other nations.

This international contest originated in England in 1853 when the schooner AMERICA first won an ornate piece of silverware, to which has been given her name. At first two masted gaff-rigged schooners were used, then gaff-rigged sloops evolved into the huge "J"-class sloops. In the beginning these were gaff rigged with topsails and later improved with the modern jib-headed rig, the best of which was probably the RANGER in 1937. Since 1958 these races have been sailed by the considerably smaller sloops known as "Twelve Meters."

12-meter COLUMBIA alongside "J"-class RANGER.

The term does not mean that they are 12 meters long, but rather that the result of a series of measurements in the formula* used gives a rating which must not exceed 12 meters (39.37 feet). Actually the water-line length is a little more than 45 feet. Because of the flexibility of the formula more of one factor must be countered by less of another. Designers have found that a large boat with a small rig will often beat a smaller boat with greater sail area (each design having the same class rating of 12 meters).

Some average figures show the development of the 12-meter class over the years.

	1930s	1938	1958–1962	1964	1967	1970
Water-line length, ft.	45.0	45.5	46.3	47.0	47.5	48.6
Displacement, lbs.	60,000	60,400	63,400	64,000	66,000	70,000
Sail area, sq. ft.	1,890	1,880	1,820	1,800	1,750	1,725
Heeling force for 30° heel angle, lbs.	3,100	3,300	3,600	3,750	3,832	4,700
Speed Made Good to Windward-knots						
Light wind	5.0	5.0	5.0	4.9	5.0	5.0
Moderate wind	6.3	6.4	6.5	6.6	6.7	6.8
Strong wind	6.5	6.7	6.9	7.0	7.1	7.5

It has been found that by putting more displacement into the afterbody the stern wave can be flattened, which is quite advantageous over a range of speeds. Nothing new about this, because AMERICA literally and figuratively reversed the design of a sailboat end for end, since she was finer forward and fuller aft than her contemporaries of the older "Cod's head-mackerel tail" type. Her success impressed her character on most yachts that followed her. Many yachts of that time had their bows lengthened—witness the many altered models on the walls of the New York Yacht Club model room, showing the quick enthusiasm with which this new hull form was accepted.

That model collection in the N.Y.Y.C. is really fascinating to anyone interested in yachts. It is unquestionably the finest collection in the U.S.A., worth at least one million dollars. A visitor has the pleasure of seeing how the design of yachts has evolved over the past hundred years by simply starting at the door and walking slowly around the room counterclockwise. For each race in the America's Cup series there is a glass case containing two fully rigged models, one of the defender, the other of the challenger. It starts with AMERICA and progresses to the present "Twelves." At one time I had the job of taking off the lines from several builders' half models there for the Smithsonian Institution. Then later it was a pleasure to serve on the model committee as a member, so I speak glowingly about these models from experience.

The growth in length and displacement, and the reduced sail area according

* 12 meters, or 39.37 ft. $= \dfrac{\text{Length} + 2 \text{ girth diff.} + \sqrt{\text{sail area}} - \text{freeboard}}{2.37}$

All dimensions in meters or feet are as defined by the International Yacht Racing Union.

to rule requirements, has made the search for lower wetted surface of the hull—hence less resistance—a necessity. The short keel came as the answer. But the rudder on a short keel is so far forward as to make steering almost unmanageable. (The 5.5 Meter Class is a case in point.) So the rudder was separated from the keel and relocated as far aft as possible with a small skeg in front of it. Nothing new about this either, as this was done at the turn of the century for the same reasons (the Star Class designed in 1903 is an example). It is interesting to note that this type was first designed without the skeg, which was added later to improve steering.

The first twelve-meter to have two rudders was INTREPID. She had one on

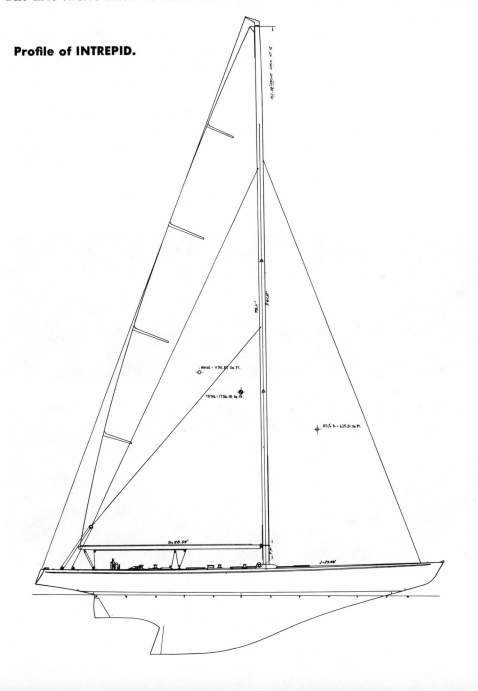

Profile of INTREPID.

her short keel, which served, like the flap on an airplane's wing, to give her an added lift to windward, when set at the optimum angle (found by helmsman Bill Ficker to be two degrees), also one well aft, and quite shallow, for steering only. The helmsman had the complication of three steering wheels to master, one inside the other. The outside, or largest, was for the aft rudder, the mid-size for the forward rudder, and the smallest for the connecting clutch. Both rudders could be used simultaneously for tight turns in maneuvering for the best starting position before the gun.

An entirely new fish's eye view, below the wave line, of dynamic water pressure on INTREPID's model, when beating to windward. Like a weather map it shows highs and lows. The highest pressure is at the bow and just abaft the rudder (where the water in these parts moves along with the boat). The lowest pressure is just above the keel amidships on the windward side (where the water speed is greatest). Also there is a low in the same spot on the leeward side, but only one third as low. The difference between these lows gives the lift pressure.

Two things are apparent that we already know. The "V" sections of the keel are doing a good job lifting her to windward, as shown by the many closely spaced contours there, and the best place to locate a speedometer hull unit is about 30% aft, the dividing contour between high and low, where there is zero pressure (true water speed).

When other models are studied in this manner the comparisons should be meaningful.

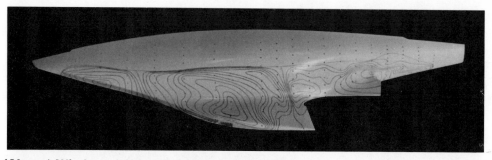

(Above) Windward Side; (Below) Leeward Side.

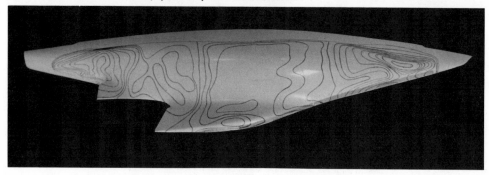

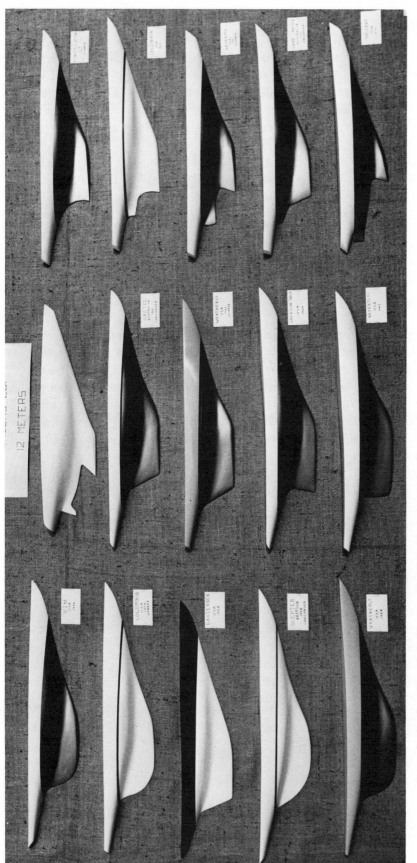

America's Cup Twelve-Meter Models by D. W. Gardiner.

VIM
COLUMBIA
EASTENER
SCEPTER
WEATHERLY

GRETEL II
GRETEL
WEATHERLY
AMERICAN EAGLE
NEFERTITI

CONSTELLATION
COLUMBIA
INTREPID
DAME PATTIE
VALIANT

When beating to windward these new short keel boats cannot point as high as their old-fashioned longer keel sisters. They slide sideways more. So they must be sailed "full and by" and never "pinched." Then by designing them with fuller ends (higher prismatic coefficients, explained on page 283) their speed through the water is enough faster to improve their speed made good to windward. That is to say, they arrive at the weather mark first.

Important to designing twelve-meters is the saving of weight, so that the saving, especially aloft, can be added to the amount of lead ballast on the keel. This increases the power to carry sail, making a marked advantage in windward ability. Spars and rigging employ special materials, such as aluminum and titanium, and streamlined rod rigging of stainless steel.

The effort put into a twelve-meter design for the America's Cup is prodigious. For example, both CONSTELLATION and INTREPID each required about 10,000 hours of design time, and each about 100 drawings of all kinds. These included the drawings of lines for seven or eight models, plus a total of over thirty model changes.

It is a good analogy to say that the America's Cup races do for yacht designing what the big automobile races at LeMans or Indianapolis do for automobile design. Improvements in things like engines and tires, which are used in stock cars, are a direct result of races like these, even at the expense of life itself. Although lives have been lost in auto races, so far none has been lost in dismastings, which do occur with the use of the lightest possible masts in yacht races.

The following are all direct contributions to yacht designing as a result of the design of America's Cup contestants.

    Outside ballast as an improvement over inside ballast.

    Keel sections developed from rectangular to U- and now to V-shape.

    The jib-headed rig.

    Cut-away profile, especially the forefoot for lower wetted area and less resistance.

    Short keel, resulting in lower wetted area.

    Use of two rudders in tandem.

    The "bustle" or "kicker" (really a bulbous stern).

    Streamlined rod standing rigging.

    Bending booms to control draft in the mainsail.

    Lighter weight aluminum masts.

    Dacron sails that hold their shape better and are lighter in weight.

    Winches, reel type, coffee grinder type, linking them together for four men to work one drum, below-deck operation.

    The reverse transom, a lighter-weight stern.

    Dacron and nylon rope.

    The ability of larger hulls to sail faster with smaller sails.

    Improved model testing in the towing tank.

CHAPTER IV

HANDICAP RULES

When a yacht club has a fleet of cruising sailboats, sooner or later its owners will want to race each other. A few years ago a handsome trophy was presented by the family of a deceased member of our club in his memory. It sparked that activity at the Cold Spring Harbor Beach Club, here on Long Island.

The cruising fleet of about a dozen boats ranged in size from about 25 feet to about 44 feet overall, and included mostly sloops, several yawls, a couple of ketches, and a large cat boat (the latter became the committee boat, because she was so slow). There were larger ocean racers, but they were formally measured and rated under the Cruising Club Rule, and their skippers declined to race against the rest of our group of craft which had no measurement certificates with ratings.

Because of the informality desired in these races (the only qualification was that boats had to have working heads), we chose a rule that is simplicity itself. It requires only a boat's principal dimensions, type of rig, and type of propeller. No costly measurements by a measurer are necessary. It may be that other clubs will have the same problem, so, for what it's worth, this rule is reproduced below.*

* COLD SPRING HARBOR BEACH CLUB
  RATING RULE

Rating = $1.5 \times (L - B) \times RA \times PA$

$$L = \frac{LOA + 2 \times LWL}{3}$$

B = Maximum Beam

RA = Rig Allowance

centerboard sloops and cutters	100%
keel sloops and cutters	98%
yawls	96%
ketches	88%
gaff rigs 8% less than above	

PA = Propeller Allowance

no propeller	100%
folding or feathering prop.	98%
two bladed solid prop.	96%
three bladed solid prop.	94%

Sail area is not a factor in this rule, but spinnakers cannot exceed maximum C.C.A. size.

A triangular course (to insure a beat, a reach, and a run) was laid out the night before the race. Based on the distance around the buoys selected, the starting times for each rating at that distance were assigned, using the Time Allowance Table shown on **page** 28.

The idea was to start the smallest boat first. Then in order of their ratings from lowest to highest, each boat would follow on her starting time signal. The largest boat would be the last one to start. A race run in this manner is really a lot of fun, because each contestant knows by observation exactly where he stands. The first boat to finish wins the race. The second boat to finish takes second prize, and so on.

It seemed to work pretty well, because when there was a breeze, all the boats finished quite close together. As a sporting gesture, which helped to equalize the boats' handicaps for the next race, we agreed to increase the winner's rating by a

YANKEE GIRL, a modern ocean racer, is the mother of a family of fast boats. Her lines, as well as her arrangement and sail plan, were done by the author at S&S. Not published are some interesting features about her hull shape such as the waterlines of her appendages (fin keel, skeg and rudder). These are taken from the formula for a curve which is used for the sections of helicopter blades.

In the old days we used to think of the ideal streamlined shape as being widest one-third of the way aft from the leading edge. This is no longer so. Now the best spot for maximum width has proven to be at a point 45% aft of the leading edge.

Her sections are very much the shape of a champagne glass, with the tumble home of a brandy glass. She doesn't have much of a bustle in her skeg, is extremely fine, and has about as little wetted surface as is possible in a keel boat. Actually she is more like a centerboarder with a fixed lead centerboard, because her hull has such a shallow deadrise, and her lead fin keel is like a slab of lead on edge.

Of welded aluminum construction, she is fairly light displacement (3000 pounds lighter than her fiberglass sister ship). This helps her to reach surfing speed. Still in all, she is easy to steer and behaves herself when some of her competitors are broaching, out of control, knocked bown by a gust in their huge spinnakers.

For ocean racing a large forepeak is provided in which to stow the many sails used. Berths are deep and narrow, and placed near amidships, where it is more comfortable to sleep in a seaway. The owner has privacy and comfort in his stateroom aft.

When he came to us, our client wanted a winning boat, especially good reaching and running. Not only is she that, but she also turned out to be good to windward, because she is so stiff. A large fore triangle with small mainsail allows a combination of head sails in a double head rig, the power of her high speed to windward.

As present ocean racers go, YANKEE GIRL is one of the best.

TIME ALLOWANCE TABLE

FOR ONE NAUTICAL MILE, IN SECONDS AND DECIMALS.

Rating	Allowance	Rating	Allowance	Rating	Allowance	Rating	Allowance
15.0	381.35	18.0	332.75	21.0	294.98	24.0	264.55
.1	379.49	.1	331.33	.1	293.87	.1	263.64
.2	377.65	.2	329.93	.2	292.76	.2	262.73
.3	375.83	.3	328.54	.3	291.65	.3	261.82
.4	374.03	.4	327.17	.4	290.56	.4	260.92
.5	372.26	.5	325.83	.5	289.48	.5	260.03
.6	370.50	.6	324.48	.6	288.40	.6	259.14
.7	368.76	.7	323.14	.7	287.33	.7	258.26
.8	367.03	.8	321.82	.8	286.26	.8	257.38
.9	365.31	.9	320.50	.9	285.20	.9	256.51
16.0	363.64	19.0	319.19	22.0	284.15	25.0	255.65
.1	361.97	.1	317.89	.1	283.10	.1	254.78
.2	360.31	.2	316.60	.2	282.07	.2	253.92
.3	358.66	.3	315.32	.3	281.04	.3	253.07
.4	357.02	.4	314.05	.4	280.02	.4	252.23
.5	355.39	.5	312.78	.5	279.00	.5	251.39
.6	353.79	.6	311.53	.6	277.99	.6	250.55
.7	352.21	.7	310.29	.7	276.99	.7	249.72
.8	350.64	.8	309.06	.8	276.00	.8	248.89
.9	349.08	.9	307.84	.9	275.01	.9	248.07
17.0	347.52	20.0	306.62	23.0	274.03	26.0	247.25
.1	345.99	.1	305.42	.1	273.06	.1	246.44
.2	344.47	.2	304.24	.2	272.09	.2	245.63
.3	342.96	.3	303.05	.3	271.13	.3	244.82
.4	341.46	.4	301.87	.4	270.17	.4	244.02
.5	339.97	.5	300.71	.5	269.22	.5	243.23
.6	338.50	.6	299.54	.6	268.27	.6	242.44
.7	337.04	.7	298.39	.7	267.33	.7	241.66
.8	335.60	.8	297.25	.8	266.40	.8	240.88
.9	334.17	.9	296.11	.9	265.48	.9	240.10
27.0	239.33	31.0	211.61	35.0	188.76	39.0	169.52
.1	238.56	.1	210.98	.1	188.24	.1	169.08
.2	237.79	.2	210.36	.2	187.72	.2	168.64
.3	237.03	.3	209.74	.3	187.20	.3	168.19
.4	236.27	.4	209.11	.4	186.68	.4	167.75
.5	235.52	.5	208.50	.5	186.17	.5	167.31
.6	234.78	.6	207.89	.6	185.65	.6	166.88
.7	234.04	.7	207.28	.7	185.15	.7	166.45
.8	233.30	.8	206.68	.8	184.64	.8	166.02
.9	232.57	.9	206.08	.9	184.14	.9	165.60
28.0	231.84	32.0	205.48	36.0	183.64	40.0	165.18
.1	231.11	.1	204.88	.1	183.14	.1	164.75
.2	230.39	.2	204.29	.2	182.64	.2	164.32
.3	229.67	.3	203.70	.3	182.15	.3	163.88
.4	228.95	.4	203.11	.4	181.66	.4	163.46
.5	228.24	.5	202.52	.5	181.16	.5	163.04
.6	227.53	.6	201.94	.6	180.67	.6	162.62
.7	226.82	.7	201.36	.7	180.19	.7	162.21
.8	226.12	.8	200.79	.8	179.71	.8	161.80
.9	225.43	.9	200.22	.9	179.23	.9	161.39
29.0	224.74	33.0	199.65	37.0	178.75	41.0	160.98
.1	224.05	.1	199.08	.1	178.27	.1	160.56
.2	223.37	.2	198.51	.2	177.79	.2	160.15
.3	222.68	.3	197.95	.3	177.31	.3	159.74
.4	222.00	.4	197.39	.4	176.83	.4	159.34
.5	221.33	.5	196.83	.5	176.36	.5	158.93
.6	220.66	.6	196.27	.6	175.90	.6	158.52
.7	219.99	.7	195.72	.7	175.43	.7	158.12
.8	219.32	.8	195.17	.8	174.96	.8	157.73
.9	218.66	.9	194.63	.9	174.50	.9	157.33
30.0	218.00	34.0	194.09	38.0	174.04	42.0	156.93
.1	217.34	.1	193.54	.1	173.58	.1	156.53
.2	216.70	.2	193.00	.2	173.12	.2	156.13
.3	216.05	.3	192.46	.3	172.67	.3	155.74
.4	215.40	.4	191.92	.4	172.21	.4	155.35
.5	214.75	.5	191.38	.5	171.76	.5	154.96
.6	214.11	.6	190.85	.6	171.30	.6	154.57
.7	213.48	.7	190.32	.7	170.84	.7	154.19
.8	212.85	.8	189.79	.8	170.40	.8	153.80
.9	212.23	.9	189.28	.9	169.96	.9	153.42

TIME ALLOWANCE—Continued.

Rating	Allowance	Rating	Allowance	Rating	Allowance	Rating	Allowance
43.0	153.04	47.0	138.71	51.0	126.10	55.0	114.90
.1	152.66	.1	138.38	.1	125.81	.1	114.64
.2	152.28	.2	138.05	.2	125.51	.2	114.37
.3	151.90	.3	137.71	.3	125.21	.3	114.11
.4	151.52	.4	137.38	.4	124.92	.4	113.84
.5	151.14	.5	137.05	.5	124.62	.5	113.58
.6	150.76	.6	136.73	.6	124.33	.6	113.32
.7	150.38	.7	136.40	.7	124.04	.7	113.05
.8	150.01	.8	136.07	.8	123.76	.8	112.79
.9	149.65	.9	135.74	.9	123.47	.9	112.53
44.0	149.28	48.0	135.41	52.0	123.18	56.0	112.27
.1	148.91	.1	135.08	.1	122.89	.1	112.01
.2	148.54	.2	134.76	.2	122.60	.2	111.75
.3	148.17	.3	134.44	.3	122.32	.3	111.49
.4	147.80	.4	134.11	.4	122.03	.4	111.24
.5	147.43	.5	133.79	.5	121.74	.5	110.99
.6	147.07	.6	133.47	.6	121.45	.6	110.74
.7	146.71	.7	133.16	.7	121.17	.7	110.49
.8	146.35	.8	132.85	.8	120.89	.8	110.24
.9	145.99	.9	132.54	.9	120.61	.9	109.99
45.0	145.64	49.0	132.22	53.0	120.33	57.0	109.74
.1	145.28	.1	131.90	.1	120.05	.1	109.49
.2	144.92	.2	131.58	.2	119.77	.2	109.24
.3	144.56	.3	131.27	.3	119.50	.3	108.99
.4	144.20	.4	130.96	.4	119.22	.4	108.74
.5	143.85	.5	130.64	.5	118.94	.5	108.49
.6	143.50	.6	130.33	.6	118.67	.6	108.24
.7	143.15	.7	130.03	.7	118.39	.7	108.00
.8	142.80	.8	129.72	.8	118.12	.8	107.76
.9	142.46	.9	129.42	.9	117.85	.9	107.52
46.0	142.12	50.0	129.12	54.0	117.58	58.0	107.28
.1	141.78	.1	128.81	.1	117.31	.1	107.03
.2	141.43	.2	128.50	.2	117.04	.2	106.78
.3	141.08	.3	128.20	.3	116.77	.3	106.52
.4	140.74	.4	127.89	.4	116.50	.4	106.28
.5	140.39	.5	127.58	.5	116.23	.5	106.04
.6	140.04	.6	127.28	.6	115.96	.6	105.80
.7	139.70	.7	126.98	.7	115.69	.7	105.56
.8	139.37	.8	126.68	.8	115.43	.8	105.32
.9	139.04	.9	126.39	.9	115.16	.9	105.08
59.0	104.84	63.0	95.78	67.0	87.52	71.0	79.99
.1	104.60	.1	95.56	.1	87.32	.1	79.80
.2	104.36	.2	95.34	.2	87.12	.2	79.62
.3	104.12	.3	95.12	.3	86.92	.3	79.44
.4	103.89	.4	94.91	.4	86.73	.4	79.26
.5	103.66	.5	94.70	.5	86.54	.5	79.08
.6	103.42	.6	94.49	.6	86.35	.6	78.90
.7	103.19	.7	94.27	.7	86.16	.7	78.72
.8	102.96	.8	94.06	.8	85.97	.8	78.54
.9	102.73	.9	93.85	.9	85.78	.9	78.37
60.0	102.50	64.0	93.64	68.0	85.59	72.0	78.20
.1	102.26	.1	93.43	.1	85.40	.1	78.02
.2	102.03	.2	93.22	.2	85.21	.2	77.84
.3	101.80	.3	93.01	.3	85.02	.3	77.66
.4	101.57	.4	92.80	.4	84.83	.4	77.48
.5	101.34	.5	92.59	.5	84.64	.5	77.30
.6	101.11	.6	92.38	.6	84.45	.6	77.13
.7	100.88	.7	92.17	.7	84.26	.7	76.96
.8	100.66	.8	91.97	.8	84.07	.8	76.79
.9	100.43	.9	91.76	.9	83.88	.9	76.62
61.0	100.21	65.0	91.55	69.0	83.69	73.0	76.45
.1	99.98	.1	91.34	.1	83.50	.1	76.27
.2	99.76	.2	91.14	.2	83.31	.2	76.10
.3	99.53	.3	90.94	.3	83.12	.3	75.93
.4	99.30	.4	90.73	.4	82.93	.4	75.76
.5	99.07	.5	90.53	.5	82.74	.5	75.59
.6	98.84	.6	90.32	.6	82.55	.6	75.42
.7	98.62	.7	90.12	.7	82.36	.7	75.25
.8	98.40	.8	89.92	.8	82.17	.8	75.08
.9	98.18	.9	89.72	.9	81.99	.9	74.91
62.0	97.96	66.0	89.52	70.0	81.82	74.0	74.74
.1	97.74	.1	89.32	.1	81.63	.1	74.57
.2	97.51	.2	89.12	.2	81.44	.2	74.39
.3	97.29	.3	88.92	.3	81.25	.3	74.22
.4	97.07	.4	88.72	.4	81.07	.4	74.05
.5	96.85	.5	88.52	.5	80.89	.5	73.88
.6	96.64	.6	88.32	.6	80.71	.6	73.72
.7	96.42	.7	88.12	.7	80.53	.7	73.55
.8	96.20	.8	87.92	.8	80.35	.8	73.39
.9	95.99	.9	87.72	.9	80.17	.9	73.23

small percentage. Also, the last boat to finish was assigned a lower rating by a small percentage, so she was helped for the next race.

Here is a theoretical example of how to use the Time Allowance Table, when starting boats on their handicaps. We will assume the race is 15 miles long, and there are only three boats in it.

Boat	Rating	Sec. per Mi. ×	15 Mi.	Starting Time
FIDELIA	21.0	294.98	4425 Secs.	10 o'clock
SANTA MARIA	29.0	224.74	3371 Secs.	10:17:34
WAUPI	33.0	199.65	2995 Secs.	10:23:50

Let's say we start FIDELIA at 10 o'clock on the dot. Then to obtain SANTA MARIA's starting time, it is necessary to take the difference betweeen FIDELIA's time allowance to sail the course and SANTA MARIA's (4425 Secs. − 3371 Secs. = 1054 Secs. Then 1054 ÷ 60 = 17 Min. and 34 Secs. So we can start SANTA MARIA at 10:17:34 o'clock). The same applies for WAUPI's starting time, using FIDELIA's allowance again as the base time. (4425 − 2995 = 1430 Secs. Then 1430 ÷ 60 = 23 Min. and 50 Secs., so we can start WAUPI at 10:23:50).

During all this race committee work, it struck me how difficult it is to be fair to all hands. I mean, using this time on distance system, how accurately the time was calculated, but how startlingly inaccurate the distance was assumed to be.

Suppose the race is almost entirely to windward, as the Annapolis to Newport Race once was, up the coast dead into a howling northeaster. To be fair the race committee must estimate a longer distance for windward work, because of the zig zag beating it entails. The Time Allowance Table shown is from the North American Yacht Racing Union and is worked out for a boat sailing under average conditions. It can be adjusted for a triangular course, where one third of the race is to windward, by adding 360 to the numbers under "Allowance."

At the other extreme from that Newport-Annapolis Race is the St. Petersburg to Fort Lauderdale Race. Because of the fair current of the gulf stream that runs up the east coast of Florida, the committee shortens the distance used in its calculations. The question in both cases is: what is the correct distance to assume that the average boat will sail through the water for that particular race?

There is another system of handicapping besides this time on distance one. It is called time on time and is used in Great Britain and Europe. It is considered fairer to the small boats, which are always stopped dead compared to large boats, when they beat to windward in heavy seas. To arrive at a boat's corrected time, the elapsed time of each boat is multiplied by a time correction factor, which at this writing is a percentage equal to:

$$\frac{\sqrt{\text{Rating}} + 2.6}{10}$$

Of course, before these calculations can be made, a boat must finish in order to get her elapsed time. The winner will be determined on the basis of corrected time.

The rule in use today, gaining worldwide acceptance, is the International Offshore Rule. It is a combination more or less of the hull measurements of the British R.O.R.C. Rule, and more or less of the sail measurements of the American C.C.A. Rule. It is not published here, because it is subject to frequent changes, as the loopholes are plugged. It is 60 pages long and contains about 145 measurements, all told, for hull and sails. To understand it I suggest reading the book, *Yachtsman's Guide to the Rating Rule* by Peter Johnson, Nautical Publishing Co., Nautical House, Lymington, Hampshire, England.

To obtain the I.O.R. Rule write the North American Yacht Racing Union, Offshore Office, 198 New York Avenue, Huntington, N.Y. 11743.

Once all the measurements are written down, it takes only about six minutes for an experienced operator to run them through a small computer to obtain a boat's rating under the I.O.R. Rule. But the measuring is not so quickly done. It is a two man job. Measurements must be taken both when a boat is hauled out, and when she is afloat.

Every competitive racing owner is interested in what he can do to reduce his boat's rating. Under the I.O.R. Rule, as of 1972, the following 19 theoretical changes in his boat will produce the probable effects on her in general, on her rating, and on her speed:

Change in Yacht	*General Effects*	*Effect on Rating*	*Effect on Speed*
Trim by bow. Move inside ballast forward.	To offset stern trim produced by crew in cockpit.	Lower slightly.	Slight improvement, if boat is more nearly parallel to D.W.L.
Trim by bow. Add inside ballast just Fwd. of mast.	To offset stern trim produced by crew in cockpit.	No change—to slightly lower.	Increased displacement should make boat slightly stiffer.
Trim by stern. Move inside ballast aft.	To offset bow trim produced by sails forward and crew amidship.	Raise, moderately.	Slight improvement, if boat is more nearly parallel to D.W.L.
Increase displacement by adding joinerwork and personal gear.	Will increase wetted area and stability.	Lower rating— slightly to moderately.	Probably none noted, except that due to increased efficiency of crew.
Increase displacement by adding inside ballast.	Will increase wetted area and stability.	Raise, moderately.	Boat will be able to carry larger sails longer in increasing wind and carry speed through waves.
Increase displacement by adding outside ballast.	Will increase wetted area and stability.	Raise, considerably.	Boat will be notably more powerful in breeze. Light air performance should not be affected.

Change in Yacht	General Effects	Effect on Rating	Effect on Speed
Decrease displacement by taking out joiner work and personal gear.	Neater and more open boat, less wetted area.	Raise, slightly.	Probably won't be noticeable, except in attitude of crew.
Decrease displacement by removing inside ballast.	A light boat will be less stiff. Heavy boat might seem more lively.	Raise, slightly, or no change.	Will depend on stiffness and ability to carry sail. Light air performance not apt to change.
Decrease displacement by removing outside ballast.	A light boat will be noticeably less stiff, and a heavy more lively.	No change—to slight decrease.	Will depend very much on stiffness in a breeze. Light air performance not apt to change.
Change propeller from solid to feathering.	Less Prop. drag.	Raise, slightly.	Very slight increase in light boat.
Solid to folding.	Less Prop. drag.	Raise, moderately.	Slight increase in light boat.
Solid to folding with strut.	Slightly less drag.	Raise, slightly.	Very slight increase in light boat.
Change to heavier engine.	Will depend on location in boat and more speed, or dependability.	Hopefully, lower, slightly.	Slight increase in stability.
Increased tankage for fuel and water.	Increased displacement and wetted area.	No change except in extreme cases.	Probably not noticeable, except boat will be less lively when tanks are all full.
Larger spinnaker pole and genoa.	Improved off wind performance. Good crew required.	Raise, considerably.	Considerable increase off the wind. Dependent in part on crew's ability. Especially effective with minimum main.
Minimum main sail.	Lowers center of effort of rig and increases ability to carry genoa. Decreases SA/WA. Increases aspect ratio.	Lower, moderately.	Probable effects: very slight loss in very light air, no change in moderate, slight gain in heavy air.
Add a bustle.	Increase prismatic co-efficient and effective L.W.L., while making boat a bit easier to handle.	No change—to raise slightly.	If the diagonals in the lines can be flattened, or straightened, a fair increase in the upper speed range may be achieved.

Change in Yacht	General Effects	Effect on Rating	Effect on Speed
Rudder at aft end of L.W.L.	Increase prismatic co-efficient and effective L.W.L., while making boat a bit easier to handle.	No change—to raise slightly.	If the diagonals in the lines can be flattened, or straightened, a fair increase in the upper speed range may be achieved.
Snub stern.	Reduces weight in end giving small trim Fwd. May give boat un-balanced look.	No change—to lower slightly.	Weight saved in ends should make hobby hors-ing less, and give sails better "platform" to operate from with very small increase in speed and comfort.

It should be apparent that to become a successful designer of competitive racing boats a person must know the current handicap rule in use backwards and forwards, and take advantage of this knowledge to prevent a competitive design from being penalized unnecessarily by a high rating.

Throughout the history of yacht racing the handicap rules have had a profound effect on yacht design. Such shapes as the following were evolved from the basic shape of the yacht AMERICA (with her long keel and plumb rudder): shorter keels with cut away forefoots and tucked under rudders, the plank on edge type with very narrow beam and deeper draft, skimming dishes with long full overhangs (the scow type being the fastest), and shallow draft centerboarders.

The ideal is to aim for a seaworthy habitable type. An example of a fast boat that is a product of the current (1972) I.O.R. Rule and does well under it is YANKEE GIRL, whose plans and pictures are shown here.

The I.O.R. Rule is a rule for boats that race across oceans, or around the buoys. It creates classes by using a fixed rating such as:

The Two Ton Class—at 9.75 meters, or 32.0 feet
The One Ton Class*—at 8.38 meters, or 27.5 feet.
The Three Quarter Ton Class—at 7.47 meters, or 24.5 feet
The Half Ton Class—at 6.60 meters, or 21.6 feet.
The Quarter Ton Class—at 5.50 meters, or 18.0 feet.

It does not cover multihulls, unballasted centerboarders, or open cockpit one designs.

The authors of this rule will be wise to plug all its loopholes and will have, I'm sure, the good judgment and common sense to author it so that it produces able boats, for the sea is no respecter of boats, or their sailors.

If a racing sailboat is to sail up to her rating, it is important to tune her. This tuning means attention to detail, shape and selection of sails, the setup of the standing and running rigging, the selection and practice of the crew, and the deck layout. Most important is maintenance of the boat itself, because the bottom must be as clean as a whistle.

* In 1898 a French Y.C. gave a cup raced for by boats qualifying under their rule giving a rating of 1 cu. meter, the volume of 1 ton of water; hence "One Ton Cup," its English nickname.

The sails must be strong, light, and correctly shaped for a range of conditions by being flexible, such as a stretchy luffed genoa. They should be full cut for light winds and flatter for strong breezes (by increasing or decreasing tension on the halyards and clews). There should be no lumps or flat spots. A uniform airfoil shape from head to foot is mandatory. Sailmakers should be consulted to perfect poorly shaped ones.

Tuning results can be proven only by sailing with another boat close alongside. The sheeting angle of jibs can be changed, and immediately results will be observed.

The mast must have its standing rigging set up so that its sail track is a straight line. To check, sight up it, when sailing on both port and starboard tacks. Upper

YANKEE GIRL's Polar Diagram

WIND SPEED	BROAD REACH	DEAD RUN
8 kn.	6½ kn.	4½ kn.
15 kn.	8½ kn.	8 kn.
22 kn.	9½ kn.	9 kn.

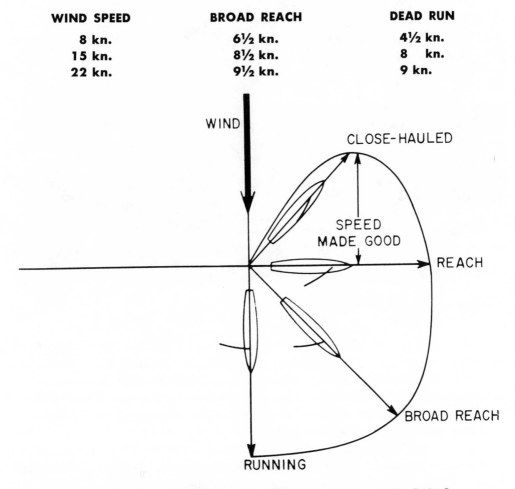

VARIATION OF SAILBOAT SPEED WITH HEADING

YANKEE GIRL racing at Cowes.

shrouds are longer than lowers, so they stretch more and should be set up a little tighter. Jib stays should be just as tight as practical, so that the luff of a jib will not sag off to leeward. The running backstay on old rigs, tightened each time a boat comes about, is an excellent way to keep the jibstay firm. Permanent backstays can be changed in tension by the use of long turnbuckles with handles, or by hydraulic backstay adjusters to tighten the jibstay.

If a skipper thinks he is not doing well in handicap racing, let him first consider how well he has tuned his boat before complaining that her rating is too high, because quite often fast boats have high ratings, and slow boats have low ratings.

Sail plan of YANKEE GIRL.

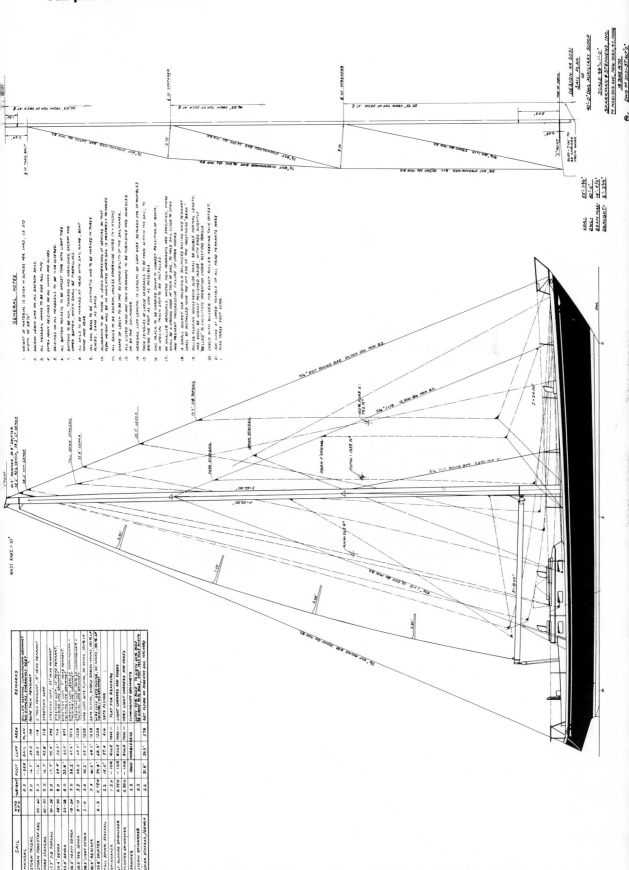

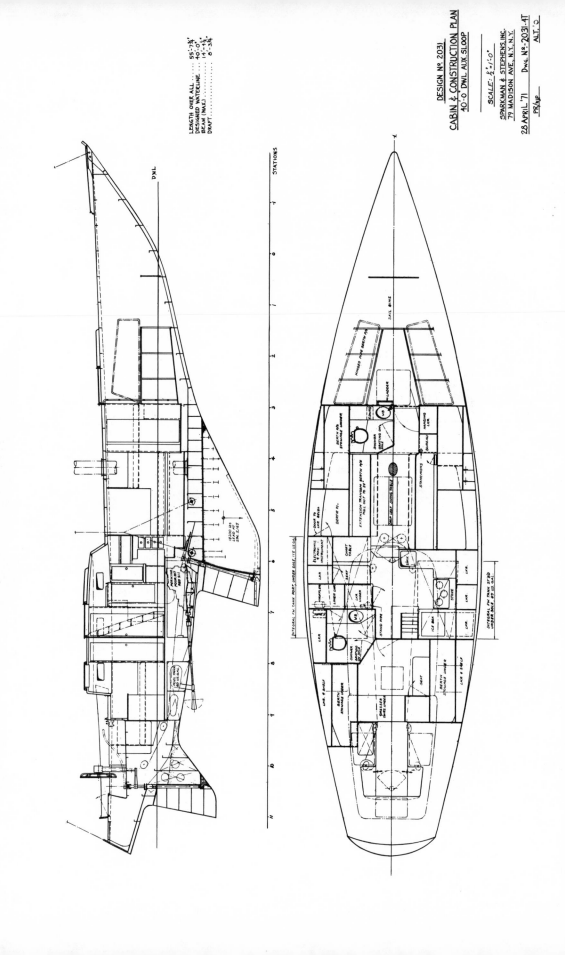

DESIGN Nº 2031
CABIN & CONSTRUCTION PLAN
40-0 DWL AUX. SLOOP

SCALE: ½'=1'-0"

SPARKMAN & STEPHENS INC.
79 MADISON AVE. N.Y. N.Y.

28 APRIL '71   DWG. Nº 2031.4T
PR/vp   ALT. 'O'

LENGTH OVER ALL .... 55'-7¾'
DESIGNED WATERLINE .... 40'-0"
BEAM (MAX.) .... 14'-4½'
DRAFT .... 6'-3¾'

STATIONS

YANKEE GIRL'S UNDERWATER
PROFILE & MIRROR IMAGE

D.W.L.

DESIGN Nº 2031
of
DECK PLAN
for
40'-0" DWL AUXILIARY SLOOP
SCALE 1/2"=1'-0"
SPARKMAN & STEPHENS, INC.
79 MADISON AVE. NEW YORK N.Y. 10016
DWG. Nº 2031-57, ALT. O PLAN

CHAPTER V

THE LAW OF MECHANICAL SIMILITUDE

This is how the law of mechanical similitude works for boats that are similar in form. If you vary the water-line length, the other particulars will vary as follows:

Speed varies as the square root of the L.W.L.

Beam, draft and length overall vary as the L.W.L.

Sail area and wetted surface vary as the square of L.W.L.

Displacement varies as the cube of the L.W.L.

Heeling moment of wind pressure on sails varies as the cube of L.W.L.

Resistance varies as the cube of the L.W.L.

Stability varies as the fourth power of the L.W.L.

Moment of inertia varies as the fifth power of the L.W.L.

As an example, let us see what happens when one boat has twice the water-line length of another similar boat; then she will have:

1.41 times the speed ($\sqrt{2}$ = 1.41);

Twice the beam, twice the draft, twice the L.O.A.;

Four times the sail area and wetted surface (2 × 2 = 4);

Eight times the displacement (2 × 2 × 2 = 8);

Eight times the heeling moment of wind pressure on sails in the same breeze;

Eight times the resistance at the faster speed;

Sixteen times the stability (2 × 2 × 2 × 2 = 16);

Thirty-two times the moment of inertia (2 × 2 × 2 × 2 × 2 = 32).

So we realize from the figure of "sixteen times the L.W.L. for stability" why the power to carry sail increases much faster than the heeling moment (eight times the L.W.L.) for a similar boat twice the water-line length. This is the reason that large sailing yachts are so much stiffer than small ones even with relatively much less draft and beam.

SOLING Class: A popular one-design class now used in the Olympics, designed by J. H. Linge.

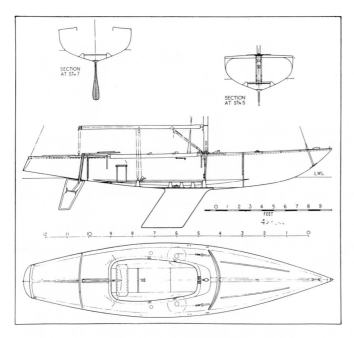

SECTION
AT ST_N 7

SECTION
AT ST_N 5

LWL

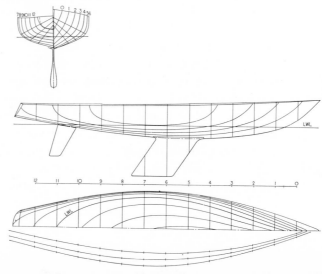

LWL

LWL

CHAPTER VI

APPEARANCE, OR THE LOOK OF A BOAT

Of all man's creations there is nothing more beautiful, I think, than a good-looking sailboat under sail. But now the question is, fellow yacht designers, just how do you go about drawing your design so that it comes out good-looking?

Let's start with the negative approach first. One of man's ugly creations in my opinion is the Volkswagen beetle. Now let's analyze why this is so. Because, it seems to me, almost all of its lines are circles.

The statue of Venus de Milo shows a combination of weak curves and strong curves, so that the hard stone seems to take on a softness and beauty like whatever lady was the sculptor's model for Venus.

The profile of a clipper bow can be like a Volkswagen beetle if it is an ugly quarter circle, or, when properly drawn, it can be a line of beauty culminated by a figurehead and flowing trail-board scrolls. It is one of the most difficult lines to get right. When you look at a pleasing one you can see that the strongest part of the curve is about at the mid-height, which flows into an almost straight line at the water, and above the mid-point flows into a small tight "S", or reverse curve, beneath the bowsprit. The late A. Loring Swaysey, a yacht designer of some renown, told me once that he spent a whole day on the design of the clipper bow on a large three-masted schooner he was designing. One entire day for one line!

The trick to making a good-looking mid-section of a boat as well as a good-looking bow profile, either spoon type or clipper, is just this. Use a curve first one way, then the other, reversing it on itself, or flipping it over. There is an illustration of what I mean, titled "How one curve may be used to draw a section," page 200.

An ellipse is a good-looking shape, which in essence is a combination of two strong and two weak curves blending into each other. Half an ellipse looks beautiful when used as the arch on a masonry bridge. Carrying this over into yacht design, half an ellipse may be used in plan view for the forward end of a deckhouse, or the after coaming of a cockpit, easily built in fiberglass, aluminum or steel, or even molded plywood. In my opinion by far the most pleasing shape for a portlight is not a circle, not a rectangle, not an oval, but an ellipse. You can buy elliptical portlights that open from Simpson & Lawrence in Glasgow, Scotland. To draw them you can buy ellipse templates with several series of different sizes, from long thin ones to short fat ones.

I think it necessary for a yacht designer to have something of the artist in his make up, because an artistic touch is needed to create a good-looking boat. And who wants to spend a fortune to build a boat that isn't good-looking? How can you sell your design to a prospective client if it does not please him to look at it?

By trial and error you can accomplish this. Use the eraser frequently. It is one of the most important tools of a yacht designer. You can sharpen it by laying it on its side and cutting it with a knife, and by using a thin steel eraser shield you can take out a single line without disturbing other lines of your drawing.

There are lots of boat-painting tricks that can help make her good-looking. Basically a light color makes a boat look bigger than she is, and a dark color makes her look smaller. It's a shame to see so many boats with interiors of teak, which is dark and makes the already small interior look even smaller.

Since the sheer line is one of the most beautiful lines on a boat, or certainly should be, you should accentuate it. This can be done by a contrasting color, like a varnished teak toe rail above white topsides, or a white bulwark above black topsides. Another good combination—white house, turquoise sheer strake, white topsides, red bottom without any boot top. To really make it look stunning, have a gilded cove line below the sheer. Now there's more to doing this than just that. The toe rail on, say, a 40-foot boat should be tapered in height from, say, 4 inches high at the bow to, say, 2½ inches high at the stern. Likewise, if the rail is a bulwark with a rail cap, the bulwark should decrease in height from the bow to the stern. And even the cove line should not be parallel to the sheer. It should be further below the sheer at the bow than it is at the stern. So, you see, there are these subtleties that are part of designing and creating a good-looking boat.

I think deckhouses should be disguised, especially high ones like those on motor sailers. One way to do this would be to paint the topsides white to make the hull look bigger and paint the deckhouse light gray, or light blue. You'd be surprised how it makes the house sort of disappear. If you have a row of portlights in the hull, which seem to cut it up esthetically, a trick is to paint a black or dark-blue band along them the way the airlines do with their planes. Another trick the designer should know is how to handle boot tops. Here again they are not parallel horizontal lines. They are sheered very slightly and also tapered. They should always be completely above the water, with antifouling bottom paint brought above the actual water line, so they will not become foul with slime, grass and barnacles.

Now for the sheer line, the one line that crowns or damns the entire creation. I've found that one of the most important tricks in making a good-looking sheer line is to have the low point tangent to a horizontal line at Station 8, or 80% of the water-line length aft. The sheer line should start out as almost a straight line at

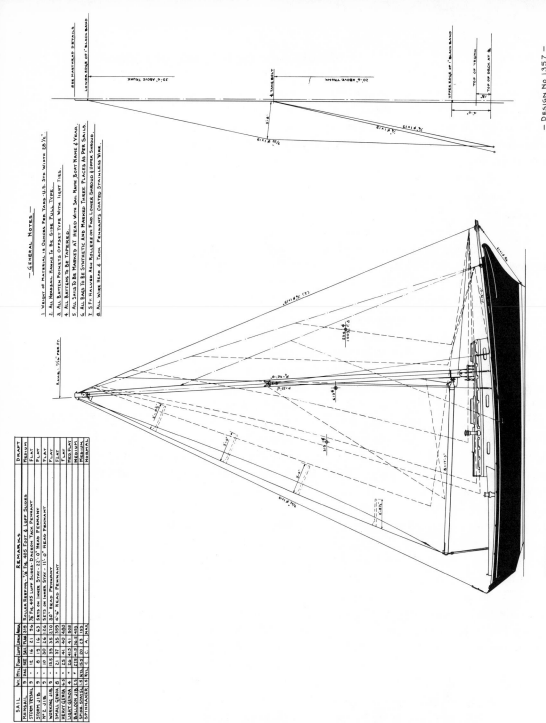

LORNA DOONE has an interesting clipper bow which gives her an outstanding character.

The lines of this little centerboarder are based on those of FINISTERRE, but compressed, so she is quite stiff. Her size is just right for Great South Bay, Long Island, New York, her original home waters.

The mast, stepped on deck in a tabernacle, can be lowered aft and raised again with strut and line to a sheet winch, which allows her to pass under a low fixed bridge.

Her design came from the drawing board of F.S.K. at S&S.

SAIL	WT.	MTL.	FOOT	LUFF	LEECH	AREA	REMARKS	DRAFT
MAINSAIL	9	DAC	SEE SAIL PLAN			319	Roller Reefing - 7/8 Fig. 405 Foot & Luff Slides	Medium
STORM TRYSAIL	3	"	12	16	21	94	7/8 Fig. 405 Luff Slides - Dacron Tack Pennant	Flat
STORM JIB	3	"	8	19	16	63	Sets on Inner Stay - 22'-0" Head Pennant	Flat
Nº 2 JIB	3	"	10	30	24	126	Sets on Inner Stay - 11'-0" Head Pennant	Flat
WORKING JIB	3	"	13.5	33	35	210	30" Head Pennant	Flat
SMALL GENOA	6	"	21	37	35	359	4'-6" Head Pennant	Flat
HENRY GENOA	6.5	"	25	41	40	460		Med Flat
LIGHT GENOA	4	"	26	41.5	41	508		Medium
BALLOON JIB	2.5	"	27.5	41.5	36.5	493		Medium
SPIN. STAYSL.	1.5	NYL	35.5	20	23	193		Medium
SPINNAKER	1.5	NYL	C.	C.	A.	MAX.		Normal

GENERAL NOTES.

1. Weight of Material is Ounces Per Yard - U.S. Std Width 28½".
2. All Headsail Hanks to be Side Pull Type.
3. All Batten Pockets Offset Type with Light Ties.
4. All Battens to be Tapered.
5. All Sails to be Marked at Head with Sail Name, Boat Name & Year.
6. All Bags to be Synthetic and Marked Three Places as Per Sails.
7. 5 Ft. Halved Ash Rollers on Fwd Lower Shroud & Upper Shroud.
8. All Wire Head & Tack Pennants Coated Stainless Wire.

DESIGN No 1357
SAIL PLAN
- of -
25'-0" W.L. AUX. CENTERBOARD SLOOP
- FOR -
MR. EDWIN THORNE
SCALE: 1/8"=1'-0"

L.W.L.	25'-0"	BEAM	10'-6"
L.O.A.	33'-0"	DRAFT	3'-0"

SPARKMAN & STEPHENS, INC.
79 MADISON AVE   NEW YORK 16, N.Y.

DATE 7/21/58 F.S.K. R.C. & E.L.N. DWG. No. 1357-G-T

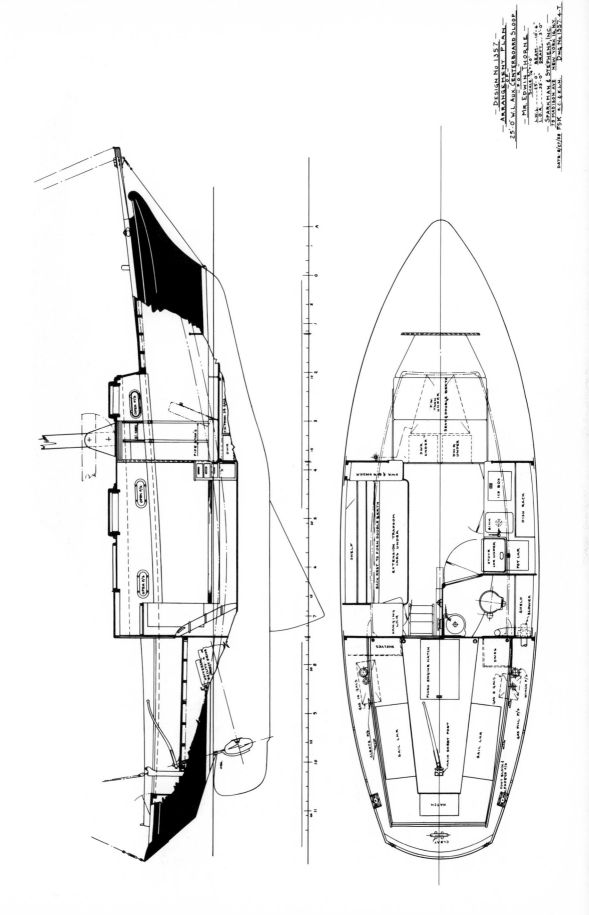

— DESIGN No. 1357 —
— ARRANGEMENT PLAN —
OF
25' 0" W.L. AUX. CENTERBOARD SLOOP
F O R
— Mr. EDWIN THORNE —
SCALE ¾"=1'-0"
L.W.L. 25'-0" BEAM 10'-6"
L.O.A. 33'-0" DRAFT 3'-0"
SPARKMAN & STEPHENS, INC.
79 MADISON AVE. NEW YORK CITY
FSK R.C. & K.H. DWG No. 1357-4-T
DATE 8/27/58

SHELF

EXTENSION TRANSOM LKR'S UNDER

BACK REST TO FORM DOUBLE BERTH

PW'R & B'IN UNDER

F'W TANK UNDER

BERTH & DOUBLE BERTH

DW'R UNDER

DW'R UNDER

ICE BOX

SINK

DISH RACK

STOVE LKR UNDER

POT LKR

SHELF

BLOWER

HANGING LKR

SHELVES

DW'RS

GAS TK IN LKR

FLUSH ENGINE HATCH

MAIN SHEET FOOT

GAS & GAS

SAIL LKR

SAIL LKR

GAS FILL F/s

PORT BLOCK & MASTER F/s

WINCH F/s

CLEATS F/s

HATCH

CLEAT

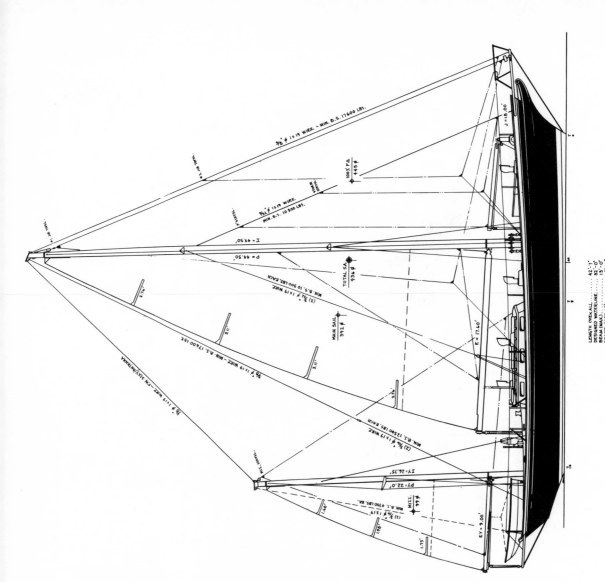

MISCHIEF OF MIAMI. This fine little sailing ship of welded aluminum is a creation that aims to combine outstanding appearance with utility. Her design and equipment are modern, in some respects advanced. Accommodations are homelike and comfortable.

She is planned and built to meet six broad requirements: (1) that she be so strong as to be almost indestructible by the elements, able to stand any sea; (2) that she be easily handled by two people; (3) that she be of minimum size to provide a great deal of comfort for extended living aboard by her owner, his wife, and frequent guests; (4) that she be good-looking in a traditional manner; (5) that she be fast and smart under sail, without regard to constraints of Racing Rules; and (6) that she be of moderate draft for use in such areas as the Bahama Islands.

The author is rewarded in learning that she actually meets these high standards, because her design came from his hand at S&S.

LENGTH OVER ALL	42'-7"
DESIGNED WATERLINE	33'-0"
BEAM (MAX.)	13'-0"
DRAFT (CBD. UP)	4'-5"
DRAFT (CBD. DOWN)	8'-5"

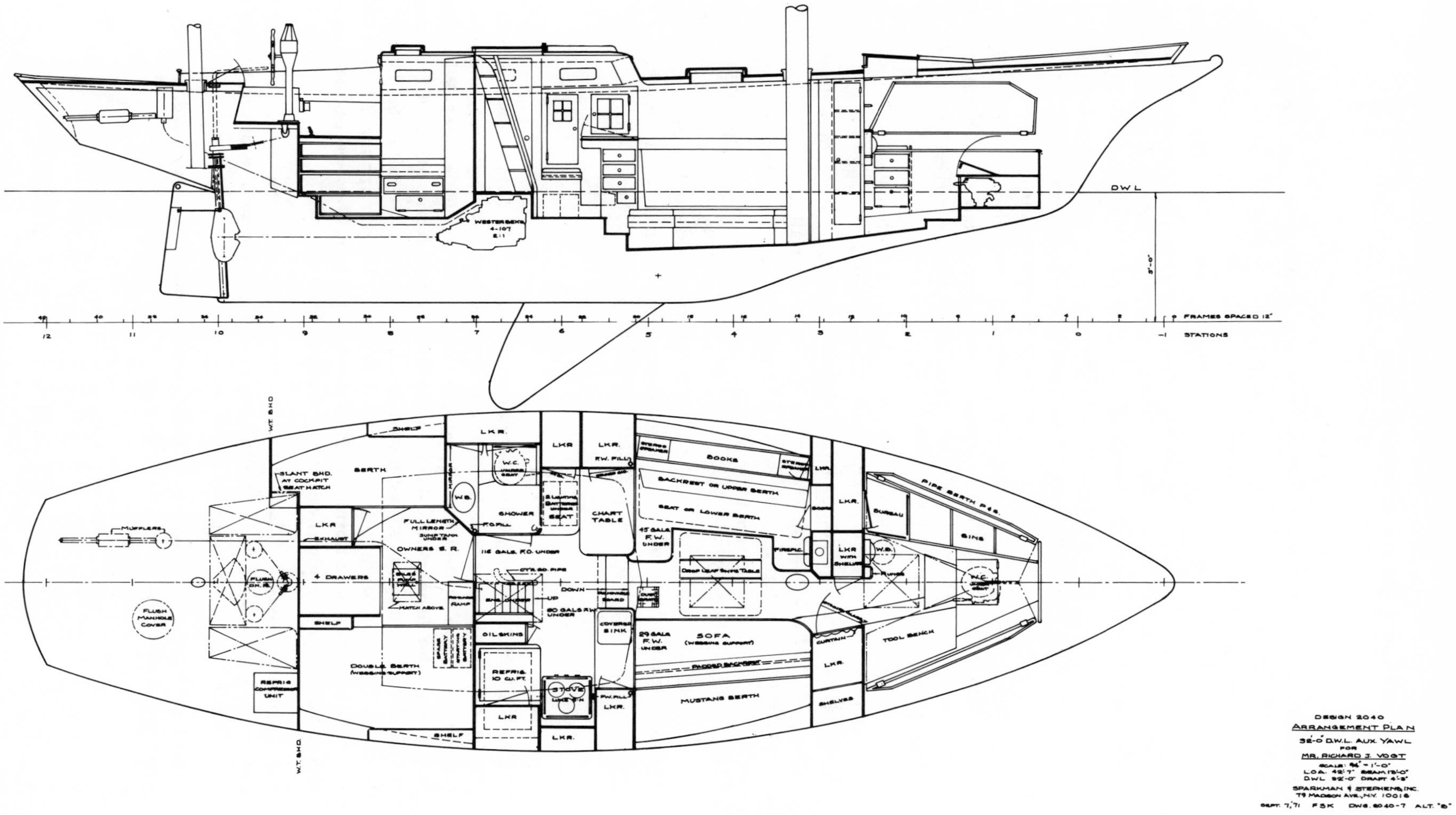

DWL
5'-0"
FRAMES SPACED 12"
STATIONS
WESTERBEKE 4-107 2:1
W.T. BHD.
SHELF
LKR.
BERTH
SLANT BHD. AT COCKPIT SEAT HATCH
MUFFLERS
EXHAUST
FLUSH MANHOLE COVER
4 DRAWERS
FULL LENGTH MIRROR
SUMP TANK UNDER
OWNERS S. R.
HATCH ABOVE
W.C. UNDER SEAT
W.S.
SHOWER
F.O. FILL
MIRROR
CHART TABLE
F.W. FILL
116 GALS. F.O. UNDER
UP
DOWN
80 GALS F.W. UNDER
OILSKINS
REFRIG. 10 CU. FT.
STOVE
COVERED SINK
29 GALS F.W. UNDER
SOFA (WEBBING SUPPORT)
PADDED BACKREST
MUSTANG BERTH
45 GALS F.W. UNDER
DROP LEAF SWING TABLE
BACKREST OR UPPER BERTH
SEAT OR LOWER BERTH
BOOKS
STEREO SPEAKER
FIREPLC.
LKR WITH SHELVES
CURTAIN
SHELVES
PUMPS
BUREAU
SINS
PIPE BERTH P & S.
TOOL BENCH
DOUBLE BERTH (WEBBING SUPPORT)
REFRIG COMPRESSOR UNIT
SPARE BATTERY
STARTING BATTERY
DESIGN 2040
ARRANGEMENT PLAN
32'-0" D.W.L. AUX. YAWL
FOR
MR. RICHARD J. VOGT
SCALE: 3/4" = 1'-0"
L.O.A. 42'-7" BEAM 13'-0"
D.W.L. 32'-0" DRAFT 4'-3"
SPARKMAN & STEPHENS, INC.
79 MADISON AVE., N.Y. 10016
SEPT. 7, '71 FSK DWG. 2040-7 ALT. "B"

the bow and increase in curvature as it approaches the stern. Theoretically, if it projected beyond the stern, the curve would continue to increase its curvature into a ram's horn.

When making your batten or spline stay in the desired curve, always have one weight at each end of the batten or spline. Otherwise the batten will straighten out beyond the last weight and spoil the line you want at the end of what you draw. I like to have a spot for the sheer line forward of the bow and aft of the stern to show the loftsman where the batten should go at each end. This makes him fasten his batten like yours, and insures that the ends of the sheer line will not deform.

The sheer in elevation must be thought of in three dimensions in connection with the deck line in plan view. A narrow boat with a sharp deck line at the bow, like a twelve-meter, should have a flat sheer. At the other extreme, a wide boat with a blunt bow should have a deep curved sheer, like a catboat. Sometimes, as seen from an angle ahead, you get a powder horn or S-curve effect. As for raised deck sheers, I submit ENDEAVOUR (page 71) as an example.

In motorboats sometimes the sheer line is drawn with a slight S shape, which I must admit looks rather well when it is done properly. A straight line sheer and a hogged sheer in my opinion look ugly. It really makes no sense, on a displacement-type vessel, to have a hogged sheer line, because, after all, the highest point should be at the bow to keep the bow wave off the deck, not amidships, where there is a hollow in the water between the bow and stern wave. The stern should be a little higher than the low point at Station 8 to keep a following sea from coming aboard.

A simple boat with a lovely sheer is the fisherman's dory. For its size it is one of the most seaworthy of all boats. (However, don't design one for a sailboat. Their water line is too narrow, so that they have little or no power to carry sail.)

ROWING DORY. Rowing is not only good exercise, it is a pleasure in a boat well designed for the purpose. But the sea requires a seaworthy boat, and so it was the combination of these two qualities I sought in this little boat. What better craft than the fisherman's dory to use as a basis? None other. A fair amount of length is needed for speed and a good run between strokes. So 12 feet was chosen. This was really too long a boat to stow aboard our then 28-foot SANTA MARIA. So there was nothing left to do but tow her. Thus we added a skeg to keep her towing straight down the second stern wave.

Spruce spoon bladed 7-foot oars are a must for an oarsman, as are the best of oarlocks, the bronze type with one horn higher than the other, so the oars won't jump out on the pulling side.

This boat is a joy to row. Her capacity is four adults, one forward, one aft, and two amidships. She's an F. S. K. design.

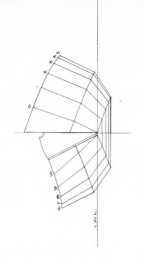

TABLE OF OFFSETS.

LINES ARE TO OUTSIDE OF PLANK.

OFFSETS ARE GIVEN IN FEET, INCHES & EIGHTHS
OF AN INCH.

	STATION	0	1	2	3	4	5	6	7	8	9	10
HEIGHTS ABOVE BASE L.	SHEER	3-6-5	3-1-0	2-11-2	3-0-4	2-10-4	2-10-2	2-10-4	2-10-4	2-11-2	3-0-3	3-0-3
	CHINE	2-6-5	2-4-6	2-3-3	2-1-7	2-0-7	2-1-5	2-1-5	2-2-4	2-3-4	2-5-2	2-5-2
	BOTTOM	2-0-0	1-10-6	1-9-6	1-8-7	1-8-3	1-8-1	1-8-2	1-8-6	1-9-5	1-10-3	2-0-0
½ BREADTH FROM L.	SHEER	0-4-7	1-0-6	1-7-0	1-10-3	1-4-3	1-5-0	1-8-1	1-8-5	1-7-3	1-5-2	1-0-3
	CHINE	0-3-2	0-8-1	0-11-7	1-2-6	1-4-1	1-4-1	1-3-6	1-2-6	1-0-3	0-8-2	0-3-4
	BOTTOM	0-0-5	0-2-4	0-4-0	0-5-7	0-6-4	0-6-4	0-6-1	0-5-4	0-4-3	0-2-2	0-0-5

CHECKED BY _____

PRINCIPAL DIMENSIONS

L.O.A. ... 12'-1"
L.W.L. ... 10'-0"
BEAM ... 3'-6"
DRAFT ... 4"

LINES & OFFSETS

12'-0" O.A. ROWING DORY

FOR

SCALE 1½" = 1'-0"

DESIGNED BY
FRANCIS S. KINNEY
COLD SPRING HARBOR
L.I.   OCT. 1, '47   N.Y.

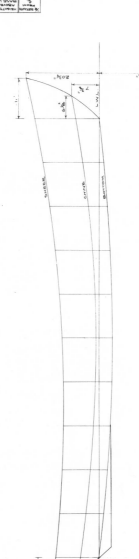

SHEER
CHINE
L.W.L.
BOTTOM

SHEER
CHINE
BOTTOM
L.W.L.

BASE LINE

STATIONS SPACED 12"

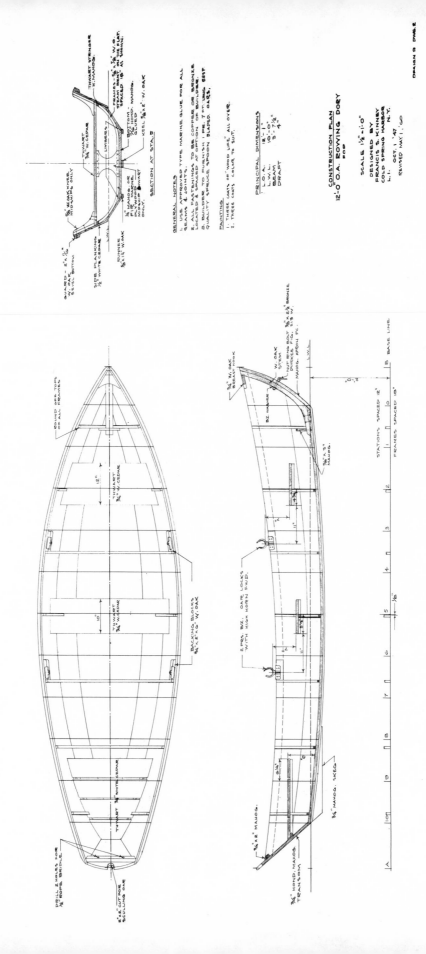

SECTION AT STA. 3

GENERAL NOTES

1. USE APPROVED TYPE MARINE GLUE FOR ALL SEAMS & JOINTS.

2. ALL FASTENINGS TO BE COPPER OR BRONZE LOCATED & SPACED AT OPTION OR BUILDER.

3. BUILDER TO FURNISH 1 PR. 7 FT. UNLG. BEST QUALITY SPRUCE SPOON BLADED OARS.

PAINTING

1. THREE COATS OF WOOD LIFE, ALL OVER.

2. THREE COATS COLOR, TO SUIT.

PRINCIPAL DIMENSIONS

L.O.A.	12'-1"
L.W.L.	10'-0"
BEAM	3'-4"
DRAFT	4"

CONSTRUCTION PLAN
12'-0 O.A. ROWING DORY
FOR

SCALE 1½"-1'-0"
DESIGNED BY
FRANCIS S. KINNEY
COLD SPRING HARBOR
L.I.   OCT. 1, '47   N.Y.
REVISED MAY 1, '60

DESIGN 9 DWG. 2

Deckhouses, to look well, should have tumble home to their sides, that is, the sides should lean in at the top. It is a subtlety of design that takes the curse off a boxlike house.

The amount of deck crown or camber has a noticeable effect on appearance. A camber of ½ inch to a foot on a flat sheered design may well raise the deck at center line so much that it will appear hogged. On the other hand, a camber of ¼ inch to a foot may be so low as to cut down on the headroom below. So the compromise camber of ⅜ inch to the foot seems to be good all around. The reason for deck camber, of course, is to give curvature to the deck, so that water will run off to the sides and overboard. Flat decks like the cockpit sole should be pitched one way or the other, so that water can run to the scuppers.

Don't pitch the cockpit sole of an after cockpit aft to after scuppers. I've been on two boats where this was disastrous. What happened was that the stern wave built up not just on the sides of the boat but through into the scuppers, and flooded the cockpit. It was embarrassing to the designers.

In summary, let me say that it is very difficult to design a good-looking boat. Let me submit our own boat, SANTA MARIA of Lloyd Harbor, in the next chapter and ask you to be the judge of the design.

SANTA MARIA.

CHAPTER VII

SANTA MARIA OF LLOYD HARBOR

Frankly, our own boat, SANTA MARIA, was designed to please my wife, so she would enjoy cruising with me.

Besides looking pretty, a classic sheer line with long drawn out lines and graceful ends makes sense for a yawl rig. This rig suits us, because it is easy to handle with just the two of us sailing. The size we like best and chose is a 29' 0" water-line length. With long ends this brings the overall length to 43' 5½". This permits a long base on the foretriangle forward, and a suitable spot aft for sheeting the larger-than-usual mizzen to the stern, thus not requiring a boomkin.

Her beam is 11' 0", which is 5 inches more than our former boat, a Herreshoff Fisher's Island 31. This is ample for stiffness and generous for room below. Draft is 6' 2½", which is the limit under C.C.A. Rule. Her sections are sea kindly, and she has a dry bow. The turn of her garboard sections is an easy curve, to allow the cabin flooring to be deep in the hull, and for greater strength. Tight curves made for broken frames.

Below we have the conventional layout of a 25' 0" water-line boat stretched to a 29' 0" water-line, so that there is more elbow room all around. Thus the arrangement is simple and roomy. We had thirteen people in the cabin at a fall rendezvous of the Crusing Club, and Rod Stephens was able to descend and ascend the easy sloped companion ladder with his accordion strapped on.

Working aft, there are two berths forward. There is a generous-sized head to port with hot and cold running water and a hot shower. The toilet bowl is 4 inches above the water-line, so that it cannot flood over and sink the boat. A large hanging locker with full-length mirror and big drawers is opposite the head. The head can close off the after side of the passage, giving additional space to the forward cabin, and the locker door can close off the forward side of the passage.

The main cabin has just two berths, although we could have had four here. My wife does not like having six or seven people cruising on board, because she feels it is just too crowded. So the main cabin berths act as seats in the daytime, and

51

have back rests that swing up out of the way to allow a good wide berth at night. A seat is too narrow to be a berth, and a berth is too wide to be a seat. The gimballed drop-leaf table on the centerline is mahogany and finished as nicely as a dining room table at home.

In the galley aft, everything is covered with flush teak covers to match the counter tops. This was one of the primary requests of my wife, and I must say it has worked out well, because these flush tops are excellent chart tables and make everything in the galley area neat and tidy. For the stove we chose the large Heritage alcohol-burning model in gimbals. It has an oven large enough to take a medium-sized roast. A great safety feature is having the shut-off valves below and inboard of the stove, so that in case there is a fire the alcohol can be shut off

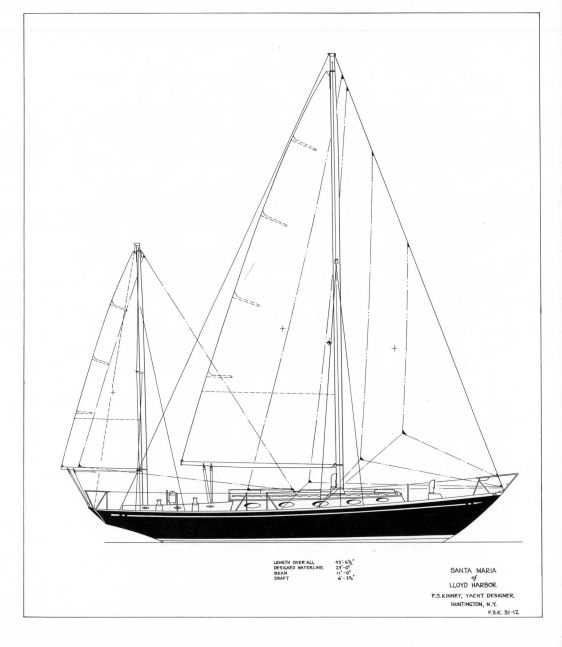

LENGTH OVER ALL	43'-5½"
DESIGNED WATERLINE	29'-0"
BEAM	11'-0"
DRAFT	6'-2½"

SANTA MARIA
of
LLOYD HARBOR
F.S. KINNEY, YACHT DESIGNER
HUNTINGTON, N.Y.
F.S.K. 31-12

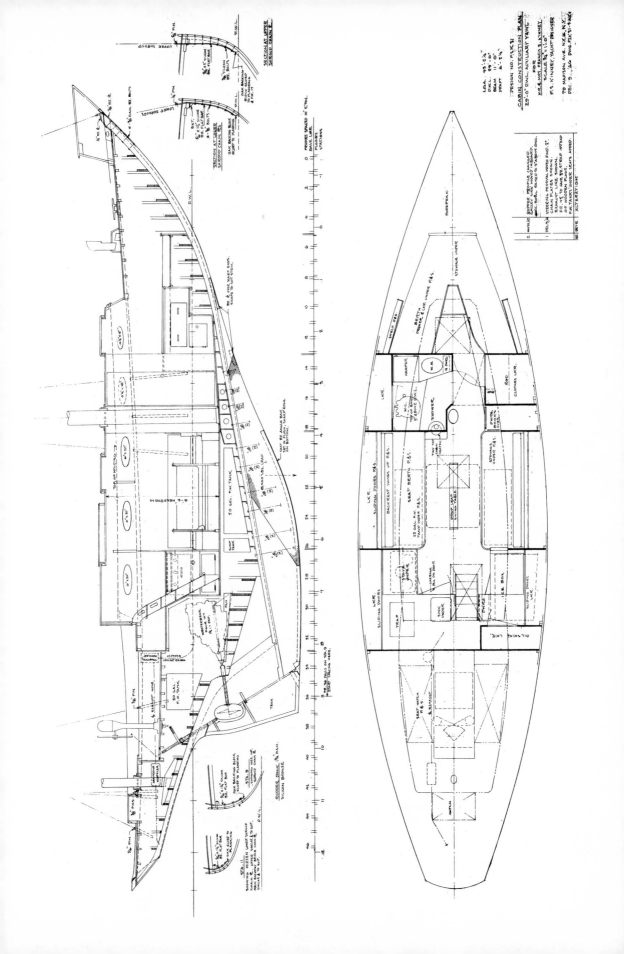

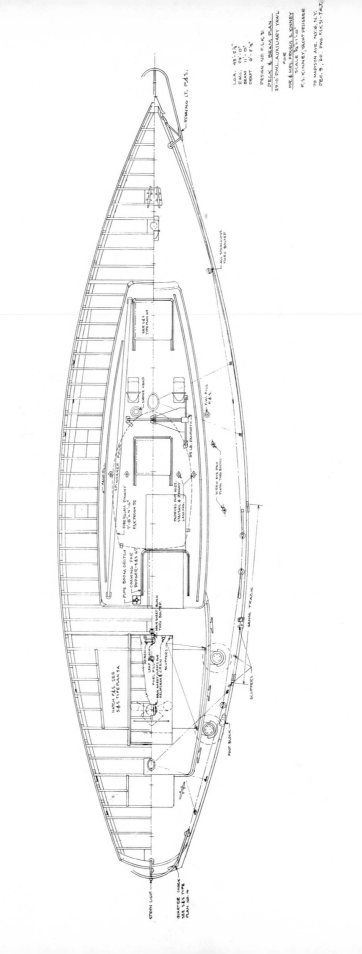

FASTENING SCHEDULE

ALL FASTENINGS TO BE SILICON BRONZE, EXCEPT WHERE NOTED.

ITEM	LENGTH	DIA.	TYPE	HEAD	REMARKS
KEEL BACKBONE —					
STEM KNEE TO STEM & KEEL	—	1/4"	BOLT	FIN	IF LAMINATION IS NOT CONTINUOUS
STEM KNEE TO KEEL	—	1/2"	BOLT	FIN	
KEEL TO DEADWOOD & STERN POST	—	5/8"	BOLT	FIN	
HORN TIMBER TO STERN POST	—	5/8"	BOLT	FIN	IF LAMINATION IS NOT CONTINUOUS
FLOORS —					
CAST BZ. FLOORS TO KEEL	—	3/8"	BOLT	FIN	TWO/FR.
CAST BZ. FLOORS TO FRAMES	1 1/4"	3/16"	SCREW	F.H.	THREE/FR. PER PLS.
WOOD FLOORS TO KEEL	—	3/8"	BOLT	FIN	ONE/FR., TWO WHERE POSSIBLE
WOOD FLOORS TO FRAMES	—	5/16"	BOLT	FIN	THREE/FR. PER PLS., FOUR WHERE POSSIBLE
MAST STEP FLOORS TO FRAMES	—	5/16"	BOLT	FIN	THREE/FR. PER PLS., FOUR WHERE POSSIBLE
MAST STEP TO KEEL	—	1/2"	BOLTS		AS REQD.
CLAMP & AUXL. SHELF					
THRU PLANKING, FRAMES, CLAMP & AUXL. SHELF	3 3/4"	5/16"	BOLT	FIN	ON ALTERNATE FRAMES
THRU CLAMP TO FRAME	3 1/4"	#18	SCREW	F.H.	ON ALTERNATE FRAMES
AUXL. SHELF TO CLAMP	—	5/16"	BOLT	FIN	AS REQD.
PECK BEAM TO CLAMP	—	5/16"	BOLT	FIN	ONE EACH END
PECK BEAM TO AUXL. SHELF	—	5/16"	BOLT	FIN	ONE EACH END
PLANKING					
OUTER PLANK TO EACH FRAME	1 3/8"	#12	SCREW	F.H.	TWO/STRAKE/FRAME.
INNER PLANK TO OUTER PLANK	3/4"	#8	SCREW	F.H.	SIX/STRAKE/FRAME. MIN.
OUTER PLANK AT WOOD ENDS	2 1/4"	#14	SCREW	R.H.	TWO/STRAKE EACH END
OUTER PLANK TO BUTT BLOCKS	AS REQD	1 1/2"	BOLT	FIN	THREE/STRAKE EACH END
DECKING					
DECK TO BEAMS	—	#12	SCREW	F.H.	SPACED ABOUT 4" C.T.C.
DECK TO SHEER STRAKE	1 1/2"	#12	SCREW	F.H.	SPACED ABOUT 4" C.T.C.
TOE RAIL					
THRU DECK TO SHEER STRAKE	4"		SCREW	F.H.	SPACED ABOUT 10", PORT BOLTS FWD.
BULKHEADS					
STRUCTURAL BHD TO FRAMES	1 1/4"	#14	BOLT		SPACED ABOUT 7", USE WASHERS
STRUCTURAL BHD TO BEAMS	1 3/4"	#14	SCREW	R.H.	SPACED ABOUT 7", USE WASHERS
JOINER BHD TO FRAME & BEAM	1 1/2"	#10	SCREW	R.H.	SPACED ABOUT 7", USE WASHERS
CABIN TRUNK					
THRU CABIN TRUNK DECK & HEADER	1/4"	5/16"	BO LT	TEE	SPACED ABOUT 20"
THRU HEADER & DECK TO CABIN TRUNK	4"	#18	SCREW	F.H.	SPACED ABOUT 5"
TIE BOLTS					
AT MAST THRU COLLAR & STEP	—	5/8"		OVAL HEAD	
CEILING TO FRAMES	3/16"	#7	SCREW	F.H.	THREE 5/8 ROWS FWD. FOURTEEN 3/4 ROWS AFT
LEAD BALLAST TO WOOD KEEL	—	3/4"	BOLTS		

NOTE: 1. HEADS OF ALL BOLTS UNLESS OTHERWISE NOTED TO BE STANDARD HEXAGONAL TYPE. ALL NUTS ON BOLTS TO BE SET UP TO BE FULLY ACCESSIBLE AND TO BE FITTED WITH OVERSIZE WASHERS WHERE POSSIBLE.

2. CHAIN PLATES, TO BE SILICON BRONZE FLATBAR WITH WHITE OAK BLOCKING THRU BOLTED TO PLANKING AND CLAMP.

3. BULKHEADS —
    STRUCTURAL BHPS.- 1/2" THK. MARINE WATERPROOF PLYWOOD.
    JOINER BHPS. - 3/8" THK. MARINE WATERPROOF PLYWOOD.

DESIGN NO. F.S.K. 31
CONSTRUCTION SECTIONS
29'-0" D.W.L. AUXILIARY YAWL
for
MR. & MRS. FRANCIS S. KINNEY
SCALE 3/4" = 1'-0"
F.S. KINNEY, YACHT DESIGNER
79 MADISON AVE., N.Y. 16, N.Y.
SEPT. 12, '66   DWG. F.S.K 31-3 ALT.1

L.O.A. 43'-5½"
D.W.L. 29'-0"
BEAM   11'-0"
DRAFT   6'-2¾"

ALT.1 - BALLAST KEEL REQUIRED
         CABIN SOLE ADDED

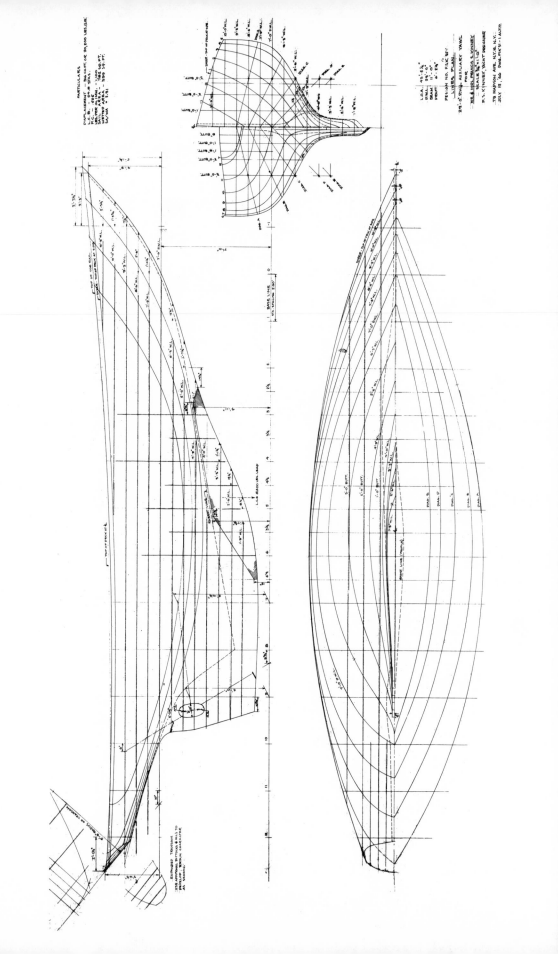

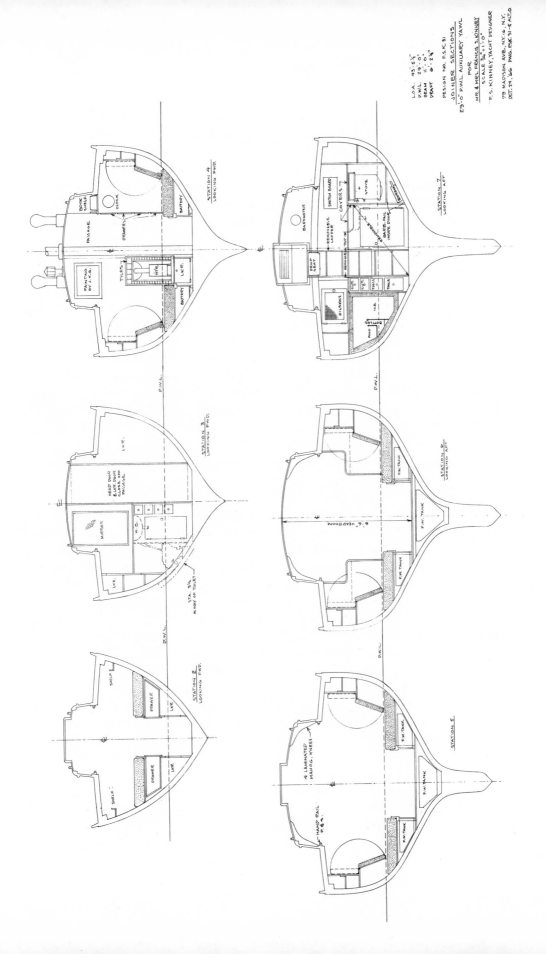

without reaching through the flames. The galley sink is large and as close to the center line as possible, so it will drain directly overboard, even when the boat is heeled. The icebox holds 290 pounds of ice, which lasts for over a week. A bottle rack and shelf for food are arranged in fore and aft partitions in the icebox. Things stay put when the boat is sailing in a stiff breeze.

One thing, a great luxury for me, a tall man, is having 6′ 6″ headroom throughout the boat. This is accomplished by having the cabin sole as deep in the boat as possible, and eliminating the cabin top beams by the use of molded plywood. The cabin top is simply made by gluing three or four layers of plywood over a form. When the glue dries, this kind of top retains its curvature. Of course, there are knees′to stiffen it and prevent racking in way of the mast. Just last year we added four laminated mahogany knees to strengthen this long trunk cabin. They do get smashed in heavy weather so I felt more stiffening of this structure was needed.

Further improvements last season include an elliptical cockpit table, and a very comfortable helmsman's back rest on the mizzen mast. The table is supported by the steering pedestal at its aft end and a folding leg forward. It stows neatly on its side under the cockpit seat hatch. This back rest came from my draftsman's stool.

There is a good oilskin locker handy to the companionway, well ventilated by a screen door. Another good feature is having four good drawers next to the companionway for cutlery, cooking utensils and tools.

The simplest design is usually the best, and so we tried to keep her that way. We have no electronic gear or suchlike instruments, having found them to be a disappointment on former boats. We are much happier without them.

Tankage is 50 gallons of diesel fuel for our Westerbeke Four 107, which at 1750 r.p.m. with its 1.5:1 reduction gear drives us at exactly 6.5 knots, and gives us a range of 390 miles under power. Top speed at 2000 r.p.m. is 7.5 knots and 8 knots under sail. Fresh water is in three tanks, total 100 gallons. These water tanks are amidships under the cabin seats and in the bilge, so that they are as low as possible and do not change the trim of the boat, when filled or empty. There is a sump tank to take the shower and icebox drain, which is pumped out by a diaphragm pump.

The power we use, taken from the Westerbeke Power Curve, is 25 h.p. at 1750 r.p.m. and is just the right amount to be absorbed by this hull.

Her lovely shaped sails were made by Hood of his soft dacron. The mainsail is only 7½ oz. dacron, which is a joy to furl, because it is so light.

Instead of having a tiller, which takes up so much room in the cockpit, we chose a pedestal steerer with a 24-inch diameter destroyer-type wheel. This aluminum wheel has a teak rim with finger notches on its forward side, and was made by Paul Luke. There is little or no friction in this steering gear, so that you can feel her balance under sail.

She is easy to sail single-handed, because all the sheets lead to the helmsman's position. The main sheet is affixed to the bridge deck and goes first to a winch with guide rod, thence through a lead block on the cockpit sole, and either up to a cleat

SANTA MARIA's cockpit table, around which her ship's company has had many a good party. It is particularly pleasant to use when the awning is rigged over the boom and one can enjoy the cool shade.

Note the helmsman's backrest on the mizzen mast. It came from the author's drafting stool and is a great comfort.

at the forward face of the cockpit, or when sailing alone, aft to a cleat at the base of the pedestal steerer.

As for the jib sheets, there are four big Lewmar winches for them, two forward and two aft on the cockpit coaming. When sailing alone, the after ones are used by the helmsman. Our working jib, which overlaps the main mast by two feet or so, is not too large to winch home without using a crank. There is a trick to coming about. You must make a slow easy turn. Then you give a mighty heave just at the last moment before she has fallen away on the next tack, and with three turns of the sheet on the winch this jib is trimmed as nicely as you please. The mizzen sheet is easy to haul or ease, because it is right behind the helmsman. So there are all four sheets leading to that one spot within the helmsman's reach.

We have a Tiny Tot heater mounted in a stainless steel semicircular recess in the head bulkhead. Its stove pipe goes up through the head to warm that compartment too. It is about the least expensive item on the boat, but worth its weight in gold, when you have a charcoal fire warming the cabin on a wet and cold day.

The workmanship is superb. Aage Walsted's Yard in Thuro, Denmark, built her with care, skill and pride. You cannot see a seam anywhere. Double-planked African mahogany set in epoxy glue literally gives her a one-piece hull.

Why wood in this day and age? We chose it over fiberglass, steel, aluminum or ferro cement, because there is something friendly about wood, a quality the other materials lack.

The deck is fiberglass over plywood, because we feel this is the lightest and the tighest material combination. Teak decks are great, but there are all those seams that leak when the boat gets older.

Building her in Denmark was just fine except for one thing. When it came time to pay the duty, the U.S. Customs insisted on charging me duty on a nonexistent architect's fee—even after I had patiently explained to them several times that I had designed our own boat myself!

After four seasons' use SANTA MARIA has proven to be an excellent boat in every respect. She is well balanced, stiff, well mannered and fast. Her lines bear study, because of all her good qualities, the most outstanding is that she is well mannered—a great source of pleasure to us.

A postscript from the designer's wife: She is a joy in every way and has completely fulfilled all my desires in a cruising boat. We have decorated the interior with gay colors, so that even on a gloomy day the cabin is cheerful, bright and warm. She is painted white throughout with varnished mahogany trim, with a thick royal blue carpet on the floor to blend with the turquoise blue mattresses and back rests, with royal blue and flowered crewel cushions for accent. We both like bright gay colors as opposed to the dark, gloomy interiors one sees on so many boats.

The cabin heater is framed with blue-and-white tiles depicting Columbus' three ships the *Nina*, *Santa Maria* and *Pinta*, under sail. It makes a well-decorated focal point for the main cabin. And above the fireplace there is an oil painting by the designer's sister of one of his favorite beaches on Martha's Vineyard.

CHAPTER VIII

MOTOR SAILERS

In my opinion, the difference between a motor sailer and an auxiliary can be determined by this example:

Let's say you are in a sailboat with power, and you start out in a calm. To make a passage you turn on the engine and power at cruising speed. Then the wind starts to blow head on. At first it is not strong enough to sail, beating to windward, and get you where you want to go, when you want to arrive. So you keep the engine on, and set the mainsail, then sheet it down flat for steadying the roll. Next the wind quickly freshens to a strong breeze (25 to 32 m.p.h.), and the head seas build up. You soon notice that with all the resulting pitching you are really not making much headway. Going slower and slower straight into it, there is only one thing left to do. Beat to windward under shortened sail.

Now, such a boat I would call an auxiliary. This condition of a strong breeze and heavy sea head on is the dividing line. If you were on a sailboat that could keep going under power into the same head seas and get there sooner, your boat should be called a motor sailer, I believe.

One insurance company gives a motor sailer a 10% lower rate than a power boat with steadying sails, because she has the ability to beat off a lee shore under sail alone! This company draws the line between such craft by using the following rule of thumb: If the boat has at least a sail area of her load water-line squared divided by two, then she qualifies as a motor sailer, instead of a power boat, and gets a lower insurance rate.

Say she is 40 feet L.W.L. Then, $40^2 \div 2 = 800$ sq. ft. If she has less than that, she might be insured at a 3% rate. But if she has more than that, this company will insure her at a rate of, say, 2.7%, because they think she will be able to save herself by sailing if the engine fails.

Perhaps the outstanding feature of motor sailers is the emphasis on having lots of motors, especially a more powerful main engine than an auxiliary has, but not necessarily less emphasis on sailing ability.

Some yachtsmen who own such a craft still cling to their dislike of the word "motor" in motor sailer, because of its association with "stink pots." So they prefer to have their vessels called not just "sailing motor sailers," but, better yet, "full-powered auxiliaries," and best of all, "ocean cruisers."

Be that as it may, motor sailers are in my opinion an excellent type of yacht in every respect. They combine the best of two worlds. The best of the world of out-and-out sailing vessels, and the best of the world of displacement-type power boats. I should say they are more seaworthy than a sailboat, because of their huskier, higher-sided hulls, and more seaworthy than a power boat, because with their sails set they do not have the uncomfortable motion of a power boat in a seaway.

You cannot appreciate how nice it is to be aboard, until you have cruised on a well-designed one. It has been my pleasure to have sailed on the 57-foot BARAKA, a ketch-rigged double-ended centerboard motor sailer. She cruised from Florida across the Atlantic, around the Mediterranean, and back across the Atlantic. On her way home she weathered a severe storm by running before it under bare poles, making a huge circle in four days. We joined her in Antigua and sailed north in the Caribbean to St. Thomas.

The first thing that impressed me was the size and complexity of her engine room. It was below the midship cockpit and had 6-foot headroom. I will take the reader on a tour of it later.

We spent the first night aboard stern to the wharf in English Harbor, Antigua, and I marveled at the lack of noise from this complex engine room, until it dawned on me that we were plugged into shore current! The electric stove, the refrigerator and the stereo tape player were all in use at the same time. These could all operate simultaneously at sea, but the 15 kilowatt auxiliary generator had to be running with its accompanying noise, vibration and exhaust, however slight each may be.

I must admit that we spent about 75% of the time on this cruise under power. But this was mostly because of the lack of wind at this time of year in that area.

We made our passage from island to island at night, like the big cruise ships, arriving at a new island every morning. When thus under power, we had the mainsail of this ketch rig set and sheeted in flat. This reduced the rolling and made for a comfortable motion in the ground swells. There was one grand sail on a close reach up the Sir Francis Drake Passage, which is protected on all sides by the Virgin Islands. I was very impressed at how well BARAKA sailed in these pro-tected waters, boiling along at 9 knots with genoa, main and mizzen set.

EGRET is a sailing motor sailer of Sparkman & Stephens design. The author was fortunate enough to be able to sail aboard her sister ship BARAKA in the Caribbean on two winter cruises, calling at almost all of the islands between St. Thomas and Grenada. During these cruises he got to know her ways pretty well, and describes her in detail in this chapter.

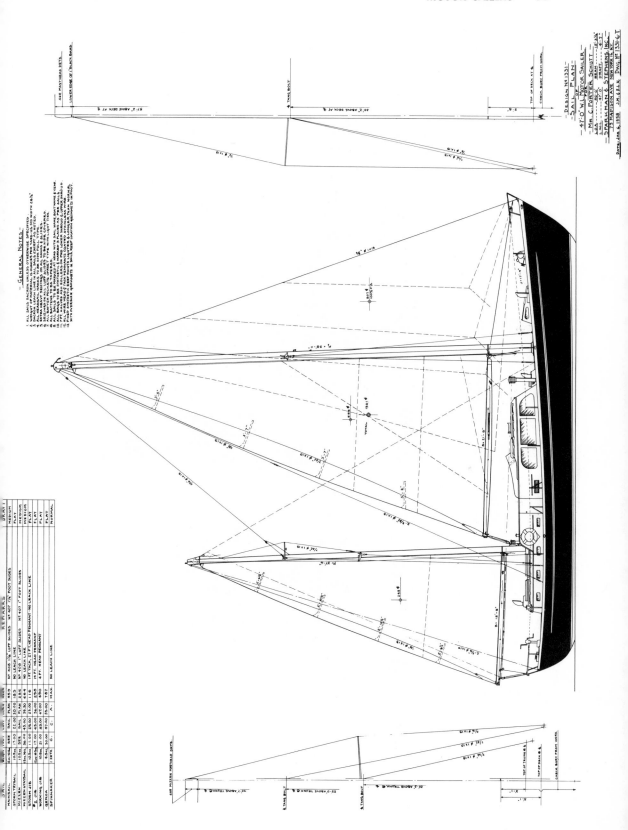

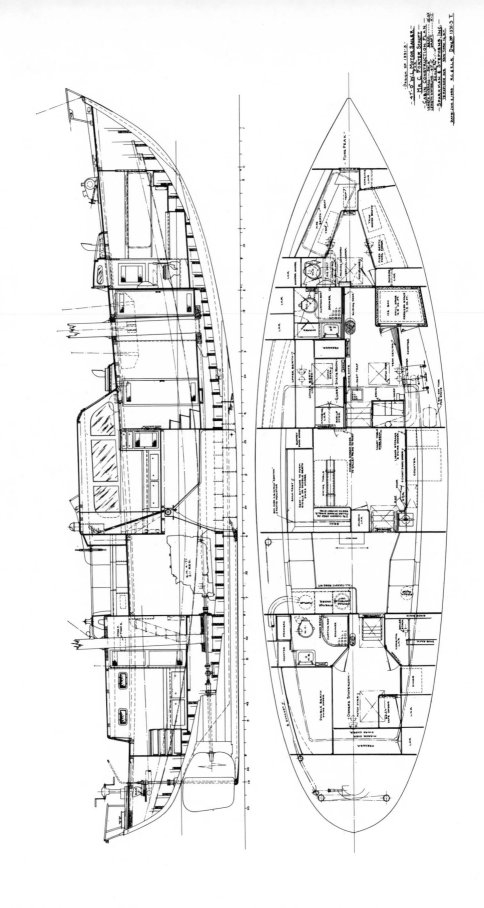

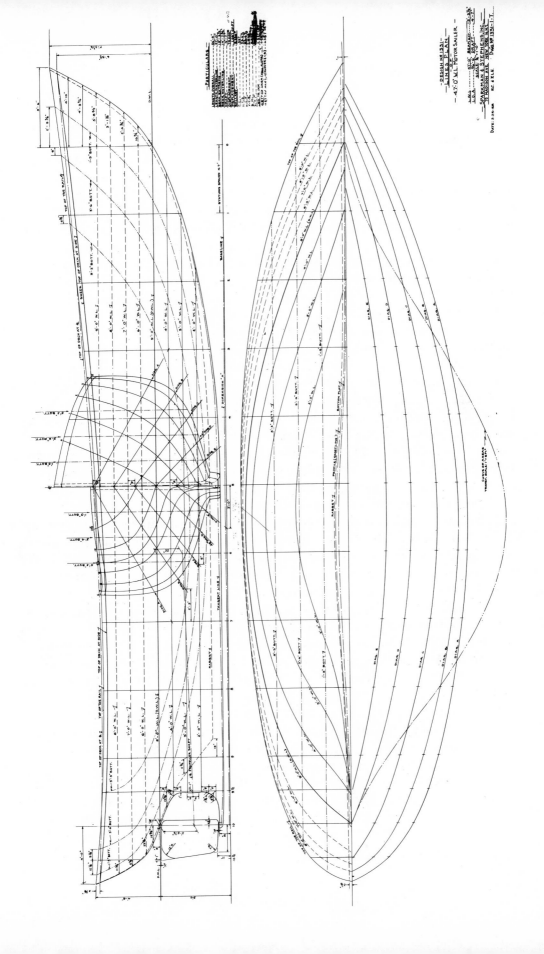

The pleasure of living aboard with all the amenities of life is just great. Hot water to shave with first thing in the morning is only a little thing, but it starts you off right for the day. Frozen foods, in every variety from orange juice to meats and vegetables, and all sorts of gourmet delights can be stored in a deep freeze and provide the ship's company with food as fine as that served in your own home ashore. A hot fresh-water shower is the greatest of luxuries on board. Then a change of clothing for the happy dinner party is really living the good life. "Music hath charms" was certainly true aboard BARAKA with her four-speaker (two in the main cabin, two in the cockpit) stereo tape player. "Summertime, and the livin' is easy" sums it up nicely. Another thing, and a very practical one too, about having an abundant supply of electricity is that the owner can have a radio-telephone and all the modern electronic navigation instruments like radar, loran, R.D.F. and depth finder, etc.

What is the best shape for a proper motor sailer hull? Well, that which comes to mind first is a vessel with the longest possible water-line length so that the maximum speed under power may be attained. This means a short-ended craft.

What about the stern? Well, a normal transom stern is probably the best, as opposed to a double-ended or pointed stern, because, again, it helps under power by reducing squatting, and drawing the stern wave further aft, thus increasing speed a little. But, on the other hand, a double-ended stern makes a more seaworthy vessel. I said to BARAKA's owner, "George, I bet you were mighty glad BARAKA had a pointed stern, instead of a transom, when you were running before that gale in the Atlantic for four days."

"I sure was," George said emphatically.

The disadvantage of a double-ended stern is one that can easily be observed. Take a look at such a boat when she is at rest. On light-colored boats you can see a line formed by dirty exhaust gases tracing the shape of the stern wave high on the stern. In fact it is difficult to locate the exhaust high enough to clear the stern wave in such cases. Such a craft usually squats under power, and thus is a little slower.

The basic theory of hull speed is to get the bow and stern wave as far apart as possible, because there is a hard-and-fast law governing the speed of waves. It is the square root of the distance between crests multiplied by 1.34. This was discovered by Admiral Taylor. So, you see, the greater the distance between crests of bow and stern wave, the faster the speed of the boat. Or for displacement-type hulls, the longer the boat, the faster she goes.

What draft should the proper motor sailer have? Well, as most of them are so large, and as most owners would like to be able to cruise to such places as the Bahama Islands, Chesapeake Bay, and the Cape Cod area, a centerboard is almost a must. Ideal for such places would be 5' 6" draft.

Bear in mind, however, that shallow draft means a shallow rudder, and this means poor steering in following seas. There is a ratio of 7 to 1 of water-line length to draft, beyond which it is dangerous to go in designing a shallow-draft boat.

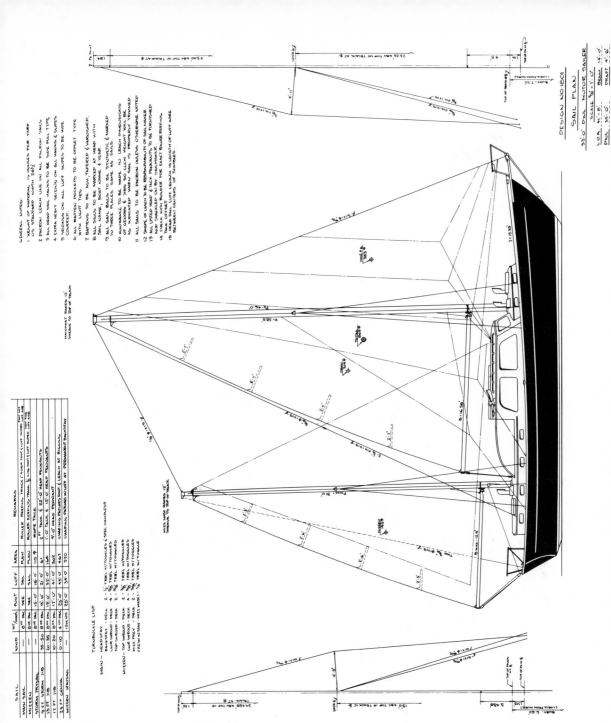

MALU is a small motor-sailer only 41 feet overall. She performs well by all reports, and is a good sailer.

The large deckhouse is a comfortable place to live below, and makes a pleasant dining room, as one can look out of the windows while eating. She is designed to accommodate two couples, one in spacious quarters aft with its head and shower, and the other in the deckhouse, with its head forward, where the galley is also located.

Her arrangement is compact because the cockpit well on deck is over a series of lockers below.

Her design came from the board of F. S. K. at S & S.

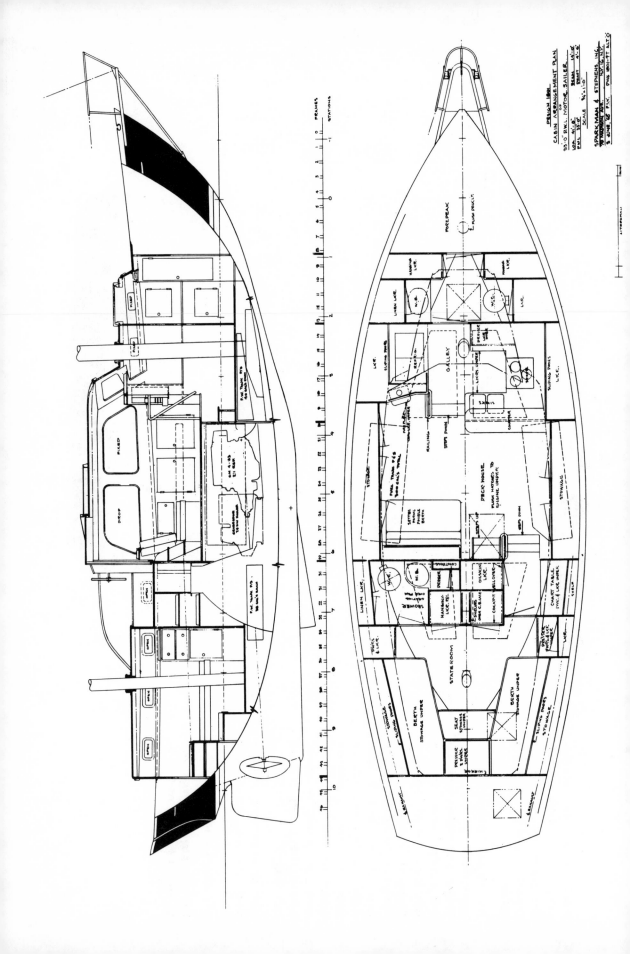

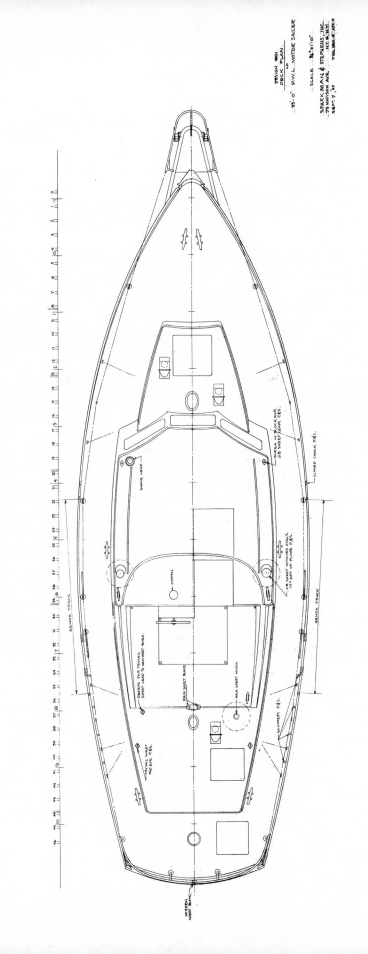

I found this out when designing the centerboard ketch ENDEAVOUR, a gunkholer's delight, because she is an extremely shallow-draft type. She broached once and was knocked over on her beam ends with her sails flat in the water. It happened when sailing before a fresh breeze against the current in a dangerous passage between Cuttyhunk and Nashawena Islands. The seas were short and steep, and were cresting. People on shore, who were watching this performance, thought she was a goner for sure. Fortunately, for the reason that she has high freeboard and inside ballast that cannot shift because it is bolted down, she righted herself and proceeded thru the passage.

Well, the point of this story is that she was 30' on the D.W.L. and drew only 2' 10" with the board up, a ratio of length to draft of 10 to 1. The centerboard sloop FIDELIA (page 97), one of my earlier designs, never had any steering problem. She was 21' 3" on the D.W.L. and drew 3' 0", a ratio of 7 to 1.

The ENDEAVOUR should have had tandem centerboards, with one well aft to act like the feather on an arrow, steering the arrow, straight.

To get back to the maximum draft desirable for the Bahama Islands of 5' 6" using the 7 to 1 ratio, we come up with $7 \times 5.5 = 38.5$ D.W.L., and if the prospective owner wants a longer boat with this draft, the designer should insist on tandem centerboards. It is the designer's responsibility to see that his client has a safe boat.

What rig is best suited for motor sailers? In my opinion a ketch rig is best, although we know that the sloop rig is fastest to windward, and next the yawl; the ketch comes third, with the schooner last. Of course nowadays with roller reefing you could say that it is easy to shorten sail on a sloop, but what could be easier than dropping the mainsail on a yawl, or ketch, and sailing on with the balanced rig of jib and mizzen? I favor the ketch rig for motor sailers, because the total sail area is more equally divided in three parts, fore triangle with headsails, mainsail and mizzen. On a yawl there is the same three-part division of sail area but the mainsail and fore triangle are larger, and thus more difficult to handle than on a ketch. In spite of the fact that I say this, our own boat, SANTA MARIA, is a yawl, but she is a lot smaller than a motor sailer and her mainsail is easy to handle.

There is also this to say about the ketch rig's being proper for a motor sailer. With all that horsepower in the main engine the great temptation, which the skipper of a motor sailer oft succumbs to, is not to tack back and forth to get to windward, but simply to push the starting button and get there quickly under power. After all, the batteries must be charged at some time. So why have the fastest rig to windward, a sloop, if you are hardly ever going to sail on that point of sailing?

Two-masted vessels are faster reaching than single-masted vessels, because yawls, ketches and schooners can set huge sails between their masts, which in the case of a golliwobbler on a schooner just about doubles the sail area. I know on our yawl we use the mizzen staysail at the drop of a hat. It is very easy to set, being lightweight,

(Below & overleaf) **ENDEAVOUR** is an explorer's delight. She can go anywhere there is only three feet of water (her draft with board up is 2'10'').

Shoal waters abound in areas around the Bahama Islands, the Florida Keys, Cheaspeake Bay, Martha's Vineyard, Nantucket, and so on. With **ENDEAVOUR** many beautiful little harbors in such places can be explored. That's good fun.

All of her interior joiner work was built (including plywood water tanks—still tight) by her owner, who is still happy with her fifteen years after she was designed for him by the author.

Full-length battens were used in the mainsail and mizzen to increase sail area. In the mainsail alone 70 square feet of area was added by their use to hold out the increased roach and fill in the space between the masts.

Her raised deck provides more space below for upper and lower berths, as well as more space on deck. Also it required fewer man-hours to build than a trunk cabin type. All inside ballast lends itself to economy too.

She is popular with her owner's friends, who often charter her, because she is so comfortable to cruise aboard. In fact she comes closer to paying her own way than any other yacht I know.

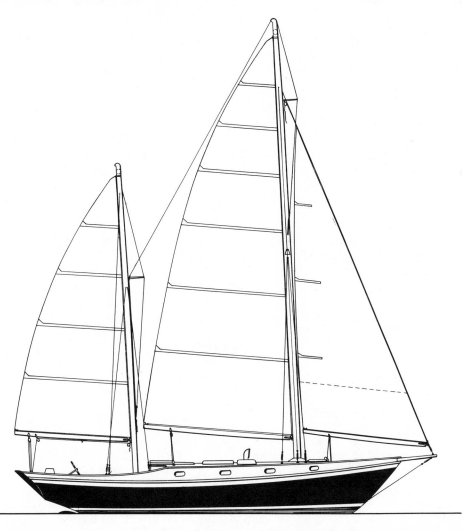

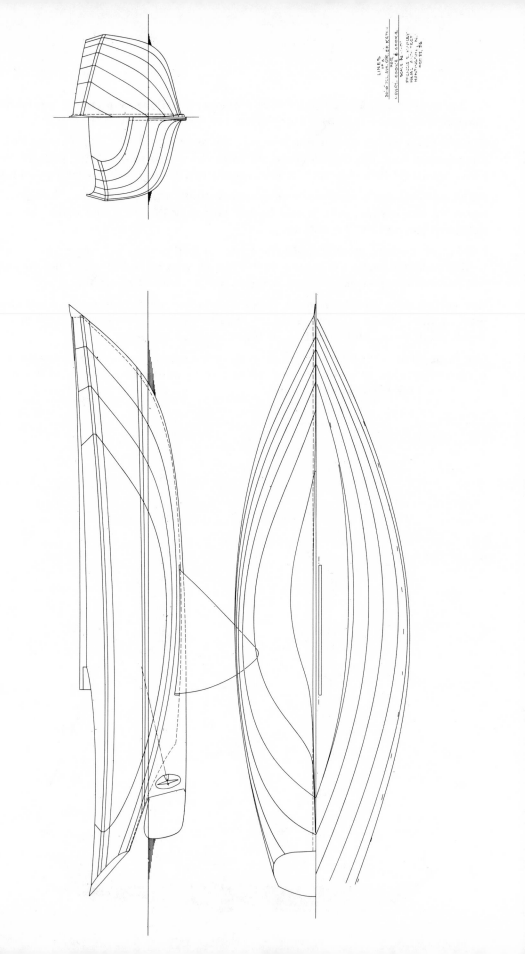

LINES
OF A
30-0 WL. AUX. OW. RD KET.
FOR
LEWIS C. COOKE & COOKE
SCALE 3/4" = 1'0"
FRANCIS S. KINNEY
N.A. ...
HUNTINGTON, N. ...
OCT 22, 56

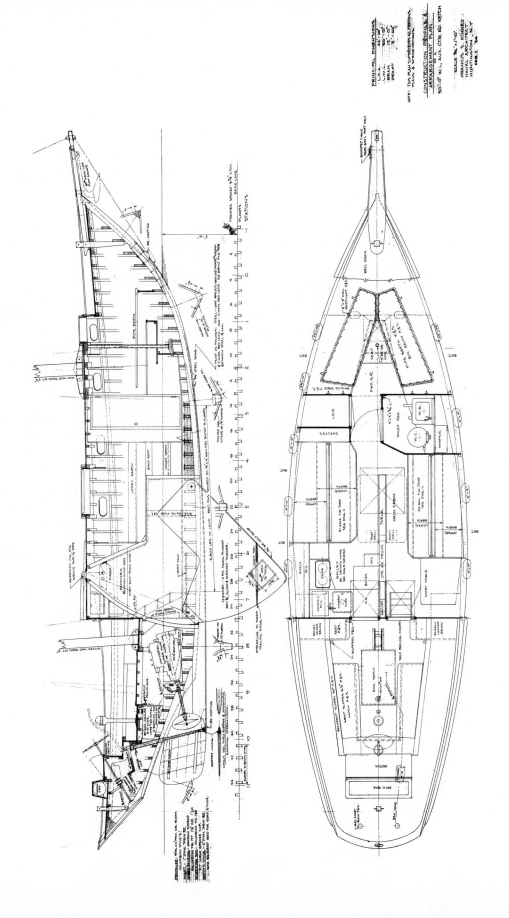

PRINCIPAL DIMENSIONS
L.O.A. .... 42'-8"
L.W.L. .... 30'-0"
BEAM .... 12'-0"
DRAFT .... 6'-3"

NOTE: THIS PLAN SUPERSEDES ALL PREVIOUS.
PLAN # SPECIFICATIONS

CONSTRUCTION PROFILE &
ARRANGEMENT PLAN
OF A
30'-0" W.L. AUX. CTR. BD. KETCH

SCALE ⅜"=1'-0"
FRANCIS S. KINNEY
NAVAL ARCHITECT
HUNTINGTON, N.Y.
S.S.Z. '46

and set flying. The result is extra speed when reaching with a mininum of effort. Sloops can't do this.

But sloops are supreme on the wind and down wind. One tall mast allows a sloop to carry a large genoa, and its driving slot effect between jib and main gives the sloop the power to get to windward first of all the rigs. When sailing down wind with the tall mast and masthead rig, the largest spinnaker of any rig is carried, and the race again goes to the sloop. But motor sailers are for cruising in comfort, not for racing.

We had a second cruise on BARAKA the following year, this time starting in the middle of the West Indies at Martinique and sailing south on the leeward side of the islands to Grenada, again demonstrating that with a motor sailer you can go anywhere with all the comforts of home.

Two ports of call on this cruise impressed me most. Perhaps Marigot Bay on St. Lucia is the most beautiful harbor I have ever seen. It is the kind of harbor a sailor dreams about, completely landlocked with palm trees and mangroves at the water's edge. My second favorite spot is the Tabago Cays, where the snorkelling is out of this world. The water is so clear you can see bottom at twenty feet, and the colors are unbelievable.

During this entire cruise we were sailing approximately south with the Northeast trade wind always blowing a strong breeze. Navigation was so simple we never had to steer a compass course, because the weather was so clear we could always see the mountains of the next island on the horizon and head for its lee side.

The weather was perfect for sailors, but poor for farmers. Although the islands in this southern half of the West Indies were greener than those we saw the year before in the northern half, they did not have really lush vegetation until we made our landfall at Grenada. There everything good to eat comes from trees—coconuts, bananas, breadfruit, grapefruit, oranges, lemons, cinnamon, nutmeg, pepper, coffee, etc. No wonder Grenada is known as the spice island.

It is interesting to note that out of the ten islands we sailed to, ice and diesel fuel are available at five of them, and only about 20% of the boats crusing this area have mechanical or electrical refrigeration. Water is not so easy to come by. It is expensive where you can get it. Our consumption for all uses averaged 8.5 gallons per person per day.

Even when we were under sail alone on BARAKA, the generator was running. It had to be run six hours a day in order to keep the electrical refrigerator and deep freeze cold enough to preserve our supply of frozen food. When our cook wanted to use the stove, it had to run to produce the 220 volts A.C. that were required. So noise, vibration and heat (the engine room was always about 110° F.) are the prices you have to pay to enjoy all the comforts of home. Our ladies liked these luxuries and didn't seem to mind the noise of the generator, but I thought to myself how glad I was to be using "silent blocks of ice" and alcohol for cooking aboard SANTA MARIA.

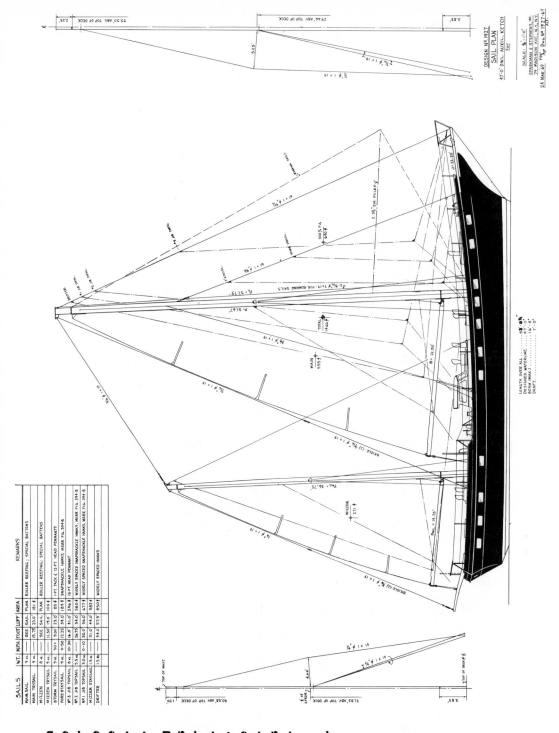

SAILS	WT.	MPH	FOOT	LUFF	AREA	REMARKS
MAIN SAIL	9 oz.	---	SEE SAIL PLAN		181#	ROLLER REEFING; SPECIAL BATTENS
MAIN TRYSAIL	9 oz.	---	15.75	23.0		
MIZZEN	8 oz.	---	SEE SAIL PLAN		104#	ROLLER REEFING; SPECIAL BATTENS
MIZZEN TRYSAIL			11.50	19.0	104#	
STORM TRYSAIL	9 oz.	50+	9.00	23.0	85#	4-FT. TACK & 12-FT. HEAD PENNANTS
FORE-STAYSAIL	9 oz.	0-50	12.75	34.0	184#	5-FT. HEAD PENNANT
No.3 JIB TOPSAIL	8 oz.	10-30	16.0	41.0	216#	SNAPSHACKLE HANKS, MERR. FIG.394.6
No.2 JIB TOPSAIL	5.5 oz.	0-10	24.75	54.0	380#	WIDELY SPACED SNAPSHACKLE HANKS, MERR FIG.394.6
No.1 JIB TOPSAIL	3.0 oz.	0-10	30.0	54.0	477#	WIDELY SPACED SNAPSHACKLE HANKS, MERR FIG.394.6
MIZZEN STAYSAIL	1.5 oz.		31.0	44.0	352#	
DRIFTER	1.5 oz.		34.0	57.5	650#	WIDELY SPACED HANKS

TOREA is a steel ocean cruiser with many of the good features of older sailing vessels, i.e., the clipper bow and the great cabin aft with windows across the stern.

She is based on Irving Johnson's YANKEE, but is larger and has a deeper keel without centerboards. Designed especially for cruising in the tropics (note the numerous airports) she has proven to be an excellent sailer.

F. S. K. had a hand in her design at S & S.

DESIGN Nº 1927
SAIL PLAN
47'-0" DWL. AUXIL. KETCH
for

SCALE: ⅜" = 1'-0"
SPARKMAN & STEPHENS, INC.
79 MADISON AVE. N.Y., N.Y.
24 MAR. 69 DWG. Nº 1927-6T

LENGTH OVER ALL .... 58'-8½"
DESIGNED WATERLINE ... 47'-0"
BEAM (MAX.) .... 16'-4"
DRAFT .... 7'-0"

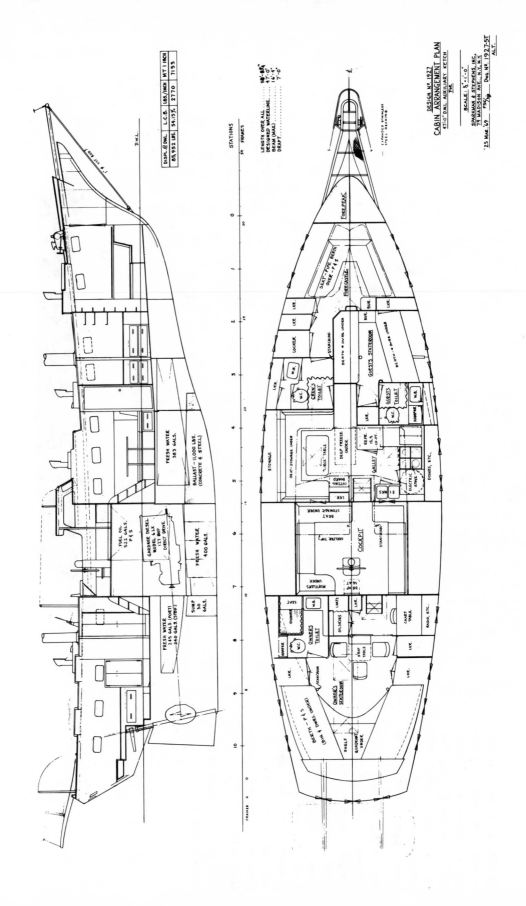

DESIGN Nº 1927
CABIN ARRANGEMENT PLAN
47'-0" D.W.L. AUXILIARY KETCH
THE

SCALE: ⅜" = 1'-0"

SPARKMAN & STEPHENS, INC.
79 MADISON AVE., N.Y., N.Y.

'25 MAR. '69   FSK/gg   Dwg. Nº 1927-ST
ALT.

DISPL. @ D.W.L.	L.C.B.	LBS./INCH	MT 1 INCH
85,952 LBS.	54.15%	2770	7153

LENGTH OVER ALL .... 58'-8¼"
DESIGNED WATERLINE .... 47'-0"
BEAM (MAX.) .... 14'-4"
DRAFT .... 7'-0"

STATIONS
34   FRAMES

FRESH WATER
393 GALS.

BALLAST — 11,000 LBS.
(CONCRETE & STEEL)

FUEL OIL
522 GALS.
P & S

GARDNER DIESEL
MODEL 6 LX
127 BHP
DIRECT DRIVE

FRESH WATER
400 GALS.

FRESH WATER 245 GALS. (PORT)
240 GALS. (STBD.)

SUMP
50 GALS.

FRAMES   A   O

FORE PEAK

SEAT - PIPE BERTH
OVER - P & S

FORECASTLE

LOCKER   LKR.   BUR.   LKR.

STANCHION

GUESTS STATEROOM

BERTH & DWR. UNDER   BERTH & DWR. UNDER

LKR.   CREW'S
W.C.   TOILET

GUESTS
TOILET

W.C.   W.B.
HAMPER

STORAGE

SEAT-STOWAGE UNDER

"ICE" TABLE

CUTTING
BOARD

REFR.
DEEP FREEZE 15.5
UNDER   CU. FT.

GALLEY

DISHES, ETC.

ELECTRIC
STOVE

SINKS   LKR.

SEAT STOWAGE UNDER

SHELTER TOP

COCKPIT

STANCHION

MRS. TABLE
MYFELLAS UNDER

DEEP
SEAT   LKR.
UNDER

SEAT   SHOWER
W.B.

OILSKINS   COATS   LKR.

HAMPER
W.C.
OWNER'S
TOILET

DROP
TABLE

CHART
TABLE

RADIO, ETC.

LKR.

LKR.   STANCHION

OWNER'S STATEROOM

BERTH - P & S
(BIN & DWRS. UNDER)

SHELF
QUADRANT
UNDER

LKR.

A tour of the engine room on BARAKA reveals the following machinery and equipment:

Main Engine—General Motors diesel (150 H.P.) with 12-volt generator for charging the starting battery and 32 v. 60 amp. alternator for charging the 32 v. lighting batteries.

Aux. Generator—Mercedes Diesel (25 H.P.) coupled to a 15 K.W. Onan generator for 220 v. and 110 v. A.C. to supply current for stove, refrigerator, deep freeze, air conditioning, hot-water heater. Also equipped with its own 12-v. generator for charging the 12-v. starting batteries of both diesels.

A rectifier to change 110 v. A.C. either from shore or ship's current to 32 v. D.C.

A 20-gallon hot-water tank with heat from engine cooling water and electric element for shore current.

A 32-v. water pressure system with 30-gallon tank.

A refrigerator compressor and deep freeze compressor, each water-cooled and air-cooled with separate 32 v. motors.

Two 110 v. A.C. air conditioning compressors.

Four 8-v. batteries for 32 v. system, for lighting and refrigeration.

Two 12-v. batteries for starting with cross-over switch.

One 32-v. air compressor for the air horn.

One 32-v. automatic bilge pump.

One 3″ bilge pump belt driven off main engine.

Four fuel tanks with 560 gallons total capacity.

A tool bench with vise on hinged top, plus a tool board.

The next tour took place on the bridge or cockpit above the engine room Here were:

Engine controls
Engine instruments
Steering wheel
Depth sounder
Automatic pilot
Compass and binnacle
Chart case with glass top
Centerboard hoisting winch
Main and mizzen sheet winches and cleats
Folding hood with clear plastic front (indispensable)
Awning over cockpit
Stowage of boarding and swimming ladders

After this we descended forward to the main cabin, where we looked around and noted the following equipment:

Switchboard with 31 circuit breakers all neatly labelled
Radio-telephone
Radar

Loran

Automatic Radio Direction Finder

Stereo tape player (110 v. A.C. with reduced voltage when other demands were made on the system, producing some sour notes)

Portable radio

Air conditioning thermostat and duct

Shore dial telephone

Additional compass

Barograph

Chronometer

Clock and Barometer

Hand Pelorus (hand bearing compass)

I asked our young English skipper what he thought about having all this machinery and equipment, and whether he would be willing to eliminate any of it, and which units were not really necessary. He said, "No, I'm happy with the lot." So the ladies were not the only ones willing to pay the price of a little noise and vibration to have all the comforts of home.

What speed did she make under power?

At 1250 R.P.M.—5½ knots

At 1550 R.P.M.—8 knots

At 1850 R.P.M.—10 knots

The distance covered at 8 knots, including the consumption of 1.5 gallons for the diesel generator used six hours per day, is 1000 miles on 550 gallons of diesel fuel.

The Most Sophisticated Yet Simple Generator. As the farmer uses the wind-driven windmill to pump water or to grind wheat, so the sailor can use the water-driven controllable pitch propeller to generate electricity silently when sailing. This has been done on two boats that I know of.

The propeller shaft has sheaves aft of the engine coupling, which with belts turn the alternator alongside it. This takes place whenever the propeller shaft is turning. The beauty of it is that as long as the boat moves, the shaft has to turn (except when the propeller is feathered for racing, or when stopped in port). The propeller spins its shaft freely under sail with the motor shut off and in neutral, and of course when under power.

Now the sophisticated part of this simple scheme is the use of a controllable pitch propeller with feathering capability. Basically, in this design, there is a shaft within a hollow shaft, which when pushed or pulled changes the pitch of the propeller blades. This pushing or pulling force is applied by turning a wheel or crank on deck with shaft and worm gear. It should be located near the helmsman. Why use the controllable pitch type? Because for any speed the boat sails through the water the necessary pitch can be cranked in to produce the optimum shaft horse power or revolutions for generating. (Note: a 100-amp. alternator requires a force of 2.4 H.P. to charge a 12-v. system. See Electrical Sec., page 305.) Just turn the pitch control and watch the ammeter for the optimum charge at the speed you are then sailing. There is no harm in the shaft turning freely in a manually operated gear box, because it has an oil-bath lubrication. However, the hydraulic type of gear box requires a specially made oil pump to lubricate the free turning shaft. The latter is a complication.

To get back to refrigeration. Suppose a client insists on being able to carry frozen foods for long voyages, yet believes in having the minimum electricity aboard his vessel. Here is a good solution, which was experimentally tried on FINISTERRE years ago. Simply eliminate the electric motor and drive an oversize compressor directly through a magnetic clutch by belts from the main engine. When the engine is run, the temperature is kept low enough in the freezer to keep frozen foods frozen. It takes only half-an-hour's running a day when the boat is in cold waters, such as in Maine, and as long as three hours a day when she is in warm water, like the Caribbean. The magnetic clutch is there to cut in, or cut out, the compressor at certain set temperatures when the engine is running for longer periods (such as in a flat calm). Many auxiliaries now have this arrangement. The skippers of craft equipped in this manner frequently carry a block of ice in their refrigerators to tide them over between times when the engine is run, and also to chip some off for drinks.

Anchoring must be thought out carefully when designing a boat. I have always thought that the weight of the anchor used was the governing factor limiting the size of a boat run without paid hands. Well, I learned a lot about how easy anchoring can be on BARAKA.

She had a sixty-pound plow anchor with a roller chock at the end of her bow sprit. It used 7/16″ chain and was let out or heaved in by an electric windlass. During our last cruise our deck hand was a twenty-three-year-old English woman. She had merely to press a button to up anchor, and the chain came in link by link, stowing itself in the chain locker below deck. Pretty soon the anchor would break the surface and be pulled over the roller with a thud, and there it stayed stowed in its roller chock. The back-straining job of lifting the anchor up over the side was thus eliminated. Anchoring was just a matter of releasing the clutch and easing off the windlass brake until the chain rattled out to the length desired. Every boat I saw in the Caribbean, with few exceptions, used this system of plow anchor housed in a roller chock. The nicest arrangement I saw was on a French auxiliary. She had her roller chock right on the center line of the bow with an inverted Y weldment over it to take the jibstay.

PALAWAN, an Ocean Cruiser. This handsome vessel can go anywhere anytime. She does nine knots with her tall rig under sail, or with her GM V6 diesel under power. Stiff when sailing, she is easily balanced with her tandem center-boards. When the after one is lowered, she steers extremely well.

Her layout provides a comfortable midship cockpit with a low shelter; a commodious owner's stateroom aft for complete privacy (with its bathroom which has a bathtub and shower); a large main cabin in which there is the galley, an articulated table with four chairs and a "L" shaped seat, chart table and drawers, lockers and office space.

Then going forward there are two double guest staterooms with head and shower, and a fo'c'sle for two in crew. Throughout the boat there is lots of stowage space.

She was constructed by Abeking & Rasmussen in Germany in welded aluminum with the shell plating, varying from ¼" at the topsides to ½" thick at the keel, welded to angle frames spaced 12" on centers. In addition longitudinals from the bow to amidships stiffen the shell against slamming into seas.

Her equipment includes: a controllable pitch 3 bladed propeller with feathering capability when sailing; a hot water heating system with radiators throughout the quarters piped to an oil burner in the engine room; electric refrigeration for 12 cu. ft. of chill space and 8 cu. ft. of freeze space; an auxiliary generator powered by a Volvo 2 cylinder diesel; an evaporator, which makes about 5 gallons of fresh water from salt water per hour of engine running, to augment the 1,000 gallons of fresh water carried. Fuel capacity is also 1,000 gallons. Radar and many electronics complete the list.

This ocean cruiser is the product of two and one-half years work (on and off) on five different designs from the board of F. S. K. at S&S. All her quarters were mocked up in plywood, first the forward part, then the after part in the owner's garage. Corrections were then made to the final design.

By all reports Mr. Thomas J. Watson Jr's. PALAWAN is an extraordinarily good boat.

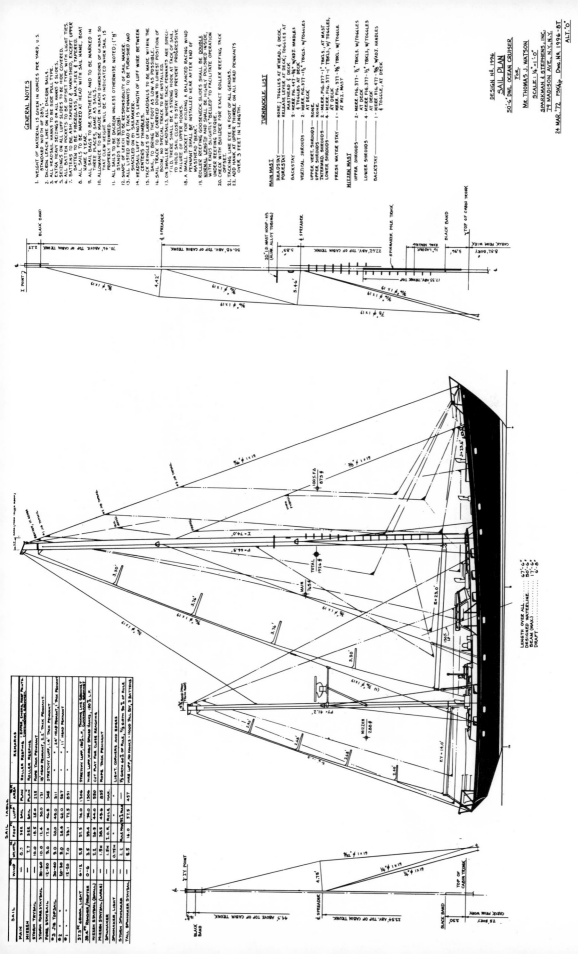

DESIGN N0. 1996
ARRANGEMENT PLAN
50'-6" DWL AUX. KETCH

SCALE : 3/8" = 1'-0"
SPARKMAN & STEPHENS INC.
79 MADISON AVE., N.Y., N.Y.
6 APRIL '72   F.S.K./yp   Dwg. N0. 1996-34T
ALTO

LENGTH OVER ALL . . . . 67'-6"
DESIGNED WATER LINE. . . . 50'-6"
BEAM (MAX.). . . . . 17'-6"
DRAFT . . . . 6'-5"

STATION NOS.
-1   0   1   2   3   4   5   6   7   8   9   10   11

D.W.L.

CABIN LKR.

DECK LKR.

DOUBLE SLIDING HATCH

FRESH WATER - 1000 GALLONS IN 4 TANKS

18,300 LBS. LEAD KEEL

648 KVS/IM 2:1 RED.

EXHAUST TRUNK

FUEL OIL - 1000 GALLONS IN 2 TANKS

3.5"DIA. x 16'4"PITCH 3-BLADE PROPELLER

OVAL PORTS IN HULL 7" x 14" FIXED TYPE

CHAIN LKR.

LOCKER.

LOCKER.

PIPE BERTH OVER SAIL BIN

UPPER BERTH

LOWER BERTH (OWNER UNDER)

PORT GUEST ST. R.

UPPER BERTH

SMALL LKR.

DRAWERS

LOCKER.

ELECTRONICS

CHART TABLE (DRWRS BELOW)

SEAT (EXTENDS FOR BERTH)

ARTICULATED TABLE

WATER WNK.

ICE BOX

LAB. LKR.

STOVE

COUNTER

LOCKER.

ELECTRICAL

MAIN CABIN

LOCKER

SMALL LKR.

SAIL STOWAGE BELOW

SEAT HATCH

SEAT

COCKPIT

SEAT HATCH

SAIL STOWAGE BELOW

SAIL BILGE HATCH

W.C.

LOCKER.

HANGING LKR.

EXHAUST

BERTH

LOCKER

SEAT (DRWRS UNDER)

OWNER'S STATEROOM

SEAT (DRWRS UNDER)

BERTH

SHELF

BOOK SHELF

FLUSH MANHOLE

11'-6" HULL DRAFT

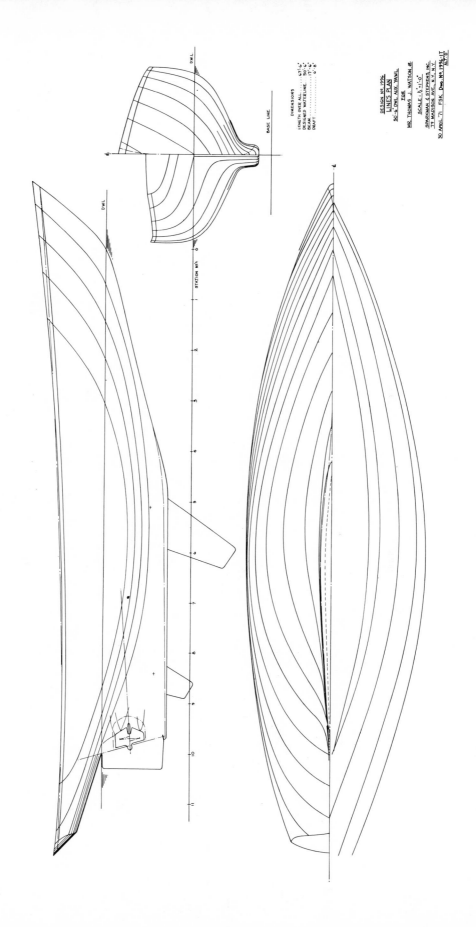

DESIGN N⁰ 1996
LINES PLAN
50'-6" DWL. AUX. YAWL
FOR
MR. THOMAS J. WATSON JR.
SCALE : ¼"=1'-0"
SPARKMAN & STEPHENS, INC.
79 MADISON AVE. N.Y. N.Y.
30 APRIL '71   F.S.K.   Dwg. N⁰ 1996-1T
ALT. "O"

DIMENSIONS
LENGTH OVER ALL .... 67'-6"
DESIGNED WATERLINE .... 50'-6"
BEAM .... 17'-6"
DRAFT .... 6'-8"

D W L
BASE LINE

STATION N⁰'S

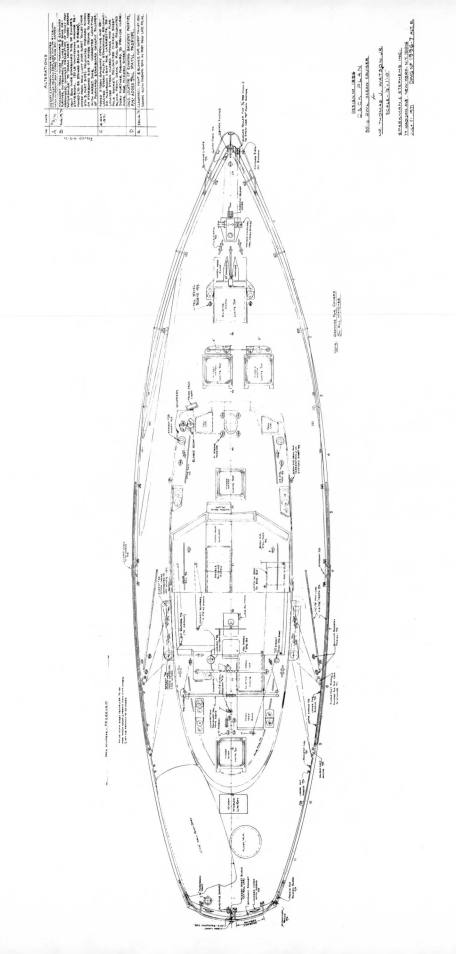

CHAPTER IX

HOW TO FIND SHAFT HORSEPOWER REQUIRED FOR DISPLACEMENT-TYPE BOATS

Let us use the 29′ 0″ D.W.L. Auxiliary Yawl *Santa Maria* and find what horsepower is needed in order to select the right engine.

At a speed-length ratio $(V/\sqrt{L})$ of 1.3 her speed will be $\sqrt{29} \times 1.3 = 5.38 \times 1.3 = 7$ knots.

Step 1—Enter chart showing "Curves Covering Range of Resistance for Displacement-Type Hulls" (Figure 1) at bottom with $V/\sqrt{L}$ of 1.3 and go up to the Upper Limit Curve, then across, reading off the resistance as 45 pounds for each long ton (2240 pounds) of displacement. Let us say the displacement of SANTA MARIA is 22,000 pounds (using a round figure) when fully loaded. So, 22,000 ÷ 2240 lbs. = 9.8 long tons. The resistance will then be 45 × 9.8 = 441 lbs.

Figure 1.

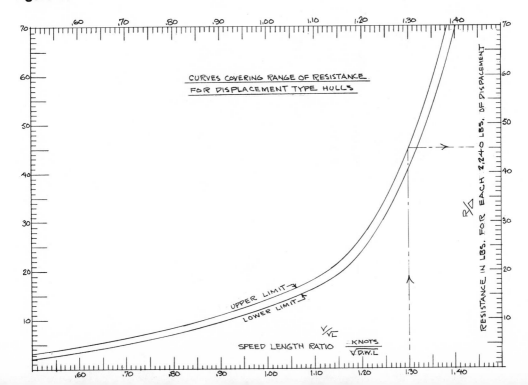

Step 2—The formula for Effective H.P. is E.H.P. = Resistance $\times$ speed $\times$ .003. So 441 $\times$ 7 $\times$ .003 = 9.26.

Step 3—Propeller Efficiencies fall in the following ranges:

Folding, 2 bladed = 10%

Auxiliaries, 2 bladed, solid = 35%–45%

Motor sailers, 3 bladed, around 50%

Displacement-type power boats, 3 bladed = 60%–66%

So for this boat we will say the Propulsive Coefficient is 35% (actually from our propeller calculations we found it to be 38%). Thus 9.26 ÷ .35 = 26.4 shaft horsepower required to drive her 7 knots.

Step 4—For SANTA MARIA we selected an engine with one-third more S.H.P., which is good practice for all displacement-type boats. So the maximum S.H.P. required is 35, and we selected the Westerbeke 4-107 Diesel rated 35 S.H.P. @ 3000 R.P.M. From its power curve (Figure 2) we see that it will deliver 26.4 S.H.P. at 2000 R.P.M., an agreeable top speed to run the engine. In practice we find we run it at 1750 revolutions, which is even more agreeable.

Figure 2.

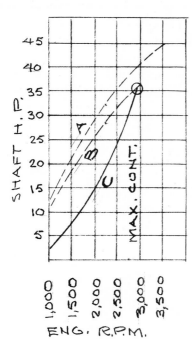

WESTERBEKE 4-107 DIESEL
POWER CURVES

A = HIGH SPEED INTERMITTENT
B = CONTINUOUS RATING
C = PROP. LOAD.

I have made a chart plotting the maximum horsepower ratings from engine catalogues versus the Designed Waterline Lengths of fifty-three displacement-type yachts (Figure 3) from the engines actually used in typical auxiliaries and motor sailers. It should be helpful to designers, builders and owners.

Figure 3.

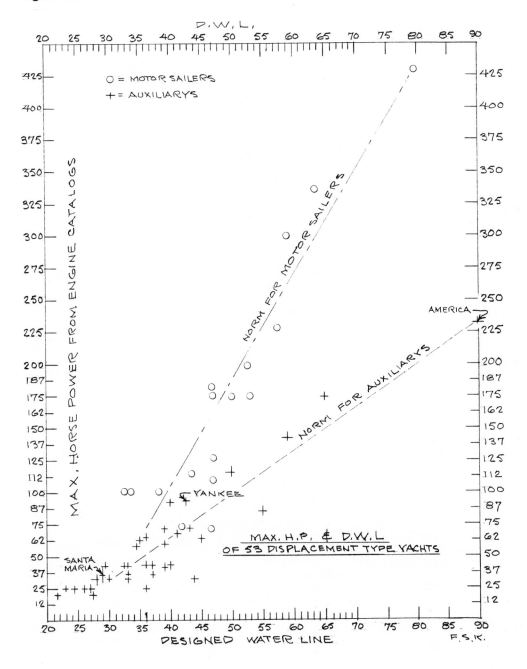

TREMELINO was one of the early designs from the author's board and turned out to be a good one.

We had her sister ship, our first **SANTA MARIA**. Although she was intended only for day sailing and weekend crusing, four of us sailed as far as Mount Desert Island, Maine, from Lloyd Harbor, New York, one of many happy cruises in her.

Every winter we had her trailered to our back yard, where I could work on her myself during spring weekends. It proved to be most economical.

She had several unusual features, among which were a convertible U-shaped seat, which became a double berth, when the backrest was set in the bosom of the U; a mast stepped on deck to provide more space below; two cockpits, the deep one converted to a tent cabin at night with two berths, the after high one for the helmsman. Also, the top of the engine box made an excellent table for picnic lunches and gave us the greatest access to the two-cylinder motor. This little engine gave her a 5¼-knot cruising speed.

SAIL DIMENSIONS

	LUFF	FOOT	LEECH	AREA
...NSAIL	32'-1"☐	15'-0"	34'-0"△	240 ◊
...KING JIB	23'-3"	10'-5"	19'-9"	105 ◊
...CHING JIB	24'-9"	14'-2"	23'-0"	161 ◊
...RM JIB	19'-0"	9'-0"	14'-4"	62 ◊

...NNAKER - AS LARGE AS POSSIBLE. PARACHUTE TYPE.
   HOIST = 24'-0". LENGTH OF POLE 9'-6". RINGS AT CLEWS.
...L SLIDES - MAIN FOOT—MERRIMAN FIG.404 ⅞"
   "   " LUFF –   "   " 406 "
...TOP OF BOOM TO TOP OF SHEAVE
...CLEW TO TOP OF SHEAVE

...TES
...EF POINTS –
...OR FIRST REEF NYLON.
...OR SECOND REEF COTTON.
...TTENS –
...APERED ASH. LENGTHS: TOP- 24", 2 MIDDLE - 36", BOT.- 30"
...RUISING CLUB RULE – MAX. WIDTH OF SPINN.- 17.6'
...E OF FORE TRIANGLE 9'-8"
   "   "   "   "   26'-7"
...E OF MAST 1½" IN 4'-0"

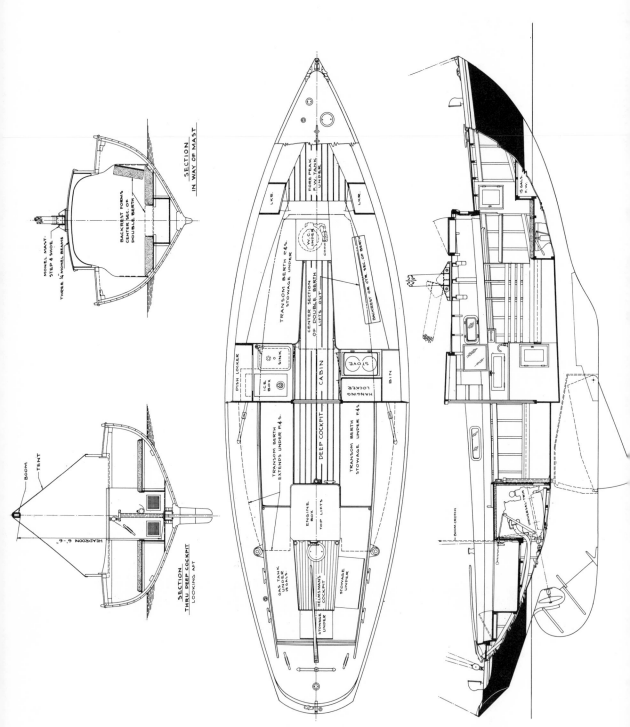

PRINCIPAL DIMENSIONS
L.O.A. 28'-7"
L.W.L. 21'-3"
BEAM 8'-4"
DRAFT 3'-0"

INBOARD PROFILE,
ARRANGEMENT & SECTIONS
21'-3" W.L. AUX. C.B. SLOOP
FOR
PHILIP LE BOUTILLIER, JR.

SCALE 3/4" = 1'-0"

DESIGNED BY
FRANCIS S. KINNEY
LLOYD HARBOR, N.Y.

SECTION
IN WAY OF MAST

MONEL MAST-
STEP & SHOE

THREE 1/4 MONEL BEAMS

BACKREST FORMS
CENTER SEC. OF
DOUBLE BERTH

BOOM

TENT

HEADROOM 6'-6"

SECTION
THRU DEEP COCKPIT
LOOKING AFT

LKR.

FORE PEAK
F.W. TANK
UNDER

LKR.

W.C.
UNDER

DISH LOCKER

ICE
BOX

SINK

TRANSOM BERTH P.&S.
STOWAGE UNDER

CENTER SECTION
OF DOUBLE BERTH
LIFTS OUT

BACKREST OR CTR. SEC. OF BERTH

CABIN

STOVE

HANGING
LOCKER

BIN

TRANSOM BERTH
EXTENDS UNDER P.&S.

DEEP COCKPIT

TRANSOM BERTH
STOWAGE UNDER P.&S.

ENGINE
BOX
TOP LIFTS

GAS TANK
UNDER 15 GALS.

STOWAGE
UNDER

HELMSMAN'S
COCKPIT

STOWAGE
UNDER

BOOM CROTCH

15 GALS.
F.W.

UNIVERSAL

CHAPTER X

THE BALANCE OF A SAILBOAT

Here is a subject that will baffle the experts. Just how a sailboat will balance can not be predicted with any degree of accuracy unless tank testing of a model is done.

The shape of a boat's sails determines her balance. We know that flat sails give a boat a lee helm, and full cut sails give a boat a weather helm. We also know that a beamy boat tends to have more weather helm than a narrow boat. With today's modern tandem rudder boats there is a need for 2% more lead of the C.E. ahead of the C.L.P.

Changing the rake of a mast will change the balance of a sailboat. The Wianno class on Cape Cod is an example. As originally designed and built they had a strong weather helm. By raking the mast way forward this was corrected.

Another of the factors which determines whether a boat will have a weather helm or a lee helm is the shape of the leading edge of the keel. An easy way to think of this phenomenon is really quite logical. If this edge is sharp, the forward part of the boat tends to bite into the water and hold its position; whereas a rounded or blunt leading edge will tend to slide off sideways when a boat is sailing to windward. So then, what we might call the true center of lateral resistance is further forward on a boat with a sharp leading edge than it would be on one with a blunt leading edge. In other words, we just don't know where this "damned elusive" center really is.

We can trace the underwater profile, cut it out with a scissors, and balance it on a pin point. This will give us the center of that area. As a rule of thumb, we can call it the center of lateral plane (C.L.P.).

Next we must find the center of all the sails. This is done by finding the center of each, using two at a time, totaling them, and taking moments about one. On a sloop it is quite simple. Find the center of the fore triangle. (To find the center of any triangle, draw a straight line from a corner to the mid point on the opposite side. Do this for all three corners. The center is where all the lines cross.) The area of any triangle is equal to one half its base times its altitude, the altitude being a line at right angles to one side and drawn to the opposite corner. Then find the center of the mainsail with its area.

Draw a line between center of fore triangle and center of mainsail (D). The center of the total of these two areas will lie on this line. Where? Well, it's the old seesaw problem. With a light person at one end and a heavy person at the other, where is the balance point? Find it by taking moments about one end—say, about the jib. Then the total (T) times dist. (X) equals main (M) times distance (D):

$$T \times X = M \times D$$
$$X = M \times D \div T$$

If there are more sails to be considered, repeat the process with the total of the first two combined with the next.

Then bring the center of the total sail area (T) down to the designed water line, and bring the center of the underwater profile (excluding the rudder) up to the water line, with lines that are at right angles to it. (See Figure 4)

For our rule of thumb, we may call one the center of effort (C.E.) and the other the center of lateral plane (C.L.P.), although neither one of them is actually that, because of the curvature of sails aloft and shape of leading edge below. When brought to the water line, the distance the C.E. is ahead of the C.L.P. is called the lead (as in "leader"). The sails lead the lateral plane.

Figure 4. Relationship between C.L.P. and C.E.

X = Dist. J to T
D = Dist. J to M
J = Jib (F. Tri.) area
M = Mainsail area
T = Total sail area
C.E. = Center of effort
C.L.P. = Center of lateral plane
D.W.L. = Designed waterline length

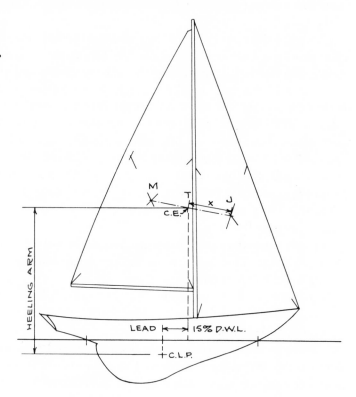

Our rule of thumb, taken with a grain of salt, is this (C.L.P. without rudder):

For Sloops—Lead = C.E. ahead of C.L.P. by 14% to 19% D.W.L.

For Yawls—Lead = about 15% (using ½ the mizzen area).

For Ketches—about 20% (using ½ mizzen area).

For Schooners—about 5% (using total sail area).

For Schooner AMERICA—Lead reversed with C.E. behind C.L.P. by 1% (using total sail area).

A clever way to balance a sailboat is by the use of two centerboards arranged one ahead of the other. By lowering one more than the other, the skipper of such a boat is able to move her C.L.P. forward or aft to suit any combination of sails, wind, and sea.

A small centerboard in way of the forefoot has also proved advantageous. With such a rig one could beat to windward well in a sloop having only her jib set.

WIND 0-3 M.P.H.
USE BALLOON JIB

WIND 3-15 M.P.H.
USE GENOA

WIND 15-25 M.P.H.
USE WORKING JIB

WIND 25-35 M.P.H.
REEF MAINSAIL,
OR LOWER IT.

WIND 35-45 M.P.H.
NO. 2 JIB & REEFED
OR LOWERED MAIN

WIND 45-50 M.P.H.
STORM JIB & DEEP REEFS
IN MAIN AND MIZZEN.

WIND 50-55 M.P.H.
STORM JIB, STORM TRYSAIL
AND REEFED MIZZEN.

WIND ABOVE 55 M.P.H.
STORM TRYSAIL ONLY

SAILING ON THE WIND

**On the wind a boat can stand more punishment than man.
Off the wind man can stand more than she can. Shorten
sail then, or she may bury her bow, pitchpole and dismast.**

SAILING OFF THE WIND

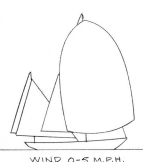

WIND 0-5 M.P.H.
LT. SPINNAKER
& MIZZEN STAYSAIL.

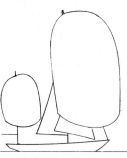

WIND 5-25 M.P.H.
MAIN & MIZZ. SPINNAKERS & SPIN.
STAYSAIL RUNNING, STAR CUT
SPIN. & MIZZ. STAYS'L REACHING

WIND 25-35 M.P.H.
NO. I JIB TOPS'L & MIZZ.
STAYSAIL REACHING,
STORM SPINNAKER RUNNING.

WIND 35-40 M.P.H.
MAIN & WORKING JIB

WIND 40-48 M.P.H.
REEFED MAIN & WORKING JIB

WIND 48-55 M.P.H.
STORM JIB & DEEP
REEFED MAINSAIL

WIND 55-60 M.P.H.
STORM JIB & STORM
TRYSAIL.
WIND ABOVE 60 M.P.H.
STORM JIB ONLY OR BARE
POLES.

VARIOUS SAIL
COMBINATIONS
TO SET IN DIFFEREN
BREEZES ABOAR
A 32'-0" D.W.L. YAW
SHOWING GOOD SEAMANS

FSK

FIDELIA has the same lines as **TREMELINO** and basically the same layout, but she is more of a seagoing type, because the deep cockpit is protected from the elements by two large telescoping hatches. And the cockpit aft, which was small in **TREMELINO**, is made larger by locating the tiny four-cylinder engine under its sole.

Several boats of this F. S. K. design have been built successfully by amateurs. They found the planking easy to do because there are no reverse curves in any of them. The lack of any hollow garboards is the reason for this.

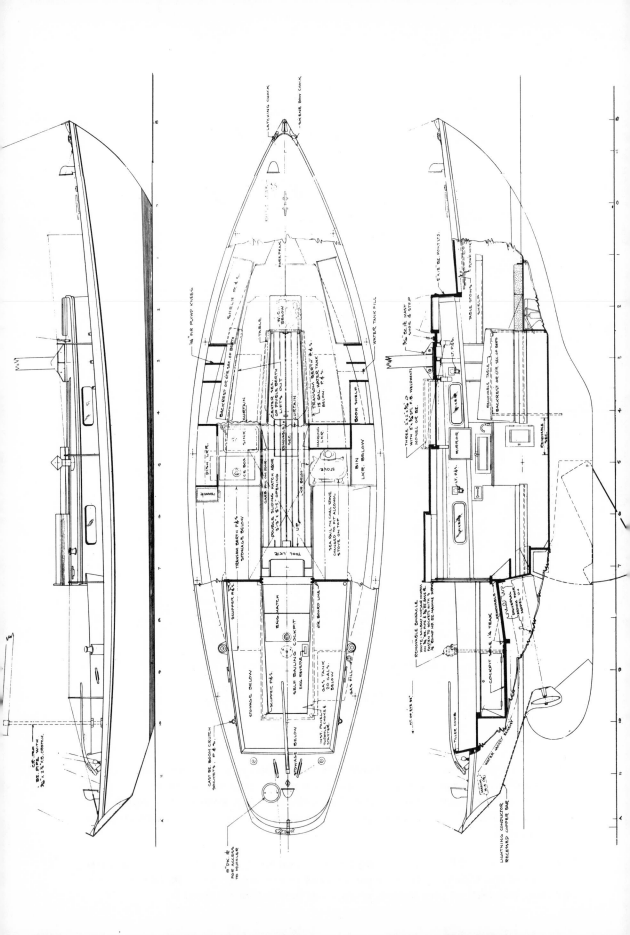

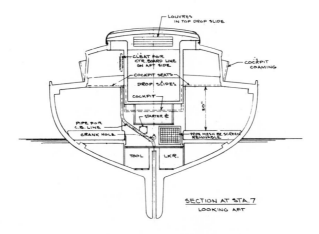

LOUVRES
IN TOP DROP SLIDE

CLEAT FOR
CTR. BOARD LINE
ON AFT SIDE

COCKPIT
COAMING

COCKPIT SEATS

DROP SLIDES

COCKPIT

30"

PIPE FOR
C.B. LINE

STARTER ⊕

CRANK HOLE

WIRE MESH BR. SCREEN
REMOVABLE

TOOL   LKR.

SECTION AT STA. 7
LOOKING AFT

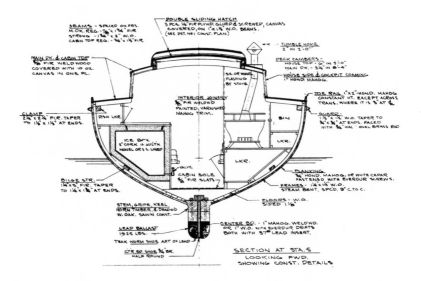

BEAMS - SPACED ON FRS.
M. DK. REG. - ⅞" x 1¾" FIR
STRONG - 1⅜" x 2" W.O.
CABIN TOP REG. - ⅝" x 1⅝" FIR

DOUBLE SLIDING HATCH
3 PCS. ¼" FIR PLYWD. GLUED & SCREWED, CANVAS
COVERED, ON 1" x 1⅛" W.O. BEAMS.
(SEE DET. №1 CONST. PLAN)

TUMBLE HOME
2" IN 2'-0"

MAIN DK. & CABIN TOP -
⅝ FIR WELDWOOD
COVERED WITH 10 OZ.
CANVAS IN ONE PC.

DECK CAMBERS -
HOUSE TOP - 6" IN 5'-0"
MAIN DK. - 3¼" IN 8'-4"

HOUSE SIDE & COCKPIT COAMING
1" HOND. MAHOG.

INTERIOR JOINERY
⅜" FIR WELDWD
PAINTED, VARNISHED
MAHOG. TRIM.

S.S. OR MONEL
FLASHING
BY STOVE

TOE RAIL 1" x 2" HOND. MAHOG
CONSTANT HT. EXCEPT ACROSS
TRANS. WHERE IT IS 3" AT ₵

DISH LKR.

CLAMP -
2¼" x 2¼" FIR. TAPER
TO 1⅝ x 1½" AT ENDS.

BIN

GUARD -
1⅜" x 1½" W.O. TAPER TO
⅞" x ⅞" AT ENDS. FACED
WITH ¾" HALF OVAL BRASS ROD

ICE BOX -
2" CORK INSUL'TN.
MONEL OR S.S. LINED

LKR.

BILGE STR. -
1¼" x 3" FIR. TAPER
TO 1¼ x 1⅜" AT ENDS.

VALVE

CABIN SOLE
⅝ FIR SLATS

LKR.

PLANKING -
¾" HOND. MAHOG. OR WHITE CEDAR
FASTENED WITH EVEROUR SCREWS.

FRAMES - 1¼ x 1¼ W.O.
STEAM BENT. SPCD. 9" C. TO C.

FLOORS - W.O.
SIDED 1⅝

STEM, GRIPE, KEEL
HORN TIMBER, & DEADWD.
W. OAK, SAWN CONST.

CENTER BD. - 1" MAHOG. WELDWD.
OR 1" W.O. WITH EVEROUR DRIFTS
BOTH WITH 37# LEAD INSERT.

LEAD BALLAST
1925 LBS.

TEAK WORM SHOE AFT OF LEAD

CTR. BD. SHOE ⅜ BR.
HALF ROUND

SECTION AT STA. 5
LOOKING FWD.
SHOWING CONST. DETAILS

PRINCIPAL DIMENSIONS	
L.O.A	28'-11½"
L.W.L.	21'-3"
BEAM	8'-4"
DRAFT	3'-0"

ARRANGEMENT PLAN
& CONST. SECTION
OF
21'-3" W.L. AUX. CTR. BD. SLOOP
FOR

SCALE 1" = 1'-0"
DESIGNED BY
FRANCIS S. KINNEY
HUNTINGTON, N.Y.
NOV. 18, '53
REVISED NOV. 26, '53 FOR CONTRACT PRICE
REVISED FEB. 7, '54

DESIGN 11, DWG. 1

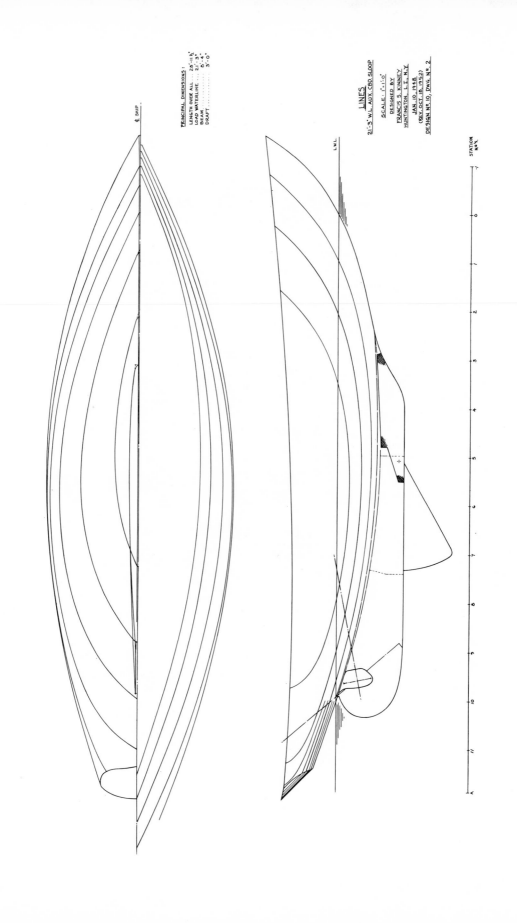

PRINCIPAL DIMENSIONS:

LENGTH OVER ALL .... 26'-11½"
LOAD WATERLINE .... 21'-3"
BEAM .... 8'-4"
DRAFT .... 3'-0"

LINES

21'-3" W.L. AUX. CBD SLOOP

SCALE: 1"=1'-0"
DESIGNED BY
FRANCIS S. KINNEY
HUNTINGTON, L.I., N.Y.
JAN. 10, 1948
(REV. OCT. 15, 1952)
DESIGN Nº 10, DWG. Nº 2

STATION Nº'S.

LWL

€ SHIP

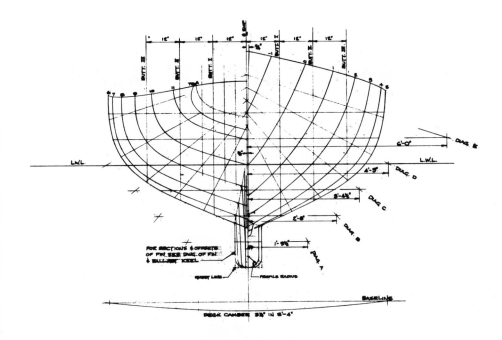

FOR SECTIONS & OFFSETS
OF FIN SEE DWG. OF FIN
& BALLAST KEEL

RABBET LINE — PROFILE RADIUS

DECK CAMBER 3½" IN 8'-4"

LINES ARE TO OUTSIDE OF PLANKING
PLANKING THICKNESS = ¾"

TABLE OF OFFSETS — IN FEET, INCHES, & EIGHTHS

STATIONS	HALF BREADTHS FROM ₵						DIAGONALS					HEIGHTS ABOVE BASE						STATIONS
	DECK AT SIDE	W.L. 2A	W.L. 1A	L.W.L.	W.L. 1B	W.L. 2B	A	B	C	D	E	DECK AT SIDE	FAIRBODY LINE	PROFILE	BUTT. I	BUTT. II	BUTT. III	
B	0-0-6	—	—	—	—	—	—	—	—	—	—	7-3-5	7-2-5	7-2-5	—	—	—	B
‑1	0-9-0⁺	—	—	—	—	—	—	—	0-1-7⁺	0-3-7	0-5-5	7-1-6⁺	5-6-7⁺	5-6-7⁺	—	—	—	‑1
0	1-9-3	1-1-1	0-7-4	0-0-8	—	—	0-9-5⁺	0-11-6	1-1-5⁺	1-3-7	1-6-1	6-11-0⁺	4-0-0	4-0-0	5-4-0	—·	—	0
1	2-7-2	2-1-2	1-7-6⁺	1-0-4	0-2-7	—	1-7-0⁺	1-9-4	2-0-0	2-2-4	2-4-7⁺	6-8-4	3-1-0	3-1-0	3-11-3	5-3-2⁺	—	1
2	3-5-1	2-11-1⁺	2-6-4⁺	1-11-3	1-1-0⁺	—	2-2-0	2-5-1⁺	2-8-3	2-11-4⁺	3-1-6	6-6-2	2-6-2	2-6-0⁺	3-2-1	4-0-4	5-8-0	2
3	3-8-4	3-6-3	3-2-7	2-8-5⁺	1-9-4⁺	0-6-7	2-6-4⁺	2-10-8⁺	3-3-1	3-6-6	3-8-4	6-4-2	2-2-4	1-10-6	2-8-7⁺	3-4-5	4-4⁻1⁺	3
4	4-0-5	3-11-0⁺	3-8-8⁺	3-3-0	2-3-6⁺	0-11-2⁺	2-9-2	3-2-1⁺	3-7-5⁺	4-0-0	4-1-0⁺	6-2-6	2-0-7	1-0-0	2-6-2⁺	3-0-4	3-8-6⁺	4
5	4-2-0	4-1-3⁺	3-11-3⁺	3-6-4⁺	2-7-2	1-0-6⁺	2-8-7⁺	3-3-6	3-8-7⁺	4-2-5	4-5-0⁺	6-1-4⁺	2-0-6	1-0-0	2-5-5	2-11-0	3-5-7	5
6	4-1-7	4-1-5	4-0-1	3-7-1	2-7-1	0-10-6⁺	2-9-2	3-3-3	3-10-1	4-3-2	4-5⁺7	6-0-4	2-2-0⁺	1-0-0	2-6-5	2-11-4⁺	3-5-6	6
7	4-0-2	4-0-1⁺	3-10-4⁺	3-5-0	2-3-4⁺	0-3-4	2-6-7	3-1-1	3-8-2⁺	4-1-6	4-2-3⁺	6-0-0	2-4-7	1-0-0	2-3-2⁺	3-2-0⁺	3-8-0	7
8	3-9-0	3-6-7⁺	3-6-7	2-11-2⁺	1-4-0⁺	—	2-2-5⁺	2-8-7⁺	3-4-2	3-10-2	3-11-1	5-11-7	2-9-4⁺	1-0-0	3-1-5	3-6-2	4-0-4⁺	8
9	3-4-2	3-4-0	3-0-4⁺	1-11-3	—	—	1-8-6	2-3-0	2-10-1⁺	3-4-4⁺	3-6-0	6-0-1	3-4-0⁺	1-0-3	3-7-6⁺	4-0-1,	4-8-1⁺	9
10	2-10-1⁺	2-9-0⁺	2-2-2⁺	0-0-0	—	—	1-1-2⁺	1-7-3	2-2-2⁺	2-9-1	2-11-3	6-0-7	—	4-0-0	4-3-2	4-7-5	—	10
11	2-2-2	1-11-2	0-1-0	—	—	—	0-4-6	0-10-1⁺	1-4-5⁺	1-11-7⁺	2-3-1	6-2-1	—	4-8-6⁺	4-11-5⁺	5-6-6	—	11
A	1-6-2⁺	0-7-1⁺	—	—	—	—	—	0-1-4	0-7-3⁺	1-2-4	1-6-6	6-3-6	—	5-4-4⁺	5-7-6⁺	—	—	A

PRINCIPAL DIMENSIONS
L.O.A.   23'-11½"
L.W.L.   21'-3"
BEAM   8'-4"
DRAFT   3'-0"

LINES & OFFSETS
21'-3" W.L. AUX. C.B. SLOOP

CHAPTER XI
GALVANIC SERIES OF METALS

If there is any one list a designer should commit to memory, it would be the list of metals in the galvanic series.

Long experience with corrosion has taught us that when two dissimilar metals are placed under salt water, the less noble metal becomes corroded while the more noble metal is protected from change. The further apart these metals are on the list, the greater is the corrosion of the less noble one. It seems that we unwittingly set up a large storage battery cell with one metal acting as the positive pole, the other as negative, and salt water as the conducting solution.

I remember so well what happened after painting a galvanized iron rudder fitting with bronze bottom paint. Up until that day the fitting had withstood the test of three or four years' time. In a matter of days after the bronze paint was applied the fitting simply dissolved to nothingness.

Another experience which shocked me had to do with strut bolts. A relatively new motor sailer suffered a broken propeller strut bolt. The strut was cast from manganese bronze. Its palm was through-bolted with silicon bronze bolts leading through planking, oak backing block, and a galvanized steel plate as an inside washer. One large bolt had broken. Why?

"Must be electrolysis," said the captain.

"Never give an opinion unless you're paid for it," I said to myself, and for once I kept my mouth shut.

The pieces of the broken bolt were chemically analyzed. The answer soon came back. "Stress corrosion caused by mercury." So we learned never again to paint a boat fastened with silicon bronze screws and bolts with mercury-bearing anti-fouling bottom paint.

Monel metal is not so affected and should be used for such stressed fastenings, if paint containing mercury is desired.

We learn what can be done and what can not be done in salt water by such mistakes.

GALVANIC SERIES

Most Noble, Electro-Negative, or Protected Metal

Mercury and Mercury Paint
Vanadium
Gold
Silver
Monel
Nickel
Stainless Steel, Passive (seldom available)
Silicon Bronze (Everdur: one trade name)
Copper and Copper Paint
Red Brass
Aluminum Bronze
Gun Metal and Admiralty Brass
Yellow Brass
Phosphor Bronze
Manganese Bronze
Tin
Lead
Stainless Steel, Active (most stainless steel fittings)
Cast Iron
Wrought Iron
Mild Steel
Aluminum
Cadmium
Galvanized Iron and Steel
Zinc
Magnesium

Least Noble, Electro-Positive, or Corroded Metal

CURRENT FLOW

You can use copper, bronze, and Monel together. They are close together on the list.

You can use aluminum, mild steel, and stainless steel judiciously together.

You can not use galvanized iron or steel next to bronze or Monel under salt water. They are too far apart on the list.

You can not use aluminum with bronze for the same reason.

You can not use yellow brass in salt water. It dezincifies.

You can not ground an electrical unit or system to an engine or underwater appendage, particularly when shore current is used. The corrosive action is speeded up as the electric current is increased.

You can use a two-wire ungrounded electrical system or a separate copper plate of the proper area, for grounding.

You should bond together inside the boat all underwater appendages—such as shafting, struts, and sea cocks—on wooden hulls, with a wire or copper tube to reduce electrolysis. But metal hulls do not require this.

To summarize then: when two dissimilar metals are submerged in salt water, an electric current will flow from the electro-positive or corroded metal towards the electro-negative or protected metal. The amount of corrosion thus caused depends on the relative positions of the metals in the galvanic series and on the exposed areas of the two metals. The further apart they are on the list, the more rapidly one will corrode while the other remains unchanged or even more protected.

CHAPTER XII

PLANING POWERBOATS

When a boat planes it lifts and skims the surface. There is definite separation of water from the stern. The wake breaks clean from the transom and the resulting flow pattern is formed as if by an imaginary extension of the hull itself.

A basic element of yacht design is that the water-line length, which is the distance between the bow wave and stern wave, limits the speed of nonplaning boats, such as sailboats, motor sailers, tugs, trawlers, etc. The speed of waves is related to the distance between crests. Admiral Taylor placed this at 1.34 times the square root of length between crests.

To go faster than this limit, a boat must leave its stern wave behind and climb up and almost over its own bow wave. To do this, separation of water at the transom must occur—a lifting of the boat for the skimming action or planing. A planing powerboat is simply like a giant water ski.

A mathematical definition of planing is simply that the speed length ratio is 2 or greater. This is Speed $\div \sqrt{\text{D.W.L.}} = 2$. For example, a 36-foot D.W.L. boat would be planing when going 12 M.P.H. or over. $(12 \div 6 = 2)$

Requirements necessary to produce a successful planing powerboat are: light weight, lots of power, and proper shape of hull. Let us discuss each in turn.

The formulas for speed are concerned with weight and power and, to some extent, length. Less weight or displacement means more speed with the same power. Greater length means more speed at the same weight and power. But lightness must be consistent with strength. By making a boat light, the designer sets in motion a chain reaction. Less weight means more speed. More speed with the same power reduces the amount of fuel required to go an equal distance. Less fuel means less weight. Therefore, once again, less weight means even more speed.

More and more powerful engines are becoming available due, to a great extent, to the auto industry. The V-8 gasoline engine has been perfected to a fine degree and probably offers more power per pound than anything else now on the market. Diesel engines have that great safety factor of using diesel oil for fuel, instead of gasoline, eliminating the ever-present danger of a gasoline explosion. Offsetting this advantage is their high cost—in some cases three times as much as a gasoline engine, and their great weight.

The Gas Turbine will in all likelihood be the popular engine of the future, I predict. It is extremely simple, having only one moving part (excepting reduction gears). It is light in weight. It is vibrationless, silent, ecologically clean, safe, and it operates at low cost.

Up to now two factors prevented its use in pleasure boating. The first was the high cost in building it of heat-resistant materials. The second was very high fuel consumption. A high proportion of the energy gained from the fuel was lost in the form of heat in the exhaust.

The first company actually to reach the market with a practical engine is Ford. They have a gas turbine engine of 373 continuous horsepower, which has been selected by Chris-Craft and Pacemaker for evaluation. The foremost problem of fuel consumption has now been solved, but the price is at present about 20% more than a diesel of equivalent power.

Use of the word "gas" in gas turbine comes from the fact that the turbine is

The new Ford gas turbine shown is one-third the size, one-half the weight, and has almost the same fuel economy as a diesel of the same power.

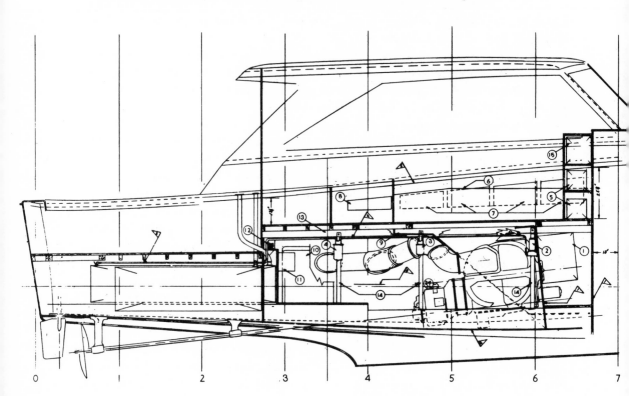

Gas turbine propulsion system arrangement.

rotated by hot gas flowing over its vanes (as opposed to steam, which is used in steam turbines for ships). It has nothing whatever to do with gasoline. Actually the engines are set up to use diesel fuel.

Engine rooms have to be ventilated more thoroughly because the volume of air passing through the engine is much greater. A very large exhaust stack is required to remove the exhaust gases. Perhaps in the future the stack will once again become an important part of the outline of a vessel, as in the old steam yachts.

Comfort is the key word to be applied to the turbine-powered motor yacht. There is nothing to compare with it now. The gas turbine engine has arrived, been tested and is here to stay.

Choosing an Engine. Before this is done, the designer should make an analysis, comparing all available engines of the size and type desired. Sometimes it may be necessary to install two or even three engines to obtain enough power for the speed desired.

Twin-engine installations are sensible because, if one should stop, there is always the other to bring you home. Two engines make a boat more maneuverable around docks and at slow speeds. With this advantage, a designer should feel free to eliminate the skeg, reducing wetted surface and resistance and thereby increasing speed. But be careful: Unless the boat is perfectly designed, she may be hard to control and not run straight.

Single-screw powerboats must have a skeg or keel to protect the propeller, which is deeper than on twin-screw boats. But it is reasonable to have a very small skeg or none at all on twin-screw craft with good deadrise, because their propellers are higher and require less protection when docking. There is always the conflict between the theoretical and the practical side of boating.

How much horsepower is required for such and such a speed, if a boat weighs so many pounds? We have two good formulas. Here they are, using the following abbreviations:

H.P. = brake horsepower (use 85% full-rated H.P.)
Disp. = displacement or weight of boat, in pounds.
M.P.H. = speed in statute miles per hour.
L = designed water-line length at rest, in feet.
C = a constant or number which varies for size and type of boat.
  For Keith's Formula, C = 1.3 to 1.5.
  For Crouch's Formula, C = 180 to 200.

Keith's Formula:

$$M.P.H. = \sqrt{L} \times C \sqrt[3]{\frac{H.P. \times 1,000}{Disp.}}$$

or transposed:

$$H.P. = Disp. \left(\frac{M.P.H.}{10\,C\,\sqrt{L}}\right)^3$$

To find the constant for Keith's Formula from trial data of similar boats, transpose it thus:

$$C = \frac{M.P.H.}{\sqrt{L}} \times \frac{1}{\sqrt[3]{\dfrac{H.P. \times 1,000}{Disp.}}}$$

Crouch's Formula does not consider length:

$$M.P.H. = \frac{C}{\sqrt{\dfrac{Disp.}{H.P.}}}$$

or the same transposed:

$$H.P. = Disp. \times \left(\frac{M.P.H.}{C}\right)^2$$

To find the constant for Crouch's Formula from trial data of similar boats:

$$C = \frac{M.P.H.}{\sqrt{\dfrac{H.P.}{Disp.}}}$$

Use constants for the above formulas with the utmost care, deriving them from trial data of existing boats of the same type. If exact predictions of a new and different design—as to speed, power, and behavior—are required, have it tank tested. There's no better way.

Let's take an example. Say we are going to design a 40-foot D.W.L. powerboat of the normal planing type. The owner likes a certain diesel engine with 165 full-rated horsepower and wants to use two. (165 + 165 = 330. Then 330 × 85% = 280 H.P. for our calculation.) Let's say she will displace 24,000 pounds. How fast will she go? Using Keith's Formula with a constant of 1.4 and substituting the above values we will have:

$$M.P.H. = \sqrt{L} \times C\sqrt[3]{\frac{H.P. \times 1,000}{Disp.}}$$

$$M.P.H. = \sqrt{40} \times 1.4\sqrt[3]{\frac{280,000}{24,000}}$$

$$M.P.H. = 6.33 \times 1.4 \times 2.27$$

$$M.P.H. = 20$$

What speed would she make if she were 4,000 pounds lighter and used the same power? According to our friend Mr. Keith, about 21.4 M.P.H.

Suppose we make the hull, say, 5 feet longer, keeping the original weight of 24,000 pounds and the same power. How fast would she go then? About 21.3 M.P.H.

Now let's see what happens if we are able to buy more powerful engines, so that we increase the H.P. of each engine by 35. Instead of 165 H.P. they are 200 full-rated H.P. each. (200 + 200 = 400. Then 400 × 85% = 340 H.P. for our calculation.) With the original D.W.L. of 40 feet and weight of 24,000 pounds, what speed can we expect? About 21.4 M.P.H.

It's pretty hard to make this imaginary boat go 1.4 M.P.H. faster. You can lighten her by 4,000 pounds. You can lengthen her 5 feet. Or you can buy 70 horsepower more, if it's available.

A lot of other factors are involved. For one thing, the constant in the formula changes. For another, seaworthiness and speed in a seaway improve with length. But, unfortunately, weight increases with length. Also, weight usually increases with power—not just the weight of more powerful engines, but the weight of more fuel to run them.

So far in this discussion we have considered weight, power, and length. There remains the most important factor at sea—the shape of the boat. Let's investigate this matter.

First of all, consider a flat-bottom skiff. With an outboard motor for power, she is one of the best planing types—that is, in protected waters only. In waves, her shape is shock creating and not shock absorbing. She will slam down and slap her bottom on each wave. There are no materials or structural methods which can withstand the punishment of such pounding. As for the crew—how long can they stand the likes of that? Not very long.

Next to the flat bottom comes the V bottom, as an improvement in shape to reduce pounding. However, there are many further subtleties which affect the riding qualities. If deadrise (the angle between the bottom in section and the base) is too flat, the boat will perform almost like our flat-bottom skiff. On the other hand, a boat having deadrise that is too steep will cut through the waves nicely but will lose so much lift that she may not plane at all. Can you imagine trying to water ski on skis shaped with a deep V section? There would be no lifting action to raise the skier above water.

A straight line in section from keel to chine is not as good as a convex one, but better than a hollow or concave section as far as seakindly qualities are concerned. A hollow section forward, with little deadrise, will let a boat cut through the water well when the sea is calm. But in rough water a boat with such a bow is antagonistic to the sea and can pound itself to a pulp. The best V-bottom shape then is one with a moderate deadrise and a convex section.

At this point it would be appropriate to mention developable surfaces. A developed surface is the surface of a cylinder or a cone. These two shapes can be easily made with flat sheets of material such as plywood or metal. On the other hand, compound surfaces, like the surface of a sphere, are difficult to make with flat sheets. Most boats have compound surfaces, being rounded in two directions. The V-bottom boat can be designed to have developed surfaces, by utilizing conical surfaces for the bottom and cylindrical surfaces for the topsides above the chine. Different combinations of cones and cylinders can be worked together cleverly. It is quite a chore for the designer, because he must use the trial-and-error method in locating the apexes of cones to produce the desired shape of bottom, but a builder can construct a boat with developed surfaces much more quickly and with less labor. This type is particularly suited to "do it yourself" amateur boatbuilders. See page 112 for an example.

When you look at the body plan of a conical surface, V-bottom boat you will see, contrary to what you might expect, that the bottom does not have sections which are straight lines. If they were straight, there would be a compound curve due to the twist in the bottom. No, they are convex, which is good.

Of all the shapes, the most seaworthy and the fastest, up to a certain speed, in waves is the round-bottom boat. During World War II the round-bottom German E boats could almost always outrun potentially faster V-bottom British motor torpedo boats in the rough waters of the North Sea. They were approximately 106' x 16' beam x 5½' draft. Their top speed was 42 knots with three diesels of 2500 H.P. each. In calm water, the British boats were faster, but the pounding and slamming they took jumping from wave to wave slowed their speed below that of their round-bottom counterparts.

Any rounding of the forward sections will cut down pounding and produce an easy-riding hull. If lines are too fine forward, there is a tendency for such a boat to dive into the waves; thus the fine, round-bottom boat is soft riding but impossibly wet. On the other hand, V-bottom, planing hulls with a wide chine kept low forward are dry but impossibly hard riding.

Spray guards are the solution to the spray problem and really make a tremendous difference. On some round-bottom boats without spray guards, a thin sheet of water will climb up the side and sometimes go as high as the top of the deckhouse. If there's a stiff breeze, this spray will soak boat and crew like water from a fire hose. If the cockpit is not designed to be self-bailing, the boat could even swamp and sink from her own spray! This is bad design. But spray guards force water, as it starts climbing up, to separate from the hull. They throw spray out and down. They also provide some lift, as well as making a planing boat more stable dynamically.

In one case, a V-bottom boat had a tendency to roll her chine under. To correct this fault her spray guards were more than doubled in width, that is they were rebuilt to project from her hull twice as far. This one change eliminated her rolling underway and did so very inexpensively.

There are two compromise types between V bottoms and round bottoms. One is the inverted ox-yoke section. It combines the soft riding qualities of a round bottom with desirable V-bottom qualities of lift and spray throwing ability. But there is a slight tendency to slam or pound waves in the concave part of these ox-yoke sections. Also, wetted surface is greater with this type.

The other compromise type of hull form has a chine for its afterbody, which gradually fades into a round-sectioned forebody. This is an excellent shape. It

**Planing powerboats. The bottom one is a form
similar to that developed by Mr. C. Raymond Hunt.**

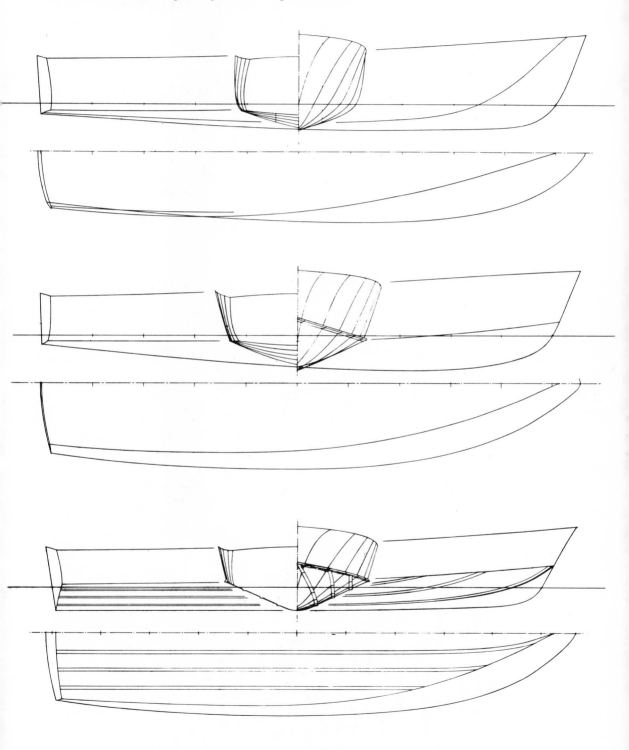

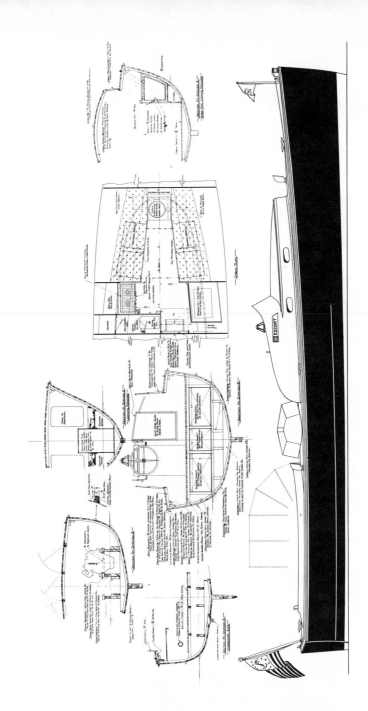

ESCORT is a smart 40-foot launch of Sparkman & Stephens design built in 1940.

With two gasoline engines her top speed is 28 mph.

She has a large open cockpit aft, engines under the large flush deck amidships, and a steering cockpit and cuddy cabin forward. The cabin is equipped with two berths and a small galley and head, but is primarily a shelter cabin, as she is seldom used for cruising.

ESCORT is an excellent example of the round-bottom type of planing powerboat. She has proven particularly easy and comfortable in a seaway.

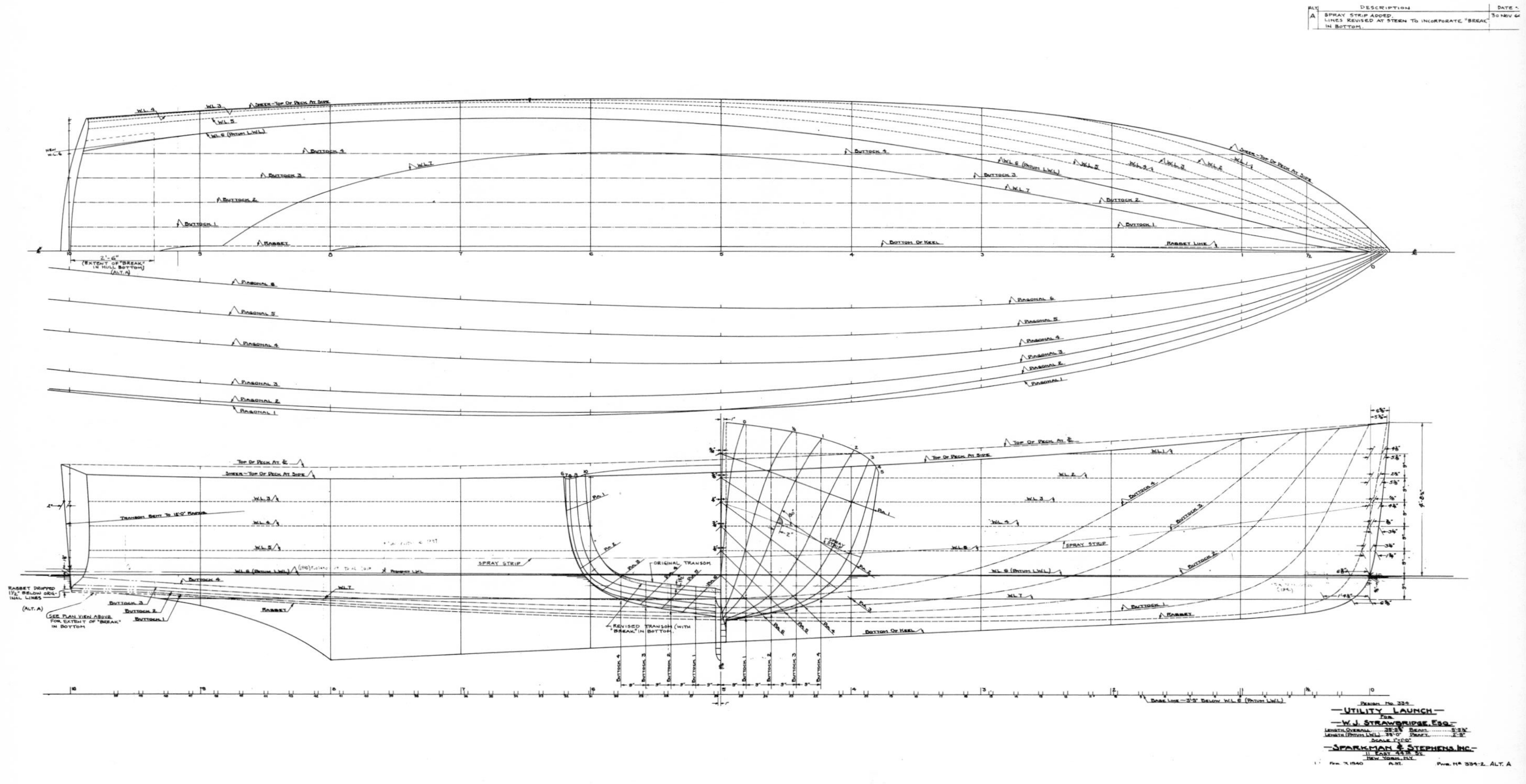
ALT. | DESCRIPTION | DATE
A | SPRAY STRIP ADDED. LINES REVISED AT STERN TO INCORPORATE "BREAK" IN BOTTOM. | 30 NOV 64
SHEER–TOP OF DECK AT SIDE
RABBET LINE
BOTTOM OF KEEL
SPRAY STRIP
ORIGINAL TRANSOM
REVISED TRANSOM (WITH "BREAK" IN BOTTOM)
2'-6" (EXTENT OF "BREAK" IN HULL BOTTOM) (ALT. A)
RABBET DROPPED 1½" BELOW ORIGINAL LINES (ALT. A)
SEE PLAN VIEW ABOVE FOR EXTENT OF "BREAK" IN BOTTOM
TRANSOM BENT TO 12'-0" RADIUS
BASE LINE–3'-3" BELOW W.L. 6 (DATUM L.W.L.)
DESIGN No. 334
UTILITY LAUNCH
FOR
W. J. STRAWBRIDGE, ESQ.
LENGTH, OVERALL 39'-3⅝" BEAM 9'-3½"
LENGTH (DATUM L.W.L.) 35'-0" DRAFT 2'-9"
SCALE 1"=1'-0"
SPARKMAN & STEPHENS, INC.
11 EAST 44TH ST.
NEW YORK, N.Y.
FEB. 7, 1940
A.M.
DWG. No 334-2 ALT. A

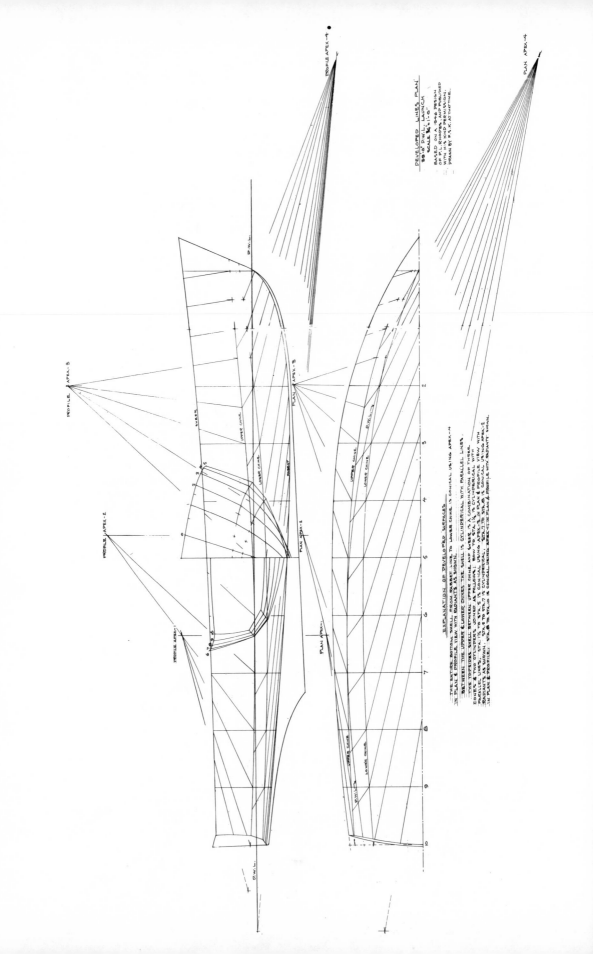

DEVELOPED LINE'S PLAN
39'-0" D.W.L. LAUNCH
SCALE ¾"=1'-0"

BASED ON A 1946 DESIGN
OF P. L. RHODES, AND PUBLISHED
WITH HIS KIND PERMISSION.
DRAWN BY F.S.K. AT THIS TIME.

EXPLANATION OF DEVELOPED SURFACES.

THE ENTIRE BOTTOM SHELL, FROM RABBET LINE TO LOWER CHINE IS CONICAL USING APEX-4
IN PLAN & PROFILE VIEW, WITH RADIANTS AS SHOWN.

BETWEEN THE UPPER & LOWER CHINES, THE SHELL IS CYLINDRICAL WITH PARALLEL LINES.

THE TOPSIDES SHELL BETWEEN UPPER CHINE AND SHEER, IS A COMBINATION OF THREE
ZONES. & THIS STUNDENT JOINED AT FALLWAL BOW TO STA. 1½ IS CYLINDRICAL WITH
PARALLEL LINES. STA. 1½ TO STA. 5 IS CONICAL USING APEX-3 IN PLAN & PROFILE VIEW WITH
RADIANTS AS SHOWN. STA. 5 TO STA. 7 IS CYLINDRICAL. STA. 7 TO STA. 8 IS CONICAL USING APEX-2
IN PLAN & PROFILE. STA. 8 TO STA.10 IS CONICAL USING APEX-1 IN PLAN & PROFILE WITH RADIANTS SHOWN.

combines a seagoing bow with an efficient planing stern form.

In any discussion on the shapes of planing powerboats it is important to consider the afterbody. On a Lines Drawing this would mean all the stations including and aft of Station 6. It has been found that if all these sections (Stations 6, 7, 8, 9, 10) below the turn of the bilge or chine coincide and show as one single line in the Body Plan, we have the best possible planing form. There will then be no twist to the bottom aft of amidships to suck up a big rooster-tail wake. The buttocks, or fore and aft lines, will be parallel and horizontal in this area.

To say that it's difficult to blend an ideal forebody into an ideal afterbody is very true. One form that does this with the least amount of twist is that which carries considerable deadrise all the way aft; or, vice versa, one that carries little deadrise all the way forward. This latter shape is not recommended. It's too much like a flat-bottom skiff, not seakindly. Have a good able boat that will take care of her crew. That's more important than speed for its own sake.

It is the responsibility of a yacht designer to put safety first. Whether his boats are sailboats or powerboats they should be designed for that unexpected violent storm. They should be, in a word, seagoing.

Speaking of seagoing ability brings to mind the double-ended hull. Lifeboats, surfboats, and whaleboats are extremely seaworthy, but they are not the proper shape to plane. They would squat too much and bury their stern with too much power. There is a shape, however, which is double ended and will plane without squatting. It is a V-bottom, planing powerboat in which the chines are brought around, in the same surface as each side of the V, to a point at the stern. Buttocks, or fore and aft lines, run out horizontally, as though to the usual transom stern, instead of curving upward as on a whaleboat. This permits separation of water from the stern, our definition of planing. But this type will have to go a few miles an hour faster before she starts to plane—that is, faster than a V-bottom boat of the same length and having a transom stern.

The advantage of this pointed stern is to reduce the tendency of broaching in a quartering sea. "Broaching" is a nasty word. It means to be inadvertently swung around out of control by the force of a following wave. This dangerous situation is a frequent cause of foundering.

Aside from its seaworthiness, the beauty of this design is that it is far more efficient at low speeds. And for one reason or another, whether it is noise, vibration, waves, or a false notion of fuel economy, most powerboats do travel at low speeds, wallowing along. This boat never drags along that low-speed brake, a submerged transom. It doesn't have one, being double ended.

Such a boat was developed by a builder on the West Coast. At the mouth of the Columbia River, nature has contrived to produce one of the roughest bodies of water in the world. The Coast Guard has found that the best boat for use in these violent waters is the double-ended V-bottom type which was evolved there.

Another important element to consider in the design of powerboats is the profile. Steering, or directional stability, is affected by it. If the forefoot is too deep and there is no skeg, it may be impossible to steer such a boat. When a boat of that profile runs down a wave, she buries her nose in water and her stern lifts high and clear. Those tiny high-speed rudders aren't much use then. Around she goes, pivoting on her deepest point, the bow. Next step in this tragedy is violent rolling in the trough of the seas. Capsizing or swamping is the last act.

If a deep forefoot is desired, then the profile must be balanced at the stern with a deep skeg and rudder. Of course, this means greater wetted surface, thus higher resistance. If the profile is cut away too much at the bow, then pounding and slamming will result. So there is a happy medium to be found. Every line must be a compromise.

Of all the different sizes and shapes of boats now afloat, probably the most popular type is the small, open, outboard runabout. There is a poor design feature which is frequently seen on these boats and, unfortunately, is the cause of many sinkings. It is the fault of the outboard engine manufacturers. They have agreed on standard shaft lengths of 24 and 28 inches from bracket to propeller. This is good for a boat about 10 feet long; but when a boat is 18 feet to 23 feet, it is too short. Here's why:

In order to submerge an outboard propeller in water, it is necessary for a boat manufacturer to design his transom sterns with a deep cutout for the outboard motor. It is a common sight to see reasonably high-sided boats with big holes in their sterns only 16 and 20 inches above the bottom.

Now let's say two men go out in such a boat on a cold morning, to go duck shooting. A breeze comes up, and the water gets rough. For some reason the outboard motor stops. One man goes aft to fuss with it. The other thinks he can help, so he goes aft also. Now this boat's stern is deep and her bow is high in the air. Like a weathervane, the bow naturally swings down wind. Instantly, water sloshes over that deep cut in the stern, now facing into each wave. Both men are so busy working on their motor they don't notice extra bilge water at first. Before they know it, it's too late. Their boat sinks. They won't survive more than ten minutes because the water is so cold.

The sad part of this story is that it is true and happens time and time again—all because outboard motor manufacturers won't increase the length of their shafts. As a group, they are so powerful that boatbuilders must adapt or quit.

Some boatbuilders producing outboard runabouts have models which incorporate a self-bailing well in way of the cut-down transom. This is safe, but it takes up so much space in a boat that it would be better to have an inboard motor in the first place. The fact is that just recently a few engine manufacturers have developed an inboard engine driving an outboard-type propeller which can be turned and raised. So the good features of both types are combined. This is driven through a "Z" drive. A rudder is not required for steering, and the propeller can be swung up and out of the way for beaching and transporting on a trailer. Since the engine is inside the boat, the transom can be as high as the sides of the hull and, therefore, safe.

(Opposite page) Where seaworthiness counts. A 52-foot motor lifeboat out of U.S. Coast Guard Lifeboat Station, Yaquina Bay, Oregon.

CHAPTER XIII

RESISTANCE

Any opposing or retarding force offered to the passage of a boat through the elements of water and air falls into the category of resistance. Nature has contrived the worst of these. A head wind, a foul current, waves, and barnacles are some of the most thwarting.

Friction is caused by a rough underwater hull surface. It's the little bumps and roughness that do the most harm. On a steel ship, for example, barnacles adhering to the bottom will result in a very real loss in speed; whereas, the large bumps and hollows of distorted plates, caused by welding, will produce almost no resistance. Barnacles can make the skipper of an ocean liner a very frustrated fellow, especially at the end of an 11-month period, before his ship goes into dry dock. His ship may be two knots slower then. This prevents him from maintaining the tight schedule his owners have set up.

Racing yachtsmen know all too well that in order to win they must keep the bottoms of their boats just as smooth and clean as possible.

Types of Resistance. Now for the man-made resistances designed into a boat. They are these:

1. Friction due to the area of surface exposed to water. This includes resistance caused by the boundary layer.
2. Wave-making resistance caused by the shape of the hull (essentially residuary resistance). This includes eddies or drag caused by appendages.
3. Windage or air resistance due to excessive rigging and, to a less extent, to the size of superstructure.

Let's discuss these one at a time. In a sailboat there is a very important relationship between wetted surface and sail area, as we have seen; also in powerboats the relationship between wetted surface and power is important. To wit, the very noticeable increase in the speed of a planing powerboat when it lifts itself and decreases the bottom area touching the water; or when, by the simple expedient of omitting the skeg, the wetted surface is considerably reduced.

Hydrofoils were developed for the express purpose of lifting a boat clear of the water, which eliminates almost entirely the friction due to wetted surface. They are successfully used on special types to increase speed. By standing on legs above these miniature wings the hull form can no longer make waves, so the resistance from this source is also eliminated.

Wave-making Resistance is the energy lost in the creation of waves. It is the principal resistance for displacement-type craft trying to go too fast, as well as for planing-type craft going too slowly. Mathematically, this would give us a boat which performed between the speed-length ratios of 1 and 2. To pin this down even more closely mathematically—the hump of greatest resistance caused by the creation of waves lies between the speed of a wave, 1.34 × $\sqrt{\text{length between crests}}$, or a speed-length ratio of 1.34 as the lower limit, and 1.65, as the upper limit.

The accompanying chart (Figure 5) shows the influence of the prismatic co-efficient on wave-making resistance at various speed-length ratios. The definition of prismatic coefficient is explained in Chapter XXIII, A Manual of Calculations. Its importance in yacht design cannot be emphasized too much, because there is an optimum prismatic coefficient for every speed.

The higher the speed-length ratio becomes, the greater the prismatic coefficient which should be used in order to obtain the least resistance. At high speed-length ratios the middle body is a great wave-making factor, so to increase the prismatic the designer must work more volume toward the ends of his craft.

On the other hand, at low speed-length ratios, a high prismatic coefficient is detrimental. For example, results of tank tests made by Admiral Taylor show the

Figure 5. Prismatic coefficient

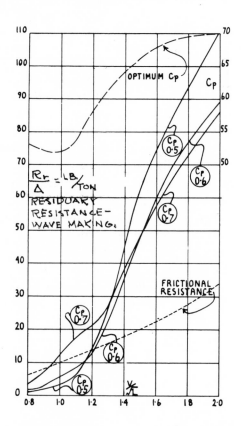

wave-making resistance of a certain model towed at a speed so as to equal a speed-length ratio of 1.0 was 4 pounds per ton with an optimum prismatic coefficient of .55. When a model of the same size was tried at the same speed but with a prismatic coefficient of .65, the resistance doubled! Therefore, there is an optimum prismatic coefficient for every speed-length ratio.

Sharp bows, with a slight hollow at the water to make the entrance even sharper, seem to reduce resistance. The surface of the water should be cut, not pushed. Underwater the problem is different. Bluntness well below the surface in some cases is beneficial. Admiral Taylor—in whose memory the David W. Taylor Model Basin near Washington, D.C. is named—discovered the advantages of a bulbous bow when experimenting with a model of a battleship type used in the Spanish American War. He found that a model with an underwater ram projecting forward could be towed with less resistance at certain speeds than a model of the same size but with a straight sharp stem. He simply cut off the ram in profile and rounded all water lines to it. The result was the bulbous bow we so often see on large ships today. The limits of speed-length ratio which show this type to be better are very narrow (0.8 to 1.1), so a careful study should be made before using a bow of this shape.

Relationship between Friction and Wave-making. It is interesting to note the relationship of the two types of underwater resistance for different speed-length ratios. It has been found by tank testing to be as follows:

Speed $\div \sqrt{Length}$	Frictional Resistance	Wave-Making Resistance
up to 1.0	50% to 35% of total	50% to 65% of total
1.0 to 1.34	30% to 20% of total	70% to 80% of total
The hump. 1.34 to 1.65	15% to 10% of total	85% to 90% of total
1.65 to 2.2	about 25% of total	about 75% of total

As we have noted before, the distance between bow wave and stern wave limits the speed of nonplaning-type hulls. Because the speed-length ratio of waves is 1.34, nonplaning or displacement types are those which operate below that speed. At speeds above a speed-length ratio of 1.34, when a vessel starts to leave the crest of her stern wave behind and is climbing the after slope of her bow crest, the planing hull form with a flat transom is the shape offering least resistance. The hump of greatest resistance, like the waves that cause it, must be surmounted by a burst of power.

For a typical planing powerboat hull, all the qualities favorable to planing are, prior to reaching the planing hump, operating to increase resistance. At low speeds the wide beam is a detriment. The wide submerged transom causes eddies. The flat angle of deadrise tends to add general clumsiness.

Seaplane hulls with their steps develop considerable suction which adds materially to the difficulty of taking off. It is necessary to aerate the surface before the excess suction can be broken. This is why heavily-loaded seaplanes commonly cross and recross their wakes in calm water take-offs.

Boundary Layer of Turbulent Water. In any discussion of underwater resistance it should be pointed out that there is great room for experiment and improvement. Particular attention should be focused on the boundary layer of turbulent water that clings to every hull moving through water. In salt water it is evident from the white froth visible on the surface close to the hull. It varies in width for different-sized boats, from nothing at the bow to:

$$5'' \text{ wide at the stern on a } 30' \text{ hull.}$$
$$12'' \text{ wide at the stern on a } 100' \text{ hull.}$$
$$24'' \text{ wide at the stern on a } 400' \text{ hull.}$$

Within this belt of frictional wake, the water has a certain forward velocity imparted to it by the motion of the ship, then transferred outward by the interlocking of molecules. The speed of wake water varies from that of a thin film which moves along next to the hull, through declining velocities as energy is dissipated, to a state of rest at the edge. The frictional resistance occurs within the wake. The amount depends on the area of surface exposed to water, the texture of the surface, the viscosity of water, and the speed of the vessel.

Porpoises do not have this boundary layer. It is believed that this is the secret of their great speed in relation to their power. These mammals swim at 25 knots—and often faster when they are about to leap out of water—and require only a few pounds of mackerel for fuel from time to time. How can they go so fast? The theory is that porpoises are able to feel the flow over their skins and to detect a transition from laminar flow to a boundary layer of turbulent water. These marine creatures must be able to change their shape to insure that the water clings to their skin. Otherwise they could not attain such high speeds so effortlessly. Their outer skin is paper thin. Beneath this comes a spongy layer about one quarter of an inch thick, next to their real skin. Perhaps the undulating motion accomplishes this change of shape. Some think an airfoil shape is created, sucking the porpoise forward. If so, a naval architect would have a hard time emulating such a feature in the design of a ship. Imagine a boat that wiggles! A rubber life raft does, but seems to get nowhere.

The late Dr. Kenneth S. M. Davidson, in whose honor the towing tanks on the campus at Stevens Institute are now named, was fascinated with the great speeds these bottle-nosed dolphins could maintain for long periods. His theory was that this was due to their streamlined shape and their smooth, oily skin. He deserves a great deal of credit for changing the hull shape of our modern submarines. Now they truly resemble the shape of a porpoise and are just about the fastest vessels afloat when traveling submerged. They seem to be almost as quick as a fish when maneuvering. Due to their circular sections they have the minimum wetted surface. No deck gun, no unnecessary appendages such as shafting and struts as used on the old twin-screw subs. There is a single propeller on the center line. To a designer's eye the first small ALBACORE was a thing of beauty—a man-made fish. These new submarines have certainly borne out Doctor Davidson's theory about the ideal shape.

As to the oily, smooth skin—well it just may be that the softness is more important, allowing the skin to change shape enough to insure that water clings to its surface, and to hold an uninterrupted laminar flow pattern. At any rate, here is a potential field for experiment.

Eddy-making Resistance occurs at the after edge of thick rudders, at propeller apertures, propeller struts, and other appendages under water. There is little reason for much resistance of this kind in a well-designed yacht where the lines are faired to sharp trailing edges like those of a fish.

Leading Edge. Resistance-wise, the leading edge is also very important. A small projection near the bow—such as a through-hull sea cock fitting for a toilet or the transducer unit of a depth finder—will act like a lump of ice on the leading edge of an airplane wing. There, fittings must be set in flush. Otherwise, the streamlines will be destroyed. Just as an airplane with too much ice on its wings cannot fly, so also a sailboat with a lumpy leading edge will perform poorly.

Displacement-Length Ratio. To complete our discussion of underwater resistance it is necessary to consider one more relationship, the displacement-length ratio. It is the displacement in tons divided by the cube of length divided by 100, expressed thus, $D \div (.01L)^3$. For example, for our **PIPE DREAM** Cruising Sloop the displacement in tons in salt water would be the displacement in cubic feet divided by 35, or $210 \div 35 = 6$ tons. The displacement-length ratio would be: $6 \div .254^3 = 6 \div .016 = 375$. (Long tons of 2,240 lbs. are used).

Although alterations of displacement-length ratios have relatively little effect on wave-making resistance, they do affect frictional resistance. For low speeds this has a noticeable effect on the over-all resistance per ton. At low speed-length ratios we are concerned principally with friction. There is a diminishing ratio of skin-friction resistance to displacement. So with straightforward logic we can deduce that an increase in length for the same displacement would have a favorable over-all effect. It has been discovered by tank testing that a decrease of displacement-length ratio usually reduces the total resistance per ton at low speed-length ratios.

Air Resistance is not important until the relative speed of a boat through the air is 30 knots or more. Air is only about 1/800 the weight of water, so the resistance under ordinary conditions is a small fraction of water resistance. Windage effect for a powerboat is not as great head-on as with the wind abeam. So streamlined deckhouses are pointless. But a sailing vessel with yardarms, topmasts, ratlines, and all such top hamper presents a great deal of windage when at anchor, head to wind. Those square-riggers had huge anchors for good reason. Excessive rigging would create so much windage as to cause a vessel to drag anchor in a fresh breeze.

The modern sailboat should be designed so that her masts and spreaders present absolutely the least amount of windage. Her standing rigging should be of the minimum diameter consistent with proper strength. If a wire or a rope can be eliminated from the design, all the better. The less windage, the faster she'll sail to windward.

When it comes to considering air resistance on powerboats, there are two design features worthy of attention. One is the Venturi wind deflector used on the bridges of ocean liners to shoot the air up and over the heads of people. Venturi wind deflectors could well be used in way of the upper steering positions on powerboats.

The other design feature involves proper smoke stack design to carry off exhaust gases no matter what the wind direction. Odd as it may sound, the best stack design is a tall narrow pipe. It will allow the gases emitting therefrom to be blown clear, without curling down on the leeward side, and it presents the least wind resistance. A low wide stack may look very smart, but it is useless as far as carrying out its proper function. The top of the stack must be higher than the pilothouse; otherwise, those on the bridge may be asphyxiated in a following breeze.

The temptation for anyone writing about resistance is to put down a lot of formulas, charts, and tables showing just how it can be calculated. But the truth of the matter is that yacht designers seldom, if ever, calculate resistance themselves. By resorting to tank testing of models they are able to obtain solutions to their speed and power problems far more accurately than by any other means.

Summary. A good designer has that certain instinct of doing the correct thing to reduce resistance. In order to do this he must:

1. Know and apply the optimum prismatic coefficient.
2. Reduce wetted surface to the minimum.
3. Eliminate appendages below water.
4. Keep underwater surfaces smooth.
5. Use the proper hull form.

For the reader who is genuinely interested in formulas showing how resistance can be calculated, there is a wealth of material based on thousands of experiments by such great scientists as Sir Isaac Newton, William Froude, R. E. Froude, Osborne Reynolds, Admiral David W. Taylor, Kenneth S. M. Davidson. Pertinent formulas, tables, and charts, based on data given by the above and many other authors, are available in one book, *Principles of Naval Architecture*, Vol. II, by Rossell and Chapman, published by the Society of Naval Architects and Marine Engineers, New York, N.Y.

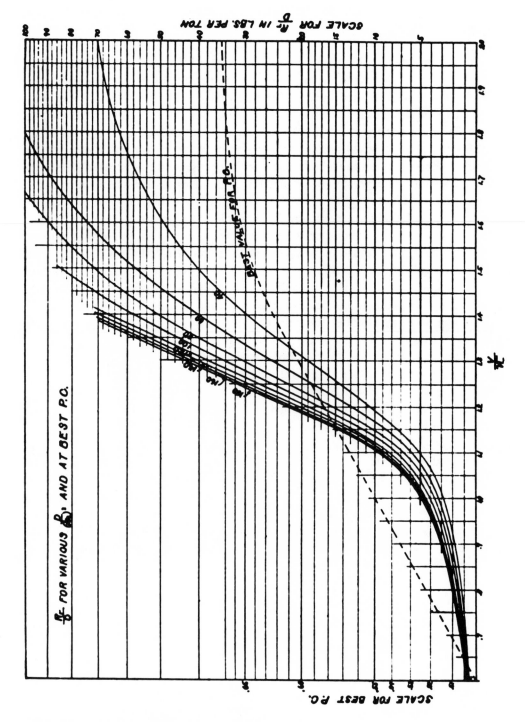

For narrow displacement-type powerboats, and for multi-hull craft without ballast.

CHAPTER XIV

TANK TESTING

Unquestionably the best way to ascertain the performance of full-size vessels before their construction is by the use of models towed in water. The model and the towing tank combine to make the most valuable tools of ship and yacht designing. The idea is quite old. Some of the oldest seagoing civilizations used this concept thousands of years ago.

Scaling Laws. Model testing is based on simple scaling laws of similitude. These are:

1. The speed of model and ship are proportional to the square roots of their lengths.
2. The wave-making resistance of model and ship are proportional to the cubes of their lengths.
3. The displacement of model and ship vary as the cubes of their lengths.

Model Speed, Resistance, and Power Requirements. Let us start right off with a simple example. In testing a model of a ship in order to determine its resistance, it is obvious that we cannot run the model at the same speed as that of the ship. For the sake of using round numbers, let's say we have designed a 64-foot motor sailer, which is expected to make 10 knots. Because she is a displacement type we can estimate her speed from the formula $\sqrt{\text{D.W.L.}} \times 1.25 = $ speed in knots. So this gives us $\sqrt{64} \times 1.25 = 10$ knots. We build a 4-foot model of her. How fast should we tow the model?

To find the speed of a 4-foot model, which corresponds to the speed of a vessel 64 feet long going 10 knots, first find the ratio of their lengths, which is $64 \div 4 = 16$. Then the speed of the model, which corresponds to 10 knots for the vessel, is $10 \div \sqrt{16} = 2.5$ knots.

Next, we tow the model at 2.5 knots and find that the towing scale registers, say, 1 pound. What would this give us for the total resistance of the 64-foot vessel? First, find the ratio of their lengths as before, $64 \div 4 = 16$. Then, the resistance of the vessel corresponding to the 1-pound resistance of the model is $1 \times 16^3 = 4,096$ lbs.

With the figure of 4,096 pounds resistance (from which subtract the calculated frictional resistance, as mentioned later), we can calculate how much horsepower is required to overcome it. The formula for effective horsepower is: E.H.P. = Resistance × Speed in Kn. × .003071. So, substituting our values in the formula:

$$E.H.P. = 4,096 \times 10 \times .003071 = 125.8.$$

Since the effective horsepower is only 50% efficient, due to friction, we will need twice that, or 125.8 × 2 = 251.6 horsepower, at the engine; so, we select an engine rated at 252 horsepower to make our 64-foot motor sailer do 10 knots.

From this simple example to an accurate determination of power requirements

Used by Stevens Institute of Technology for tank testing models.

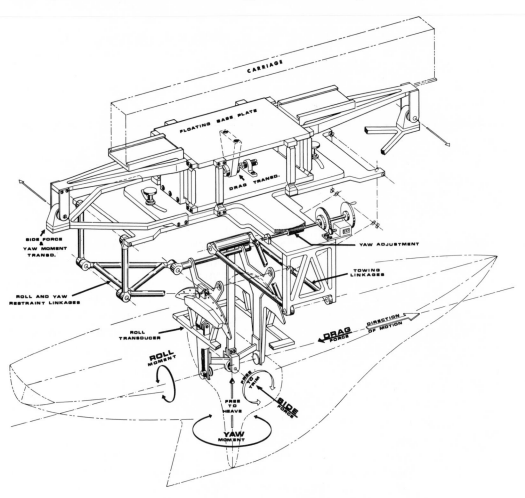

YACHT DYNAMOMETER D.L.

or sailing performance, the calculations become more and more complex. Many corrections must be made to allow for differences in model and ship behavior.

Lack of Boundary Layer Around a Model. Principal among these differences is the existence of a boundary layer of turbulent water around a ship, and the lack of a correspondingly proportionate amount around a model. Water breaks away from the ship but clings to the model. It is necessary, then, to create turbulence artificially in the flow of water around the model.

Two methods of introducing initial disturbances are presently in use, as follows:
1. Towing a small vertical rod or wire submerged just ahead of the model; and
2. Applying a narrow vertical strip of coarse sand to the leading edge of the model.

Wave-making. A model is tested for wave-making resistance only. Frictional resistance must be calculated separately and then subtracted from the total resistance, which is recorded by the scale or dynamometer on the carriage towing the model.

To Calculate Frictional Resistance based on the findings of William Froude, the celebrated English physicist, use his formula, which is:

Frictional Resistance = Speed in Knots to the Power 1.83 $\times$ Wetted Surface $\times$ a Small Number to allow for the different effect of friction on short and long surfaces. (This is .013 for a 4-foot model, .012 for 8 feet, .011 for 15 feet, .010 for a 33-foot craft, and .009 for a 200-foot vessel.) Now, to find the value for speed to the power 1.83, consult logarithm tables in the back of this book.

To raise a number to a given power, multiply the logarithm of the number by the exponent of the power, and find the number whose logarithm is the product. Example: $9^{1.83} = ?$, $1.83 \times$ log. $9 =$ log. ? Look up in the logarithm tables the logarithm for 9. It is equal to .95425. Then $1.83 \times .95 = 1.74$. Then find the number whose logarithm is 1.74. From the table it is 55. So $9^{1.83} = 55$.

Equipment. For wind-tunnel work on model airplanes it has been found convenient to hold the model stationary and move air past it. But the large volumes of water which would have to be pumped make this scheme impractical for testing ship models. So the model is moved through the water.

A simple method of model testing is to tow two models side by side from the ends of a yoke connected at its mid point to an outrigger on a launch. A bowsprit rigged way forward pointing down would serve better to avoid any interference from the launch's wake. In this case the model with the greater resistance would pull back on its end of the yoke, allowing the better model to surge ahead as the yoke pivoted. The results of such tests would only show the superiority of one model over the other, not the amount of resistance.

An arrangement which has been used successfully for small tanks is to tow the model by means of a falling weight of a known amount and to measure the speed. In this case the resistance of the model at its attained speed would equal the same number of pounds as the falling weight. Change the model a little; use the same weight. Then measure the speed to see if it goes any faster. Simple but effective.

Chapman's testing tank

Another method of model testing is the use of a revolving arm. An arm about 30 or 40 feet long is mounted on an island in the center of a small pond. It is rotated by a motor at any desired speed. Knowing the length of the arm and its R.P.M.'s, the speed of the model can be readily computed. The towline is led to a sensitive scale so that exact resistance can be read. Trim and flotation of the model may be recorded by photography.

In the modern towing tank there is a carriage which travels on rails down the length of the tank, carrying various scales for measuring resistance of the model at different speeds. Accelerating and decelerating must be done in a short space, and the speed of the carriage accurately regulated during its run, with particular attention to maintaining a constant rate of speed.

Fresh water is used to avoid the corrosive action of salt water. Special equipment, including lateral scales and other apparatus, is provided for testing sailing boat models when heeled and making leeway, as under actual sailing conditions. Other equipment is provided for the study of stability, propeller design, the influence of waves, rolling and pitching, seaworthiness, and the interaction of hull and propeller. Self-propelled models are often used to study steering characteristics.

Significance. To modify the hull form; to try it again; to find its new resistance; to check the figures against other designs previously tested; to strive to improve design from boat to boat—herein lies the great worth of tank testing. It is the best insurance an owner can buy when he intends to build an expensive boat. How simple to change hull form at model size. How impossible to make such changes on a full-sized vessel.

Controlled Tests. Another factor to be considered in tank testing is to see that the water in the tank is kept stirred up at exactly the same rate. With this in mind, it is interesting to note the schedule at the Davidson Laboratory. In their tank Number 1, the model being tested is run precisely on schedule, once every two minutes on the dot. Even at lunch time there is no pause; someone else takes over.

Other corrections which must be applied include: an allowance for the different densities of fresh and salt water at a certain temperature; a correction for shaft struts, shafting, and various appendages; a correction for the roughness of the shell of the hull.

The average reading on the towing scale for a four-foot sailboat model is only about three-quarters of a pound. So it is easy to understand why such great accuracy is required. It is surprising how the most subtle changes in hull form of the model can register noticeable differences in the resistance. A little refining here or a little fattening there will change the performance. It is a matter of trial and error. But when the performance of a new model is compared to those which have been tested before, it can be predicted accurately whether the full-size boat will perform poorly, about as well as the average, or very well indeed.

A prominent naval architect is quoted as saying, "It is very difficult to design a boat much better than existing good ones, but it is very easy to design one ten per cent worse."

The Pioneers. Sailing yacht tank testing now being carried out at the Davidson Laboratory is based directly on the work of the late Dr. Davidson. In the 1930's Dr. Davidson began by towing models in a swimming pool and developing his proof that models of small size, 4 to 5 feet in length, could give test results comparable to those of larger models. Up to that time it had been considered necessary for models to be 15 to 20 feet long for accurate results.

With the help of a young fellow by the name of Olin Stephens, and using a boat called GIMCRACK, certain coefficients were evolved, which enabled Dr. Davidson to correlate the performance of the full-size GIMCRACK with her model. After a period of intensive research, Dr. Davidson and his staff, working from vast amounts of data gathered from models of sailing craft, were able to establish values for heeling and driving wind forces. They devised mechanical means to apply these known forces to the model, and to measure the unknown forces.

Sailboat Tests. For sailboats, the total wind forces on the rig must be exactly equal but opposite to the total water forces on the hull, in direction, strength, and point of application. In the actual testing procedures, a range of rig forces are impressed upon the model by weights. The model is run repeatedly down the tank at various speeds, angles of heel, and angles of leeway, until a state of equilibrium is reached between the total water forces and each of the impressed rig values. Complex calculation then permits selection of the optimum performance for any given wind and speed.

The picture of ideal symmetrical equilibrium between wind and water would be a sailing vessel with a square sail set, running dead before the wind in a smooth sea. In this case all forces and effects are symmetrical about the center plane. The hull is upright. The rudder is at 0° angle. The sail is square across the hull, with the same area on each side. Here we have a case very similar to that of a boat operating under power, except that the wind force is applied relatively high above the boat and so has a tendency to depress the bow.

As the wind shifts to her quarter, beam, and bow, a great multitude of complex factors affect our vessel: her stability, her hull form, the size and shape of her

Model of PIPE DREAM Cruising Sloop being tested at the Davidson Laboratory, designer watching stern wave

lateral plane, the size and shape of her rig, and the displacement. These factors acting on each other in different ways produce the resultant heel angle, leeway angle, trim, and balance (weather or lee helm).

The testing of powerboat models is relatively simple compared to the complications involved in the testing of sailing yacht models. A powerboat model is towed straight forward and in the upright position over a wide range of speeds; whereas a sailing yacht model must be towed heeled over and at an angle to her

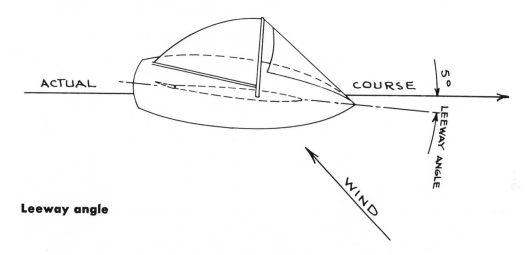

Leeway angle

fore and aft center line. This crab-like direction corresponds to that certain amount of leeway that every sailboat makes when close hauled, beating to windward. It may be from 3° to 5° in a 7-knot breeze, and from 5° to 8° in a 20-knot breeze.

The Davidson Laboratory tests sailing yacht models at three angles of heel—10°, 20°, and 30°—as well as upright. For close-hauled results, wind velocities of 7.5, 13.0 and 19.5 knots are used independently of the above, giving a result in angle of heel. A graph of the curve of upright resistance versus speed is given. A graph of heeled resistance versus speed is given after the leeway angle for each of the three heel angles is determined. A tabulation of close-hauled results is given both for fixed values of heel angle and for fixed values of true wind speed. The position of the center of lateral resistance is plotted. The balance is worked out for each angle of heel, showing weather helm or lee helm as the case may be. Finally, the meat of all the testing is summarized on one chart showing the best speed made good to windward. (See Figure 6) This does not mean the speed through the water back and forth as the boat tacks on her zigzag course to windward. No, it is concerned with the winner in a sailboat race from a leeward mark to a windward mark.

We learned a very interesting fact about stability when testing the model of a

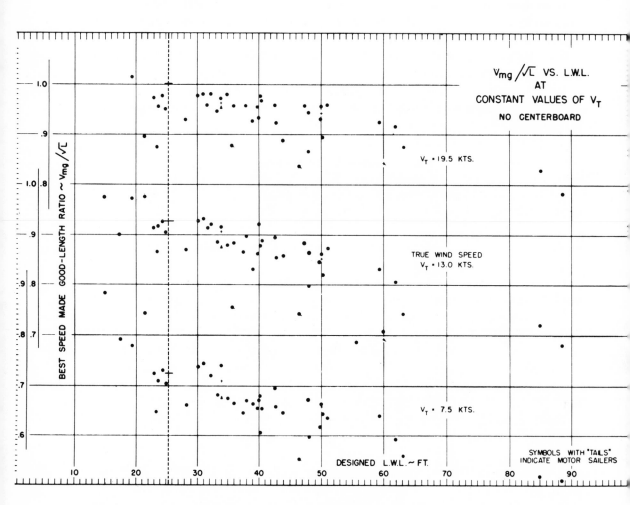

Figure 6. Best speed made good—PIPE DREAM test

fat centerboarder. Our stability calculations were way off, because they represented static conditions. The static stability calculations do not take into account what happens dynamically. On paper our design was worked out to be reasonably stiff for her size and type. Yet when her model was tested she proved to be tender. What happens as a boat moves is that its bow wave builds up in front, and the stern wave rises aft, leaving a large trough or hollow in the water at the middle of the boat. The boat literally digs a hole for herself in the water and sinks into it. There is then less water amidships to buoy up those wide midship sections. Thus, when she moves she is not as stiff as she would be if heeled over at anchor.

Powerboat Tests. The testing of planing powerboat models presents some interesting problems. Chief among these is the correct estimate of wetted surface when planing. It has been found that the running wetted areas are sometimes as little as 50% of the wetted areas when the boat is at rest, thus their importance in a friction correction is considerable.

By painting section lines on the model, as reference points, the point where solid water, not spray, breaks clear of the chine may be estimated from photographs of the model underway. But, due to spray, the extent of the wetted bottom cannot be clearly seen. Spots of wet paint have been applied to models, after which they were run to determine the flow lines. Where they smudge out sideways determines quite closely the forward boundary of the wetted bottom.

Good practice in the towing of planing powerboat models calls for the towing equipment to be attached to a point on the designed propeller shaft line. This is to provide an upward force to compensate for the upward thrust of the propeller at the angle of the shaft line. But this angle must be determined when the model is moving, to allow for trim.

Trim is an important factor. Observe what happens to the bow, the center of gravity, and the stern of a planing boat as speed is increased. At low speeds she behaves like a displacement boat, settling down in the water, with the bow usually deeper than the stern. As speed is increased, trim angle increases sharply and the center of gravity rises. Continuing increase of speed results in a leveling off and slowly decreasing angle of trim. As this happens, the center of gravity remains fixed. As speed changes, the trim adjusts itself to retain a condition of equilibrium between gravity, buoyancy, dynamic lift, drag, and propeller thrust.

When planing, the minimum resistance lies between a 2° and 4° angle of trim. Wave-making resistance increases with an increase of trim angle, but frictional resistance decreases as the trim angle gets larger. This, of course, is due to the wetted surface decreasing as the bow lifts. This conflict of interests, so to speak, seems to compromise at a trim angle of between 2° and 4° for planing-type hulls.

The trim angle, if too low, can be increased by moving the center of gravity aft. But it must be borne in mind that too high a trim angle might result in porpoising.

Power Required for Planing Powerboats. The chart giving minimum resistances for planing hulls (Figure 7) is presented here with thanks to its creator, Allan B. Murray. By consulting it the designer may work out the horsepower needed to drive a planing powerboat at a certain speed.

Example: A 50-foot D.W.L. planing-type powerboat displaces 44,800 pounds at rest. She is required to go 20 knots. Find effective horsepower. First, find her speed-length ratio: $20 \div \sqrt{50} = 2.83$. Next, her displacement-length ratio: $44,800 \div 2240 = 20$ tons. $20 \div .5^3 = 160$. From the chart, for a speed-length ratio of 2.83 we look up the intersection at the curve for displacement-length ratio

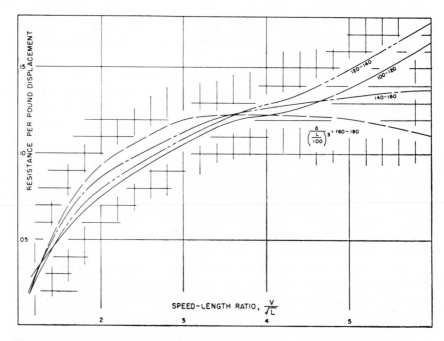

Figure 7. Resistances for planing hulls

of 160. So R = .113, from this chart, which means resistance per pound. Resistance for this boat would then be .113 × 44,800 lbs. = 5,060 lbs. Then substituting in the formula for effective horsepower which is:

$$\text{E.H.P.} = R \times V \times .003071$$
$$\text{E.H.P.} = 5,060 \times 20 \times .003071$$
$$\text{E.H.P.} = 310$$

Since E.H.P. is only 50% efficient, 310 × 2 = 620 H.P. is required to drive this boat 20 knots.

Models of Canals. Models are used to investigate the behavior of ships in narrow waters, such as rivers and canals. A model of the Panama Canal was built at the Taylor Model Basin, and model ships were maneuvered through it by remote control. Now that giant-size tankers are in operation their movement through such bodies of water as the Suez Canal becomes more and more of a problem.

This lack of elbow room for supertankers in the Suez Canal has prompted a very large oil company to build a scale model of a section of the canal in France, where navigation problems can be worked out in advance. Through the mock canal a 20-foot model supertanker is taken some 600 feet by a trainee pilot, who looks as if he were sailing a large kayak. The model vessel is maneuvered by the pilot himself, so that he may check the response of the ship to certain difficult situations similar to those that would arise when the ship actually traversed the

Canal. The worst among these is the very fact that such large ships must move so close to the banks.

Close to a ship's sides the water flows more rapidly, causing suction If a ship is traveling along, let us say, the right-hand bank of a canal and tries to turn to the left, when she puts her rudder to port her stern will not swing to starboard in the normal manner; it will swing to starboard a great deal more, due to suction; and because of this suction, it may run aground, damaging her propeller and rudder. This phenonemon—as well as winds, currents, and curves in the canal—is simulated at the research basin.

A figure illustrating the moment the rudder must overcome while running downwind with spinnaker

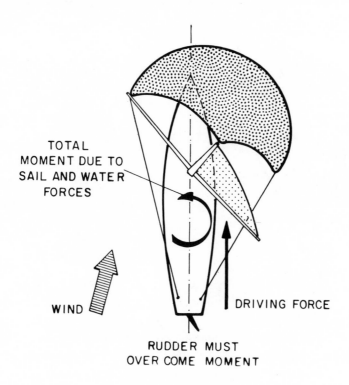

TOTAL MOMENT DUE TO SAIL AND WATER FORCES

WIND

DRIVING FORCE

RUDDER MUST OVER COME MOMENT

KEEL PROFILE VARIATIONS
5.5 METER CLASS

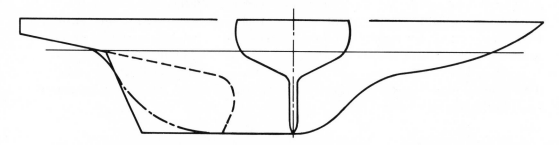

Keel Profile Variations for the 5.5-Meter Class. This shows the development of the keel profile over the last 10-12 years, indicating a major reduction in lateral plane which also resulted in bad handling characteristics.

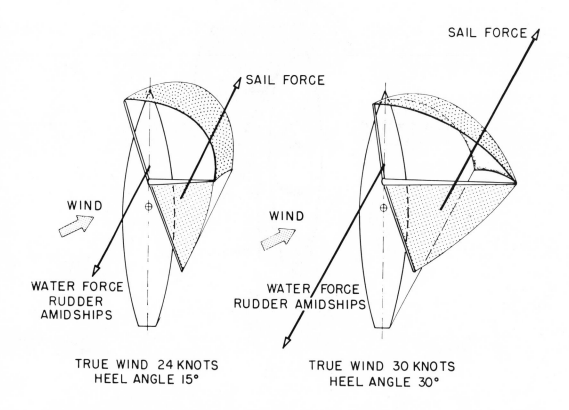

SAIL FORCE

SAIL FORCE

WIND

WIND

WATER FORCE
RUDDER
AMIDSHIPS

WATER FORCE
RUDDER AMIDSHIPS

TRUE WIND 24 KNOTS
HEEL ANGLE 15°

TRUE WIND 30 KNOTS
HEEL ANGLE 30°

A figure showing the increase in moment on a reach for a relatively small increase in wind speed from 24-30 knots; the heel angle doubles and the moment acting on the hull more than doubles.

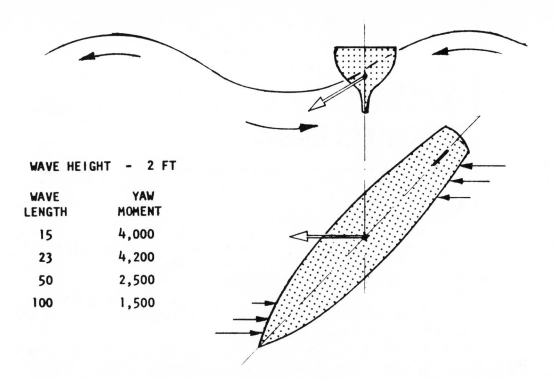

WAVE HEIGHT - 2 FT	
WAVE LENGTH	YAW MOMENT
15	4,000
23	4,200
50	2,500
100	1,500

A figure showing a broaching or yawling moment acting on a hull in a seaway.

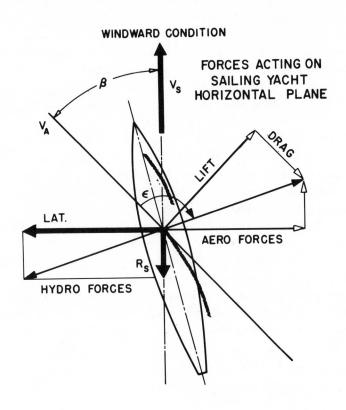

WINDWARD CONDITION

FORCES ACTING ON SAILING YACHT HORIZONTAL PLANE

CHAPTER XV

PROPELLERS

To calculate, by scientific methods, the correct size of the propeller to use on a certain boat is a long and tedious process, requiring a mass of detailed information. When applied to motorboats, motor sailers, and auxiliaries, it is none too satisfactory. So many coefficients which are correctly known for large ships must be guessed at for smaller craft. It is rare that the first propeller chosen is the final one used on a new design.

In order to drive a boat at her expected speed, the motor must deliver the proper amount of power at a particular number of revolutions. To avoid cavitation and its detrimental effect on power and speed, the revolutions must be kept within bounds. The propeller must produce a thrust which is exactly equal to the resistance of the boat at her expected speed. The diameter, pitch, and slip must all be related to each other to give this result.

Diameter of a propeller is the diameter of the circle swept by the tips of the blades.

Diameter is the most important single factor in propeller calculations. A slight change in diameter has more effect on power absorption than a considerable change in pitch or blade area. The most common error is to install a propeller of too large a diameter for the power available. In such a case, revolutions are held down. Power and speed are lost.

Early in the design stage it becomes necessary to know the approximate diameter of the propeller that will be used. This dimension affects draft, angle of shaft line, location of rudder, position of struts and bearings, and if our design is for an auxiliary, the size of the propeller aperture.

The chart for propeller diameter (Figure 8) may be used with a considerable degree of accuracy. It is based on Admiral Taylor's experiments and is plotted for propellers having a blade width of 30% of the diameter. It checks with a diameter chart devised by Mr. George F. Crouch and published in *Yachting*, March 1932. His chart goes as high as 10,000 R.P.M. and is useful for very high-speed racing

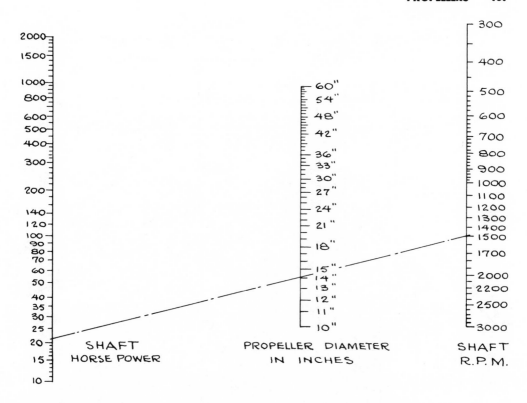

Figure 8. Propeller diameter—three bladed (Short Method)

powerboats. In each case suitable allowance, based on experience, has been made for friction.

Simply run a straight line from the selected figure for shaft horsepower on the left to shaft R.P.M.'s on the right; then read off the diameter of propeller (given in inches) where it crosses the line in between. These figures will have to be selected from figures given by the engine manufacturer for brake horsepower at different R.P.M.'s. Allowance has been made in the chart (Figure 8) for friction. Shaft revolutions must take into account any reduction gear; for example, a 2:1 reduction gear would mean half the number of shaft revolutions as engine R.P.M.'s.

Remember, this chart is for three-bladed propellers of moderate blade width, so the reading for diameters of two-bladed propellers should be increased by 5%. The diameter given by the chart must be modified somewhat by experience. It is evident that a diameter suitable for a light runabout having a 30 H.P. motor turning at 3500 R.P.M. would not be suitable if that same motor were to be used in a heavy auxiliary. Do not expect to get maximum power and maximum speed in heavy, slow boats in which high speed motors are used, unless a reduction gear is installed. For instance, if a motor which develops 30 H.P. at 3500 R. P. M. is used

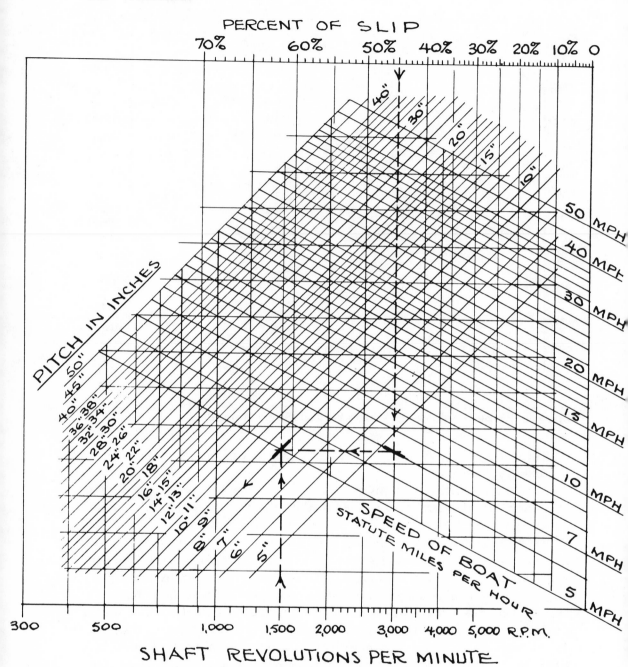

Figure 9. Propeller pitch chart (Short Method)

in an auxiliary, and, due to lack of space, direct drive is desired, then select the propeller for the power which the motor will develop at about half that speed, say 16 H.P. at 2,000 R.P.M. Specify a low compression head with this engine.

Pitch. Like a screw turning and advancing into a piece of wood, the pitch of a propeller is the distance it will advance in one revolution through water, assuming there is no slippage. Thanks to Mr. George F. Crouch, who has devised the accompanying chart (Figure 9), it is possible to pick off the amount of pitch required on a certain propeller. This chart shows the relationship between boat speed in M.P.H.; shaft revolutions and propeller pitch in inches; and apparent slip in percentage. Knowing any three of these, it is possible to find the fourth. We can assume the slip for the type of boat under consideration.

Experience shows that there are certain slips appropriate for different types of boats as follows:

> High speed powerboats—around 20%
> Light power cruisers   —about 24%
> Heavy power cruisers   —about 26%
> Auxiliaries   —from 40% to 55%

To determine the pitch, select the point at the top of the chart on the scale for "percent of propeller slip." Start there and drop a vertical down to the diagonal representing the estimated boat speed. From this intersection carry a horizontal over to meet the vertical drawn up from the shaft revolutions. The point where they meet must be read off on the diagonal giving the answer—propeller pitch in inches. A glance at the chart shows the variation in these quantities when any one of them is changed.

On an existing boat it is easy to determine from this chart just what the slip is, since revolutions, speed, and pitch are known.

Precise Calculations for Size. A more precise method using Propeller Charts A, B, C, and D.

As an example let's use the 29′ 0″ D.W.L. SANTA MARIA with her 35 H.P. diesel @ 3000 R.P.M. having a reduction gear of 1½:1. Find her propeller dimensions.

There is a loss in power of 1½% for each shaft bearing outside the engine, plus a loss of 3% for the gear box. But the S.H.P. for this engine covers the gear box. So we have one bearing = 1½% loss, and thus:

$$98.5\% \times 35 = 34.5 \text{ H.P. at propeller}$$

$$\frac{3000 \text{ R.P.M.}}{1.5 \text{ Reduction}} = 2000 \text{ shaft R.P.M.}$$

$$\text{Speed } 1.25 \times \sqrt{29} = 6.7 \text{ knots}$$

Step 1—Find the speed of the water at the propeller using Propeller Chart A. The SANTA MARIA has her propeller in an aperture, so it is .85 of the boat's speed. $6.7 \times .85 = 5.7$ knots. Find this value to the $2\frac{1}{2}$ power (for 5.7 knots, it is equal to 77), which we need for the next formula, which is:

$$BP = \frac{\text{Shaft R.P.M.} \times \sqrt{\text{H.P. at Prop.}}}{\text{Speed of water at Prop. To the } 2\frac{1}{2} \text{ power}}$$

$$BP = \frac{2000 \times \sqrt{34.5}}{77} = 153$$

PROPELLER CHART A

KNOTS	VALUES OF SPEED OF WATER AT PROP, TO $2\frac{1}{2}$ POWER									
	TENTHS OF KNOTS									
	.0	.1	.2	.3	.4	.5	.6	.7	.8	.9
5	56	59	62	65	68	71	74	77	81	84
6	88	92	96	100	104	108	112	116	120	125
7	130	134	139	144	149	154	159	164	170	175
8	181	187	192	198	204	211	217	223	230	236
9	243	250	257	264	271	278	286	293	301	308
10	316	324	332	340	349	357	366	374	383	392
11	401	410	420	429	439	448	458	468	478	488
12	499	509	520	530	541	552	563	575	586	598
13	609	621	633	645	657	670	682	695	707	720
14	733	746	760	773	787	801	814	828	843	857
15	871	886	901	916	931	946	961	977	992	1008
16	1024	1040	1056	1073	1089	1106	1123	1140	1157	1174
17	1191	1209	1227	1245	1263	1281	1299	1318	1337	1356
18	1375	1394	1413	1432	1452	1472	1492	1512	1532	1553
19	1574	1594	1615	1636	1658	1679	1701	1722	1744	1767
20	1789	1811	1834	1857	1880	1903	1926	1950	1973	1997
21	2021	2045	2069	2094	2118	2143	2168	2193	2219	2244
22	2270	2296	2322	2348	2375	2401	2428	2455	2482	2509
23	2537	2565	2592	2620	2649	2677	2706	2734	2763	2792
24	2822	2851	2881	2911	2941	2971	3001	3032	3063	3094
25	3125	3156	3188	3220	3251	3283	3316	3348	3381	3414
26	3447	3480	3514	3547	3581	3615	3649	3684	3718	3753
27	3788	3823	3859	3894	3930	3966	4002	4038	4075	4111
28	4148	4186	4223	4261	4298	4336	4374	4413	4451	4490
29	4529	4568	4607	4647	4687	4727	4767	4807	4848	4888
30	4929	4971	5012	5054	5095	5137	5180	5222	5265	5308

SPEED OF WATER AT PROP. = .60 BOAT SPEED - SMALL SHIPS
.85 BOAT SPEED - BOATS WITH PROP, IN APERATURE
.90 BOAT SPEED - BOATS WITH PROP, IN CLEAR
1.00 BOAT SPEED - HIGH SPEED POWER BOATS

Step 2—Use Propeller Chart B, which has curves for three-bladed propellers. Enter with BP = 153 and spot it just above the Max. Efficiency Line. Then pick off Pitch Ratio = .57 at side of chart, Efficiency = .38 on line slanting up to the left; Delta = 435 on line slanting up to the right.

Now we can calculate the diameter from this formula:

$$\text{Diam.} = \frac{\text{Speed of Water at Prop.} \times \text{Delta}}{\text{Shaft R.P.M.}}$$

$$\text{Diam.} = \frac{5.7 \times 435}{2000} = 1.24' \text{ (3 bladed)}$$
$$= 14.9''$$

For two-bladed Props. add 5%. 14.9 × 1.05 = 15.6″
And we can calculate the pitch as follows:
Pitch = Pitch Ratio × 3 Blade Diam.
.57 × 14.9″ = 8.5″

So the two bladed propeller to use will be 16″ Diam. × 9″ Pitch.

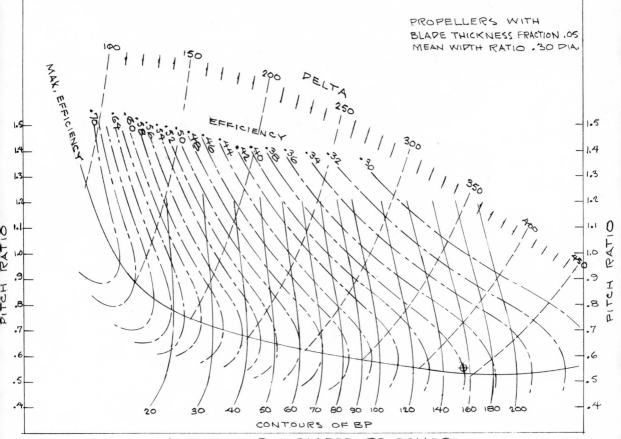

CURVES FOR 3 BLADED PROPELLERS

PROPELLER CHART B

Step 3—To find slip use Propeller Chart C. Enter with Pitch Ratio = .57 on the side and Delta = 435 on line slanting up to the right. Spot where they cross and on a line slanting up to the left read off the Slip = .59.

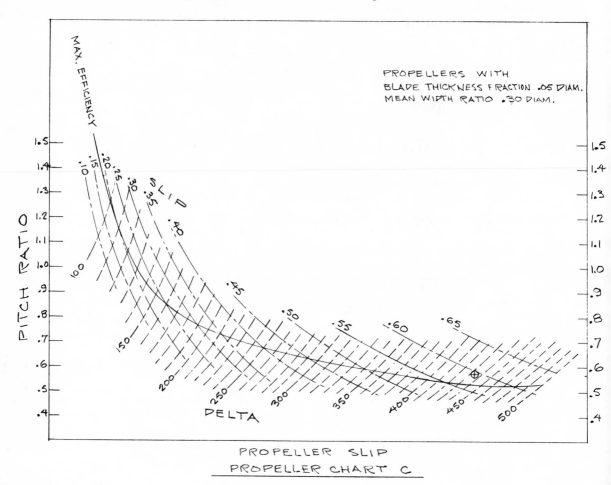

PROPELLER SLIP
PROPELLER CHART C

Step 4—To find the R.P.M.'s above which this propeller will cavitate use Propeller Chart D.

Determine Pitch in feet × Diam. in feet .70′ × 1.33′ = .93.

Enter bottom of chart with .93 on a vertical line to the contour for $\dfrac{\text{M.W.R.}}{\text{B.T.F.}}$

for this common type used in all these charts, which is $\dfrac{.30}{.05}$ = 6. At the side read

off NC = 3,000. Then enter small graph at top right corner of chart with

Slip = .59 and read off on its side $\dfrac{\text{NC}'}{\text{NC}}$ = .63.

Then solve $\dfrac{\text{NC}'}{\text{NC}}$ × NC = Cavitation R.P.M.

.63 × 3000 = 1890 R.P.M.

Thus this propeller willl start cavitating at 1890 shaft R.P.M., which is below its maximum shaft R.P.M. of 2000. The engine tachometer connected for engine revolutions would read 1890 × 1.5 (reduction) = 2835.

Since we want to keep the narrow two-bladed propeller for low drag under sail, it would be good to increase the pitch 1″ to hold down the R.P.M.'s to avoid cavitation, instead of using a wide-blade propeller.

Thus we use a 16″ Diam. × 10″ Pitch two-bladed propeller with narrow blades.

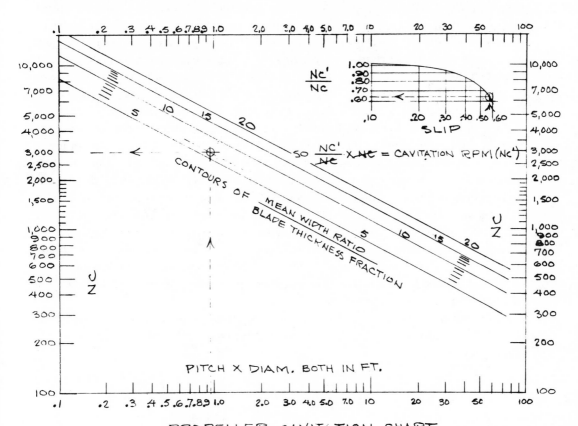

PROPELLER CAVITATION CHART

PROPELLER CHART D

Slip. There are two kinds of slip. Apparent slip is the difference between the advance observed and that calculated by pitch times revolutions. It is what we are concerned with. True slip is greater than apparent slip, due to wake moving with the boat. The wake that affects slip is a body of water surrounding the propeller and moving along with the boat. Sometimes this wake is drawn along at a speed as high as 20% of the boat's speed, depending on the fullness of the hull. The lowest wake speed is made by a high-speed, planing powerboat, which draws almost no water along with it at all. Under dock trial conditions there is absolutely no wake drawn along, so apparent slip and true slip are identical.

Example: Find apparent slip, knowing boat speed, revolutions, and propeller pitch. Let's say our boat makes 7 M.P.H. with a propeller having a 9-inch pitch, turning at 1500 R.P.M.

$$\text{Prop. Slip Stream Speed in M.P.H.} = \frac{\text{Pitch} \times \text{R.P.M.}}{1056}$$

So

$$\frac{9'' \times 1500}{1056} = 12.7 \text{ M.P.H. Slip Stream}$$

$$\text{Apparent Slip in } \% = \frac{\text{Slip Stream Speed} - \text{Boat Speed}}{\text{Slip Stream Speed}}$$

So

$$\frac{12.7 - 7}{12.7} = 45\% \text{ Apparent Slip}$$

Cavitation. Excessive propeller-tip velocity is the chief cause of the creation of cavities or voids in the water, the phenomenon called cavitation. Other contributing factors are airfoil-section propeller blades (sections with even curvature are more desirable), insufficient tip clearance (12% of the diameter is good), and a disturbed flow of water to the propeller. Disturbances are easily created by a wide sternpost that is not faired to a sharp edge, or struts that are too near the propeller. Clearance ahead of a propeller should be at least 20% of its diameter.

Back in 1894, engineers became interested in cavitation in connection with the trials of the British torpedo boat DARING. They discovered that the phenomenon causes a sharp and progressive increase in R.P.M.'s without a commensurate increase in thrust and together with a loss in efficiency. When fully developed, cavitation was found to limit the speed reached by a vessel regardless of engine power available. The DARING was designed for a speed of 27 knots, but on her first trial reached only 24 knots with full power. The propellers were exchanged for others of the same diameter and nearly the same pitch but with more blade area. Finally, after the sixth set, having 45% more area, was tried, the designed speed was attained. At this time the relationship between pressure and blade area was believed to be the correct theory.

Later, Admiral D. W. Taylor experimented with model propellers and concluded that a tip speed of 12,000 feet per minute was the limiting criterion for the blades to grip the water.

The limits vary widely with the slip and pitch ratio, as well as with blade width and shape of leading edge. This entire field is such a lengthy subject in itself that we will not attempt to go into it too deeply here.

As an example, let's say we want to check whether or not an 18-inch (or 1.5-foot) diameter propeller turning at 2,000 R.P.M. will be below the cavitation range. The tip velocity in feet per minute is simply the circumference of the circle swept by the tips of the propeller blades, or feet traveled in one revolution, times the revolutions per minute. The circumference of a circle is 3.14 times the diameter, so:

Tip Speed = Diam. in Ft. × 3.14 × R.P.M. = Ft. per Min.

Tip Speed = 1.5′ × 3.14 × 2000 = 9,420 Ft. per Min.

This propeller is too close to cavitating speed. If it had a pitch ratio of 1.0, a slip of 17%, and was a 3-bladed type with blades having a mean width ratio of .38, then according to our chart for "Maximum Allowable Tip Velocities to Avoid Cavitation" (Figure 10), it would fall within the cavitating speed and thus should not be used.

Figure 10. Cavitation. Folding prop. Pitch sketch

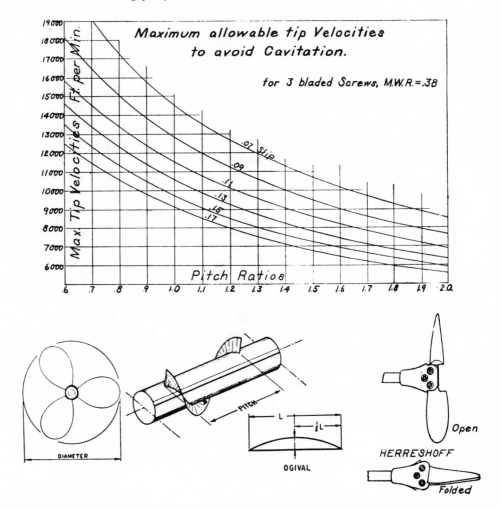

We have learned that water can sustain only a very small amount of negative pressure or tension, and that when this limit is exceeded disruption takes place, and cavities or bubbles are formed. When this happens the propeller runs wild in a pocket. In order to delay cavitation, it is desirable to use sections with even curvature (ogival sections) rather than sections with uneven curvature (airfoil sections), and wide blades.

Erosion and blade pitting occur as a result of the tremendous impact pressures created when the cavities collapse on the propeller blade surfaces. The necessity of frequent propeller replacement is another good reason to avoid cavitation.

Pitch Ratio is the ratio of pitch to the diameter, or the pitch divided by the diameter. Practicable pitch ratios range from .5 to 1.5. Below and above these limits the efficiency is very low. For auxiliaries, the pitch seems to work out well at about ¾ of the diameter (Pitch Ratio = .75). For planing powerboats, the pitch is frequently almost the same as the diameter (Pitch Ratio = 1.0). Some people call such a propeller a "square wheel." For very high-speed craft, the pitch may be higher than the diameter, especially in racing motorboats that have stepped-up or multiplication gearing on their engines.

For best efficiency, the pitch ratio should be in the following range:

.55 to .80 for tugs and trawlers.
.65 to 1.00 for heavy and average cruisers.
.80 to 1.20 for medium and fast cruisers.
.90 to 1.50 for very fast powerboats.

Pitch ratios outside these ranges generally will indicate an unsuitable shaft speed.

Mean Width Ratio is the ratio of the average width of the blade to the diameter of the propeller. Average width is arrived at by dividing the area of the blade by its length from hub to tip. Two-bladed propellers used on auxiliaries may have narrow blades with a mean width ratio as low as .21, to reduce drag when sailing. An even lower ratio is .18, used on certain five-bladed propellers. But the standard mean width ratio for three-bladed propellers is about .31, used on moderate speed powerboats. On high-speed planing boats, wide blades with a ratio as high as .42 can be used to advantage to delay cavitation. These are small screws 12 to 14 inches in diameter and three-bladed, designed to turn between 3,600 and 5,000 R.P.M. when driven by a high-powered engine.

Rotation. When viewed from aft, a right-hand propeller turns clockwise, a left-hand counterclockwise. Most engines require right-hand propellers, but the rotation may be changed by a reduction gear. Just to confuse things, the engine manufacturers view the rotation of their products from forward. So a left-hand engine takes a right-hand propeller!

With a single right-hand screw driving on the center line the boat will turn to port. Perhaps this is caused by the blades biting into the denser water below the shaft with more effect than when turning in a less dense fluid above. One can imagine the stern being forced sideways to starboard on such a boat, as if the propeller were a roller under the bottom. If for some reason an engine must be installed off center, the location can be used to counteract this tendency of a single propeller to turn the boat. One degree of the shaft line off center does it. Engine to port for right-hand propeller, *vice versa* for opposite hand. In both cases the propeller is on the center line of the boat.

Twin screws should have engines of opposite rotation to avoid this veering off to one side. Each propeller should be turning out; that is, a right-hand screw, or one turning clockwise when viewed from aft, is best for the starboard side, and a left-hand one is best for the port side.

During the war a large troop carrier was dry-docked for propeller repairs in a repair yard in Alaska. The officer in charge somehow or other became confused about right-hand and left-hand rotation for this twin-screw vessel. The propellers were replaced with new ones, the ship launched and prepared for sea. "Slow ahead," ordered the skipper. But the ship went astern! There was one officer wishing he were somewhere else just then. The wrong propeller had been installed on the wrong side!

Temperature. Just to show how many factors are involved, it is interesting to note that even the temperature of water is of importance. As the water temperature drops, its density increases, so a propeller suitable for warm water operations can no longer be turned to its designed R.P.M.'s. It was found during World War II that propellers on PT boats stationed in the freezing Aleutian Islands should be as much as two inches less in diameter, to allow the same R.P.M.'s as for similar boats in South Pacific waters. Based on a 70° temperature, reduce the diameter approximately 1% for each 10° drop in water temperature.

Shafting. Two useful charts are included. One is a nomogram for use in selecting the minimum diameter shaft of bronze or Monel when given the shaft horsepower and shaft R.P.M.'s. The other is a chart to show maximum allowable spacing for shaft bearings. If bearings are spaced too far apart, the shaft will vibrate. Figure 11 shows both charts.

Emphasis should be placed on the importance of filleted keyways. Shafts tend to break at the sharp right-angle corners made by a keyway at the propeller or coupling. Rounding or filleting this sharp corner relieves the stress.

Shafts must be absolutely straight, so it follows that the very stiffest noncorrosive material is the best to use. Monel is highly recommended for shafting.

Bearings located inside the boat should be roller or ball bearing of the sealed type, with a provision for axial movement of the shaft. Stern bearings outboard can be rubber or lignum vitae and must be lubricated by water. Stuffing boxes should be repacked with flax packing at least once a year. When tightened too much, a stuffing box will cause a good deal of friction, getting hot and slowing down the R.P.M.'s. It is good practice to loosen the nut on a stuffing box, so that it leaks a drop of water at a time when the shaft is revolving but remains tight

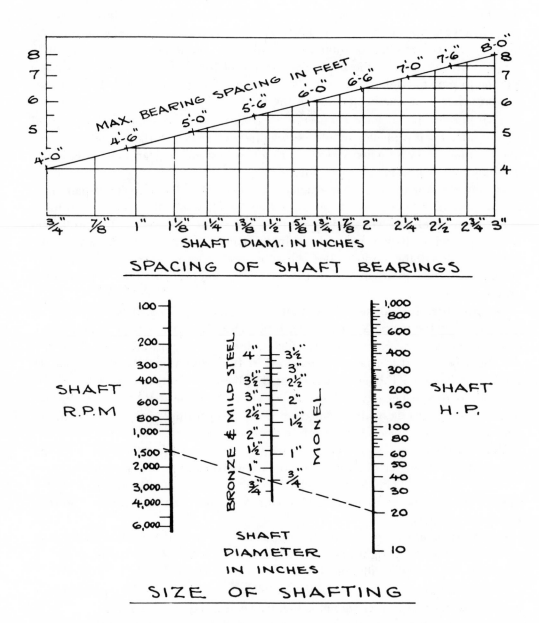

SPACING OF SHAFT BEARINGS

SIZE OF SHAFTING

Figure 11. Spacing of shaft bearings. Size of shafting.

when the engine is shut off. Herreshoff used to make a stuffing box with a knurled nut which could be turned by hand only. This was held in position by a standard lock nut. Such a foolproof arrangement prevented overtightening with a wrench.

Propellers for Sailboats. The object here is to have a propeller that will give the minimum drag or least resistance when a vessel is under sail. The old Herreshoff folding propeller still has no equal when it comes to minimum drag. The next best thing is a two-bladed feathering propeller. Next in order, and the most common of all used today, is a two-bladed solid propeller with narrow blades. Installed behind the deadwood with the two blades vertical in an aperture, the drag from such a propeller is not very great, but when this solid screw and its shafting are suspended on a strut clear of the ship, say aft of the rudder or to one side, then the dray is something to worry about.

The question often asked by owners of motor sailers is whether or not they should allow their propellers to revolve freely when under sail. The answer is: The shaft should be locked so that the propeller cannot revolve. It has been found that a revolving propeller creates more drag and slows the boat down noticeably when under sail.

Controllable Pitch Propellers. Here is another field where the aviation people can teach naval architects a thing or two. For a good many years airplanes have been using controllable pitch propellers. The pitch can be altered. The blades can be feathered, and the pitch can be reversed. Without this reversing it would be impossible for some of our large airplanes to land in a relatively short space. Without the feathering blade, an airplane with a stalled engine in flight would be in serious trouble.

Controllable-pitch propellers have been used by the marine industry in Europe for a good many years, but in the U.S.A. their use has been sadly neglected. Just think of the advantages. In the first place, such a propeller does not require the use of reverse gears on the engine. So the engine can be shorter, lighter, and less expensive! The R.P.M.'s can be kept the same at all times, and the vessel's direction and speed simply controlled by adjusting the pitch of the propeller. On a sailing vessel the blades could be feathered to advantage. Why are not more of these controllable-pitch propellers for sale in this country?

Jets. In this age of jet airplanes it is not surprising that water jets should be used to propel boats. They are used. At this writing it is possible to buy two types of pumps designed to direct a jet of water astern as the sole means of propulsion. One is a propeller-type pump which operates axially in a pipe. The other is a centrifugal pump which sucks water up through a sea chest in the bottom and forces it out through an elbow-type nozzle. This jet nozzle is turned for steering and reversing.

The propeller-in-pipe type discharges through the transom, which means a water jet is pushing against air at planing speed. The momentum of this water forces a small boat forward at high speed, just as a large stream of water pumped through the nozzle of a fire hose pushes the fireman backwards. Steering and reversing for this type are accomplished by turning baffles.

The centrifugal pump is always discharging its water jet against water, which has been found to be less effective. The manufacturers claim that with their centrifugal pump their jet can deliver more thrust on heavy, slow craft, such as self-propelled barges, small tugs, small fireboats, small ferries, amphibious vehicles, and fishing boats.

The elimination of shafting, struts, propeller, and rudder saves on repairs, reducing lay-up time, which is of prime importance for a work boat. Shallow draft is permitted. Unusual maneuverability results from the use of this jet, permitting vessels such as ferries to crab along diagonally when approaching their slips through a crosscurrent.

There can be no cavitation. This results in a constant thrust over the entire speed range and accounts for these water jets being able to drive slow, heavy craft faster than a propeller can. Another advantage is that a jet stream can not damage a fishing net. And another is that there is no underwater propeller noise to scare fish or be picked up by sonar. (Perfect propulsion for a submarine.)

Like anything new, these pumps are expensive—many, many times as expensive as the normal shafting, propeller and rudder. Then, too, there is the unfortunate disadvantage, for small boats, of great intake suction, which pulls a small boat down into the water, making it difficult to lift and plane.

Tip Clearance. To prevent vibration in the propeller area, propellers should be located so that the tips of the blades clear the hull as follows:

15% Prop. Diam. of clearance for auxiliaries.

20% Prop. Diam. of clearance on motor sailers and powerboats.

CHAPTER XVI

RUDDERS

In designing rudders there are a great many features to be studied and co-ordinated. Area, size of rudder stock, shape, amount of balance, location, rake, and shape of rudder water lines are important. The function of a rudder is to steer the boat, but in performing this necessary duty, it will increase resistance through eddy-making and friction. The problem is to obtain good steering qualities with the least resistance.

Each type of yacht requires its own particular kind of rudder. So let's divide all boats into different groups and discuss the best form of rudder for each. Classify them as: sailboats, auxiliaries, motor sailers, low-speed powerboats, and highspeed powerboats. (See Figure 12)

Sailboat Rudders. An area of between 8% and 10% of the total lateral plane or underwater profile is the desirable size of a sailboat rudder.

What diameter should we make the rudder stock? We have a good rule of thumb for solid bronze rudder stocks on normal sailboat rudders supported at top and bottom. It is:

Stock Diam. in Inches = .16 × D.W.L. Beam in Ft.

Turning radius

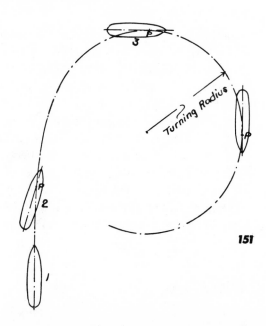

A figure which illustrates the actual test data for the three variations on BAYBEA. (See page 6). Note that the maximum average rudder moment is more than doubled with the final separate rudder as compared to cut-away keel.

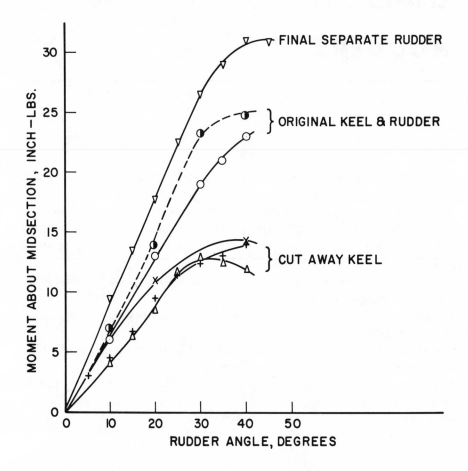

Sailboats should have unbalanced rudders. That is, the axis of rotation must be at the forward edge and attached to the fin keel.

It has been found that balanced rudders hung independently, well aft of the fin, steer poorly and increase resistance. The uniform flow of water, so necessary in way of a rudder, is broken up. But by the introduction of a narrow skeg immediately ahead of an unbalanced rudder excellent control is obtained. The skeg for such an independently-hung rudder arrangement may be even as small as one-third the rudder area and still be effective. Consider both bending and twisting strains when calculating rudder stocks of this type, because little, if any, support will be given by a narrow skeg.

A raking rudderpost gives the best shape of lateral plane for a deep-keel sailboat. Just how much rake? As much as 45° has proven successful. On the other hand, a

Figure 12. Rudder designs

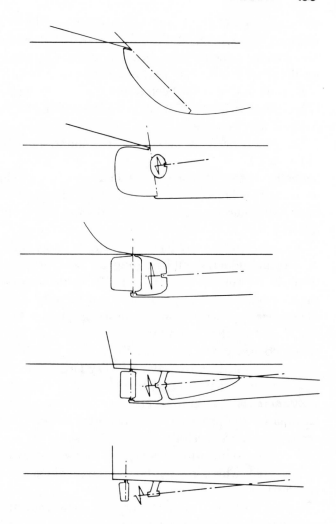

shallow-draft sailboat presents an entirely different problem. Plumb rudderposts, or nearly vertical ones, make sense here, because what these boats lack in depth of lateral plane must be made up for in length of keel.

The standard sailboat rudder shape has a fair curved after edge with its greatest width near mid-depth. A little width at the top helps to fair the rudderpost as it emerges from the hull, preventing eddies at that point. Aspect ratio has a greater effect on rudder efficiency than outline shape, so the designer should use squared-off, rectangular outlines when they permit the necessary area to be disposed in a narrow blade of higher width-depth ratio. The deep, narrow rudder does a better job than the long, shallow one.

It is interesting to study the influence of a rudder's aspect ratio on the stalling angle—that is, the point at which the streamline flow of water breaks down. Without an attached fin ahead of the rudder, a deep, narrow blade of 1 to 5 ratio will stall at an angle of only 12°, whereas a square rudder of 1 to 1 ratio will stall at, say, 30°. A long, shallow rudder will stall at 45°. But with the fin attached ahead of the same rudders the stalling angle is raised for all types, from 12° to 30° for the deep 1 to 5 ratio, and proportionate amounts for the others.

By tank testing it has been found that a little weather helm, between 2° and 3°, is beneficial in lifting a boat to windward. If the rudder must be held at 4° or more, it acts as a brake.

Lee helm, even in the slightest amount, increases resistance rapidly. Every sailor well knows how difficult it is to steer a boat to windward when she has a lee helm. It can be alarming. A boat with a lee helm will bear off in a puff and let herself be knocked down, but a well-designed sailboat with a slight weather helm will round up, spilling the wind when you let go of the wheel or tiller. She'll luff in a puff.

The shape of the rudder water lines is important, particularly in racing boats. A sailboat rudder should fit snug to the deadwood and offer the least possible break in the surface at that point. It should thin down to a sharp after edge. If the aft edge is left blunt, not only will there be more drag, but at certain speeds the rudder itself will begin to vibrate or chatter. Both of these undesirable occurrences may be eliminated by having a knife-like trailing edge. A sailboat designer would do well to fair the water lines of the hull directly to the trailing edge of the rudder, even if it means having a very large-diameter rudderpost. Streamline the flow of water—that's the goal.

Rudders for Auxiliaries. The question on this type of craft is what is the best location for the propeller? The practical answer: just ahead of the rudder on the center line in an aperture.

The main thing with this type is to try and avoid having an aperture in the rudder itself. There is a big hole through which water pours when such a rudder is turned.

Undoubtedly the most streamlined arrangement of all is to locate a folding propeller aft of the rudder and just enough off center for the propeller shaft to miss the rudderstock. The drawback is that you have little or no control of your boat when trying to maneuver at slow speed under power, around docks and the like.

Aside from the consideration of the best propeller location, rudders for auxiliaries can be treated exactly like those for sailboats.

Motor Sailer Rudders. Because, by their nature, these vessels require a larger propeller than do auxiliaries, the sailboat-type rudder must be abandoned. Usually it is necessary to have the rudderstock plumb vertical to provide room for the propeller. And because of the added pressure of a larger propeller slip stream and the difficulty in steering large rudders by hand, it makes sense to use a balanced rudder on motor sailers. The larger the rudder, the quicker the turn.

How much rudder area should be ahead of the axis for a properly balanced rudder? Say, between 17 and 20%.

Low-Speed Powerboat Rudders. The required area of a rudder for such vessels as ferries, club launches, work boats, and the like is less than that required for sailboats. How much should it be? Say 2 to 5% of the total lateral plane. The reason for this is added pressure caused by the propeller slip stream, assuming the rudder is located directly behind the propeller, where it should be.

What diameter should we make the rudderstock for such vessels? No rule of thumb here. We must use a more complicated formula. Let's take two cases, one where the rudder is supported top and bottom, so that we are concerned with twisting only, and the other where we have a spade-type rudder, unsupported at the bottom, so that we must consider both twisting and bending of the stock. Many a spade-type rudder has broken off because the rudderstock was too small in diameter, so bending must be prevented by providing ample diameter.

Calculation for Diameter of Rudderstock, Twisting Only, Solid Stock

$$\text{Diam. (Inches)} = \sqrt[3]{\frac{10.9\ ATS^2}{F}}$$

Twisting and Bending for Spade Rudders, Solid Stock

$$\text{Diam. (Inches)} = \sqrt[3]{\frac{10.9\ AS^2(B + \sqrt{T^2 + B^2})}{F}}$$

A = Area of rudder, in square feet.
T = Arm for twisting, in inches, center of rudder to center of stock.
B = Arm for bending, in inches, center of rudder to hull.
S = Speed of vessel, in knots.
F = Allowable fiber stress, 7,500 to 10,000.

The above formulas incorporate certain constants and factors of safety to allow for the most severe strain on a rudderstock, when a vessel is going full speed astern with her rudder hard over. A table comparing the tensile strengths of metals used for rudderstocks follows:

Tobin Bronze	22,000 Pounds per Square Inch
Manganese Bronze	30,000
Aluminum	40,000
Mild Steel	60,000
Monel	75,000
Silicon Bronze	80,000
Stainless Steel	85,000

Planing Powerboat Rudders. Rudder size for this type is the smallest of all. The faster a boat goes, the smaller the rudder has to be. The size is only 1% to 2% of the total lateral plane. It should be greater for outboard rudders and less for twin rudders.

The same formulas used for low-speed powerboats apply to high-speed planing powerboats. Give particular attention to allowing ample diameter for the rudderstocks of spade-type rudders.

On very high-speed powerboats, the usual streamlined rudder tends to form a cavity by its rapid passage through the water. With a balanced spade-type rudder this cavity may start as far forward as the stock, resulting in poor steering. To overcome this trouble, a rudder with water lines shaped like a wedge—sharp forward, blunt aft—is effective.

Since wetted surface should be reduced to increase speed, it follows that a boat without any rudder would be best. What? Steer without a rudder? Of course. Outboard motors require no rudders. The motor turns directing the propeller slip stream all the way around 360°. There are "Z"-drive installations now available which require no rudder either, operating somewhat like an outboard, but with an inboard engine for power.

General. In connection with rudders a designer should bear in mind the following outline, as a check list:

> Bearings—hull, upper, and carrier bearings; sleeves in way of bearings on
> steel stocks.
> Pintles—arrangement for removal of rudder.
> Tillers—emergency tiller and stowage.
> Quadrants.
> Rudderposts, stuffing boxes.
> Rudder stops.
> Lifting eye bolts.
> Deck plates.
> Provision to prevent rudder lifting.

Steering Gear—Hand

> Entire installation must be free of friction.
> Roller bearings or ball bearings required throughout.
> Lubrication of sheaves. Guards on sheaves.
> Minimum number of sheaves, 16 wire diameters each.
> Worm gear steerer with push-pull rod and tiller is good for powerboats. Bell
> cranks. Torque shafts.
> Roller chain with small sprocket, cables, sheaves, and quadrant is good for
> sailboats.
> Hard over to hard over—number of turns required:
>> Powerboats—3 turns, more for larger vessels.
>> Sailboats—1¾ to 2 turns, more for larger boats.
>> Direction of turning: Wheel clockwise, rudder to starboard.
>> Rudder angle indicator. Wheel position indicator.
>> Nonmagnetic steering gear near compass.
>> Bulkhead stuffing tubes.
>> Steering cables—size and type, with turnbuckles for take-up.
>> End terminals to permit easy replacement.
>> Stops to prevent rudder from turning beyond 35° from center.

Steering Gear—Power

> Type—electrical, hydraulic.

Torque—speed ahead, speed astern.

Automatic Pilot—ram, motor, amplifier, compass, controls.

Disconnect device to prevent drag on hand steering.

Backing Rudders. Certain special situations require the installation of a separate rudder solely to steer the vessel when going backwards. For example, river tugs, which are not towboats but push boats, must turn a long string of barges. Because they are shallow draft they require twin screws. This dictates twin rudders. And for backing, it has been found advantageous to add a rudder on each side of each shaft ahead of the propellers. This makes a total of six rudders, two for going ahead, four for going astern or sideways which are also called flanking rudders.

One yacht owner's requirement was that his new motor sailer be designed so that she could turn quickly when backing out of her slip on the bank of a narrow river. She was a single-screw vessel. So the designers incorporated a small rudder above the shaft and ahead of the propeller. It was faired right into the shape of the hull. Reports are that it accomplished its purpose well. When going astern, the slip stream from the backing propeller is thrown to the desired side by the backing rudder.

Trim Tab on Rudder. Much as in an airplane, a small rudder or tab incorporated in the trailing edge of the rudder itself may be utilized to do the work. The Flettner rudder, which has been used on ships, is a true servo, having the steering gear attached solely to the small rudder. It is connected by horizontal rod linkage to a vertical shaft inside the hollow rudder stock. When the small rudder is turned to port, it swings the main rudder to starboard, and the ship turns to starboard. The area of this small rudder may be 1/20 of the area of the main rudder.

Trim tabs may be incorporated in sailboat rudders to balance the helm. And like an airplane pilot, the sailboat skipper is then able to take the load off his tiller, or wheel, by turning a small crank to change slightly the angle of the rudder tab. In an airplane, the elevators may be controlled by just such an arrangement. When a group of passengers moves aft on a large plane, the pilot would have to keep pushing the control stick forward to hold the tail up but for the minor adjustment he can make with the control tab. As a plane is supported by the flow of air over the wings and elevator, in a very similar manner the flow of water over the keel and rudder of a sailboat enables it to overcome the sideward pressure of the wind.

A sailboat with a properly designed trim tab on its rudder can sail itself to windward automatically. The tab is set at a slight angle to just balance the weather helm, and the helmsman takes hands off. As the wind increases, the weather helm force also increases. But the boat begins to move faster, resulting in a corresponding increase in the counteracting influence of the trim tab. Conversely, if the wind becomes lighter, the process is reversed, and the helm remains balanced, as long as there is reasonable steerage way. Because of inertia, changes in the speed of the boat lag slightly behind sudden changes in the wind. Thus the boat will find the wind, sailing off in the headers, and coming up in the puffs.

The proper size for the tab, and its influence on the rudder, is governed by its distance from the center line of the rudder stock. This distance, or moment arm, is in a sense the length of lever upon which the area of the tab acts to swing the rudder. Mathematically, this relationship is known as the first moment of area, taken about the rudder stock axis. Experience with sailing yachts has shown that the tab should have a value of first moment of area which is very close to 1/5 the first moment of area of the main rudder, both moments being taken about the main rudder stock axis. If the moment of the tab is too large for the rudder, the tendency will be for the tab to overcontrol the rudder, losing the wind. If the moment of the tab is too small, it will fail to balance the helm.

For a given rudder, the trim tab should be located as far as possible from the rudder stock; be mindful that it is desirable to keep it clear of the propeller stream. The tab should have as high an aspect ratio as is mechanically practical, and it should be recessed to form an integral part of the trailing edge of the rudder. Tests have shown that the tab should be faired to the rudder with no aperture or slot at the tab stock.

Some unique problems are likely to be encountered in the design of the control linkage. Important considerations are as follows:

The trim tab should be designed to swing at least 15° each side in respect to the rudder. The tab control handle should be readily accessible to the helmsman, mounted on the wheel or tiller, for he must reverse it with each tack.

The rudder stock must usually be hollow to convey the necessary control shaft or cables.

And, finally, the tab stock will be located in a very thin section of the rudder, so that the operating lever or quadrant may necessarily project out, necessitating streamline form or fairing enclosure. Experience has shown that linkages using connecting pins or bolts under salt water should not be less than $\frac{3}{8}''$ in diameter to prevent them from falling apart by corroding.

WAUPI has a clever linkage system, designed and built by her owner, F. George duPont. The helmsman simply rotates the grip on the tiller, like a motorcycle handle bar, and the trim tab turns exactly as desired.

At this time automatic pilot steering is beind developed utilizing a boat's trim tab. You will be able to have your boat steered automatically by either magnetic compass or wind vane at the masthead. Only a minute amount of electric power is needed, since the force required to turn a trim tab is so small.

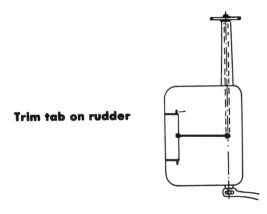

Trim tab on rudder

WAUPI running before the wind.

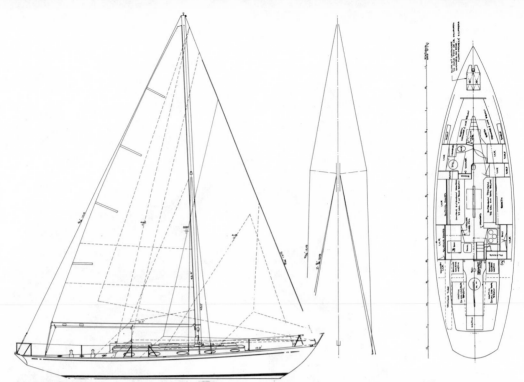

WAUPI. Able, stiff and well proportioned describe this design from the drawing board of F. S. K.

Her owner has sailed her to Bermuda and back twice so far, and is quite happy about her performance.

Below, her layout has an interesting double berth, which basically is a large extension transom with a backrest fitting alongside to double its width. The forward cabin has its own wash basin.

Her diesel engine has a Vee drive, which puts it aft in its own space, easily accessible from seat hatches and a manhole in the cockpit sole.

She has a true trim tab on her rudder with linkage to the tiller hand grip worked out by her owner and described in the chapter on rudders.

When they see her, most people think she is a fiberglass boat. There simply are no visible seams anywhere, she is so smooth. Bob Derecktor, her builder, used a unique method of constructing her. He planked her in the single planked manner glued and screwed to laminated frames, then laid a long vertical strip of mahogany plywood fitting exactly in each frame bay, gluing and back screwing it to the inside of the planking. A hull that was virtually one piece, showing no seams, was the result.

Another interesting detail on WAUPI is her anchor stowage bin. She carries two Danforth anchors standing on edge in a special box in her forepeak with a flush deck cover. They are accessible and in the right spot when you want them, yet out of the way of flying sheets and moving feet on deck—there, not to snare one, or stub the toes of the other.

I had a great time sailing her in the Edgartown Regatta recently. Her stiffness compared to other boats was astounding! When beating to windward we were holding our own with larger boats, which, we observed by lining up our mast with theirs, were heeling at least 10° more. And we were passing boats our own size heeling at least 15° more!

WAUPI is one of the rare boats about which one can truthfully say, "She is an excellent boat in every respect."

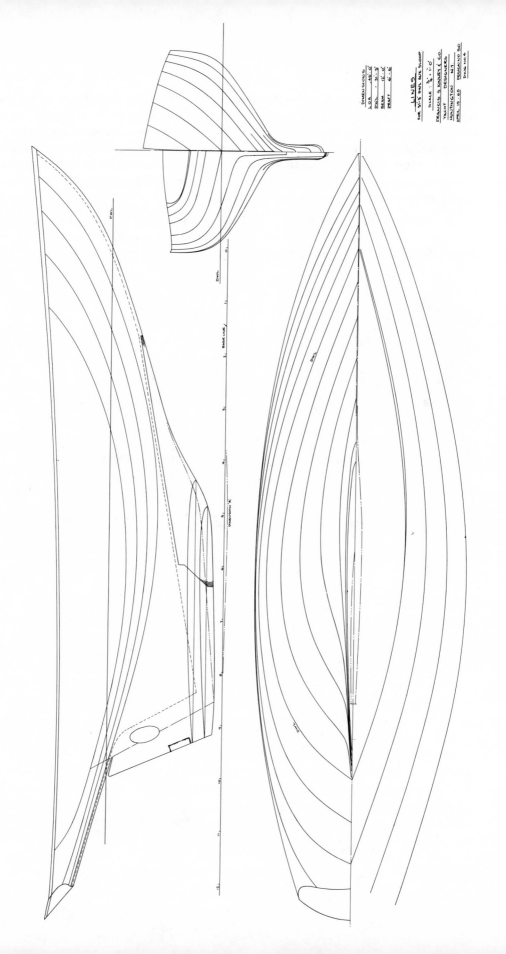

LINES
FOR 30'5 DWL BLK SLOOP
SCALE: 3/4" = 1'-0"
FRANCIS S. KINNEY & CO.
YACHT DESIGNERS
HUNTINGTON N.Y.
APRIL 19 - 65   DWG NO 4

DIMENSIONS
L.O.A. 49'-0"
DWL. 31'-5"
BEAM 12'-0"
DRAFT 6'-6"

Self-steering gear by Gustav Plym on ELSELI IV, with masthead Wind Vane and Trim Tab. Wind vane on top of mizzen mast is 5 sq. ft. in area. It is in free air and cannot be damaged by waves. A stainless steel transmission tube was found to be better than an aluminum one to reduce the give between vane and servo rudder. Minimum friction in the system was needed. The linkage between vane and servo rudder has a 1.5:1 ratio between the arms to increase the speed of action of the servo rudder.

Shock cords on the tiller were found to be necessary to reduce the tendency to over steering, when sailing off the wind in a seaway. A balance weight in front of the wind vane should make it even better.

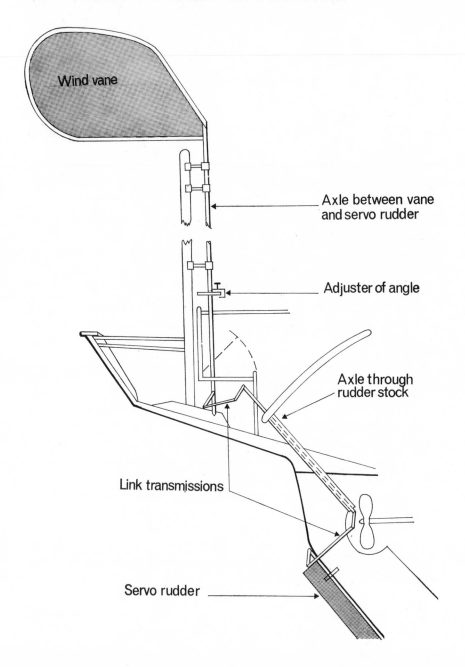

CHAPTER XVII

SPARS AND RIGGING

To harness the wind the seafaring man must hoist his sails on spars held by rigging. Sails, spars, and rigging are to a sailing craft what propellers and shafting are to a power vessel. They harness the propulsive force.

Knowledge on the subject of spars and rigging has been handed down through history from ancient times. Have yacht designers added much? I wonder.

Consider the ancient Egyptian feluccas, still very much in evidence, sailing up and down the Nile as they have done for thousands of years. They use one large loose-footed sail most efficiently. Upon close examination it appears to be almost exactly the same shape as a sail thought of as a modern development—a large Genoa jib!

The Chinese junk is another wonderful rig. It may even be older than the Egyptian felucca, for all we know. Unfortunately the English language has a derogatory meaning for the word "junk," but if you called the junk a Chinese yawl or a Chinese ketch, then you might start thinking about how good it is.

In this chapter our purpose is to explain the available methods of calculating spar sizes. Masts, booms, spinnaker poles, bowsprits, spreaders, and sizes of rigging will be considered.

As the song goes, "Old man Noah thought he knew a thing or two. Because he thought he knew a thing or two, he thought he knew it all," so our use of formulas must be modified by the feel and judgment that comes with experience. But we need the formulas to start with.

All spars are in compression. Masts (except unsupported ones), spinnaker poles, and spreaders may be considered to be in pure compression, while booms are subject to bending.

Attention to lightness of weight aloft, consistent with strength, is important. For example, suppose a masthead light 50 feet above the water can be reduced in weight by two pounds; the moment is thus reduced by 100 foot-pounds.

In ancient times all spars were solid, except the bamboo ones of the East. A hollow spar is roughly half the weight of a solid one and, if given about a 10% increase in diameter or sectional dimensions, is just as strong.

Scale

0   10   20   30   40   50   60 feet.

The LORCHA was a type developed in China by a Portuguese colony about 1550, which used the Chinese junk rig combined with a Portuguese modeled hull. Note the lines from the aft end of each batten so the sails can set without a twist. She sailed faster than pirate vessels and carried more cargo. Such a craft would make an uncommonly excellent yacht.

Mr. Skene worked out an example illustrating the advantage of a hollow spar: Two spars are compared. Each is made of spruce and is 10 feet long. Each is designed for the same strength, 8500 pounds. One is hollow, the other solid. The hollow one has an outside diameter of 4 inches and an inside diameter of 3 inches. Its weight is only 11½ pounds. Now for the contrast: the solid one is only ⅜ inch smaller with a diameter of 3⅝ inches, but it weighs 21½ pounds, or about *twice as much*!

Hollow masts should be varnished or shellacked inside. They do take in rain water, probably through the cut for the sheaves at the masthead, so it is good practice to provide a hole at the bottom for drainage to prevent rot.

Perhaps the most severe of all strains for spars and rigging occurs in light weather when a vessel is rolling in a seaway. Dr. Gifford Pinchot tells how, when sailing across the Atlantic in his wooden yawl LOKI, she began to open up in a calm spell when big swells were running. The garboard seam started leaking below the mast step. He was able to caulk her somehow and thereby reduce the time required for pumping, but as soon as he reached port, he had a metal mast step installed, incorporating metal floors. He tells me this experience was the chief reason why he has chosen welded aluminum construction for his new boat.

Clear, dry, Sitka spruce was one of the very best materials we had for spars. Aluminum alloy in the form of extrusions and tubing is now our best, in terms of weight and upkeep.

It is interesting to note the comparison between a spruce and an aluminum mast, as worked out for the PIPE DREAM Cruising Sloop. Both are 46 feet long. The wooden one weighs 206 pounds, the aluminum one 193 pounds, a saving of 13 pounds or 6%. The maximum section of the aluminum mast is smaller, being 4½″ × 7½″ with a wall .188″ thick. The wood mast section works out to 5½″ × 8″ with 1⅛″ and 1⅝″ walls.

Now let's consider our first formula.

Unsupported Masts. To find the diameter of a solid spruce mast designed to stand without shrouds or stays, consider it as a cantilever which must resist bending. The simplest rig of all, a catboat, uses such a mast. The factors which make up this formula are:

P = wind pressure (sq. ft. of sail area × 1.15 for small boats and up to 1.5 for large boats).

L = length of mast in inches.

Safety factor = from 1.5 for small boats up to 3.5 for large catboats with gaff rigs.

15,700 = Pi × the fiber stress of spruce, which is 5,000.

The formula is:

$$\text{Diam. (Inches)} = \sqrt[3]{\frac{16\ PL \times \text{Safety Factor}}{15,700}}$$

Figure 13 gives average proportion of solid spars and taper.

Supported Masts are those held in place athwartships by wire shrouds, and fore and aft by wire stays. We are concerned with designing the unsupported lengths, called "panels," to carry the loads imposed. The amount of compression on a mast is the product of many factors. These are the same factors that affect stability, namely: the beam of the boat, the amount of sail carried, the strength of the wind, the location of the center of gravity, and the displacement of the boat. In a nutshell, the righting moment contains all these factors. So we use it as a starting point.

Figure 13. Average proportions of solid spars and taper

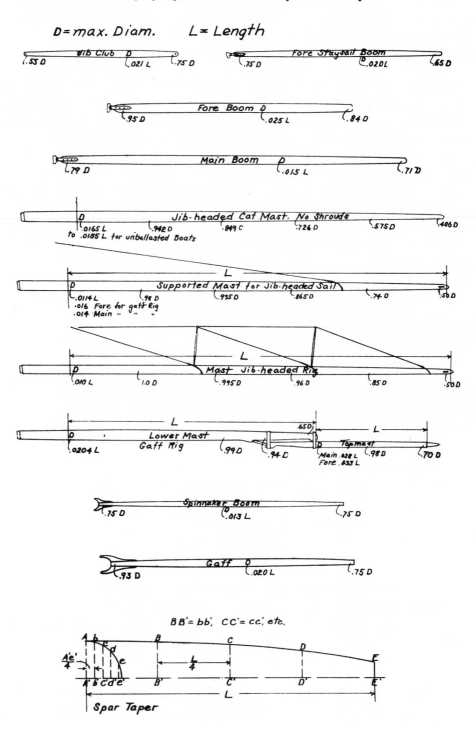

D = max. Diam.   L = Length

Jib Club   D
.55 D   .021 L   .75 D

Fore Staysail Boom   D
.75 D   .020 L   .65 D

Fore Boom   D
.95 D   .025 L   .84 D

Main Boom   D
.79 D   .015 L   .71 D

Jib-headed Cat Mast. No Shrouds
D
.0165 L   .942 D   .849 C   .726 D   .575 D   .406 D
to .0155 L for unballasted Boats

L
Supported Mast for Jib-headed Sail
D
.0114 L   .98 D   .935 D   .865 D   .74 D   .50 D
.016 Fore for gaff Rig
.014 Main "   "   "

L
Mast Jib-headed Rig
D
.010 L   1.0 D   .995 D   .96 D   .85 D   .50 D

L   650   L
D   D   Topmast
Lower Mast
Gaff Rig   .99 D   .94 D   .98 D   .70 D
.0204 L   Main .828 L
                                     Fore .833 L

Spinnaker Boom
D
.75 D   .013 L   .75 D

Gaff   D
.93 D   .020 L   .75 D

BB' = bb', CC' = cc', etc.

A b c d
e'/4   e
A' b c d e'   B'   C'   D'   E'
L
Spar Taper

The stiffer the boat or the greater her power to carry sail, the more the compressive load on her mast will be. The total compression pushing the mast down into the boat will be opposed by an equal amount of tension pulling up on the weather chain plates.

Short Method to Determine Maximum Section of Supported Masts

Step 1—From the chart of righting moments (R.M.) at 30° heel (Figure 14), choose an approximate righting moment for the designed water-line length of the boat. This chart is sufficiently accurate for most present-day cruising auxiliaries. For highly competitive types where greater accuracy is desired, the actual righting moment can be worked out for the individual boat by use of the formula—

$$\text{Righting Mom. } 30° = \frac{30° \times \text{Disp. in Lbs.} \times \text{GM}}{57.3}.$$

Step 2—Substitute the righting moment at 30° (R.M.) thus obtained in the following formulae:

Mainmast Load = R.M. × 2.78 ÷ ½ beam main mast to chain plate.

Yawl & Ketch Mizzen Load = R.M. × .50 ÷ ½ beam mizzen mast to chain plate.

Mizzens with radar = R.M. × .75 ÷ ½ beam mizzen mast to chain plate.

Figure 14. Righting moment at 30°

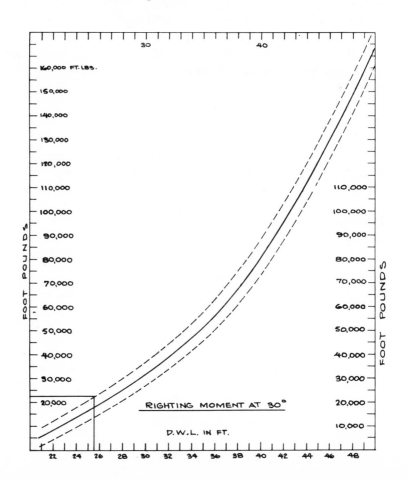

Step 3—Determine the panel lengths in inches. The length from deck to lower spreaders (L_T) is the length we need for transverse stiffness. The length from deck to jibstay (L_L) is what concerns us for longitudinal stiffness. Square each.

Step 4—Moments of Inertia (I) about the transverse (I_{TT}) and longitudinal (I_{LL}) axis of the mast are then obtained from the following formula with the result expressed in inches to the fourth power.

$$I_{TT} \text{ (in}^4) = C \text{ Transv.} \times \frac{L_T^2 \text{ (in }^2)}{10,000} \times \frac{\text{Load (lbs.)}}{10,000}$$

$$I_{LL} \text{ (in}^4) = C \text{ fore \& aft} \times \frac{L_L^2 \text{ (in }^2)}{10,000} \times \frac{\text{Load (lbs.)}}{10,000}$$

C stands for constants for the above as follows:

Mast Material	C. Transverse		C. Fore and Aft with Double Lowers					
	Single Spreaders	2 or 3 Sets Spreaders	Up to 32' D.W.L.		32'–45' D.W.L.		45' and over D.W.L.	
			Masthead	⅛	Masthead	⅛	Masthead	⅛
Spruce	6.78	8.11	3.9–4.2	3.74	2.9–3.2	3.74	2.2–2.5	3.74
Aluminum	.94	1.13	.54	.52	.40	.52	.30	.52

NOTE: The above data is for use with masts stepped through the deck, which are considered as columns with one fixed end and one pin end. For masts stepped on deck, we have a situation which is more like a column with two pin ends, so the constants should be increased, say by 50%, depending on the stiffness of the step. (See Illustration below)

Step 5—From the oval mast chart (Figure 15 for wood; Figures 16, 17, 18, 19, for aluminum), with the figures obtained in Step 4, start at the side with I_{LL}, go across horizontally to meet a vertical line from I_{TT} at the bottom. Then read off the value for A, which will be the fore and aft dimension, and B, the athwartship dimension of the mast at its maximum cross section. This gives the ideal section. If aluminum, pick out the nearest size from the list of aluminum extrusions at the end of this chapter.

Behavior of columns under compression

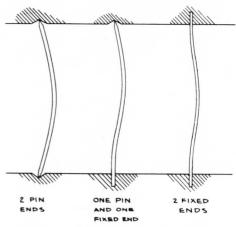

2 PIN ENDS   ONE PIN AND ONE FIXED END   2 FIXED ENDS

It is easy to see that by trying different combinations of panel lengths the most favorable section of the mast may be obtained. The oval mast charts (Figures 15–19) allow for a variation in shape, from a circular section to an oval. The normal section for a modern rig may have a fore and aft dimension 1.5 times the athwartship diameter. This is to stiffen the mast fore and aft where the staying is less and the panels are longer.

Wall thickness of a hollow spruce mast is proportioned to the major dimensions. Thus the port and starboard walls are usually 20% of the athwartship dimension, and the forward and after walls 20% of the fore and aft dimension.

For a section at the top of a mast, use 50% of the maximum section; for the bottom, 95%. The question remains—Where is the best spot for the maximum section? About 70% of the height above the deck is good practice for a masthead rig.

Short Method to Determine Standing Rigging Loads. Obtain the transverse load on the mast for the shrouds as follows, using righting moment at 30°:

Main Transv. Load   = R.M. × 1.5 ÷ ½ beam mainmast to chain plate.

Mizzen Transv. Load = R.M. × .5 ÷ ½ beam mizzen mast to chain plate.

Multiply the transverse loads by a factor of safety as given on pg. 174.

Then multiply by a percentage to distribute the loads as given in the table below:

Load Distribution on Shrouds from Tests

Mast	Rig	Sets of Spreaders	Load on Shrouds in % of Transv. Mast Load		
			2 Lowers	Intermediates	Uppers
Main	⅞ F.T.	1	60	—	45
Main	Masthead	1	65	—	45
Main	Masthead	2	55	30	30
Mizzen	Yawl and Ketch	1	42	38	20

With the load thus obtained, look up the breaking strength of the type of wire to be used (1 × 19 is best) and find the diameter given for the nearest strength.

For the stays, we have to go pretty much by instinct. We have a rule of thumb and not much more. Use the largest shroud size for the head stay, no less; and about that for the permanent backstay. Jib stays and running backstays fall in the same category. (See Figure 20 for strength of wire)

If there is only one head stay, it should be the strongest wire in the rig. If it should part, or its turnbuckle or toggle should break, the whole rig will fall directly aft and may injure the crew. Head stays or jib stays must be kept just as tight as possible to prevent the jib from sagging off to leeward or moving in or out as the boat rises and falls in a seaway.

Figure 15. Oval mast chart: spruce

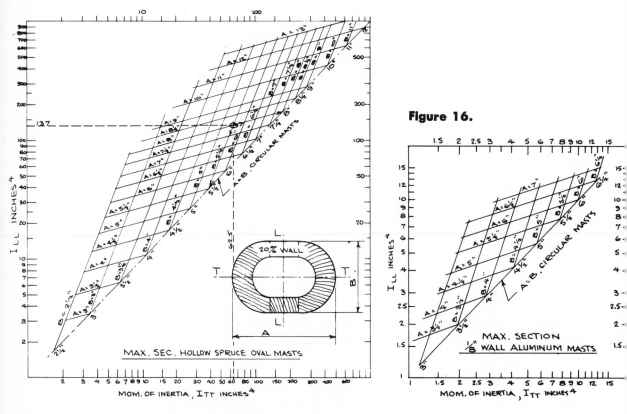

Figures 16, 17, 18, 19. Aluminum mast charts

⅛" should be the minimum wall thickness for all aluminum spars.

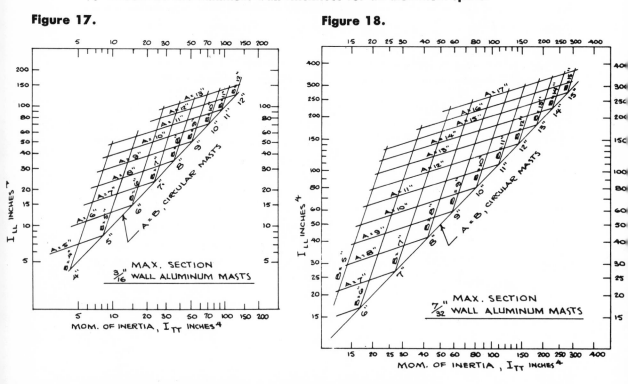

Figure 19.

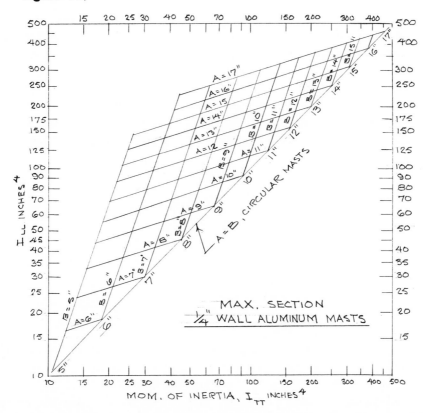

MAX. SECTION
¼″ WALL ALUMINUM MASTS

MOM. OF INERTIA, I_{TT} INCHES⁴

Running Rigging. Running backstays should be attached close to the attachment of the jib stay on the mast and as far aft as possible on deck. In writing up a block and rigging list for a new design, it is always well to refer to previous designs for sizes of running rigging, using good judgment. "What did we use on such and such a boat?" is a common question heard in design offices.

Wire rope is one of the most reliable structural materials known—particularly plow steel. The best for standing rigging is 1 × 19 strand; and 7 × 19 strand, which is flexible, is the best for running rigging where wire rope is required.

Care should be taken to provide a large enough sheave, when using wire halyards or steering cable; otherwise the tiny strands will break. Sixteen diameters seems to be the minimum size sheave allowable for 7 × 19 wire where it makes a 90° turn; 20 diameters where a 180° turn is required. Thus, if a ¼-inch diameter wire halyard were used, the sheave should be no smaller than 20 × ¼, or 5 inches in diameter.

Winches should be thought of as sheaves when wire is used. Too small a drum diameter will have the same bad effect on the wire, breaking the strands, decreasing the strength, and cutting the hands of the crew.

Blocks. There are wooden blocks, bronze blocks, plastic blocks, and rubber-shelled blocks. Each has its advantages. But the best block is the one that is strong, and kind to the rope at the same time. This is the wooden-shelled block. Of these the choice rests between certain hard woods, such as ash or lignum vitae. Because lignum vitae contains a certain natural oil in its pores, it is the best of the best.

Lubrication of the sheaves is vitally important. In my opinion, there is nothing quite so nice on sheet blocks as roller bearings. They make such a pleasant sound "tick ticking" away when you haul or slack-off a sheet.

Be careful never to have too small a block for the size of rope used. Don't be trapped by the old seaman's curse, "Large lines and small blocks to you."

Cleats should be sized according to the diameter of the rope used on them. $\frac{1}{16}$ inch diameter for each 1 inch of cleat length, thus for

$$
\begin{array}{rcl}
\frac{1}{4}'' \text{ rope} & = & 4'' \text{ cleat} \\
\frac{5}{16}'' & = & 5'' \\
\frac{3}{8}'' & = & 6'' \\
\frac{7}{16}'' & = & 7'' \\
\frac{1}{2}'' & = & 8'' \\
\frac{9}{16}'' & = & 9'' \\
\frac{5}{8}'' & = & 10'' \\
\frac{3}{4}'' & = & 12'' \\
\frac{7}{8}'' & = & 14'' \\
1'' & = & 16'' \\
\end{array}
$$

Black locust, white oak or teak are used for wooden cleats for running rigging. Well-rounded cast bronze cleats are the strongest and should be used for mooring cleats. In the large sizes they are hollow and use four bolts.

For small racing sailboats cam-action jam cleats made of fiber are popular for use with main and jib sheets. They save work and time for the crew, but are unkind to the rope.

Halyards of Manila, linen, or cotten stretch when dry and shrink when wet. Wire halyards prevent this. Dacron is excellent, as the come-and-go of this material is comparatively small. Nylon is wonderfully strong and should be used for anchor lines, docking lines, and where elasticity is necessary. But a wire halyard on a reel winch does that job best of all.

A good arrangement which eliminates the expensive winch is one where the wire halyard has a snatch block with becket at its end. The single part rope spliced to the becket is used to haul the sail most of the way up. Then it is looped around a snatch check block at the base of the mast, up over the sheave of the snatch block at the end of the wire, and hauled down to a cleat, thus giving a three-part mechanical advantage for the last few feet.

Resolving a Force. At this point it would be well to explain the principle involved in resolving a force. It is a graphic system. By drawing a diagram to scale, in which each line is parallel in direction to a given force, the length of the lines may be scaled off to indicate the magnitude of the force.

For example, let us find the required diameter of a bobstay wire. (See Figure 21) We are given the head stay size as $\frac{9}{32}$ inch, 1 $\times$ 19 wire with a breaking strength of 10,300 pounds. First, draw parallel lines at exactly the same angles as the

Figure 21. Force on bobstay

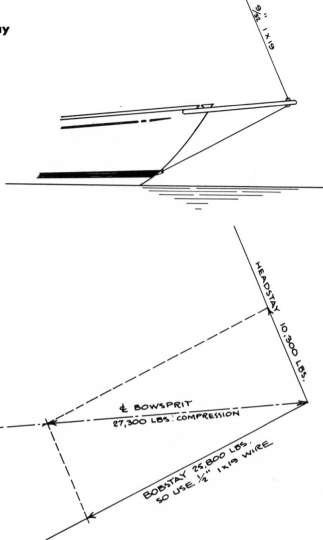

head stay, the center line of the bowsprit, and the bobstay. Second, starting at the bottom of the head stay, lay off 10,300 units upward along it, using any convenient scale (say, engineers scale 60). Third, draw a line aft from this spot, exactly parallel to the bobstay. Fourth, from where it intersects the center line of the bowsprit, draw another line down exactly parallel to the head stay until it intersects the bobstay. Fifth, using the same scale, measure off the length of the bobstay line thus obtained. This length, read off in the same units, is the required breaking strength for the bobstay. Look this up in the wire table and pick out the diameter. (Figure 20)

If the compression on the bowsprit were required, this would simply be the resultant force as measured along the bowsprit line in the diagram using the same scale.

To calculate the size of a shroud, lay out a diagram to scale as in Figure 22. By ratio and proportion:

$$\frac{\text{Shroud Tension}}{\text{Shroud Length}} = \frac{\text{Load}}{\text{Spreader Length}}$$

Solving then,

$$\text{Shroud Tension} = \frac{\text{Load} \times \text{Shroud Length}}{\text{Spreader Length}}$$

Multiply the shroud tension by a factor of safety of from 1.5 to 3 as follows:

1.5 for Yawl Mizzen Shrouds
2.0 for Ketch Mizzen Shrouds
2.5–2.75 for Main Upper Shrouds
3.0 for Main Lower Shrouds

Then look up the breaking strength of 1 × 19 wire and use the diameter given. (Figure 20)

Long Method to Determine Shroud and Mast Loads. The question now is—How much is the mast loaded and where? The answer is that nobody really knows. There are theories on the subject, however, and the best of them seem to be these:

For a mainmast, assume a wind pressure of one pound per square foot of sail area. For a mizzenmast on a yawl rig, use two pounds per square foot of sail area. These are the limits.

BREAKING STRENGTH IN POUNDS

DIAMETER	WIRE			ROPE			CHAIN GALV. PROOF
	1 x 19	7 x 19		MANILA	NYLON	DACRON	
	STAINLESS	STAINLESS	GALV.				
1/16"	550	480					SAFE WORKING LOAD
3/32"	1,200	920					
1/8"	2,100	1,900	1,800				
5/32"	3,300	2,600	2,500				
3/16"	4,700	3,900	3,800	450	850		520
7/32"	6,300	5,200	5,100				
1/4"	8,200	6,600	6,500	600	1,100	1,200	900
9/32"	10,300	8,000	7,900				
5/16"	12,500	9,000	9,700	1,000	1,800	1,800	1,360
3/8"	17,600	12,000	14,300	1,300	2,600	2,600	1,860
7/16"	23,400	16,300		1,700	3,700	3,500	2,500
1/2"	29,700	22,800		2,600	5,000	4,500	3,300
9/16"	37,000			3,400	6,400	5,500	4,100
5/8"	46,000			4,400	8,000	6,800	5,000
3/4"				5,400	10,500	9,300	7,100
7/8"				7,700	14,000	12,600	9,600
1"				9,000	18,800	16,100	12,400
1 1/8"				12,000	22,300		
1 1/4"				13,500	27,500	24,400	
1 1/2"				18,500	38,300	34,200	

Figure 20. Table of strengths for wire, rope and chain

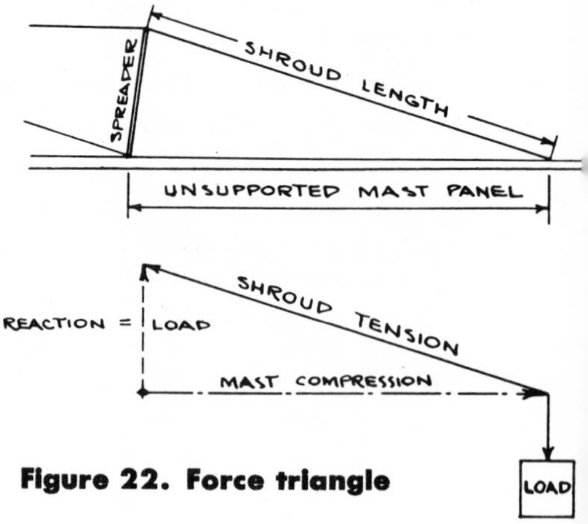

Figure 22. Force triangle

Figures 23, 24, 25.
Shroud loads

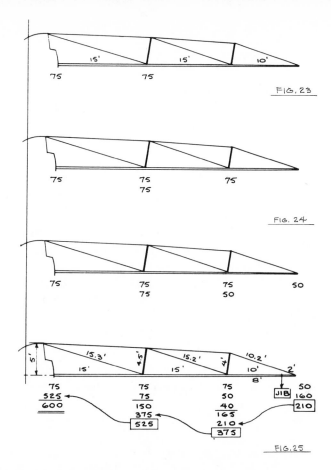

FIG. 23

FIG. 24

FIG. 25

The load of the jib will be concentrated at one spot on the mast, just where the jib stay is attached. But the load of the mainsail and its distribution is open to question. It seems to work well if we assume that the load is evenly distributed along the mast, regardless of the fact that most sails are triangular, not rectangular as would follow from our assumption. So take the area of the mainsail, divide it by the height of the mast, multiply by one, and you have the load per lineal foot of mast, due to the wind pressure on the mainsail.

For the sake of using round numbers, then, if there were a 400-square-foot mainsail set on a 40-foot mast, the load would be 10 pounds per lineal foot.

Now take the length of each panel, multiply it by the load per lineal foot, then assume that each end of the panel takes half the strain. If we have a 15-foot bottom panel, 10 lbs. × 15′ = 150 lbs. Put down 75 pounds for the load at one end, the deck, and 75 pounds for the load on the other end, the lower spreaders. (See Figure 23)

Next in our example, the middle panel also has 150 pounds, so add 75 pounds to the lower spreaders and 75 pounds to the upper spreaders. (Figure 24)

The top panel has 10′ × 10 lbs. = 100 lbs. load. So add 50 pounds to upper spreaders and 50 pounds to top of mast.

Now we come to the jib. Let's say the jib stay or forestay, as the case may be, is attached 2 feet below the masthead and that we have a 200-square-foot fore triangle. We have 200 pounds load at a point 2 feet from the top of this 10-foot panel. Like the old seesaw problem (page 280), we resolve these forces by moments to find what proportion of the load goes at the upper spreaders and what proportion at the masthead.

Taking moments about the left end, we have

$$10X = 8 \times 200$$
$$X = 160 \text{ lbs.}$$

So put down 160 pounds at the top, and the remaining 40 (200 — 160 = 40) at the upper spreaders.

Next, each column should be added, bringing forward the total to each succeeding panel, starting at the masthead and working down to the deck. (Figure 25)

Now the last figure in each column represents the athwartship load on the mast at that point. So when we have scaled off the lengths of the spreaders and the diagonal length of each shroud, we can calculate the size of the shroud by ratio and proportion, as in our simple diagram.

$$\text{Shroud Tension} = \frac{\text{Load} \times \text{Shroud Length}}{\text{Spreader Length}}$$

In this example—(in practice too light)

$$\text{Upper Shroud} = \frac{210 \times 10.2}{4} = 535 \text{ lbs.}$$

With a factor of safety of 4, $4 \times 535 = 2,140$ lbs.

So use $\frac{1}{8}''$ 1 $\times$ 19 wire which has a breaking strength of 2,100 lbs.

$$\text{Intermediate Shroud} = \frac{375 \times 15.2}{4.5} = 1,270 \text{ lbs.}$$

$$4 \times 1270 = 5,070 \text{ lbs.}$$
So use $\frac{7}{32}''$ 1 $\times$ 19 wire (6,300 lbs.)

$$\text{Lower Shroud} = \frac{525 \times 15.3}{5} = 1,600 \text{ lbs.}$$

$$4 \times 1600 = 6,400 \text{ lbs.}$$
So use $\frac{7}{32}''$ 1 $\times$ 19 wire (6,300 lbs.)

If two lowers are desired, use two $\frac{5}{32}''$ wires.

By our rule of thumb then, the jib or forestay would be no less than $\frac{7}{32}''$ diameter and so would the backstay, because $\frac{7}{32}''$ is the largest shroud size.

Spreaders. The strength of a spruce spreader is worked out for a streamlined section whose length is $2\frac{1}{2}$ times its height and where the area is 81% of the rectangular outline. By using the chart (Figure 26), it is only necessary to work out the compression on the spreader and then pick off the proper section for the length that will be used.

To find the compression on a spreader, we use the same graphic system of scaling off the forces. For example, use the strength of the wire shroud selected

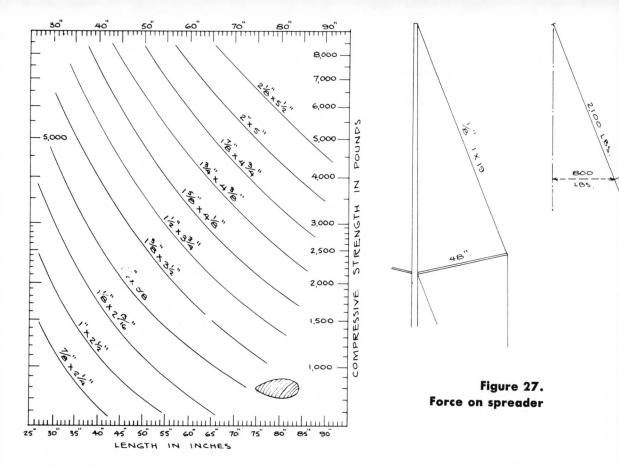

Figure 27.
Force on spreader

Figure 26. Spruce spreader sizes. In practice the fore and aft dimensions given should be increased to prevent a spreader from breaking should any running rigging snare it.

previously, say the upper shroud, ⅛″ diameter, 1 × 19 wire, which has a breaking strength of 2,100 pounds. So lay off 2100 units from the mast, along the shroud line. Using the same scale, measure from the spot on the shroud thus found directly inboard to the mast. (Figure 27) With an engineer's scale it works out to 800 pounds in this case. We know from the drawing that it is to be 48″ long. Entering the chart (Figure 26) with 800 pounds and 48″ we come up with a streamlined section slightly less than 1″ × 2½″ for the upper spreaders, in this example.

The outboard end of spreaders should be tapered to provide a substantial slot (sheathed with metal) to push against the wire. It should have a good lashing hole so that the shroud may be seized to it to prevent slippage, which if allowed may lead to dismasting.

The inboard end of a spreader should have two pins, one forward, one aft, to prevent swinging. Otherwise the pitching motion of the boat, combined with the slack leeward shrouds, will tend to shake off such a swinging object as a spreader with a single pin end. We can recommend the same treatment for jumper struts.

Booms. We have seen how mast sizes, shrouds, stays, and spreaders are figured.

Now let us consider booms. We have a helpful chart (Figure 28 for booms) that is based on boom sizes that have proven successful on many boats that have gone before.

Note that rectangular hollow booms usually have the proportion of a height 1.4 times the width using a 20% wall thickness. (A 10% wall thickness is sometimes used in highly competitive classes.) It is sometimes advisable to make the top plank, say, 25% thick in relation to the height, because greater thickness is needed here to hold the sail track screws. Small sizes, say below 1½″ wide, may just as well be solid or made with two planks forming a tee section. It is interesting to note the extremes on the boom chart.

The round roller-reefing main boom must have the greatest section of all because it is so weak in bending. Square booms may be used for roller reefing and can be 84% less in width. Roughly speaking, where a 6″ diameter hollow spruce boom is required for roller reefing, a 5″ × 5″ square hollow boom can be used instead. But because the mainsheet must be at the after tip of the boom on the roller outhaul fitting, these booms always seem to bend in a strong breeze. The after section should be larger than the forward one on rectangular booms, with the maximum section proportionately aft of the mid point.

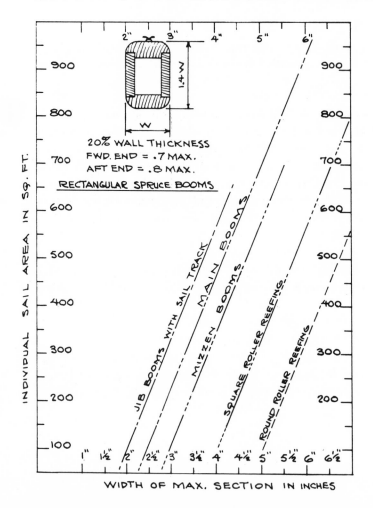

Figure 28. Rectangular spruce booms

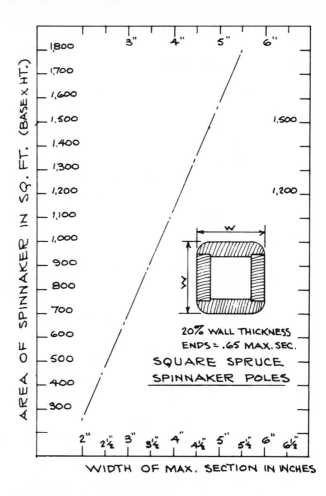

Figure 29. Square spruce spinnaker poles

Spinnaker Poles. Now we come to spinnakers. These sails play a very important part in sailboat racing, not only around short triangular courses of an afternoon, but also in long ocean races. It is safe to say that spinnakers may be used for 60% of a race, for running down wind and close reaching. By setting a spinnaker you practically double the total sail area.

Yacht designers should pay particular attention to the size of the fore triangle they lay out on their sail plans. If it exceeds a ratio of 3 to 1, height to base, it will produce too high and narrow a spinnaker. Masthead rigs must have a long base to avoid this failing. Notice the beautifully-shaped spinnakers on the 5.5-meter and 12-meter boats. Their ratio of height to base is between 2 to 1 and 3 to 1.

The area of a spinnaker in this day and age is very nearly equal to the rectangle formed by the base of the fore triangle and its height, which is the distance from the main deck up along the front of the mast to the spinnaker block. By the time the spinnaker is all made up with its built-in curves there is very little material wasted from this rectangle.

Based on this area of base times height, the spinnaker pole chart (Figure 29) may be consulted for maximum section. This should be a square section. For it to be round, the diameter would have to be 16% greater, so there is no point at all in using a round-sectioned spinnaker pole. The maximum stiffness is required because this spar is in pure compression. And lightness consistent with proper strength is important.

The maximum section on spinnaker poles should be located midway between the ends, which should be tapered to about 65% of the maximum section, or to suit the fitting which is generally made for a round pole.

Long Method to Determine Mast Section. The method most commonly used to calculate mast sections is a trial-and-error system. The compression on the mast is calculated using our simple example to determine shroud sizes:

Mast Compression for Each Panel = Load $\times$ Panel Length $\div$ Spreader Length.

So then, the mast compression for the upper panel = 210 $\times$ 10 $\div$ 4 = 525 lbs.; for the intermediate panel = 375 $\times$ 15 $\div$ 4.5 = 1,250 lbs.; for the lower panel = 525 $\times$ 15 $\div$ 5 = 1,575 lbs.

The sum of all forces on the mast then is:

Due to Uppers	525
Due to Intermediates	1,250
Due to Lowers	1,575
Weight of Mast and Rigging	200
Weight of Sails	100
Weight of Boom	20
Pull of Halyards (3 $\times$ wt. of sails)	300
Pull of Sheets (3 parts $\times$ 50 lbs.)	150
Total Compression on Mast	4,120 lbs.

It should be noted that the pull of sheets and halyards is dependent upon the number of parts of the halyard or sheet. A single-part main halyard would have to pull down with a tension of at least 100 pounds to lift a sail weighing 100 pounds. This 100 pounds pulling down on each side of the sheave would put a 200-pound compressive force on the mast. In practice, halyard winches are used to hoist the sails as tight as possible. So it would be better to multiply by 3 or 4 to find the compression on the mast due to a single-part halyard. The compression on a mast due to a main halyard is reduced by at least 50% by the use of a catch designed to hold the head of a mainsail.

Now multiply the total compression by a factor of safety between 2.7 and 4. Guess at a section that looks strong enough, and calculate its area; then calculate its radius of gyration from the formulas given for each shape. (See Chapter XXIII, A Manual of Calculations and Figure 30.)

Convert the longest panel length of the mast to inches. Divide this length by the radius of gyration. This ratio is called the L/R, or slenderness ratio.

The L/R for a 1″ diameter spruce strut is shown plotted on the chart (Figure 30) against compressive strength in pounds. This is for a strut with one pin end and one fixed end.

Choose on the chart the L/R corresponding to the calculated one, and obtain the strength per square inch from the chart. (Strength ÷ Area.)

Now the strength of the guessed-at section = strength per sq. in. × area of guessed-at sec. ÷ .785. (.785 is the area of a 1″ spruce strut.)

Compare the result with the calculated load, and increase or reduce the guessed-at section, repeating the process, until by trial and error a section is found to support the load.

Testing a Model to Destruction. Mr. Clinton Crane in his *Yachting Memories* tells how Nat Herreshoff figured the strength of the large steel masts he built for his early cup defenders. Rather than relying on Euler's* long column formula he was largely guided by the strength of similar small structures. He believed it was much simpler mathematics to test a small model to destruction and determine from that what a full-sized structure would stand.

The mathematical relationship between a small structure and a similar large one is this: weights of similar structures of the same material vary as the cube of the dimensions, while the structure itself will carry a load which varies as the square of the dimensions. This cube to square relationship places a definite limiting size on every kind of structure.

Tangs. Sheet metal tangs or pads held to the mast by tube bolts and round-head screws are, without doubt, the best way to attach shrouds and stays to a mast. If properly designed, they will not crush the wood, nor slip. They permit detachment of the rigging by the removal of a pin.

All parts of the rigging should be designed like links in a chain, each with the same strength. No one member should break before the others. As "A chain is no

Figure 30. L/R for 1″ diam. spruce strut

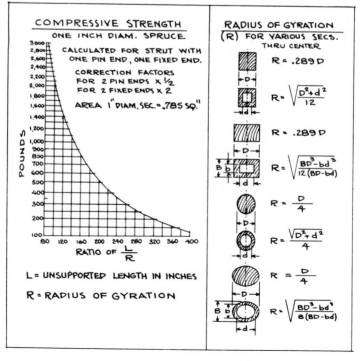

stronger than its weakest link," so each tang should be designed for the strength of the wire shroud or stay it holds. The proper number of screws, the proper-size tube bolt, the proper length and thickness of the metal are all related. For those who are interested, an example of tang design is given in the calculations for the PIPE DREAM Cruising Sloop.

* EULER'S FORMULA: $W = (3.14 \div L)^2 EI$ for column with 2 pin ends.

  W = Compression in pounds on mast or column.
  L = Length in inches of unsupported panel.
  I = Moment of Inertia of maximum section of mast or column in inches to the fourth.
  E = Modulus of elasticity, a measure of stiffness, being a ratio within the elastic limit of a material of the unit stress to the unit strain, or deformation. In compression:

      E for spruce   =   1,310,000 pounds per sq. in.
      E for aluminum = 10,000,000 pounds per sq. in.
      E for steel   = 29,000,000 pounds per sq. in.

EULER'S FORMULA: $W = 2 (3.14 \div L)^2 EI$ for column with 1 pin, 1 fixed end.

EULER'S FORMULA: $W = 4 (3.14 \div L)^2 EI$ for column with 2 fixed ends.

Note: See page 168 for an illustration of the behavior of columns under compression.

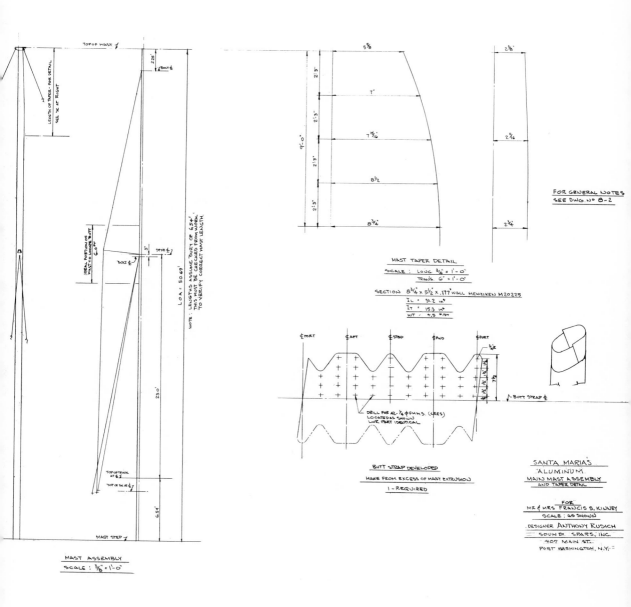

MAST TAPER DETAIL

SCALE : LONG 3/4" = 1'-0"
         TRANS 6" = 1'-0"

SECTION 8 3/4 x 5 1/2 x .177 WALL MENZIKEN M20225

FOR GENERAL NOTES
SEE DWG. N° B-2

BUTT STRAP DEVELOPED

MAKE FROM EXCESS OF MAST EXTRUSION

1 - REQUIRED

SANTA MARIA'S
ALUMINUM
MAIN MAST ASSEMBLY
AND TAPER DETAIL

FOR
MR & MRS FRANCIS S. KINNEY
SCALE : AS SHOWN

DESIGNER ANTHONY RUSICH
SOUND SPARS, INC.
407 MAIN ST.
PORT WASHINGTON, N.Y.

MAST ASSEMBLY
SCALE : 3/8" = 1'-0"

The details of SANTA MARIA's aluminum mast (pages 183-187).

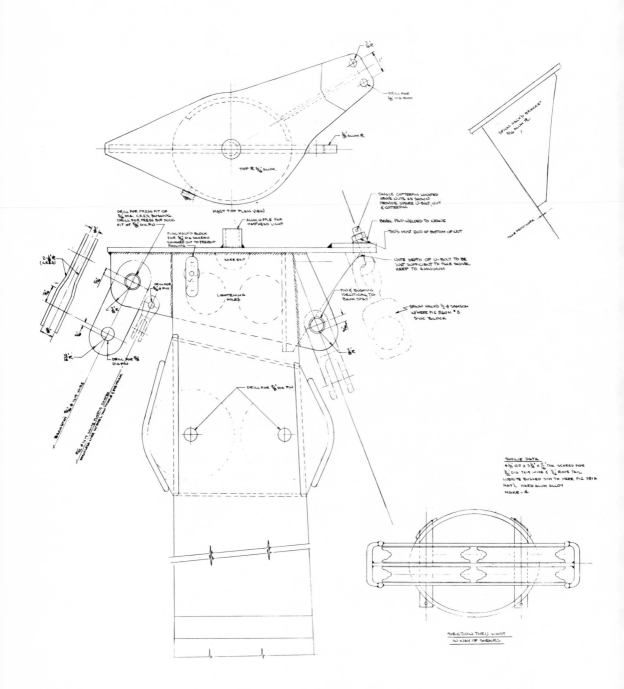

MAST TOP PLAN VIEW

SECTION THRU MAST
IN WAY OF SHEAVES

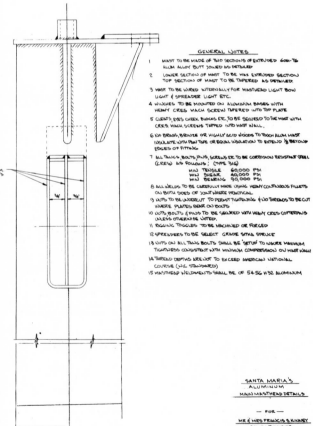

GENERAL NOTES

1. MAST TO BE MADE OF TWO SECTIONS OF EXTRUDED 6061-T6 ALUM ALLOY BUTT JOINED AS DETAILED

2. LOWER SECTION OF MAST TO BE MAX EXTRUDED SECTION TOP SECTION OF MAST TO BE TAPERED AS DETAILED

3. MAST TO BE WIRED INTERNALLY FOR MASTHEAD LIGHT BOW LIGHT & SPREADER LIGHT ETC.

4. WINCHES TO BE MOUNTED ON ALUMINUM BASES WITH HEAVY CRES MACH SCREW TAPPED INTO TOP PLATE

5. CLEATS, EYES CHEEK BLOCKS ETC. TO BE SECURED TO THE MAST WITH CRES MACH. SCREWS TAPPED INTO MAST WALL.

6. NO BRASS, BRONZE OR HIGHLY ACID WOODS TO TOUCH ALUM MAST INSULATE WITH PBW TAPE OR EQUAL INSULATION TO EXTEND ⅛ BEYOND EDGES OF FITTING

7. ALL TANGS, BOLTS, PINS, SCREWS ETC TO BE CORROSION RESISTANT STEEL (CRES) AS FOLLOWS : (TYPE 316)

        MIN TENSILE   60,000 PSI
        MIN SHEAR   40,000 PSI
        MIN BEARING   90,000 PSI

8. ALL WELDS TO BE CAREFULLY MADE USING HEAVY CONTINUOUS FILLETS ON BOTH SIDES OF JOINT WHERE PRACTICAL

9. NUTS TO BE UNDERCUT TO PERMIT TIGHTENING & NO THREADS TO BE CUT WHERE PLATES BEAR ON BOLTS

10. NUTS, BOLTS & PINS TO BE SECURED WITH HEAVY CRES COTTERPINS UNLESS OTHERWISE NOTED.

11. RIGGING TOGGLES TO BE MACHINED OR FORGED

12. SPREADERS TO BE SELECT GRADE SITKA SPRUCE

13. NUTS ON ALL TANG BOLTS SHALL BE "SETUP" TO INSURE MINIMUM TIGHTNESS CONSISTENT WITH MINIMUM COMPRESSION ON MAST WALL

14. THREAD DEPTHS ARE NOT TO EXCEED AMERICAN NATIONAL COURSE (N.C. STANDARD)

15. MASTHEAD WELDMENTS SHALL BE OF 5456 H32 ALUMINUM

SANTA MARIA'S
ALUMINUM
MAIN MASTHEAD DETAILS

— FOR —

MR & MRS FRANCIS S KINNEY
SCALE : FULL SIZE
DESIGNER ANTHONY RUSCH
SOUND SPARS, INC.
707 MAIN ST., PORT WASHINGTON

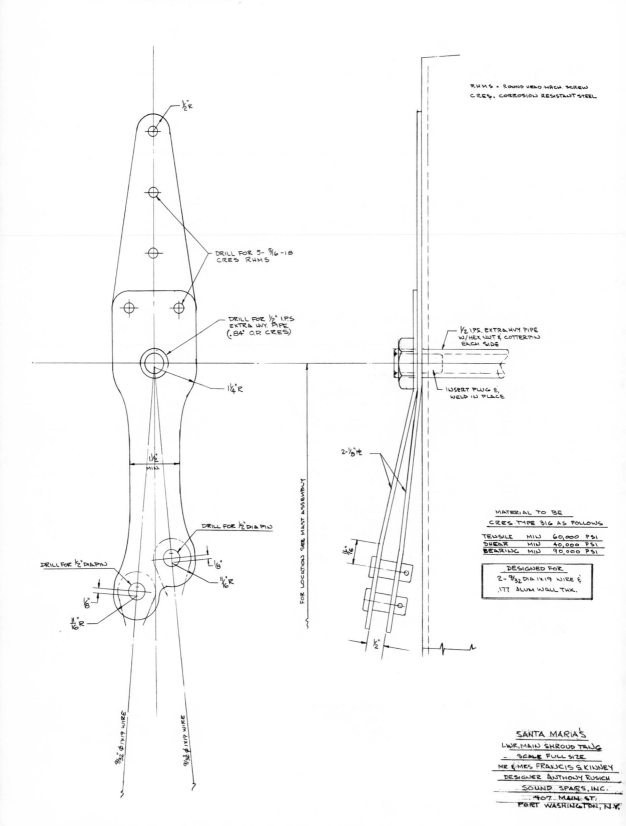

½"R

DRILL FOR 5- 5/16 -18
CRES RHMS

DRILL FOR ½" IPS
EXTRA HVY PIPE
(.84" O.D CRES)

1¼"R

1½"
MIN

DRILL FOR ½" DIA PIN

⅛"

11/16"R

DRILL FOR ½" DIA PIN

⅛"

11/16"R

9/32"Φ 1X19 WIRE

9/32"Φ 1X19 WIRE

FOR LOCATION SEE MAST ASSEMBLY

RHMS - ROUND HEAD MACH SCREW
CRES. CORROSION RESISTANT STEEL

½ IPS. EXTRA HVY PIPE
W/ HEX NUT & COTTER PIN
EACH SIDE

INSERT PLUG &
WELD IN PLACE

2-⅛"±

½"

½/16"

MATERIAL TO BE
CRES. TYPE 316 AS FOLLOWS

TENSILE	MIN	60,000	PSI
SHEAR	MIN	40,000	PSI
BEARING	MIN	90,000	PSI

DESIGNED FOR
2-9/32" DIA 1X19 WIRE &
.177 ALUM WALL THK.

SANTA MARIA'S
LWR. MAIN SHROUD TANG
SCALE FULL SIZE
MR. & MRS FRANCIS SKINNEY
DESIGNER ANTHONY RUSICH
SOUND SPARS, INC.
407 MAIN ST.
PORT WASHINGTON, N.Y.

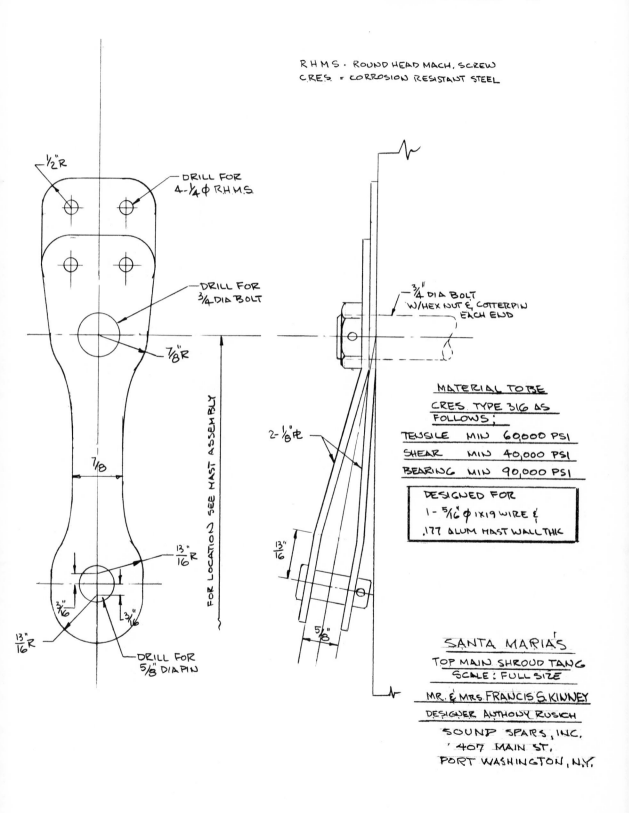

R H M S · ROUND HEAD MACH. SCREW
C.R.E.S. = CORROSION RESISTANT STEEL

½"R

DRILL FOR
4-¼ φ R.H.M.S

DRILL FOR
¾ DIA BOLT

⅞"R

7/8

FOR LOCATION SEE MAST ASSEMBLY

13"/16 R

3"/16

3"/16

13"/16 R

DRILL FOR
5/8 DIA PIN

¾" DIA BOLT
W/HEX NUT & COTTERPIN
EACH END

2-⅛" ℄

13"/16

5/8

MATERIAL TO BE

CRES TYPE 316 AS
FOLLOWS:

TENSILE   MIN 60,000 PSI
SHEAR   MIN 40,000 PSI
BEARING MIN 90,000 PSI

DESIGNED FOR
1- 5/16 φ 1X19 WIRE &
.177 ALUM MAST WALL THK

SANTA MARIA'S
TOP MAIN SHROUD TANG
SCALE: FULL SIZE
MR. & MRS. FRANCIS S. KINNEY
DESIGNER ANTHONY RUSICH
SOUND SPARS, INC.
407 MAIN ST,
PORT WASHINGTON, N.Y.

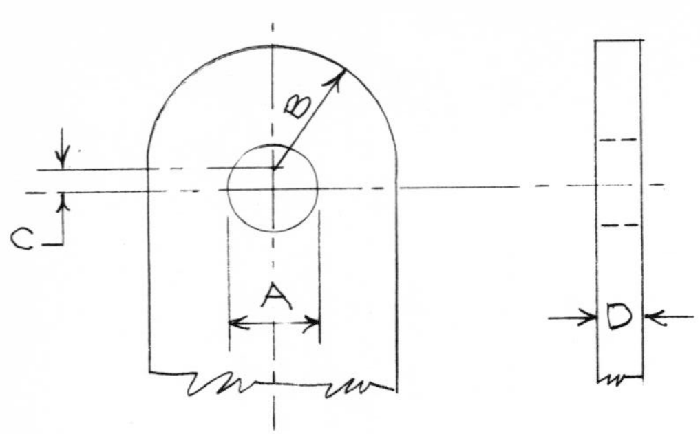

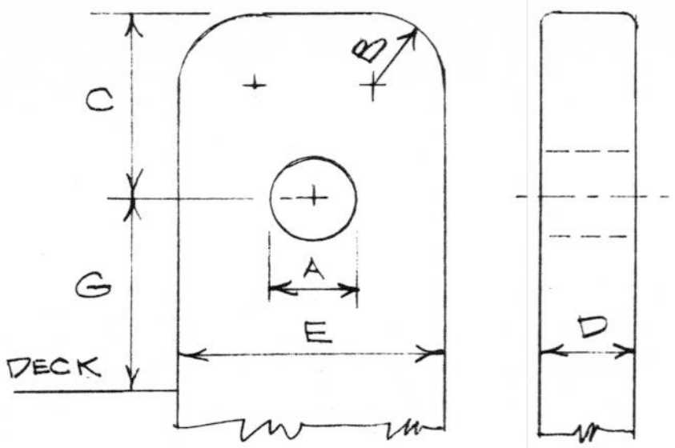

ULTIMATE STRESS

TENSION	40,000	P.S.I.
SHEAR	24,000	P.S.I.
BEARING	78,000	P.S.I.
WELD	21,000	P.S.I.

FACTOR OF SAFETY = 2.5 FOR EACH

SILICON BRONZE OR STAINLESS STEEL CHAIN PLs

LOAD IS 4/3 BREAKING STRENGTH OF WIRE

WIRE DIAM.	BREAKING STR. IN LBS. 1X19 S.S.	A PIN	B RADIUS	C OFFSET	D* THICK
1/8"	2,100	1/4"	3/8"	1/16"	1/8"
5/32"	3,300	5/16"	7/16"	1/16"	3/16"
3/16"	4,700	3/8"	1/2"	1/8"	3/16"
7/32"	6,300	7/16"	9/16"	1/8"	1/4"
1/4"	8,200	1/2"	11/16"	1/8"	1/4"
9/32"	10,300	1/2"	11/16"	1/8"	5/16"
5/16"	12,500	5/8"	13/16"	3/16"	5/16"
3/8"	17,600	5/8"	7/8"	3/16"	7/16"
7/16"	23,400	3/4"	1"	3/16"	1/2"
1/2"	29,700	7/8"	1 3/16"	1/4"	1/2"
9/16"	37,000	7/8"	1 1/4"	1/4"	5/8"
5/8"	46,800	1"	1 3/8"	1/4"	11/16"
3/4"	59,700	1 1/4"	1 5/8"	1/4"	3/4"
7/8"	76,700	1 1/2"	1 3/4"	5/16"	7/8"

* FOR JIBSTAY & BACKSTAY LUGS ADD 1/16" THICKNESS

ALUMINUM CHAIN PLATES (ALLOY 5086-H32)

(SEE BRONZE OR S.S. CHAIN PLs FOR WIRE STRENGTH)

WIRE 1X19 S.S.	A PIN	B RADIUS	C	D THICK	E WIDTH		LENGTH OF WELD			G
							3/16" 2,790*	1/4" 3,720*	5/16" 4,640*	
1/8"	1/4"	3/16"	7/16"	5/16"	11/16"		3 3/4	2 3/4		11/16
5/32"	5/16"	1/4"	1/2"	3/8"	1"		6"	4 1/2	3 1/2"	3/4"
3/16"	3/8"	5/16"	3/4"	7/16"	1 1/16"		8 1/2	6 1/4	5"	13/16"
7/32"	7/16"	3/8"	13/16"	1/2"	1 1/4"		12"	8 1/2"	7"	7/8"
1/4"	1/2"	7/16"	7/8"	5/8"	1 3/8"		15"	11"	9"	1"
9/32"	1/2"	1/2"	1 1/16"	5/8"	1 1/2"		19"	14"	11"	1 1/8"
5/16"	5/8"	1/2"	1 1/8"	3/4"	1 5/8"		23"	17"	14"	1 1/4"
3/8"	5/8"	5/8"	1 1/2"	3/4"	2 1/8"		32"	24"	19"	1 3/8"
7/16"	3/4"	5/8"	1 5/8"	7/8"	2 3/8"		42"	32"	25"	1 1/2"
1/2"	7/8"	3/4"	1 7/8"	1"	2 5/8"		54"	40"	32"	1 1/2"
9/16"	1"	1"	2"	1 1/8"	2 7/8"		66"	50"	40"	1 5/8"
5/8"	1"	1 1/4"	2 3/8"	1 1/4"	3 3/8"		84"	62"	50"	1 5/8"
3/4"	1 1/4"	1 1/4"	2 1/2"	1 1/2"	3 3/4"		108"	81"	65"	1 3/4"
7/8"	1 1/2"	1 3/8"	2 5/8"	1 3/4"	4 1/8"		136"	104"	82"	1 7/8"

* STRENGTH OF WELD IN SHEAR, LBS. PER LIN. INCH.

List of Aluminum Spar Extrusions Available in the U.S.A.

	Section in inches	Wt. in Lbs./Ft.	Inertias
	13.50 × 8.50 × 0.22	8.76	145.0 & 72.0
	12.0 × 8.0 × 0.22	7.94	105.3 & 56.4
	11.5 × 8.0 × 0.22	7.74	100.0 & 55.0
	11.5 × 8.0 × 0.188	6.50	82.0 & 47.0
	11.43 × 6.44 × 0.22	7.08	81.0 & 33.3
	11.0 × 7.0 × 0.188	6.00	67.5 & 33.6
	10.0 × 6.0 × 0.22	6.32	56.0 & 25.37
	9.5 × 6.0 × 0.188	5.30	42.8 & 21.0
	9.5 × 5.0 × 0.125	3.29	25.89 & 9.63
	9.25 × 5.5 × 0.188	4.99	37.92 & 17.0
	8.75 × 5.5 × 0.188	4.80	33.0 & 16.0
	8.75 × 5.5 × .157	4.00	27.8 & 13.6
	8.5 × 5.75 × .188	4.81	31.90 & 17.43
	8.5 × 5.0 × .188	4.56	29.03 & 12.73
	8.5 × 4.8 × .188	4.48	28.26 & 11.61
	8.5 × 4.5 × .133	3.12	19.63 & 7.34
	8.0 × 4.8 × .138	3.29	18.3 & 8.25
	8.0 × 4.5 × .188	4.21	23.39 & 9.53
	7.5 × 4.5 × .188	4.05	20.08 & 9.05
	7.5 × 4.0 × .156	3.22	15.6 & 5.86
	7.5 × 4.0 × .100	2.08	10.27 & 3.90
	7.0 × 3.75 × .094	1.83	7.80 & 3.00
	6.0 × 3.5 × .130	2.21	7.03 & 3.04
	5.62 × 4.07 × .110	2.10	5.7 & 3.45
	5.0 × 3.5 × .188	2.90	6.3 & 3.59
	5.0 × 3.5 × .13	1.98	4.54 & 2.61
12 meter	11.925 × 9.652 × .23	9.208	131 & 92
8 meter	8.25 × 6.5 × .16	4.27	27.8 & 19.3
6 meter	6.04 × 4.89 × .095	1.928	6.58 & 4.61
5.5 meter	5 × 4.125 × .10	1.670	3.98 & 3.0
	8.00 × 4.56 × 0.14	3.25	17.9 & 7.5
	7.75 × 4.75 × 0.125	3.25	15.0 & 7.2
	6.5 × 4.375 × .125	2.75	10.4 & 5.2
	6.7 × 4.1 × 0.14	2.72	10.9 & 5.1
	6.0 × 4.0 × .14	2.51	8.24 & 4.4
	6.0 × 3.5 × .13	2.34	6.95 & 3.05
	5.5 × 3.375 × .125	2.17	5.75 & 3.25
	5.5 × 3.375 × .110	1.71	4.76 & 2.23
	5.0 × 2.75 × .125	1.83	3.72 & 1.46

List of Aluminum Spar Extrusions Available in the U.S.A. (continued)

Section in inches	Wt. in Lbs./Ft.	Inertias
4.5 × 2.75 × .110	1.43	2.5 & 1.4
4.375 × 2.81 × .09	1.48	2.21 & 1.26
4.0 × 2.625 × .10	1.18	1.71 & 0.89
3.85 × 2.37 × .080	0.90	1.19 & 0.56
3.75 × 2.25 × .10	1.07	1.32 & 0.59
3.56 × 2 × 0.094	1.05	1.01 & 0.41
2.84 × 2 × .085	0.87	0.75 & 0.385
2.65 × 1.75 × 0.085	0.80	0.43 & 0.22
3.315 × 2.5 × .085	0.98	1.50 & 0.71
2.75 × 2.12 × 0.070	0.75	0.58 & 0.335

CHAPTER XVIII

TOOLS REQUIRED FOR DESIGNING

The following list is given to help the beginning designer acquire the proper basic tools needed to produce a good drawing.

1. A roll of vellum—Keuffel & Esser Co. Albanene Number 195L, or equal.
2. Two mechanical pencils—one with a soft lead, such as HB; the other with a harder lead for drawing—5H for lines, 2H for other plans.
3. Erasers—Pink Pearl, or equal—Eberhard Faber.
4. Erasing shield and dusting brush.
5. Pencil sharpener suitable for mechanical pencils.
6. A good straightedge, about 30 inches long, of stainless steel, because wood usually warps.
7. Splines or battens of various thicknesses and lengths. These are hard to come by. The best I have seen were made in France, some tapered at each end, some tapered in the middle, some tapered at one end, and some parallel-sided. Wooden battens are usually too stiff, so a plastic material, such as celluloid, is preferred.
8. Lead weights or ducks, such as K & E Number 1936. These can be home-made. A dozen is a good round number to have. Weight about three and a half lbs. each. These are used to hold the battens to the curve desired. (See Figure 31)
9. The following curves, in my opinion, are the best ones and are used the most often: K & E Copenhagen ship curves, pattern Numbers 37, 40, 49, 53, 54,

**Figure 31. Spline
with lead weights**

55, 60, 104, 109, 150. There ought to be a whole family of curves, such as Number 150, manufactured, but all the ones I have seen were homemade. Of the irregular French curves, I have found pattern Numbers 26 and 29 most useful. (See Figure 32)

10. A simple 180° protractor.
11. Two 45° triangles, about 8″ x 8″.

Figure 32. Curves most frequently used

CURVES MOST FREQUENTLY USED   F. S. K.

12. One large 30°–60° triangle, say 9″ x 12½″. No T-square is required. To draw parallel lines, lay out one straight line, measure to others, and use the system of sliding one 45° triangle on the other, holding the left one fixed.

13. A set of architect's flat scales. One 6″ and one 12″ long, both sides beveled and divided: ⅛″, ¼″, ½″, 1″; ⅜″, ¾″; 1½″, 3″ to the foot.

14. A planimeter—K & E Number 4212. This is an ingenious mechanical device used to ascertain the area of plane surface drawn to any scale. This is done by tracing its boundary line, in a clockwise direction, with the tracing point of the instrument, then reading the result computed on the calibrated measuring wheel. It is important to have this instrument to save labor in calculating not only areas, but volumes, displacement, stability, amount of ballast, etc. (See Figure 33)

**Figure 33. Planimeter:
reading directly
in square inches**

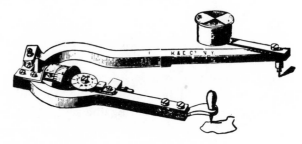

15. A template to draw circles of many sizes.

16. A good compass to draw larger circles.

17. A 10″ simple slide rule, such as K & E Number 4055.

18. A drawing board, with horses, movable fluorescent lamp, foot stool, and stool.

19. Scotch drafting tape and scissors. Scissors will not be used simply to cut paper from a roll, but will be used to cut out the underwater profile and heeled sections of the full body plan. By balancing these cutouts on a point, two important centers are found: the center of lateral plane and the center of buoyancy, respectively—thus saving long, tedious mathematical calculations.

These methods will be treated in Chapter XXIII, A Manual of Calculations.

CHAPTER XIX

THE DRAWINGS

In order to obtain price estimates from several different boat builders, it is necessary to have a minimum of three preliminary drawings of any design, together with a set of specifications. In the case of a sailboat or motor sailer, these would be the Sail Plan, the Arrangement Plan, and the Midship Construction Section, showing the size of frames, frame spacing, planking thickness, keel, floors, decking, beams, house sides, centerboard trunk and gear, stringers, clamp and shelf, rail, amount and type of ballast—in short, all the materials to be used and their sizes. In the case of a powerboat, a drawing of the Outboard Profile would take the place of the Sail Plan.

The specifications should cover everything not shown on the drawings. On some large yachts I have seen specifications as long as fifty or sixty pages, covering every imaginable item. Personally, I feel the shorter these can be made, the better, because they usually collect dust in the foreman's desk, and the men actually building the boat don't ever see them. The old Chinese saying, "One picture is worth ten thousand words," applies here. The more plans, the better; and the more information on each plan, the better.

In this respect it is wise for a designer to build up a file of standard plans which can be applied to suit any design, such as:

Typical Hatch Details—sliding and box types.
Details of Water Trap Vent Box—several sizes.
Extension Transom Berth.
Gas Tank and Piping.
Lifeline Stanchion and Base.
Bow Pulpit Rail.
Masthead Light and Wiring.
Ice Box Lining and Insulation.
Soundproofing in Way of Engine.
Engine Compartment Blower Installation.
Typical Spreader Clips.

Mast Tangs for Several Wire Sizes.
Typical Bilge Piping System.
Typical Rudder Details.
Genoa Sheet Lead and Track.
Winch Bases.
Cockpit Scuppers.
Typical Toilet Piping.
Typical Wash Basin Piping.
Spinnaker Pole Fittings.
Typical Switchboard Layout.
Typical Chain Plates—several sizes.

After the designer obtains prices from several yards, the client may decide to have his new boat built at one of them on a fixed contract price basis. A contract is then drawn up and signed by all parties concerned. A Standard Builder's Risk Insurance Policy should be taken out to protect the owner in the event of fire. And then the designer has to produce the working drawings as fast and as accurately as possible. These consist of the following:

Lines Drawing.
Table of Offsets.
Construction Plan.
General Arrangement Plan.
Deck Plan.
Joiner Sections.
Machinery Arrangement.
Sail Plan and Standing Rigging.
Spars.
Mast Fittings.
Wiring Diagram.
Piping Diagram.
Other details not covered by the architect's standard or type plans.

With all this work you may well ask How does anybody in this business ever make any money? The answer, just as you thought, is that no one ever made a fortune at it, but it *is* possible to make a living and most rewarding to see one's creations come to life.

Running down the list of plans, I would like to mention a few helpful hints which may assist the amateur in making his drawings.

The Lines Drawing. An accurately laid-out grid on the back of the paper (transparent vellum) is important as a starter. By drawing the grid on the reverse side and the lines themselves on the front, the grid will remain when you erase the lines on the front, and erase you must do—many, many times. It is far easier to draw the body plan or cross sections on a separate small piece of paper, with its grid also on the back, because this allows one to turn the drawing sidewise or upside down more easily, which is helpful in drawing curved lines.

Figure 34. Steps in drawing lines

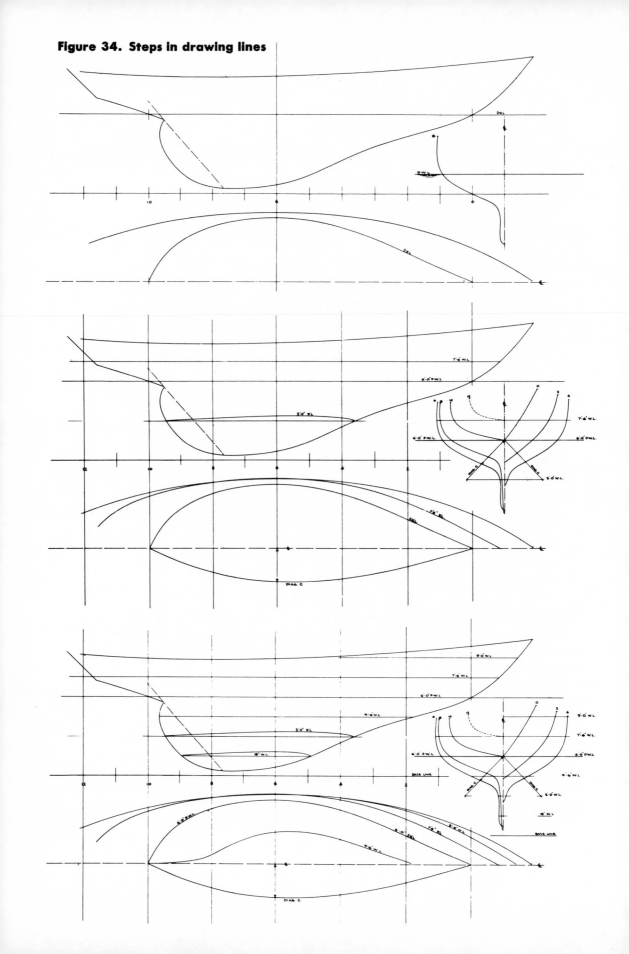

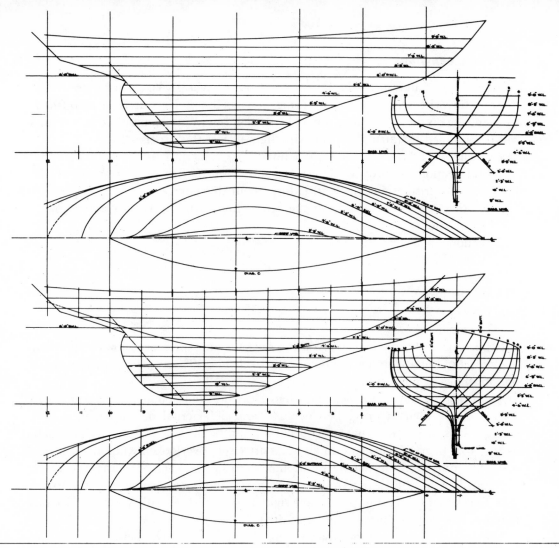

Figure 35. Lines of the PIPE DREAM Cruising Sloop

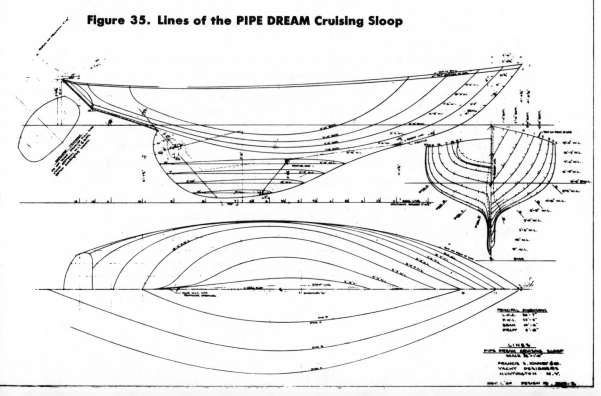

After trying different methods over a period of several years, I have arrived at my own favorite sequence in preparing a set of lines. Here it is in a nutshell: Concentrate on the water lines. I may be wrong, but in my opinion the best results can be obtained by fairing the following lines in just this order:

1. Profile, deck line, designed water line.
2. Mid section to proper underwater area for desired displacement at the required prismatic coefficient. (More about this later.)
3. 45° diagonal from D.W.L. at the center line with widest part at Station 6.
4. Water lines.
5. Sections.
6. Water lines.
7. Sections.
8. Water lines.
9. Buttocks.
10. Diagonals.

It takes between five and ten working days for an experienced man to produce a good set of lines, whether the boat is 25' over-all or 95' over-all. (See Figures 34, 35, 36, showing how to draw lines.)

Another good hint is to keep the Lines Drawing small enough so that you can see the entire boat at once. Between 24" and 30" actual measurement is long enough. It is surprising what great accuracy can be obtained from scales as small as $\frac{3}{8}'' = 1' 0''$. Mistakes and unfair spots are easily overlooked when the drawing is too big, but stand out like a sore thumb, so to speak, when the same drawing is reduced. It is helpful in determining whether a line is "eye sweet" or not, to lay your cheek right near the paper and sight along the line with your eye. In this manner, flat spots or bumps can be located.

A set of lines must be more than just pretty and eye sweet; they must have the proper prismatic coefficient and the proper location for the center of buoyancy. These fall within a narrow range and will be treated later on in Chapter XXIII, A Manual of Calculations.

The Table of Offsets is simply a collection of horizontal measurements from the center line and vertical measurements from the base line to as many points as possible on the Lines Drawing. With this list of measurements the builder can then lay out the lines full size in his mold loft, fair them, and make his templates. Offsets are customarily given to the outside of the planking, in a wooden boat, and to the inside of the shell plating, in a metal boat. Feet, inches, and eighths of an inch are used, with one-sixteenth of an inch added where required by adding a plus sign. Thus $4-7-7+$ would mean $4'$ $7\frac{15}{16}''$. (See following table.)

The Construction Plan will be dealt with in great detail in the chapter on Construction, since a whole book could be written on this subject alone.

The General Arrangement Plan, showing the layout of the interior, is a test of the designer's ability to utilize the maximum space available in the most efficient manner. The phrase "inch juggling" is most appropriate. Here it is important to

Table of Offsets

Note deck cambers for SOUTHERLY in upper right hand corner, 4″ in 10′ 6″ for main deck, and 6″ in 6′ 0″ for top of cabin. A camber of 3/8″ per foot of beam, more or less, is normal for the main deck of most yachts.

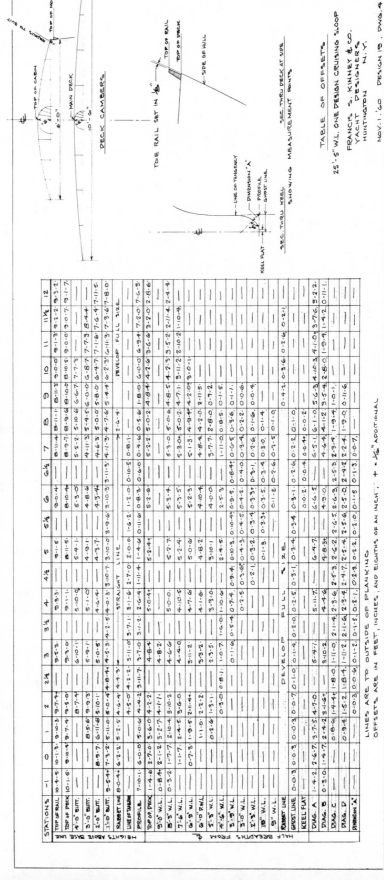

	STATIONS	-1	0	1	2	2½	3	3½	4	4½	5	5½	6	6½	7	8	9	10	11	11½	12
HEIGHTS ABOVE BASE LINE	TOP OF RAIL	10-4-5	10-1-3	9-10-3	9-7-4+	—	9-5-3	—	9-3-3	—	9-1-5	—	9-0-4	—	8-11-4	8-11-1	8-11-3	9-0-0	9-1-3	9-2-2	9-3-2
	TOP OF DECK	10-1-5	9-10-4	9-7-4	9-5-0	—	9-3-0	—	9-1-1	—	8-11-5	—	8-10-4+	—	8-9-7	8-9-6	8-10-0	8-10-5	9-0-0	9-0-7	9-1-7
	4′-0″ BUTT.	—	—	—	8-7-4	—	6-10-1	—	5-10-0+	—	5-4-1	—	5-9-0	—	5-5-2	5-10-6	6-6-7	7-7-3	—	—	—
	3′-0″ BUTT.	—	—	8-5-6	9-9-3	—	5-9-1	—	5-1-0	—	4-9-1	—	4-8-6	—	4-11-3	5-4-5	6-0-0	6-8-7	7-7-3	8-4-4	—
	2′-0″ BUTT.	—	8-9-7	6-11-6	5-10-1	—	5-0-5	—	4-6-4	—	4-3-7	—	4-3-4+	—	4-6-3	5-0-0	5-8-0	6-4-7	7-1-6	7-6-4	7-11-5
	1′-0″ BUTT.	9-5-4+	7-3-2	5-11-0	5-0-4	4-8-4+	4-5-3	4-2-5	4-0-3	3-10-7	3-10-0	3-9-6	3-10-3	3-11-3	4-1-3	4-7-6	5-4-4	6-2-3	6-11-3	7-3-6	7-8-0
	RABBET LINE	8-0-4+	6-2-2	5-2-5	4-6-4	4-4-3	← STRAIGHT LINE →									2-6-4	DEVELOP FULL SIZE				
	LINE OF TANGENCY	—	—	—	4-5-0	4-2-2	3-11-0	3-7-1	3-1-6	2-7-0	2-0-0	1-6-2	1-2-0	0-10-5	0-8-1	—	—	—	—	—	—
	PROFILE	7-10-1	6-0-0	5-0-6	4-4-2	3-11-7	3-7-0	3-1-2	2-6-4	1-11-4	1-4-6	0-11-6	0-8-3	0-6-0	0-4-6	0-5-6	1-8-0	6-0-0	6-9-4	7-2-0	7-6-3
HALF BREADTHS FROM ℄	TOP OF DECK	1-4-6	2-7-0	3-6-0	4-2-2	—	4-8-4	—	5-0-4+	—	5-2-4+	—	5-2-6	—	5-2-2	5-0-2	4-8-4	4-2-6	3-6-6	3-2-0	2-8-6
	9′-0″ W.L.	0-8-4+	2-1-2	3-2-7	4-1-1	—	4-8-2	—	—	—	—	—	—	—	—	—	—	—	—	—	—
	8′-3″ W.L.	0-3-2	1-7-7	2-10-4	3-10-2	—	4-6-6	—	5-0-0	—	5-2-7	—	5-3-4	—	5-3-0	5-0-6	4-8-5	4-2-3	3-5-2	2-11-4	2-4-4
	7′-6″ W.L.	—	1-1-7	2-4-5	3-6-0	—	4-4-0	—	4-10-5	—	5-2-4	—	5-3-5	—	5-3-0+	5-0-2	4-7-1	3-11-2	2-10-2	1-10-4	—
	6′-9″ W.L.	—	0-7-3	1-9-5	2-11-4+	—	3-11-2	—	4-7-6	—	5-0-6	—	5-2-3	—	5-1-3	4-9-4+	4-2-0+	3-0-1	—	—	—
	6′-0″ D.W.L.	—	—	1-1-0	2-2-2	—	3-3-2	—	4-1-6	—	4-8-2	—	4-10-4	—	4-8-4	4-2-0	2-11-5	—	—	—	—
	5′-3″ W.L.	—	—	0-2-6	1-3-1	—	2-3-5	—	3-3-0	—	3-10-1	—	4-0-0	—	3-7-7	2-8-0	0-7-2	—	—	—	—
	4′-6″ W.L.	—	—	—	0-3-0	0-8-1	1-0-7	1-6-0	1-10-6	—	2-4-5	—	2-5-3	—	1-11-0	0-8-5	0-1-5	—	—	—	—
	3′-9″ W.L.	—	—	—	—	—	0-1-6	0-5-4	0-7-4	0-9-4	0-10-3	0-10-4+	0-9-5	0-8-4+	0-6-5	0-3-6	0-1-1	—	—	—	—
	3′-0″ W.L.	—	—	—	—	—	—	—	0-2-5	0-3-6+	0-4-3	0-4-5	0-4-2	0-4-0	0-3-4	0-2-2	0-0-6	—	—	—	—
	2′-3″ W.L.	—	—	—	—	—	—	—	—	0-2-1	0-3-2	0-3-4	0-3-3+	0-3-1	0-2-6	0-1-6	0-0-4	—	—	—	—
	18″ W.L.	—	—	—	—	—	—	—	—	—	0-1-3	0-3-3+	0-3-5	0-3-4	0-3-0	0-1-4	—	—	—	—	—
	9″ W.L.	—	—	—	—	—	—	—	—	—	—	—	0-1-2	0-2-6	0-2-5	0-1-0	—	—	—	—	—
	RABBET LINE	DEVELOP FULL SIZE															0-4-2	0-3-6	0-2-6	0-2-1	—
	GHOST LINE	0-0-3	0-0-3	0-0-3	0-0-7	0-1-0	0-1-4	0-2-0	0-2-5	0-3-1	0-3-4	0-3-4	0-3-1	0-2-6	0-2-2	0-1-0	—	—	—	—	—
	KEEL FLAT	—	—	—	—	—	—	—	—	—	—	—	0-0-2	0-0-4	0-0-4+	0-0-2	—	—	—	—	—
	DIAG. A	1-4-2	2-6-7	3-7-5	4-7-0	—	5-4-1	—	5-11-7	—	6-4-7	—	6-6-5	—	6-5-1	6-1-0	5-6-3	4-10-3	4-1-0+	3-7-6	3-2-2
	DIAG. B	0-3-0	1-4-7	2-4-2	3-1-6+	—	3-10-2	—	4-4-6	—	4-8-3+	—	4-9-0	—	4-6-4	4-1-2	3-5-4	2-8-0	1-9-4	1-4-2	0-11-1
	DIAG. C	—	—	0-8-6	1-4-4+	1-8-0	1-11-0	2-1-4	2-3-6	2-5-3	2-6-2	2-6-5	2-6-3	2-5-3	2-3-4	1-9-4	1-0-1	—	—	—	—
	DIAG. D	—	—	0-9-4	1-5-2	1-8-4	1-11-2	2-1-6	2-3-4	2-4-7	2-5-4	2-5-6	2-5-0	2-4-2	2-2-4	1-9-0	0-11-6	—	—	—	—
	DIMENSION "A"	—	—	—	0-0-3	0-0-6	0-1-2	0-1-5	0-2-1	0-2-3	0-2-2	0-2-0	0-1-5	0-1-3	0-0-7	—	—	—	—	—	—

LINES ARE TO OUTSIDE OF PLANKING
OFFSETS ARE IN FEET, INCHES, AND EIGHTHS OF AN INCH. + = 1/16″ ADDITIONAL

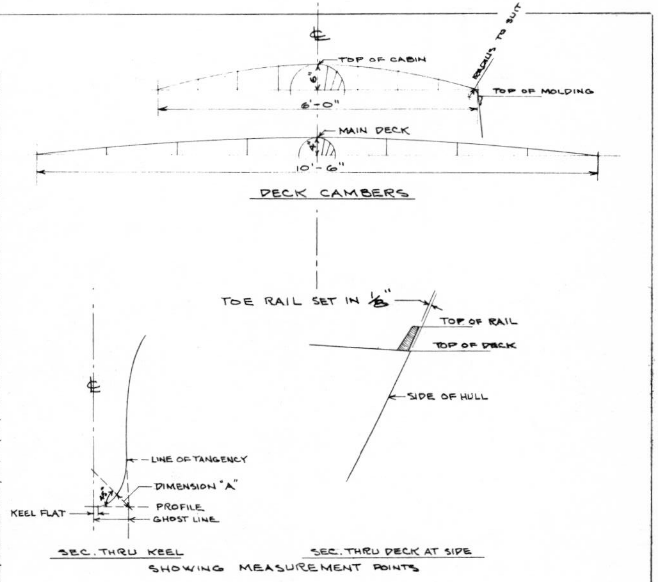

TABLE OF OFFSETS

25′-5″ W.L. ONE DESIGN CRUISING SLOOP

FRANCIS S. KINNEY & CO.
YACHT DESIGNERS
HUNTINGTON N.Y.

NOV. 1. '60 DESIGN 19, DWG. 4

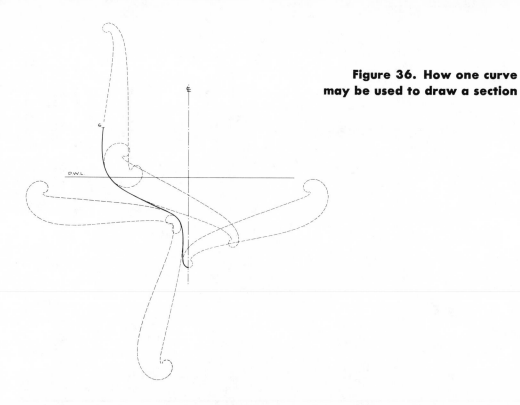

**Figure 36. How one curve
may be used to draw a section**

be well versed in the dimensions of the human form and fixed measurements of various familiar household objects, such as: a dining room chair, 17″ high; a dining room table, 30″ high; kitchen dresser, 37″ high; stairs, ladders, doors, beds, etc., etc. Keep a folding six-foot rule handy to check the actual dimensions you are going to use and, after a little experience, one gets to be an expert. A compartment door narrower than 21″ is not wide enough. More than 12″ spacing for the steps of a ladder is too great. A hatch 18″ x 18″ is the minimum size for a person to squeeze through, etc., etc.

Dimensions of the Human Figure. Boats should be designed around people, so people sizes are important.

A yacht designer, like an architect, deals with spaces for people, hence the illustration "Dimensions of the Human Figure" is one of the most useful pieces of data for him.

This illustration is an old one and shows a 5′9″-tall man. (Nowadays, I would say, Mister Average Man is much taller.) To change the dimensions shown proportionately to those of a taller man, use the following conversion factors:

Height of Man Shown	Multiply By	To Obtain
5′-9″	101.4%	5′-10″ man
5′-9″	102.8%	5′-11″ man
5′-9″	104.3%	6′-0″ man
5′-9″	105.9%	6′-1″ man
5′-9″	107.1%	6′-2″ man
5′-9″	108.7%	6′-3″ man
5′-9″	110.1%	6′-4″ man

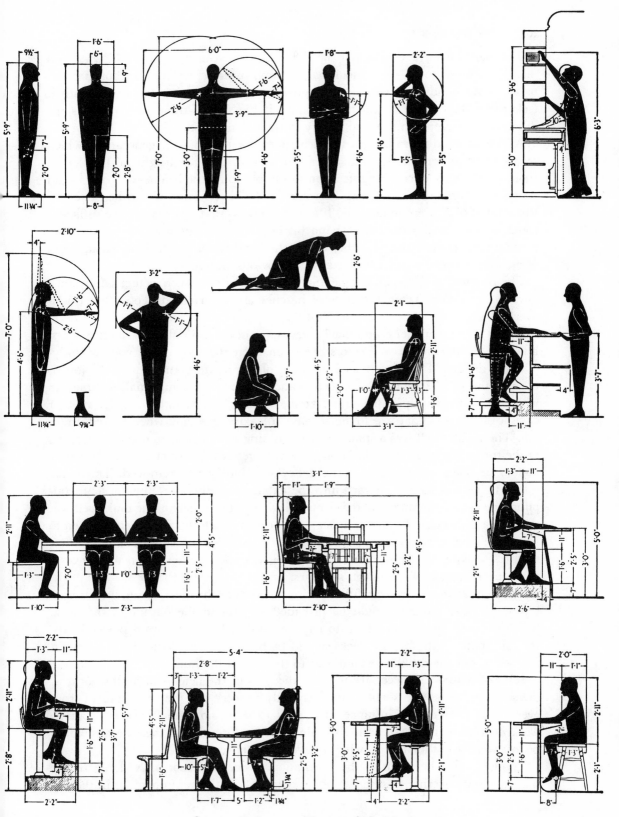

Scale of Human Figure 1/4" = 1'-0"

These dimensions are based on the average or normal adult. As clearances are minimum they should be increased when conditions will allow.

The most effective way to tell the difference between a passage 24″ wide and one 27″ wide is to set up a mock passageway, using screens or cardboard boxes or anything handy—then walk through it yourself, changing the width until it feels right. This effort is worthwhile. This is the sort of thing which makes the difference between comfort and misery in the finished boat.

Adequate head room is a must, particularly for the younger generation, which seems to be growing taller and taller. For a man 6′ 2″ in height, 6′ 1½″ head room can be very uncomfortable! Constantly bumping the beams with one's head brings this home the hard way! Therefore, 5′ 10″ head room would be better for this man, if 6′ 3″ were impossible. If a person knows that he doesn't have sufficient room he will stoop, rather than bang his head continually, and will stand up in areas under hatches and skylights where the head room is sufficient. Head room or clearance above stairs is important, for obvious reasons.

The removal of the main engine and other large items, such as fuel tanks, must always be foreseen when the sizes of hatches are determined. Too often this is overlooked!

Access to compartments and machinery is one of the most obvious requirements, but sad to say, some real horrors occur on even the most otherwise carefully-planned designs. The cursing and swearing of engine mechanics on repair jobs is not without good reason. I have seen brand-new boats, costing small fortunes, in which it is almost impossible to get at the stuffing box to tighten it. In another case, a brand-new boat was found to have a leaking gas tank when heeled under sail. The repair itself was a small matter—adding more solder to one or two rivets at the top of the tank. But what a job it was to get at those rivets! First, the galley had to be taken apart. Second, the galley sink piping was removed. Third, the main engine was moved forward into the cabin, after disconnecting the shaft coupling, the exhaust piping, and the electrical wiring. Then, fourth, the tank itself was slid forward through the engine space, lifted out through the main hatch, taken to the shop, and steamed free of gas fumes. The soldering job itself took only a few minutes. Taking the boat apart and putting it back together again took several days and hundreds of the owner's dollars.

The Deck Plan requires careful attention to produce the ideal, clean, uncluttered layout. A clear passage should be provided all around the outside of the deck, with no raised objects on which to trip or stub one's toe. Even on power boats, the minimum width for side decks should be fifteen inches. With anything less, it is wiser to put the deckhouse right out to the side of the hull.

Joiner Sections are necessary to show the builder the heights of berths, lockers, dresser tops, seats, and shelves, and generally to work out the arrangement from every aspect. Here, for instance, it is easy to show how small drawers can be worked in below the wash basin for toilet articles. Attention to these details would be lost were it not for the drawing of several joiner sections.

Thought must be given to the ventilation of enclosed spaces. A clause in the specifications covering this item is not enough. Show the vent openings in the top and bottom of the locker doors, and they will be built into the boat because the man building the doors will see the openings shown on the drawing. Some big yards will draw up every detail of joiner work in their own drafting department. See that they send the plans to the architect for his approval before starting construction.

The Machinery Arrangement is a drawing which for small boats may be incorporated in one of the other plans, such as the General Arrangement. For large, complicated vessels having all the comforts of home, the arrangement of machinery requires a great deal of thought. A separate drawing will be worth a great deal to ensure a good design. The main engine, the auxiliary generator, the exhaust piping, batteries, switchboard, fresh water pressure system, bilge and other pumps, valve manifold, refrigerator compressor, automatic pilot units, hot water heater, heat exchanger for fresh water cooling, fuel piping system, CO_2 fire extinguisher system, etc.—all these must be located so as not to interfere with one another. For example, the auxiliary generator should be located so that it may be started by hand cranking and should be equipped with a crank, for the time when all the batteries are dead and there is not even enough electricity to start this key piece of machinery.

Careful attention to the best layout for the main engine exhaust is too often forgotten, with the result that either salt water or fresh water from condensation runs back into the engine manifold, causing all kinds of trouble and expensive repairs. There should be a low point in the line just aft of the engine to collect any such undesired water. Have also a high trap against waves, such as a high loop in the exhaust line or a stand-up muffler. Take into consideration its location during the heeled condition of the boat—the stern wave builds up to a surprising height and is apt to enter the end of the exhaust when the vessel is sailing hard. Use a wooden plug on a lanyard or a valve in the end of the exhaust line, if you like, but don't forget to open it before starting the engine!

While we are thinking about the stern wave, let's consider the location of scuppers for a self-bailing cockpit. Don't put them at the after end of the cockpit, because the stern wave builds up to such a height that water will flood up through them. The forward end of the cockpit is the only place to locate them.

The Sail Plan is the basic drawing by which the designer judges the final appearance of his creation. It should be developed concurrently as the design progresses, to check the sheer line, the size of deckhouses, the location of deck erections, etc. In this respect, it is good practice to draw in the location of the helmsman's eye when he is standing or sitting. You must make sure he will have good visibility. A roomy deckhouse, first drawn on the Arrangement or Construction Plan at a large scale, may look all right, but, when drawn on the Sail Plan at its smaller scale, it may spoil the appearance of the entire boat. Check for appearance on the Sail Plan when drawings for such as these are being made.

Aspect ratio, or the ratio of the foot of the sail to its hoist or luff, now runs as high as one to three and one-half, but the average effective ratio seems to be about one to

Deck plan and outboard profile

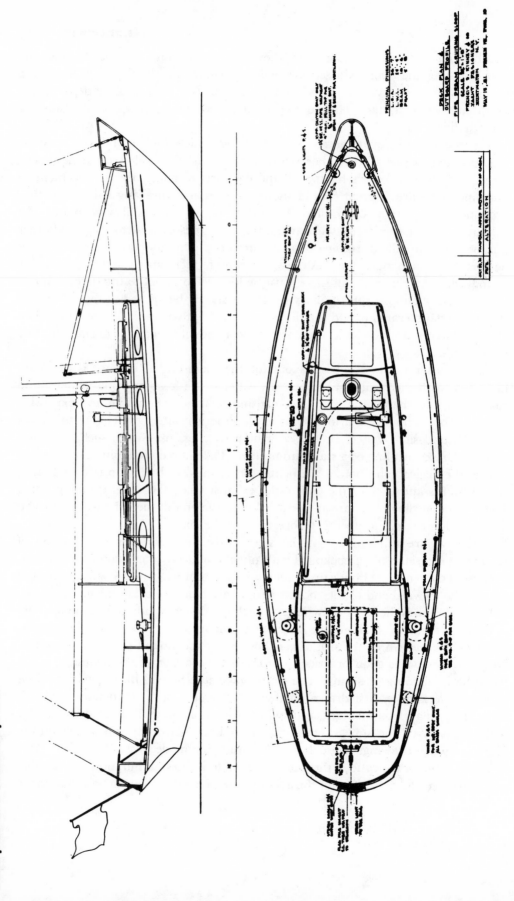

Inboard profile and arrangement plan

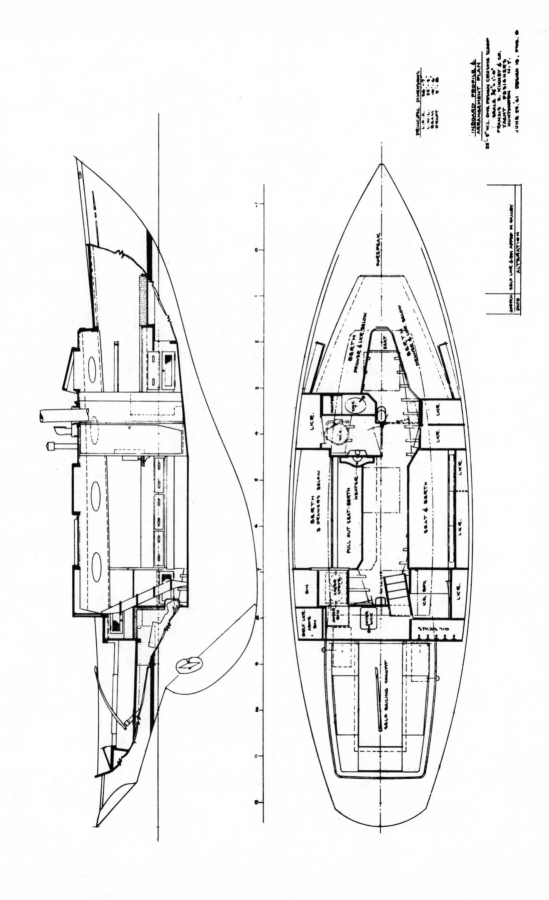

Joiner sections

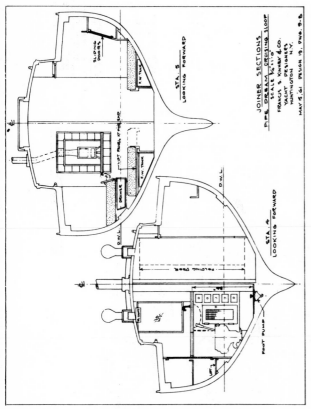

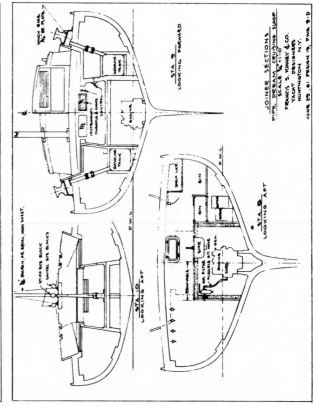

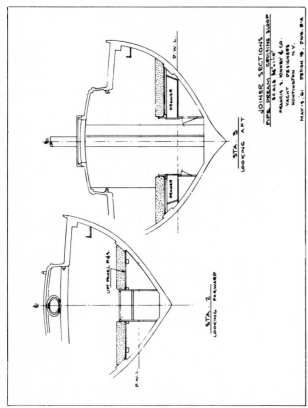

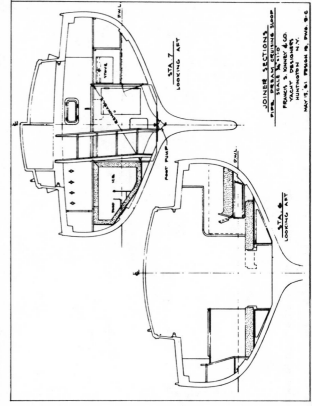

Sail plan

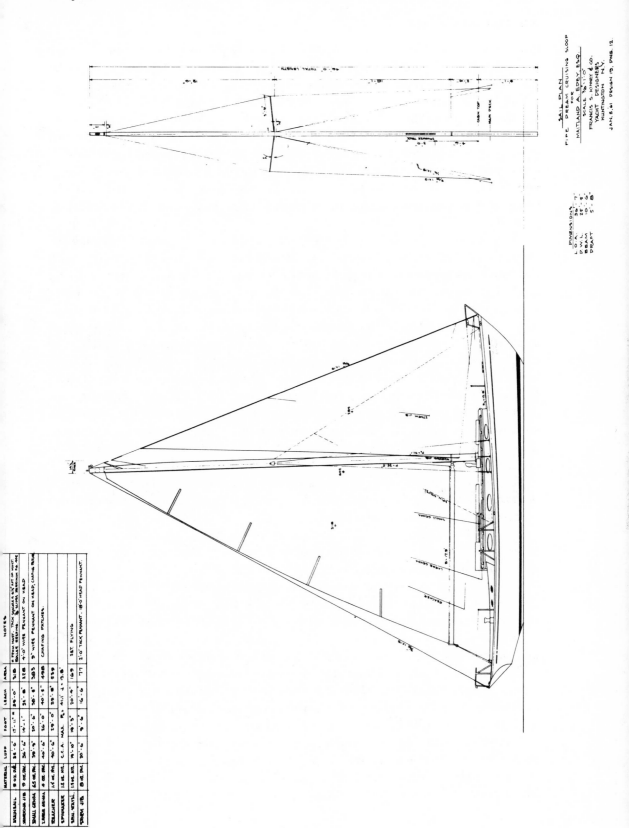

three. The length of battens in a mainsail is what determines the amount of roach or curvature in the leach of the sail. The longer the battens are, the greater the roach may be and, thus, the more area for given foot and hoist lengths.

Full-length battens are effective in light air and a ground swell. They prevent the airfoil shape of the sail from collapsing when the boat rolls. Also, they make reefing easier, if the reef points are located on a batten. The usual flapping and shaking of a sail when a boat comes about or lies at anchor into the wind is eliminated on a fully-battened sail. This should make a sail last longer, it would seem to me. On the other hand, full-length battens make a sail heavier, as well as being heavily penalized under the Cruising Club rule. (See ENDEAVOUR, page 71)

The masthead rig is now the most popular, and for good reason. By placing the jib stay at the masthead, the need for running back stays and jumper stays with their struts is eliminated. The permanent back stay does the work directly. Being able to go down wind with a huge spinnaker set from the masthead is another advantage. If you are in a boat with a seven-eighths fore-triangle rig, the spinnaker must be set close to the attachment of the jib stay at the mast and is that much smaller. How maddening it is, if you are aboard such a boat, to watch your competitors with a tremendous masthead spinnaker slide past on the down wind leg of the course! Needless to say, the same advantage applies on a reach. The boat with a masthead rig can carry a larger Genoa jib. Of course, the mast itself must be stouter to take the greater loads, but even so, it appears that the advantages more than outweigh the disadvantages of larger mast dimensions and extra weight. Aluminum masts are superior here to wood, in almost every respect. The exception is their greater cost.

The soundest ratio to work out from the Sail Plan and Lines Drawing is one of sail area to wetted surface area. This is a relationship of power to resistance and is important in comparing sailboats.

The standing rigging should be shown on the Sail Plan, giving wire diameters and type. For standing rigging with swaged terminal fittings, 1 x 19 stainless steel wire is now used almost exclusively.

It is important to have the spreaders cocked up at an angle of about 7° from the horizontal, so that the angle formed by the wire shroud is bisected by the spreader. A common sight on the water is the sailboat with its spreaders horizontal or, worse yet, drooping down a bit. This is a risky situation because the spreader may slide down easily. In fact, unless that outboard angle is bisected, the tendency of the spreader to slip increases. If the spreader collapses, the shroud it used to support becomes slack, and the mast breaks. Seizing with marline over tape makes a secure connection between wire shroud and spreader, holding the leeward spreader in place when a boat is sailed hard and the lee shrouds become slack.

A problem requiring forethought is sheet leads. One method to obtain the proper lead for jib sheets is done in the following manner. In plan view, come aft at a 10° angle from the center line, starting at the jib stay on deck. In profile, take a point 40% up the luff of the jib, and from here through the clew draw a straight line. Where this line intersects the 10° line on deck will be the spot from which the jib sheet should be led. (See Figure 37) Another method is to take a point in profile 50% up the luff of the jib and another point at the intersection of the luff and a perpendicular from it to the clew. Then from halfway between these two, draw a straight line through the clew to the deck. Some designers use a 12° line on deck and even 14° for a Genoa jib. For the ends of a main sheet traveler, an angle of 3° from the mast is used by one designer. Sheet travelers on a two-masted vessel can be treated generally as follows: The further aft, the flatter the sheets should be trimmed, because each sail tends to backwind the one aft of it when close hauled. Thus the jib sheet traveler could be laid out with a 10° angle on deck, the mainsheet, say, 5°, and the mizzen sheet secured directly on the center line without a traveler. In fact, leading the mizzen sheet to a wire bridle or from the top of a stern pulpit rail allows it to be trimmed even flatter—a desirable feature.

The sheet leads and the location of winches and cleats should be worked out using the Deck Plan in conjunction with the Sail Plan. Allow space for winch handles to turn a complete circle! If the vessel is to be a single hander, lead all sheets close to the helmsman's reach.

The topic of the balance of a sailboat is such a fascinating and all-engrossing subject to me that I have written a separate chapter about it.

Figure 37. Jib sheet lead

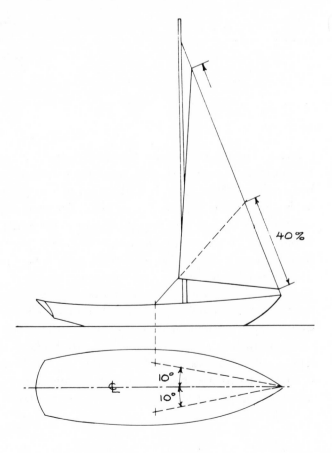

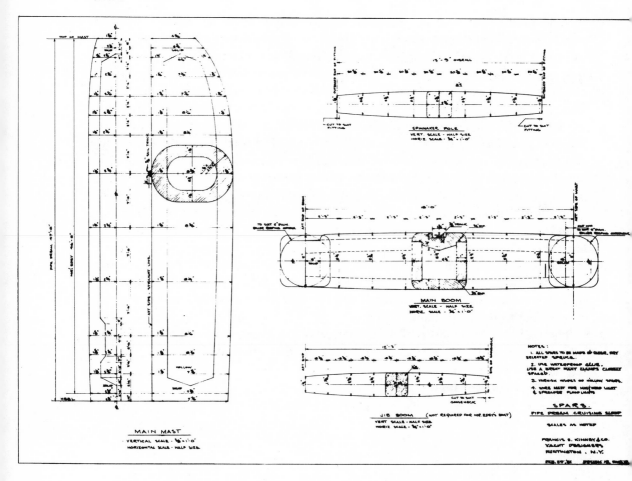

Spars. The least expensive type—after the solid spruce spar, which should not be considered (except for very small sizes, because of its excessive weight)—is the box-section, hollow spar. It is glued up of four pieces. Its corners can be rounded so that its section approaches an oval. The oval section mast offers less windage, but the box section is stiffer. A case in point is the spinnaker pole. Because it is a spar under pure compression only, it should have a square section with slightly-rounded edges. A circular section on a spinnaker pole makes no sense whatever. The sides of spars, where sail tracks are attached, should be straight. Thus, the after side of a mast and the top of a boom having sail track should be in a straight line. The track should be mounted on a spruce feather or block about ½″ high so as to clear various projections, such as the heads of screws and bolts.

When making a spar drawing, use two different scales, say ⅜″ = 1′ 0″ for the length, and a half-size one of 6″ = 1′ 0″ for the breadth. In this way, the drawing is foreshortened and more accurately dimensioned. The calculations required to arrive at the proper size for spars will be treated in a separate chapter.

The attachment of wire shrouds and stays to masts is now accomplished by the use of tangs, screws, and tube bolts. Each tang should be carefully designed to take the same load as the wire it secures, unless the wire is oversized to reduce stretching. It must be the proper width in way of the pin for the tensile strength of the material used. The bearing required in the wood is allotted between the proper diameter tube bolt and the proper number of screws. Various other devices, such as small ladder-type rungs and large washer-type rings recessed in the wood, have been used to increase the bearing area of a tang on a wooden mast. For the bearing surface of a screw, one third its diameter times its length is used. An example on how the tang size is calculated is given for the PIPE DREAM Cruising Sloop. We will use this design, with all its drawings and calculations, to illustrate how various problems such as this are worked out.

Detail at aft end of jib boom

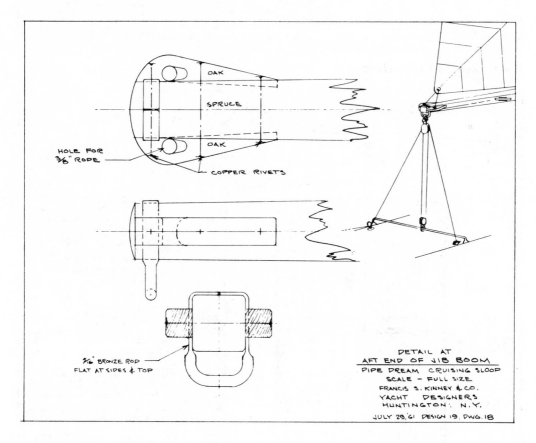

Masthead details

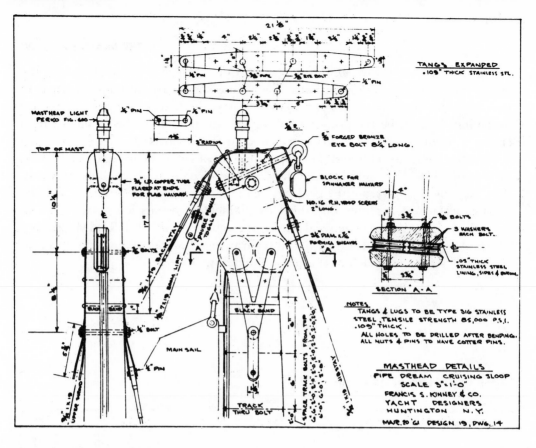

Mast tangs and spreaders

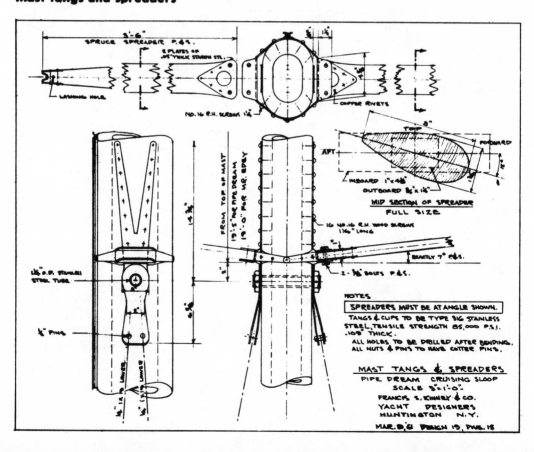

CHAPTER XX

SPECIFICATIONS

"Built out of so much chaos
Brought to Law ... "

When you consider the thousands of different items that go into the building of a yacht and the variety of materials and equipment needed to complete her, that line about "so much chaos" is indeed true. A good set of specifications can "police" this chaos and bring it to law.

The specifications must be complete, accurate, and correct. At the same time they should be brief. In practice, they are almost never any of these things.

There is one contract clause which covers a multitude of sins, and that is the one about omissions which goes something like this: "Omission from the plans or specifications, or both, of any items, which according to generally accepted practice are necessary for the proper operation of the yacht, shall not release the builder from supplying and installing such items." Just how a builder can be held to this legally is beyond me. The thing to do, of course, is to pick a builder by his reputation for integrity; to look over boats that he has constructed; and to satisfy oneself by talking to owners of his products.

With the thought that an example might be helpful, I have included a set of specifications for a 25' 5" water-line cruising sloop at the end of this chapter. The designer can simplify or elaborate on these specifications as he chooses, but I submit them as reasonable specifications for a medium-sized boat.

In general, if a definite size for an item is given, and it must be given somewhere in the design, it should only appear in one place and not be repeated in two or three places and again in the specifications. Sooner or later a change is made, and if the change needs to be made in each of several places, things really get fouled up!

It seems to me that about the best place for the size of scantlings or parts of the ship's structure is on the Midship Construction Section and just in that one place. On this drawing, for example, the note would read "planking ⅛" Honduras

Interior of PIPE DREAM Cruising Sloop, *SOUTHERLY*. *(Top)* Main cabin looking aft; *(middle)* forward cabin; *(bottom)* main cabin looking forward.

mahogany". In the specifications, the subject would be covered as follows: "Planking—as shown on plans." Now here in the specifications a long dissertation on the subject of planking could be set forth, covering details such as proper seasoning (air-dried for at least three years), maximum width of plank, spacing of butts, bedding for double planking, kind of glue and type of joint for strip planking, size and type of fastenings per plank per frame, whether the fastenings are to be counterbored and plugged, material for the plugs, plugs set in glue or white lead, grain of plugs running in same direction as parent member, etc., etc.

This sort of thing could go on for every item in the specifications, and you would end up with something 40 pages long. Let's face it, a good builder knows more about planking than the designer, anyway. And if he is not a good builder, no amount of writing in the specifications is going to give him the know-how. So it makes sense to be brief and just say, "Planking—as shown on plans."

On the other hand, a thorough description of how the boat will be painted is most appropriate for the specifications. So is a complete list of equipment and a lengthy paragraph on electrical grounding. Exact sizes of running rigging, blocks, cleats, winches, turnbuckles are better listed in the specifications than on the plans.

It is worth the time to have an index as well as a list of catalogues used, together with the addresses of the manufacturers. For example, there were 23 different catalogues used for the design of a 30-foot water-line auxiliary centerboard ketch, and these were listed at the beginning of the 14-page specifications. The index contained 98 items and formed a good check list to guard against omissions.

So, the perfect set of specifications (if such a thing could ever exist) would be written by many professionals, each an expert in his own field: a good sea lawyer; an expert on wooden boat building, or aluminum or fiberglass construction; a good piping man; an expert on ventilation; an expert on machinery and propellers; someone who really knows about painting; an electrical engineer; and an expert rigger and sailor. All these experts must have one thing in common—experience at sea in small boats.

For example, our expert electrical engineer may specify a superb switchboard with all the very best equipment. But if it is located directly beneath a hatch, beneath a porthole, or beneath a weather door, the entire electrical system may be shorted out by salt spray during a storm—the very time when it is needed most. And again, he may specify the very best grade of marine electrical wiring—but if he locates it in the bilge, alas! Anyone who has been to sea knows how easily a lot of water can get below and how high the bilge water can slosh up on the inside of the hull.

SPECIFICATIONS

Design No. 19

25′ 5″ D.W.L. PIPE DREAM CRUISING SLOOP

INDEX FOR SPECIFICATIONS DESIGN NO. 19

LIST OF CATALOGUES AND ADDRESSES USED IN THESE SPECIFICATIONS

Aeroquip Corp., Jackson, Mich.
Columbian Bronze Corp., Freeport, L.I., N.Y.
The Durkee Co., Inc., 29 South St., New York

The Edson Corp., 334 South Water St., New Bedford, Mass.
Elasto-Muffle-Elastomer Co., Vancouver, B.C.
Essex Machine Works Inc., Essex, Conn.
Federal Propellers, Grand Rapids   Mich.
Getty Marine Hardware Co., Philadelphia, Pa.
The Kraissl Co. Inc., 299 Williams Ave., Hackensack, N.J.
Manhattan Marine & Electric Co., 116 Chambers St., New York
Merriman Bros., 185 Amory St., Boston   Mass.
Murlin Mfg. Co., 200 Block S. Ambler St., Quakertown, Pa.

Perko-Perkins Marine Lamp & Hardware Co., 1943 Pitkin Ave., Brooklyn, N.Y.
Revere Supply Co. Inc., 30 Front St., New York
Rostand Mfg. Co., Milford, Conn.
Simpson-Lawrence Ltd., St. Andrews Square, Glasgow, C 1, Scotland
South Coast Co., Newport Blvd. at 23rd St., Newport Beach, Calif.
Stow-A-Way Ladder—The Crows Nest, 16 East 40 St., New York
Universal Engine Co., Oshkosh, Wis.
Whale Pump-Munster Sims & Co. Ltd., Imperial House, Donegall Square East, Belfast, Ireland
Whitehead Metal Products Co., 303 West 10 St., New York
Wilcox-Crittenden Division, North & Judd Mfg. Co., Middletown, Conn.

Dimensions L.O.A.   Approx. 36' 6"
            D.W.L.   Approx. 25' 5"
            Beam   Approx. 10' 6"
            Draft   Approx. 5' 8"

General Conditions—It is the intent and purpose of these specifications to cover all items for the construction of an economical yet sound type of auxiliary sloop, designed for minimum upkeep.

Workmanship—To be sound throughout. All members of the boat's structure shall fit together properly in accordance with good marine practice. All defective workmanship shall be replaced.

Materials—Of good quality as specified. The term "or equal" shall denote that an item of similar quality may be substituted. All equipment to be U.S. Coast Guard approved where required. Building of the boat shall take place under cover of a permanent roof. Before delivery the boat shall be tried under power and sail to the satisfaction of both Architect and Owner.

Items Furnished by Owner—The following items shall be furnished by the Owner and installed by the Builder:
  Tiller Fitting
  Hatch Fittings (hinges, cam strap locks, friction
    skylight openers)
  Swimming Ladder
  Sea Cocks
  F.W. Tanks
  Toilet
  Wash Basin and Pump
  Galley Sink and Pump
  Bilge Pump
  Engine and Instrument Panel
  Controls
  Muffler
  Propeller
  Shafting, Stern Bearing, Stuffing Box
  Gasoline Tanks
  Gasoline Valves, Filter, Flexible Fuel Line
  Chocks and Bronze Cleats
  Cowl Vents
  Blower, Ignition and Blower Switch
  Lifeline Wire, Turnbuckles, Pelican Hook
  Compass
  Stove
  Anchor
  Fire Extinguishers
  Miscellaneous Equipment is listed on page 221
  W.T. Electric Outlets, Electric Wiring and
    Fuse Panel
  Lights as listed on page 221
  Wire for Standing Rigging
  Turnbuckles
  All Items on Block and Running Rigging List
    (except wooden cleats)
  Winches
  Everdur Bronze Fastenings

Insurance—During construction the boat shall be insured for account of Owner & Builder, the insurance being furnished by the Owner. To commence with the arrival and storage of the first items of material or equipment, increasing in value with progress of construction until delivery of boat, copy of said policy to be sent to the Builder.

Alterations—Before any changes from the plans or specifications are made they shall be discussed with the Architect and approved by him.

Cleaning—Before painting, and again before launching, all sawdust, shavings, dirt, loose nails or screws are to be cleaned out of bilge. Use of a vacuum cleaner is recommended.

Cradle—Builder to provide temporary wooden cradle for shipment of boat.

Cover—Builder to provide suitable canvas cover to protect boat during shipment, and to be used later as a winter cover by Owner.

Drawings—Drawing #1, the Preliminary Sketch showing Sail Plan, Arrangement Plan, and Midship Construction Section, together with these specifications, both dated May 25, 1960, are the basis on which the Builder is to quote a fixed price. In addition, the Architect shall furnish the following working drawings:
  Lines, Body Plan, and Offsets.
  Construction Profile and Deck Plan.
  Inboard Profile and Arrangement Plan.
  Joiner Sections.
  Spars.
  Mast Details, Tangs, Spreaders.
  Other Miscellaneous Details as required.
Alternate layouts for 4, 5, and 6 berths to suit individual owner's requirements. All drawings are the property of the Architect.

Laying Down—Lines to be laid down and faired full size. Special attention to fairness of sheer line. Particular care taken to eliminate any bumps or unsightly hollows throughout. Matching parts shall be laid down full size to insure proper fit.

Access to Compartments—Every part of the boat shall be accessible for cleaning, painting or repairs, especially in way of engine and stuffing box.

Safety Requirements—The Builder shall follow the standards of the National Fire Protection Association, Booklet No. 302 (60 Batterymarch St., Boston 10, Mass.) and the standards and recommended practices of the Yacht Safety Bureau, 21 West St., New York 6, N.Y.

Draft Marks—At the bow and stern a round-head screw shall be located at the D.W.L. and another set at a W.L. 6" above the D.W.L.

HULL CONSTRUCTION

Materials—All wood to be quartersawn, dressed on all sides, seasoned (air-dried for 3 years, if possible), and free of knots, sap pockets, checks and other defects. A moisture content of 12% is recommended. (Kiln dried lumber is not approved.)

  If the Builder has preference for certain items he considers equivalent to those specified, he must list each request for substitution and be prepared to submit samples.

  Any substitutions of wood must be of equal strength, weight and hardness, and approved by the Architect.
  Mahogany—Best quality Honduras, African, or
               Philippine
  Cedar   —Alaskan Yellow Cedar
  Oak   —White Oak (unseasoned, for frames)

Fir   —Rocky Mountain Douglas Fir
Teak   —Best quality from Burma
Spruce   —Sitka Spruce
Plywood   —Best grade, waterproof exterior type of fir, faced with mahogany or plastic (Harborite) on exposed or visible surfaces; or light-colored wood as selected for interior finish, or all plys of mahogany. All plys to be same thickness—3 plys up to ⅜″ and 5 plys ⅜″ to ¾″ thickness.

Glue—Waterproof Weldwood or Elmer's waterproof. To be applied in strict accordance with manufacturer's instructions.

Galvanizing—of steel shall be of the hot dip process after fabrication. Welds shall be chipped clean and holes drilled with allowance for thickness of zinc before galvanizing.

Bronze—castings to be manganese bronze, Tobin bronze for rudder stock and ballast keel bolts, Silicon (Everdur) bronze elsewhere, as specified.

Aluminum—corrosion-resisting alloy, Alcoa 5154, or equal.

Fastenings—(Furnished by Owner, installed by Builder) To be Everdur bronze throughout. See Fastening Schedule for sizes.

Welding—By qualified skilled welders. Strength of welded joints to be 100% strength of surrounding metal. A proper sequence of welding shall be followed to avoid distortion.

Ballast—Lead keel casting of about 5,500 lbs. to have 4% antimony (by volume) and 2 lbs. of caustic soda per ton added, to facilitate skimming off impurities. Provide 200 lbs. of lead in pigs of 20 lbs. to fit bilge for inside trimming ballast.

Keel Backbone—White oak. Allow 1¾″ minimum back rabbet for planking.

Stop Waters—White pine dowels fitted at joints in keel backbone to prevent these joints from leaking.

Mast Step—Galvanized steel weldment of ⅛″ plate, forming an I-beam about 3′ long and incorporating about 4 steel floors.

Bilge Stringers—As shown, tapered at ends. Locate top on Diagonal A.

Clamp—As shown, tapered at ends.

Limber Holes—1″ x 1″ minimum size in floor timbers, to allow water to run entirely from all points in hull to low point of bilge.

Frames—As shown on plans.

Floors—As shown on plans.

Planking and Butt Blocks—Planking to be in as long lengths as possible. No plank to be wider than 5″. Material and thickness of planking, as shown on plans. Single planking to be caulked with cotton. Double planking to be set in heavy orange shellac.

Butts to be well spaced throughout. Butts of inner planking to be on frames. Butts of outer planking and single planking to be through-bolted to ⅝″ thick oak butt blocks, which shall be beveled on their inboard edges and kept clear of frames, for drainage.

Transom—Double planked. Outer planking ⅝″ wood, same as topsides, set in heavy orange shellac over ¼″ plywood curved to a radius as shown.

Joint between planking and transom to be mitered. Fashion piece bounding transom to be oak.

Rudder—Plywood covered with fiberglass and tapered to a sharp trailing edge. Rudder stock 1⅝″ diameter Tobin bronze with keyway in head to take tiller fitting. Straps of ³⁄₁₆″ bronze, as shown, to be welded to rudder stock and riveted to rudder. Rudder heel fitting to be removable of cast manganese bronze, as shown. Rudder tube to be red brass pipe with welded flange plates fastened to keel and cockpit sole.

Tiller—Ash, as shown. Tiller fitting—Merriman Fig. 483, size 3, with keyway. (Tiller fitting furnished by Owner, installed by Builder.)

Chain Plates—¼″ x 1½″ Silicon bronze (Everdur) flat bars carefully bent to line up with rigging and fastened as per plans. To have welded bronze lug fitted tightly under clamp.

Ceiling—To be plywood in way of berths and lockers, to prevent bilge water from splashing up on bedding or clothing. Outside of ceiling to be **painted with preservative (page 221) before fastening** in place. To be fastened with oval-head screws so as to be removable.

Bulkheads—To be plywood, as specified under "Materials" (page 218) and "Joiner Work" (below). Structural bulkheads ⅝″ thick. Joiner partitions ⅜″ thick. Small shelves ¼″ thick. Butts and seams to be backed with plywood of same thickness, through-fastened and glued.

Decks—½″ plywood, as specified under "Materials" (page 218), covered with fiberglass laid in strict accordance with manufacturer's instructions. Avoid the use of oil-based compounds to insure adhesion. Provide a roughened fiberglass surface for nonskid paint. Butts and seams in plywood to be located at option of Builder and to be through-fastened and glued to plywood of same thickness. Deck blocking of ¾″ oak under all deck fittings as per plans.

Deck Beams—Laminated spruce as shown on plans. Ends of beams to be through-bolted to heads of frames. Headers to be oak as shown.

Cabin Sole—⅝″ teak resting on floor timbers and left bare. To be made up in removable sections so that entire bilge is accessible. Finger holes for lifting.

Cockpit Sole—1″ thick quartersawn teak laid in narrow planks. Seams to be caulked with cotton and filled with Woolsey's rubber deck seam compound. Surface to be left bare.

Engine Beds—Oak as shown. Securely fastened to frames and floors to make a firm foundation.

Toe Rail—As shown on plans.

JOINER WORK

General—All deck joiner work to be teak. To have well-rounded corners to prevent injury to crew. Interior joiner work finish to be a light-colored wood, such as ash, oak, prima vera, knotty pine, or as selected from samples suggested by Builder.

Deckhouse—Size and material of sides and corner

posts as shown. Fixed portlights of $\frac{3}{16}''$ plate glass to be installed as shown, using lead quarter-round beading as a seal.

Doors—Toilet room and forward cabin doors to be house-type $1\frac{3}{8}''$ thick with hollow core and light-colored wood-faced plywood surfaces. Other locker doors to be plywood with vent openings top and bottom. Bronze hardware to be used as manufactured by Getty, or equal.

Drawers—Type that must be lifted $\frac{3}{16}''$ to open. Allow ample clearance for swelling. Slots for four fingers instead of handles.

Hatches—(Hatch fittings consisting of hinges, cam strap locks, friction skylight openers to be furnished by Owner, installed by Builder.)

Forward Hatch—Simple box type with $\frac{5}{8}''$ thick Plexiglass top and loose pin hinges at forward and after ends. Two Rostand No. 2318 cam strap locks. Two Simpson-Lawrence No. 1886, size 2, friction skylight openers.

Midship Hatch—Simple box type, similar to forward hatch with same fittings.

Main Companion Hatch—Sliding type as shown with $\frac{5}{8}''$ plywood top, fiberglass covered, brass-faced runners and $\frac{3}{16}''$ aluminum plate hood. Hasp with combination padlock to be installed. Drop slide with louvre, to close companionway. To be large enough to permit removal of main engine.

Cockpit Seat Hatches—To be slightly raised type with brass flat bar coaming. Top to be plywood, fiberglass covered; to have bounding brass angle set in flush and containing rubber gasket. To have two hinges, one cam strap lock and one friction skylight opener on each.

Ladders—Main companion ladder to have teak treads left bare. Swimming & Boarding Ladder—(Furnished and installed by Owner.) Stow-A-Way folding aluminum ladder with brackets, for starboard side, set in flush.

Cockpit—Seats to be plywood, fiberglass covered, similar to those on main deck. Sides to be plywood faced with mahogany.

Mirror—$\frac{1}{4}''$ plate glass. In wood frame over wash basin.

Table—Folding mahogany top and removable legs, to store in toilet room.

Handrails—To be located on house top as shown, and through-bolted to every other beam.

Galley—Shelves, lockers, bins, dresser as shown. Dresser tops to be sheathed with stainless steel. Galley sink flush, covered to match.

Ice Box—To be lined with stainless steel watertight removable lining. 2'' thick Styrofoam insulation all around. 3 layers of tar paper between stainless steel and insulation. $\frac{1}{2}''$ copper tube drain to accessible faucet—high enough to allow for large container below. Top to be sheathed to match galley dresser top and to have flush lifting handle—Wilcox Fig. 615.

Garbage Container—To be made of stainless steel with handle. Located on back of door under galley sink. To be removable.

Soundproofing—In engine compartment all surfaces in way of engine, including underside of bridge deck, underside of cockpit sole, and vertical surfaces, except for sides of hull, shall be insulated with 2'' fiberglass—Owens-Corning Type PF 334—and sheathed with $\frac{1}{8}''$ perforated masonite (close perforations) with rough side showing.

PLUMBING

Sea Cocks—(Furnished by Owner, installed by Builder.) To be provided in an accessible location for all through hull openings. To be Wilcox, or equal, bronze full-way type. Through hull fittings to have bronze plate set in flush on outside of planking. Neoprene hose with stainless steel hose clamps to be used.

Fresh Water Tanks—(Furnished by Owner, installed by Builder.) 3 tanks required of Monel (approx. 50 gal. total capacity) as follows:

One tank under port extension transom, of about 15 gal. capacity, made of .043'' Monel and with 3 transverse baffle plates (shaped to fit space available).

One tank under starboard settee berth, of about 20 gal. capacity, made of .043'' Monel and with 2 transverse baffle plates (shaped to fit space available).

One tank under forward berths, of about 15 gal. capacity, made of .043'' Monel with one longitudinal and one transverse baffle (shaped to fit space available).

Tests—Each F.W. tank to be tested to a head of water of 5 ft.; any leaks found, to be fixed before installation.

Fresh Water Piping—To be copper tubing, $\frac{1}{2}''$ supply lines, with shut-off valve at each tank; $\frac{3}{8}''$ vent lines for tanks with gooseneck high under deck. Tank fills to be $1\frac{1}{2}''$ with neoprene hose connection at deck. Each tank to have separate fill to deck. Deck fill plates to be marked "water." Install sounding plug in accessible location over deepest part of each tank. Provide marked measuring stick for each tank. All piping to be fitted with brass unions laid out for easy winter drainage.

Toilet—(Furnished by Owner, installed by Builder.) Wilcox "Imperial" to be installed as shown. Locate intake as close to keel as possible. Discharge through vented loop—Wilcox Fig. 1548, on bulkhead (15'' above D.W.L.). Neoprene hose may be used with stainless steel hose clamps. Sea cocks required.

Toilet Room Fixtures—Soap dish, tooth brush and glass holder, paper holder, towel bars to be selected. Wooden medicine cabinet to be built as required.

Wash Basin and Pump—(Furnished by Owner, installed by Builder.) Legion Model S 135 U stainless steel oval bowl installed flush in dresser top as shown. F.W. supply pump to be Rostand foot pump. Supply line to have shut-off valve accessibly located. To discharge directly overboard through neoprene hose and sea cock.

Galley Sink and Pump—(Furnished by Owner, installed by Builder.) Perko Fig. 356, size 2, stainless steel, with Fig. 357 cup strainer. F.W. supply pump to be Rostand foot pump. Supply line to have shut-off valve accessibly located. To discharge directly overboard through neoprene hose and sea cock.

Scuppers—Toe rail to have 4 openings each side as shown. Cockpit to have 1¼″ I.D. neoprene hose with flush bronze or copper cockpit fittings and sea cocks; 2 required as shown.

Bilge Pump—(Furnished by Owner, installed by Builder.) Whale 2½″ nonchoke pump to be installed in bridge deck. Strainer on suction at low point. To discharge through nonsiphon-vented loop as high as possible, and through nondrip hull fitting in transom next to exhaust outlet.

MACHINERY

Engine—(Furnished by Owner, installed by Builder.) Universal Aqua-Pak Atomic Four Model UJ–VD, 4-cylinder gasoline engine (30 H.P. at 3500 R.P.M.) with 1.67 to 1 reduction gear, 12 volt starting and ignition.

Cooling Water Piping—Sea cock, zinc pencil (Chrysler Marine) on ½″ plug in tee pipe fitting; neoprene hose with stainless steel hose clamps required in raw water line.

Instrument Panel—(Furnished by Owner, installed by Builder.) Standard panel furnished with engine, mounted out of weather in cabin, as directed, visible to helmsman. To include oil pressure gauge and ammeter; replace key ignition switch with watertight combination ignition-blower switch, Perko Fig. 149.

Controls—(Furnished by Owner, installed by Builder.) Choke and throttle—simple push-pull cable type, mounted near helmsman. Reverse lever to be 12″ handle Columbian Fig. 440 C, or equal, mounted on starboard side of cockpit, with required mechanical control linkage parts, Columbian, or equal.

Exhaust—(Muffler furnished by Owner, installed by Builder.) Copper tube water jacket section—inside tube 1¼″ I.D. x .109″ wall, outside tube 2″ I.D. x .109″ wall—to have low point aft of engine, to trap condensation with drain plugs for inner and outer tube. To be made up in sections with flanged connections for easy removal. High point under afterdeck as shown. Water to enter exhaust line on downward slope just ahead of muffler. Muffler to be neoprene Elasto Muffle, located near transom. Short tail pipe of red brass to extend 1″ beyond transom to act as a drip lip. Entire exhaust line to be securely held in place with suitable rubber-lined straps.

Propeller—(Furnished by Owner, installed by Builder.) Federal Tru-Pitch, 2-bladed, 15″ diam. x 9″ pitch. (Check rotation of engine reduction gear for right-hand or left-hand propeller with Architect before ordering.)

Shafting—(Furnished by Owner, installed by Builder.) ⅞″ diam. Monel with standard taper for propeller. Stern bearing—Essex for auxiliaries with Cutless Rubber bearing. Stern tube—lead pipe flanged out at each end. Stuffing box—Columbian Fig. 160.

Gasoline Tanks—(Furnished by Owner, installed by Builder.) 2 stock Aquamaid, or equal, Monel rectangular tanks, 12″ x 12″ x 26″. Each has a 14-gal. capacity, with one transverse baffle; total 28 gals. To be mounted under cockpit as low as possible, port and starboard.

Gasoline Piping, Valves and Filter—(Furnished by Owner, installed by Builder.) Kerotest diaphragm packless valve required at each tank, with reach rod to accessible location, if necessary. Filter to be galvanized duplex-type Kraissl Class 72. Piping of Aeroquip No. 1502 flexible oiltight hose required between tanks, filter and engine. Tank fills to be 1½″, to have neoprene hose connections just below deck, with 2 stainless steel hose clamps at each connection. Fill plates to be marked "GAS." Provide marked measuring stick for sounding tank through fill pipe. Vents to be ¼″ copper tubing with gooseneck to atmosphere. (See Safety Requirements, page 217.)

Drip Pan—Copper oiltight pan mounted under engine as shown, to extend under carburetor.

EQUIPMENT

General—Suitable bedding compound—Dolphinite, or equal—to be applied under all deck fittings to prevent leaks.

Chocks and Cleats—(Furnished by Owner, installed by Builder.) 1 pr. Skene bulwark chocks, Perko Fig. 752, located P & S at bow, to be brazed to a common bronze plate. 1 pr. closed chocks in rail amidships, 1 pr. Skene stern chocks, Perko Fig. 161, size 11, located P & S on top of stern rail. Edges of all chocks to be well rounded to prevent chafing rope.

Two 12″ cleats, Wilcox 4020, forward, through-bolted to oak backing block below and with a ⅛″ common bronze plate above. Two 8″ similar cleats on afterdeck. (All other cleats mentioned in Block & Rigging List, page 222.)

Ventilators—(Cowl vents furnished by Owner, installed by Builder.) 2 cowl vents, cast aluminum Moyle pattern, 3″ size, as manufactured by Paul Luke, East Boothbay, Maine, to be mounted on Dorade-type watertrap vent boxes, P & S on house top as shown.

Louvres required on after face of cockpit, on drop slides, and on locker doors, top and bottom.

Blower—(Blower furnished by Owner, installed by Builder.) One 4″ Manhattan Fig. T 703, 12-volt 300 CFM, to be mounted high under bridge deck, to draw air through a duct from low point of drip pan and discharge through large-size clamshell vent on top of house. Use combination blower-ignition switch on instrument panel.

Life Rail—(Wire, turnbuckles, pelican hook furnished by Owner, installed by Builder.) Single lifeline of white plastic covered ¼″ 7 x 7 stainless steel wire running from bow pulpit to stern pulpit, with 5⁄16″ turnbuckles. Stanchions to be 1″ O.D. x .083″ wall Monel or stainless tube, with cast bronze heads with eyes, and bases with ears, through-bolted to oak backing blocks. Gangway opening starboard side, with pelican hooks and eyes for wire, braces for stanchions. Bow and stern pulpits to be weldments of same, tubing as stanchions with brackets for running lights and stern light. Bow pulpit to have eye for anchor line snatch block.

Compass—(Furnished by Owner.) Wilfred O. White & Sons—Sailboat Corsair W–102, or equal. To have top-lighting light 12 V bulb and W.T. electric outlet. Compass to be mounted on wooden removable pedestal on bridge deck.

All items within a 4-ft. radius of the compass are to be nonmagnetic, and all electrical wiring within this radius, to be twisted.

Stove—(Furnished by Owner, installed by Builder.) Shipmate 2-burner pressure alcohol stove, mounted in gimbals, Manhattan Fig. T 1843. Insulate surrounding woodwork with asbestos sheathed with stainless steel; allow ¼″ between asbestos and woodwork. Sheathing to be oiltight pan under stove, to retain spilled alcohol, with lip.

Mattresses—Urethane foam, covered with material selected by Owner. To be 6″ thick on built-in berths, 4½″ thick on extension transom and port settee berth. Covers to have zippers for easy removal.

Anchor—(Furnished by Owner.) One 22-lb. Danforth Standard.

Anchor Line—¾″ spun nylon, 150 ft. long, with a 4-ft. length of ⅜″ galvanized chain with shackle.

Fire Extinguishers—(Furnished by Owner.) One 4-lb. Ansul dry chemical type; one 5-lb. CO_2 portable extinguisher for galley.

Miscellaneous Equipment—(Furnished and installed by Owner.)

Life preservers—5 kapok-filled orange U.S.C.G.-approved, Revere Fig. 4101.

Foghorns—1 large-size Guest Products, or equal, with 3 spare cans of Freon; 1 brass mouth-type.

Screens—mosquito netting—to fit all hatch openings.

Docking lines—two 35-ft. and two 50-ft. lengths of ⅝″ Manila rope.

Dinghy—as selected by Owner; maximum size for stowage on deck, 8′ 7″.

Flag staffs—2 spruce poles 3 ft. long, with revolving wires to take 12″ flags. Pole at stern 4′ 6″ for 24″ x 36″ ensign; stand-up socket.

Boat hook—10-ft. spruce pole shaped to have a pear section to indicate direction of hook; bronze ball-pointed hook.

Fenders—4—Durkee Fig. 5667—4″ x 24″, or equal.

Bell—6″ lightweight pattern.

Lead line—4 lb. lead with marked line.

Navigational equipment—clock, barometer, charts, protractors, taffrail log, binoculars, parallel rule.

Tools—to include wrench to tighten stuffing box.

Cooking Utensils, Cutlery, China, Glassware.

Sails—Sail Covers, Sail Stops, Awning.

Blankets, Linen, Pillows.

PAINTING

Preservative Treatment—3 coats of a solution of pentachloriphenol, such as Wood Life, Chemi-Seal, or equal, to be applied to all wood surfaces.

Bottom—2 coats antifouling paint as selected.

Boot Top—Check with Architect for final location; 3 coats enamel, color as selected.

Topsides and Transom—2 coats flat, 2 coats semi-gloss, color as selected.

Name and Port—Name painted on transom in 3″ letters, in contrasting color; name of hailing port below in 2″ letters.

Spars—If painted, 2 coats flat, 2 coats semigloss.

Bilge—2 coats red lead.

Below Decks—2 coats flat, 2 coats enamel on overhead surfaces. Bulkheads, where visible in quarters, to be light-colored wood as selected, which shall be hand rubbed and lacquered to produce a dull or satin finish.

Bright Work—Toe rail, hatches, handrails, cabin sides, interior trim to have 5 coats of Interlux spar varnish.

Cove Stripe—To be carved out and gilded. Arrow design as per Sail Plan.

ELECTRICAL

General—12-volt D.C. 2-wire ungrounded system, powered by standard 12-volt generator supplied with engine and storage batteries listed below.

Batteries—Two, required to be Exide Sure-Start 2 SM, or equal (rated 50 AH at 20 hrs.), about 11″ x 7″ x 10″ high and weighing 42 lbs. each. One to be used for starting and lighting, the other kept as a spare, through the use of a single-pole triple-throw vapor-proof switch—Durkee Fig. 4206—which also will serve as a master switch to disconnect all power and for the operation of both batteries in parallel.

Batteries to be mounted in a fiberglass-lined wooden box with vented cover for protection, to be located under seat in forward cabin.

Wiring—Stranded copper wire insulated with neoprene—Simplex Tirex No. 14, or equal. Black for positive, white for negative. Mast wires, smaller.

Switchboard—Wires to enter bottom with drip loops. All units to be accessible for service. Voltmeter and switch. Master transfer switch as described under "Batteries." Toggle switches. Phenolic nameplates. Rheostat for compass light.

Outlets—(Furnished by Owner, installed by Builder.) W.T. outlets in cockpit, one for portable searchlight, one for compass light, to be Perko Fig. 477. Outlet in toilet room (on mirror light) for electric razor.

Light List—(Furnished by Owner, installed by Builder.)

2 side lights—Perko Fig. 910 on bow pulpit rail.

1 bow light—Perko Fig. 911 on mast 9′ above deck.

1 stern light—Perko Fig. 912 on stern pulpit rail.

1 masthead light—Perko Fig. 600 at main masthead.

2 spreader floodlights—Perko Fig. 254 at main spreaders.

6 bracket lights—Perko Fig. 450 with shades.

1 mirror light—Murlin No. 906 with outlet.

1 portable spotlight—Wilcox Fig. 8 with 15′ of cable and plug to suit W.T. sockets.

1 anchor light—Wilcox Fig. 21-A, or equal, oil burning.

Grounding—For lightning protection, all chain plates, jibstay fitting and backstay fitting, to be grounded to ballast keel bolts with $\frac{3}{8}''$ copper tubing flattened at ends.

Electrical System Ground—To minimize electrolysis due to electric leaks and for personnel protection, an electrical ground shall be installed, consisting of a No. 6 wire connected to the ballast keel bolts. Where located close to lightning grounds the two systems should be cross-connected. The following shall be connected to this ground:

Propulsion and auxiliary engines.
Large metallic enclosures of all electrical apparatus, motors, pumps, compressors, etc.
Fuel tanks. Rubber hose sections in the fill pipe shall be bridged by belden braid jumpers.
All through hull fittings, such as sea cocks.
Ground terminals on electronic units.

SPARS AND STANDING RIGGING

Mast and Boom—Hollow box-type section with well-rounded corners, as per plans, of clear spruce glued together. Scarphs to have a ratio of 12 : 1 length to thickness. Main mast to be wired inside for mast-head light, bow light, and spreader floodlights. $\frac{1}{2}''$ spruce feather required under sail track on mast. Mast to have tangs and spreader clips of bronze as per detail plans. Spreaders of spruce to be streamlined as shown.

Boom to have furling hooks—Merriman Fig. 519—and eyes—Fig. 520—with $\frac{1}{4}''$ shock cord all set in flush for roller reefing. (Furnished by Owner, installed by Builder.)

Spinnaker Pole—Hollow square section of spruce as shown.

Sail Track and Slides—$\frac{7}{8}''$ Merriman Fig. 406 for mast and main boom. Joints to be brazed together and filed smooth. Through-bolts in way of head of sail when fully hoisted and in reefed positions. Track gate required Merriman Fig. 548, mounted above furled mainsail. Slides on luff and foot to be Merriman Fig. 405 (furnished by Sailmaker).

Boom Crutch—Main boom to be held up by single wooden boom crutch to match deckhouse. Bronze flat bar sockets at forward end of cockpit to take boom crutch.

Standing Rigging—(Wire furnished by Owner, installed by Builder.) 1 x 19 stainless steel wire with swaged Truloc fittings, sizes as per plans.

Turnbuckle List—(Furnished by Owner, installed by Builder.) Subject to development. Check with Architect before ordering. All toggles to be machined from solid stock.

Jibstay—one $\frac{1}{2}''$ turnbuckle—Merriman Fig. 378—with toggle.
Main lowers—four $\frac{1}{2}''$ turnbuckles—Merriman Fig. 378—with toggles.
Main Uppers—two $\frac{1}{2}''$ turnbuckles—Merriman Fig. 378—with toggles.
Main Permanent Backstay—one $\frac{7}{16}''$ turnbuckle—Merriman Fig. 377L—with toggle.

BLOCK AND RUNNING RIGGING LIST

(All items, except for wooden cleats, to be furnished by Owner, installed by Builder.)

All blocks to be rubber shelled, roller bushed, unless otherwise noted. All fittings to be through-bolted.

Merriman Fig. numbers = Merr. South Coast Fig. numbers = S.C.

Winch List—(Furnished by Owner, installed by Builder.)
Jib Halyard—1 Merr. 395 No. 2 with handle and holder.
Main Halyard—1 Merr. 545 B, size 2, with handle and holder.
Genoa Jib Sheets—2 Merr. 397 No. 5, mounted on bases on cockpit coaming.

Main Sheet—$\frac{3}{8}''$ dacron, 3″ blocks.
1 S.C. 106 double on boom outhaul fitting.
1 S.C. 119 stiff eye singles on deck at centerline.
2 S.C. 118 swivel eye single lead blocks P & S.
2 6″ wooden cleats for double-ended sheet.

Working Jib Sheet—$\frac{3}{8}''$ dacron, 3″ blocks.
1 S.C. 106 double front shackle on boom bale.
1 S.C. 100 on traveler.
1 Merr. 416 #1 eye plate.
1 Merr. 442 $\frac{3}{8}''$ rod traveler, 4′ 6″ long.
1 S.C. 118 swivel-eye single lead block.
1 6″ wooden cleat.

Genoa Jib Sheets—$\frac{1}{2}''$ dacron with 2 Merr. 391 #3 stiff snap shackles.
2 Merr. 477 G Genoa Tee tracks, $1\frac{1}{4}''$ x $\frac{3}{16}''$ x 8 ft. long.
4 Merr. 477 F track eye slides.
4 S.C. 108 3″ snatch blocks.
2 8″ wooden cleats.
2 Merr. 655 latching cheek snatch blocks for $\frac{1}{2}''$ rope.

Storm Jib Sheets—$\frac{1}{2}''$ dacron tied in clew.
2 S.C. 120 D 4″ wide mortise blocks, with screw eye deck plates with screw plugs.

Main Halyard—$\frac{7}{32}''$ diam. 7 x 19 stainless steel wire to reel winch and eye splice on shackle.
1 Sheave as per main masthead detail scored for $\frac{7}{32}''$ wire.
1 Merr. 420, size 0, fairlead on starboard spreader forward side.
1 Merr. 390 $\frac{3}{8}''$ headboard shackle.

Jib Halyard—$\frac{7}{32}''$ diam. 7 x 19 stainless steel wire with $\frac{7}{16}''$ dacron tail. Halyard to be long enough to reach stem head with 2 turns on winch, with enough left to make fast to cleat with bitter end knotted through eye.
1 Merr. 420, size 2, eye.
1 Sheave as per main masthead detail scored for $\frac{7}{32}''$ wire and $\frac{7}{16}''$ rope.
1 Merr. 391 No. 3 stiff eye snap shackle.
2 Merr. 388 $\frac{5}{16}''$ shackles.
2 Merr. 392 No. 3 swivel snap shackles at tack.
1 8″ wooden cleat at mast.

Spinnaker Halyard—$\frac{3}{8}''$ dacron.
1 Merr. 560 M 2 $\frac{5}{8}''$ wide mortise single swivel eye.
1 Merr. 388 shackle to suit above block.
1 Merr. 392 No. 3 swivel eye snap shackle.
2 Merr. 420, size 3, eye straps, fairlead and bitter end.
1 8″ wooden cleat on mast.

Spinnaker Lift—$\frac{5}{16}''$ dacron.
1 Merr. 645 fairlead in place of block.
2 Merr. 391 No. 0 stiff eye snap shackles, 1 each end.
1 5'' wooden cleat on mast.

Spinnaker Sheet and Guys
2 $\frac{7}{16}''$ dacron lines—one for sheet, one for after guy—made up with 2 interlocking Monel rings $\frac{1}{4}''$ x $1\frac{1}{2}''$ I.D., and Merr. 392 No. 2 swivel snap shackle at end of each.
1 $\frac{3}{8}''$ dacron fore guy with Merr. 391 No. 1 stiff eye snap shackle.
2 Merr. 347 3'' snatch blocks.

Spinnaker Pole Fittings
1 Merr. 450 T $1\frac{1}{4}''$ x $\frac{3}{16}''$ track screwed to mast.
1 Merr. 450 S, size 3A, slide.
2 Merr. 450 L sockets, one at each end of pole.
Trip line on pole.
Lift bridle on pole.

Goosenecks—Forestaysail boom—Merr. 659—9'' above deck.

Main boom—Merr. 485 A, size 3B for 5'' diam. roller reefing boom.

Main Boom Downhaul—$\frac{5}{16}''$ dacron.
1 Merr. 352 #0 single with becket.
1 Merr. 356 #0 check block.
1 5'' wooden cleat.

Clew Outhauls—Forestaysail outhaul—Merr. 409 C No. 2—$\frac{1}{8}''$ 7 x 19 stainless steel wire with $\frac{5}{16}''$ dacron tail.
1 Sheave for $\frac{1}{8}''$ wire in end plate.
1 5'' wooden cleat on boom.
Main Clew Outhaul—1 Merr. 538 Roller reefing swivel clew outhaul for 5'' diam. boom.

Boom Lifts—Forestaysail—use spinnaker pole lift.
Main boom—$\frac{1}{8}''$ 7 x 19 stainless steel wire, Truloc eye fitting with toggle at upper end. Lower end to have eye splice on thimble and $\frac{3}{16}''$ nylon lashing to clew outhaul shackle.

Flag Halyard—Tube bushing athwartships at masthead, with well-flared end to reduce chafe. $\frac{3}{16}''$ braided nylon halyard.

CHAPTER XXI

INSPECTION CHECK LIST USED BY ROD STEPHENS, JR.

This list includes many of the individually small, but collectively bothersome, items that come up on the majority of boats in the course of final inspection and trials.

It is obviously more economical to avoid the problem areas in the course of planning and construction, rather than adding to the burden of last-minute corrections at the time of delivery.

PROBLEM AREAS TO BE CORRECTED

A—Cabin

1. Unsatisfactory friction catches on doors. Elbow catches with finger holes best.
2. Floor boards tight, and not beveled, and absence of margins at vertical surfaces.
3. Bilge access poor, and poor floor lifts.
4. Quarter berth ventilation (inadequate).
5. Bunkboards—weak and/or low.
6. Dangerous location and inadequate marking of stove fuel master valve.
7. Inadequate marking of individual stove burner valves.
8. Inadequate insulation over stove area.
9. Alcohol stove pressure system that fails to hold pressure—poor pump, poor valve, poor gauge.
10. Inadequate fiddles on tables and dressers and counters.
11. Inadequate dresser area in toilet rooms.
12. Inadequate dresser area in galley.
13. Inadequate clearance in drop-sash drawers.
14. Inadequate clearance in doors.
15. Galley slop pail inadequate or missing.
16. Lack of fixtures in head for soap, towels, toilet paper.
17. Fire extinguishers not stowed near stove and engine.
18. Not enough hanging knees in trunk cabin.
19. No through bolts fore and aft of ports in trunk cabin.
20. No long hooks to hold head door 2″ open for ventilation.
21. Extension berths hard to extend. No locking, in or out position.
22. No drain for icebox.
23. Inadequate dish and glass racks in galley.

B—Deck

1. Leaky hatches. No holding down fittings. No groove for cover.
2. Dorade vents weak, small, low and badly scuppered (should never be screened).
3. Spongy life lines—inadequate diagonal braces at pulpits and gangways. Closed center turnbuckles without toggles.
4. Dangerous gangways.
5. Tillers with heavy grip but weak hinge fittings with lost motion.
6. Inadequate winch handle holders.
7. Incorrect angling and/or spacing of cleats.
8. Bow chocks—weak and/or small and/or sharp, which will chafe rope.
9. Inadequate hatch cover provision.
10. Genoa sheet track holes not numbered, and slides not free.
11. Poor compass installation for visibility, bearings, deviation.
12. Avoid built-in compass correction.

13. Leaking mast coats.
14. Missing boat hook chocks.
15. Running lights wiring not water tight, not parallel to center line.
16. Mooring cleats not large enough, not thru-bolted.
17. Life line stanchion bases not thru-bolted, no eyes.
18. Anchor windlass. Chain doesn't fit. No chain stopper.
19. Spinnaker pole chocks missing. No chafing strips on pole.

20. Anchor chocks missing.
21. Dinghy chocks missing.
22. Smoke head and stove pipe not tight. No water deck iron.
23. Midship chock missing. No eye on it for boom tackle.
24. Foot or turning blocks not thru-bolted.
25. Fiberglass deck too slippery.
26. Companion ladder too steep. Steps too far apart and slippery. No hand holds in sides.

C—PLUMBING

1. Restrictive or missing scupper guards.
2. Inadequate drainage of coaming lockers.
3. Inadequate drainage of cockpit seats.
4. Bilge pump intakes—incorrect screening and/or poor location.
5. Bilge pump piping that may allow sea water to enter.
6. Deck pumps located so they may admit water when in use.
7. Sinks (and basins) that can admit sea water thru drains when heeled.
8. Top of W.C. bowl below flotation line. Can sink boat.
9. W.C. intakes too high and/or too near outlets.

10. W.C. discharge loop too far outboard (can admit sea water when heeled).
11. Inadequate tank sounding provision.
12. No way to clean out tanks, especially sump tank. Never gasoline tank—dangerous.
13. Poorly located tank vents (may admit rain or spray).
14. Poor location of, and marking of, seacocks. Not on all thru hull fittings.
15. Omission of effective check valves in F.W. supply lines.
16. Tanks don't have individual shut-off valves (packless type valve needed on fuel tank).
17. Marked sounding stick for each tank missing.

D—RIGGING AND RIG FITTINGS

1. Cotter pins, too long, too sharp, excessively opened.
2. Omission of toggles.
3. Incorrectly beveled mast tangs (all bevel in outer plate).
4. Closed barrel turnbuckles and/or lock nuts (dangerous).
5. Blind terminals on rod rigging and/or lock nuts (dangerous).
6. Turnbuckles upside down (right-hand thread should be down).
7. Internal wire outhauls (impractical to repair).
8. Gooseneck interference when boom all the way out.
9. Slides that are rough and inadequately belled.
10. Slides on roller reefing goosenecks not long enough.
11. Luff tracks that do not come right down to lowest possible boom position.
12. Poor track gates, badly located and badly retained.
13. Poor track switches, badly located and badly retained.
14. Incorrect mast wedging (use tight rubber).
15. Poor provision for mast wiring at partners.
16. Incorrect mast heel position and poor provision for moving and for stepping. Bevel surfaces to help mast heel enter easily.
17. Bad rope and wire splices.
18. Incorrect serving of wire halyard eye splices.
19. Careless control of length of wire halyards.
20. Careless control of length of all running rigging.

21. Inadequate provision for bitter-end attachment.
22. Inadequate provision for wire attachment to all reel winches.
23. Omission of halyard marking.
24. Careless arrangement of internal halyards.
25. Mast (track) must be straight before stepping.
26. Bosun's chair—no varnish—short synthetic straps with ring.
27. Absence of necessary small lines and sail stops.
28. Inadequate lubrication and covering of turnbuckles (anhydrous lanolin best).
29. Inadequate screw-in blocks for heavy weather headsail sheet leads.
30. Unnecessary splicing running rigging, and excessive serving on rope splices.
31. Standing rigging not tuned up.
32. Poor winch layout on mast for handle clearance, halyard leads.
33. Poor cleat location for sheet leads.
34. No bitter-end fittings for halyards.
35. No winch handle stowage.
36. Halyards won't reach rail or stem head fitting.
37. No halyard fair leads.
38. Mast track not bolted at sail head when fully hoisted, or when reefed, or at storm trysail head.
39. Halyard sheaves don't turn freely.
40. Spinnaker crane not strong enough.
41. Mainsheet lead poor. Sheet too short.
42. No boom crutch. No stowage for it.
43. Boom doesn't clear backstay when raised in a jibe (can capsize a boat).

E—SAILS

1. Battens (top one tapered fiberglass to allow top of mainsail to curve).
2. Leach Lines.

3. Sail bags (size), and sail folding.
4. Correct head and tack pennants on smaller headsails. Always shackle on.

F—Hull

1. Stiff steering, rudder tight, steering gear and sheaves not lubricated. Sheaves out of line, too small and too many of them. (Little finger on spoke should be able to turn wheel easily).
2. Poor limbers and bilge drainage.
3. Omission of reference marks necessary to control trim (flotation).
4. Unguarded sheaves in cable steering gear.
5. Poor access to steering gear for adjustment and cable replacement.
6. Sharp corners on quadrants and inadequate stops.
7. Omission of complete lightning grounding.
8. Omission of propeller shaft marking (2-bladed props—solid in vertical position, folding in horizontal).
9. Omission of shaft locking, when generating may be required.
10. Presence of sharp corners—both wood and metal.
11. Dirty bilges—rough finish impossible to clean.
12. Fiberglass cabin liners that prevent access to fastening of deck fittings, and inspection of interior of hull (to be removable).
13. Inadequate exhaust system.
    Consider:
    a) Resistance to flooding (as high and as near center line as possible).
    b) Unnecessary heat in cabin.
    c) Noise suppression.
    d) Ease of repair and replacement.
    e) Above-water outlet at full speed (keep high above stern wave).
    f) Side exhaust better.
14. Exposed electric switches.
15. Avoidance of magnetic items near compass. (Must be outside 6 ft. radius.)
16. Strong non-magnetic emergency tillers with convenient stowage, missing.
17. Incorrect chainplate bevels (to align with shrouds).
18. Need of elkhide on destroyer-type steering wheel rims.
19. No center kingspoke on wheel, inadequately marked, and no center line mark on quadrants.
20. No generous access to engine.
21. Not large enough, or any, pan under engine.
22. No carburetor drip pan on gasoline engine.
23. No sound insulation around engine.
24. No exhaust blower taking suction from low point in gasoline engine compartment.
25. Not good enough fairing ahead of propeller.
26. Rudder not sharp enough at trailing edge.
27. No worm shoe at bottom of keel.
28. No drip lip on exhaust thru hull fittings.
29. Centerboard leading and trailing edges not tapered properly.
30. Centerboard pin does not have cover plates to prevent working loose.

CHAPTER XXII

BOAT BUILDING IN WOOD, FIBERGLASS, STEEL, ALUMINUM AND FERRO CEMENT

General. A boat should be considered as a box section girder that will take care of the strains of hogging and sagging. Hogging occurs when a boat is supported by a wave amidships, or when she is hauled out and stored for the winter (the ends droop—like a hog). Sagging occurs when the ends are supported by waves or lifted by slings (the middle sags, like the back of an old horse). Thus, the sides, the deck and the bottom form the box girder. In small boats without decks, such as canoes, a little tumble home (inward sloping sides) increases rigidity tremendously. The American Indians knew this when they built their birch bark canoes.

Sailboats require additional strength in way of the mast, shrouds, and ballast. Power boats require additional strength in way of the engines, as well as in the forefoot to resist pounding and slamming at high speeds.

The outer skin is the principal member of a boat's structure. It is not there just to keep the water out, but forms the sides of the box girder and, together with the keel backbone, provides the longitudinal stiffness. Other longitudinal members which contribute to the box girder effect are: the stringers, clamp and shelf, sides of the deckhouse, and the cockpit coaming. Cutting such a member would destroy its effectiveness. The frames and deck beams are the transverse members.

Systems of longitudinal framing are used in vessels such as welded steel tankers. But in small boats there is no great advantage in longitudinal framing. The members in a longitudinal system of framing are deeper, thereby using valuable space inside the boat without any appreciable saving in weight.

Wood Construction. The illustration of the cross section of a log (Figure 38) shows the characteristic shrinkage and distortion of flats, squares, and rounds, as affected by the direction of the annual rings in the tree. The tangential, or across-the-grain, shrinkage is about twice as great as the radial, or with-the-grain,

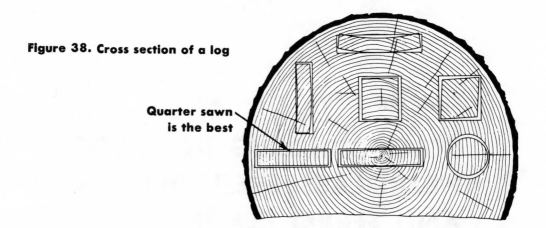

Figure 38. Cross section of a log

Quarter sawn
is the best

shrinkage. For this reason, quartersawn wood should always be used in boat building.

The original caveman's log canoe is still used by natives on the island of Jamaica. These boats last about six years, whereupon another tree is cut down, split in half, hollowed out, pointed at the ends, and launched. Probably the next simplest type of wood construction is the flat-bottom rowboat.

After this comes the V-bottom type which, if it has a developed surface, can utilize plywood sheets—that is to say, if the bottom is a part of a cone, and the top sides a part of a cylinder or combination of cone and cylinder. Beware of the V-bottom boats which have straight-line sections! These appear to be easy to build, but if the surface is not developed, compound curves will result, making it impossible to use plywood because of the great twist which can not be forced without buckling.

The next type of wooden construction to be considered is the lapstrake method. Boats built this way have their planking lapped like the clapboards on a house. A great deal of longitudinal strength is added by these laps. For this reason, the framing can be reduced and a strong, light boat is the result. Many power boats are built in this manner. Spray is deflected by the many ridges on the bottom and sides of such a power boat; this is a great advantage. Fastenings are copper rivets, brass or bronze bolts, or clenched nails. The disadvantages are: a shorter life, because once the laps start to leak it is almost impossible to caulk them; and a greater surface—thus, more resistance—because of the ridges formed by the laps. The Scandinavians use this method for many of their craft. But it does not make for fast sailboats.

The carvel plank method is the one in which the planks are laid flush so as to be smooth-sided. The planks run fore and aft and are fastened to frames more closely spaced than in the other methods of construction mentioned. The seams are caulked with cotton and sealed with seam compound. This method allows for contraction and expansion and so provides a longer life for a boat than does any other type of wooden construction. It is also easy to repair. Planking may be

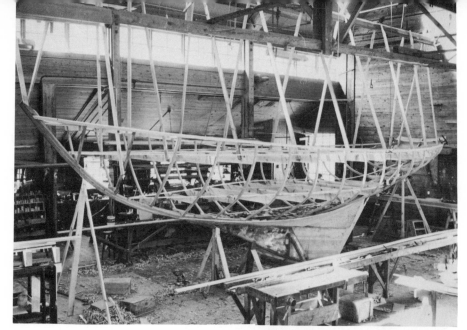

PIPE DREAM Cruising Sloop, *SOUTHERLY,* under construction. *(Top)* One third of frames in place; *(middle)* planking completed; *(bottom)* planking half done.

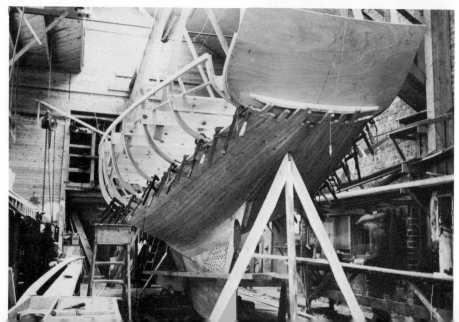

double thickness bonded together by heavy orange shellac, no caulking being required.

Another method of construction is the strip plank method. This is an old method which has been used in Maine for years and years. The planks are strips of wood, sometimes square in section, edge nailed and glued to each other, starting from the bottom and working upward. This is an easy method, but it is not labor saving, because there are so many more pieces required. It gives a smooth surface like the carvel planking, but requires fewer frames, giving a clear, uncluttered appearance to the inside of the boat and providing more room. The weight saved by using fewer frames is not great. Two disadvantages come to mind: first, because of the locked up stresses—formed by the cumulative expansion of the many strips of planking with no caulking to squeeze against—I am always afraid of a loud crack occurring on a hull built in this manner; second is the difficulty in making repairs.

Decks. There are two kinds of decks to be considered in wood construction. A narrow plank teak deck, where the surface is left bare, is probably the epitome of beauty. It has the advantage of providing the very best nonskid surface. But alas, it is heavy, it is liable to leak, and it is expensive! The plywood deck covered with canvas or fiberglass is undoubtedly the best. It is tight, lightweight, strong, and relatively inexpensive. Sometimes the two types have been combined, that is, a thin layer of teak planking set on plywood. This is not recommended, because water is liable to be trapped between the two and cause trouble.

Deck Beams. The strongest and lightest beams are of laminated spruce. Deck beams for a plywood deck must be properly spaced according to the following table; otherwise plywood will not support, without bending, the load of a person walking along the deck.

Plywood Thickness	Beam Spacing
¼''	5¾''
⅜''	8''
½''	10''
⅝''	12''
¾''	14''

Keel Backbone. A hard wood, such as white oak, should be used for the keel not only because of its great strength, but also to hold the fastenings better. Laminated oak is not recommended. There is apparently some acid in the oak which does not like glue. I had some experience with this on a little boat, built thirteen years ago by one of the best builders in the country. He could not get a big enough piece of oak for one part of the keel backbone, so he laminated about six layers of oak, using an approved marine waterproof glue. Everything was fine until about five years later when the keel began to show signs of coming apart. This was rather disturbing. We held it together with a lot of additional fastenings, but I never felt very comfortable about laminating oak after that.

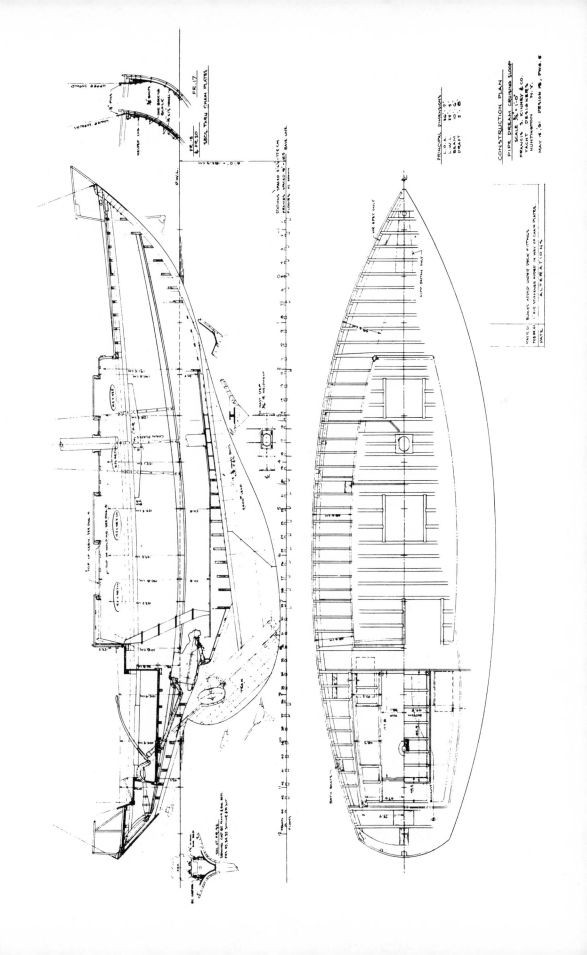

Frames. White oak again is the best wood for frames. Steam-bent oak gives the strongest type of frame and should be used right up to the very largest possible sizes. Larger than this, double-sawn oak has been used in standard framing. These large double-sawn frames are perfectly tremendous pieces of wood. There is plenty of size and weight in such framing, but the strength is open to question. It was to overcome this lack of strength that the large laminated frame of fir was developed for large wooden vessels. The steam-bent frame can be given a twist to conform to the mold around which it is bent. Where such a twisted steam-bent frame joins a floor timber, a poor connection will occur unless the floor timber is beveled to take the frame.

Frames used to be boxed into the keel. That is, there was a box-shaped opening hollowed out of the keel to take the end of the frame. The frame was then securely held in this box which, shaped like a keystone, could not pull out. This was a good system because it held the planking to the keel in a most rigid manner, preventing leaks along the garboard seam.

I have seen the wrecks of many old catboats with frames still held tightly in the keel, like the bones of a fish attached to its spine.

Floors. White oak again should be used. The most common method is to lay the floors alongside the frames, fastening by through bolts. Another method which has great merit is to lay the floor timbers on top of the frames, fastening with long screws through the planking and through the frames to the floor. The floors, of course, should be through-bolted to the keel, their main purpose being to act as a connecting bracket between frames and keel.

Fastening the outside ballast casting with long rods through thick floor timbers used to be the accepted practice. But it is more advantageous to fasten the ballast directly to the keel between floor timbers; and to fasten the floor timbers, which can then be thinner, independently to the keel.

In talking about ballast, it should be pointed out that lead, of course, is the best—not just because of more weight in less space, but because it is soft and can absorb the shock of collision with the ground. This was brought home to me the hard way last spring when I was taking our boat around to the shipyard. I was alone, traveling under power at full speed (7¼ knots). To save time, I cut inside a buoy marking the end of a rocky reef. Having lashed the tiller, I was returning to the cockpit from below when the bow struck a submerged rock. With a resounding crash, she was lifted four feet into the air, throwing me flat on my back. I thought I'd had it, and I thought the boat had had it that time! But half an hour later, when I arrived at the boatyard, no leaks had developed. The next day, when she was hauled out, I found the front of the lead keel had been gouged out and flattened, but that was all.

Ceiling. The ceiling is like another skin on the inside of the frames and gives additional strength to the boat as well as providing a smooth, clear surface inside the hull. Lightweight woods, such as cedar, should be used here. Bilge stringers provide longitudinal strength and should be used when ceilings are omitted.

Midship construction section

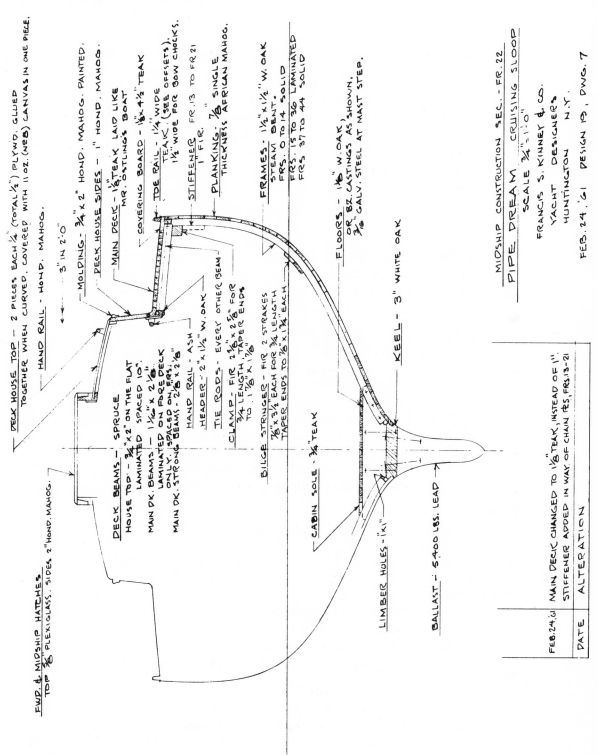

NEVINS' SCANTLING RULES FOR WOODEN YACHTS

Nevins' yard at City Island, New York, was, in my opinion, one of the best boat yards we had for many years in this country. The late Mr. Henry B. Nevins left us a great contribution by working out all the different sizes of members and fastenings for a wooden boat's structure.

His rules, given below, are easy to follow. If strictly adhered to, they will produce an excellently built wooden boat, not too heavy, and not too light.

General Clause. The cube root of the displacement in cubic feet, $\sqrt[3]{\text{Disp. cu. ft.}}$, (with the yacht in load condition) is the basis upon which scantlings are calculated. (See table of functions of numbers in the back of this book for cube roots.)

Keel

Material: White Oak, Teak, or Mahogany.
Molding: Not less than $\sqrt[3]{\text{Disp. cu. ft.}}$ multiplied by .7.
Siding: Not less than double the molding at the widest point of keel.

Stem

Material: White Oak, Teak, or Mahogany.
Molding: Not less than siding.
Siding: At head not less than four times the thickness of the planking. Below head the siding of stem and bow timber shall be gradually increased to siding of keel to provide proper back rabbet.

Sternpost

Material: White Oak, Teak, or Mahogany.
Molding: Not less than siding.
Siding: Not less than four times thickness of plank.

Horn Timber

Material: White Oak, Teak, or Mahogany.
Molding: Not less than twice the thickness of plank.
Siding: Not less than twice the molding.

Frames

Material: White Oak, steam-bent.
Sectional Area: At heel in accordance with table sizes. May be straight-tapered to head to not less than 75% of the heel area. (See page 239)

Where untapered frame is used, rule size shall be maintained for ¾ of D.W.L.

length. Fore and aft of the ¾ length, the area may be gradually reduced to the ends of the yacht where it may be 15% less than amidships.

Where tapered frame is used, the rule shall be applied to the longest frame in the yacht, establishing thereby a standard taper for all other frames. The head size of the longest frame shall be maintained throughout the yacht, and the established taper applied therefrom to the heel, thereby decreasing the areas at the heel as the frames grow shorter fore and aft of the longest frame.

Spacing: To be in accordance with table. (See page 239)

Molding: Optional. Table dimensions are recommended. In no case less than is required to entirely bury the plank fastenings of the length specified for screws.

Siding: Optional. Table dimensions recommended.

Where severe bends are encountered, making it impractical to use a solid frame, it is recommended that the frame be split, in a fore and aft direction, from the end to just beyond the point of extreme bend; or a double frame may be used, one member bent inside the other. In both instances, plank fastenings should extend through outer member well into inner member and the two be drawn tightly together.

If *sawn frames* are to be used, they shall be double, with the members adequately bolted or riveted together. *Sectional Area*—50% heavier than the table size of frames.

Belt Frames

Material: White Oak, steam-bent.

Molding: ¾ that of frames.

Siding: Equal to frames.

Belt frames are to be applied to yachts which are ceiled and there must be at least four on each side. They shall be applied after ceiling is installed.

In the case of single-masted vessels and yawls, one set of belt frames are to be located immediately forward and one immediately aft of main mast, and are to be kneed to heavy partner deck beams.

Belt frames should be used whenever possible, but, should they interfere with any unusual condition inside the yacht, may be omitted, provided the regular frame at that location is doubled in sectional area, or two frames of rule size placed alongside each other and bolted or riveted together. Yachts which are not ceiled are to be fitted with heavy frames having a sectional area of 1¾ times the area of main frames and located in a like manner to the belt frames of ceiled yachts.

In the case of two-masted schooners or ketches, one set of belt frames are to be located immediately forward and one immediately aft of each mast and are to be kneed to heavy partner deck beams.

In the case of three-masted yachts, there shall be 6 pairs of belt frames, one set located immediately forward and one immediately aft of each mast and kneed to heavy partner deck beams.

Planking

Material: Teak, Mahogany, Long Leaf Yellow Pine, and Douglas Fir.

Thickness: In accordance with table. (See page 239)

Butts to be shifted so that no two butts shall come on same frame or in same frame space, except there be 3 clear planks between, and in no adjacent plank be nearer than 3 frame spaces.

If teak is used, thickness may be reduced 10%.

Ceiling

Material: Long Leaf Yellow Pine, Douglas Fir, or Spruce.

Thickness: 40% of the table thickness of outside planking. No reduction allowed where teak planking is used.

Ceiling shall be fitted in all yachts having a $\sqrt[3]{\text{Disp. cu. ft.}}$ of over 10, and shall extend for at least the water line length of the vessel and from cabin sole to underside of clamp.

Bilge Stringers

Material: Long Leaf Yellow Pine or Douglas Fir.

Sectional Area: Equal to 3 times the table area of frames for $\frac{3}{4}$ of D.W.L. length.

Bilge stringers shall be used in all yachts which are not ceiled. There shall be one on each side, to extend from stem to stern wherever possible, and they may be straight-tapered to ends to not less than 50% of the area amidships.

Clamp and Shelf

Material: Long Leaf Yellow Pine or Douglas Fir.

Sectional Area: $3\frac{1}{2}$ times the table area of frames for $\frac{3}{4}$ of the water line length.

They shall extend the full length of the yacht but may be straight-tapered to the ends to not less than 50% of the area amidships.

A single clamp, or a clamp and shelf of required area, may be used.

Deck Beams

Material: Oak, Chestnut, Douglas Fir, Long Leaf Yellow Pine, Teak, Mahogany, and Ash.

Sectional Area: At center line of boat in accordance with table and may be reduced at ends to 75% of the sectional area at center.

Spacing: Same as table for frames.

Molding: Optional. May be reduced at ends to 75% of the molding at center.

Siding: Optional, but to be not more than 65% of the molded depth at center.

There shall be partner beams and hatch beams whose siding shall be $1\frac{3}{4}$ times the siding of the main beams.

Half beams and beams beyond the ends of the D.W.L. may be reduced to 75% of the area of the main beams.

(Opposite page) PIPE DREAM Cruising Sloop, SOUTHERLY. (Top) Ready for launching; (bottom left) just before launching; builder, Oscar Schelin, and designer discuss location of draft marks; (bottom right) streamlined underbody.

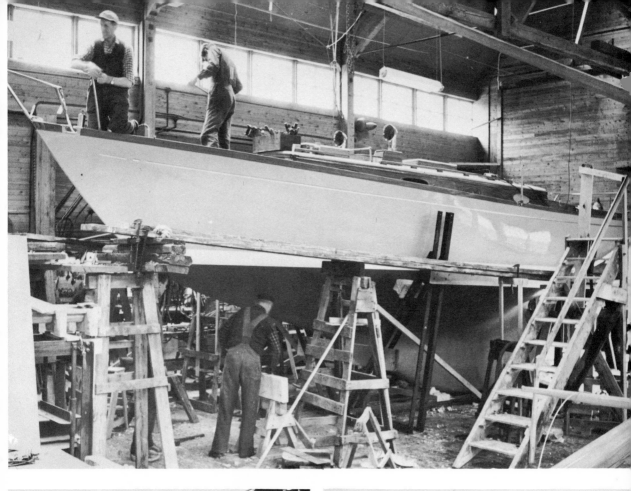

Decking

Material: White Pine, Cedar, Spruce, Cypress, or Douglas Fir.

Thickness: Same as outside planking

If teak is used, the thickness may be reduced 10%. If covered with canvas, thickness may be reduced ⅛″.

Floors

Material: White Oak, Teak, Mahogany.

Spacing: One to each pair of frames.

Molding: To be sufficient to allow at least 4 fastenings to heels of frames, whose spacing shall be not less than 1½ times siding of floor, but in no case shall the sectional area over the keel be less than 2 times the sectional area of frames.

In way of lead keel, siding of floors taking keel bolts shall be increased to regular siding, plus the diameter of the keel bolt. Molding to be same as regular floors.

There shall be no concave on top of any floor to show up cross grains at ends.

In any yacht where it is necessary to use the space occupied by wooden floors to install tanks or to meet any special conditions, metal floors—of approved design and of equal weight and strength to the wooden floors—may be used.

Siding: Not less than frame.

Hull Straps

Material: Bronze of not less than 60,000 pounds per square inch of tensile strength.

Width: Twice the planking thickness.

Thickness: .1 the plank thickness. (Other dimensions may be used but shall produce an equal cross-sectional area.)

There shall be 2 diagonal straps on each side at each mast, extending from underside of deck to keel between outside of frame and inside of planking.

Straps shall be fastened at each crossing of frame and between frames to the planking.

Deck Straps

Material, Width, Thickness: Same as hull straps.

Deck to be fitted with 2 diagonal straps at each mast, extending from gunwale to gunwale between top of deck beam and under side of deck and not cut by deck openings.

To be fastened at each beam crossing and between beams into deck.

Hanging Knees

Material: Wood, cast bronze, steel, or bronze plate flanged to frames or deck beams.

Length of Arms: 1.75 times table frame spacing.

Shall be fitted to all belt frames, all extra heavy frames, and partner beams.

Plank Fastenings

Material: Wood screws of noncorrosive metal. (See Figure 39)

Length: Twice the plank thickness from heel to turn of bilge; from turn of bilge to head may be shortened to suit molding of frame.

Size:

Plank Thickness	Gauge No.	Plank Thickness	Guage No.
⅝″	9	1½″	20
¾″	10	1¾″	22
⅞″	12	2″	24
1″	14	2¼″	26
1⅛″	16	2½″	28
1¼″	18		

Should other type of fastening be used—such as bolts, rivets, or drift fastenings—they shall be of equal cross-sectional area to those in the table for wood screws, and of suitable length.

Lead Keel Bolts

Material: Bronze, having a tensile strength of not less than 60,000 pounds per square inch.

The number and size to be sufficient to give not less than 1 square inch of sectional area of bolt for 1500 pounds of outside ballast.

Nevins' Table for Size and Spacing of Frames, Deck Beams, and Planking

$\sqrt[3]{Disp.\ cu.\ ft.}$	Planking Thickness In.	FRAMES			Deck Beam Area Sq. In.
		Area Sq. In.	Siding and Molding In.	Spacing In.	
3.8	0.56	0.65	0.81	6.03	0.75
4.0	0.56	0.65	0.81	6.03	0.75
4.2	0.59	0.75	0.87	6.30	0.88
4.4	0.62	0.86	0.93	6.58	1.03
4.6	0.66	1.00	1.00	6.84	1.18
4.8	0.69	1.13	1.07	7.12	1.33
5.0	0.72	1.28	1.13	7.38	1.49
5.2	0.75	1.43	1.20	7.64	1.65
5.4	0.79	1.60	1.27	7.91	1.81
5.6	0.82	1.80	1.34	8.18	1.98
5.8	0.86	1.98	1.41	8.44	2.15
6.0	0.90	2.20	1.48	8.70	2.33
6.2	0.93	2.40	1.55	8.97	2.50
6.4	0.96	2.61	1.62	9.22	2.67
6.6	1.00	2.83	1.69	9.49	2.85
6.8	1.04	3.10	1.76	9.73	3.03
7.0	1.08	3.34	1.83	10.00	3.22

$\sqrt[3]{Disp.\ cu.\ ft.}$	Planking Thickness In.	FRAMES			Deck Beam Area Sq. In.
		Area Sq. In.	Siding and Molding In.	Spacing In.	
7.2	1.12	3.59	1.90	10.25	3.42
7.4	1.15	3.84	1.96	10.50	3.62
7.6	1.18	4.12	2.03	10.75	3.82
7.8	1.22	4.40	2.10	11.00	4.02
8.0	1.25	4.70	2.17	11.25	4.22
8.2	1.29	5.00	2.24	11.50	4.43
8.4	1.32	5.30	2.30	11.75	4.64
8.6	1.36	5.60	2.34	12.00	4.86
8.8	1.40	5.90	2.43	12.25	5.09
9.0	1.43	6.23	2.50	12.50	5.32
9.2	1.46	6.53	2.56	12.75	5.55
9.4	1.50	6.89	2.63	13.00	5.78
9.6	1.53	7.22	2.69	13.23	6.02
9.8	1.56	7.58	2.76	13.47	6.27
10.0	1.60	7.92	2.82	13.72	6.53
10.2	1.63	8.30	2.88	13.95	6.79
10.4	1.66	8.70	2.95	14.20	7.05
10.6	1.70	9.10	3.02	14.44	7.31
10.8	1.73	9.50	3.09	14.68	7.58
11.0	1.76	9.92	3.15	14.92	7.85
11.2	1.80	10.36	3.22	15.16	8.12
11.4	1.83	10.80	3.29	15.40	8.41
11.6	1.86	11.29	3.36	15.63	8.70
11.8	1.90	11.78	3.44	15.88	9.00
12.0	1.93	12.30	3.51	16.12	9.30
12.2	1.96	12.80	3.58	16.35	9.60
12.4	1.99	13.31	3.65	16.60	9.91
12.6	2.02	13.87	3.73	16.83	10.22
12.8	2.05	14.42	3.80	17.07	10.53
13.0	2.09	15.00	3.88	17.31	10.84
13.2	2.12	15.55	3.95	17.55	11.16
13.4	2.15	16.14	4.02	17.80	11.49
13.6	2.18	16.74	4.09	18.03	11.82
13.8	2.22	17.33	4.16	18.28	12.16
14.0	2.25	17.95	4.24	18.50	12.60
14.2	2.28	18.60	4.32	18.75	12.84
14.4	2.31	19.20	4.39	19.00	13.18
14.6	2.34	19.87	4.46	19.22	13.52
14.8	2.37	20.50	4.53	19.45	13.86
15.0	2.40	21.12	4.60	19.70	14.21
15.2	2.43	21.80	4.67	19.95	14.58
15.4	2.46	22.50	4.75	20.18	14.95
15.6	2.50	23.17	4.82	20.42	15.31
15.8	2.53	23.90	4.89	20.65	15.68
16.0	2.55	24.60	4.96	20.88	16.05
16.2	2.58	25.30	5.03	21.12	16.43
16.4	2.60	26.00	5.10	21.36	16.80

Figure 39. (opposite page) Flat head wood screws for planking

PLANKING THICKNESS & GA. (1)	LENGTH & GA. (1)	DIAM. (3)	LENGTH & GAUGE -- FULL SCALE	DRILL (2)	DRILL (2)	BUNG DIAM.
$\frac{1}{4}''$	$\frac{1}{2}''$ NO. 6	.137"		$\frac{1}{8}''$	NO. 47	NONE
$\frac{3}{8}''$	$\frac{3}{4}''$ NO. 7	.150"		$\frac{9}{64}''$	NO. 44	NONE
$\frac{1}{2}''$	$1''$ NO. 8	.163"		$\frac{5}{32}''$	NO. 40	NONE
$\frac{5}{8}''$	$1\frac{1}{4}''$ NO. 9	.176"		$\frac{11}{64}''$	NO. 37	$\frac{3}{8}''$
$\frac{3}{4}''$	$1\frac{1}{2}''$ NO.10	.189"		$\frac{3}{16}''$	NO. 33	$\frac{1}{2}''$
$\frac{7}{8}''$	$1\frac{3}{4}''$ NO.12	.216		$\frac{13}{64}''$	NO. 30	$\frac{1}{2}''$
$1''$	$2''$ NO.14	.242		$\frac{15}{64}''$	NO. 25	$\frac{1}{2}''$
$1\frac{1}{8}''$	$2\frac{1}{4}''$ NO.16	.268		$\frac{17}{64}''$	NO. 18	$\frac{5}{8}''$
$1\frac{1}{4}''$	$2\frac{1}{2}''$ NO.18	.294		$\frac{9}{32}''$	NO. 13	$\frac{5}{8}''$
$1\frac{1}{2}''$	$3''$ NO.20	.320		$\frac{5}{16}''$	NO. 4	$\frac{3}{4}''$
$1\frac{3}{4}''$	$3\frac{1}{2}''$ NO.22	.347				
$2''$	$4''$ No.24	.374				

HEADS OF NO.9 AND UNDER ARE USUALLY PUTTIED.
SOAP CAN BE USED AS A DRIVING LUBRICANT.
ALWAYS CHECK SIZE OF BIT WITH SIZE OF BUNG.
TRY SMALLER LEAD HOLE FOR "PHILLIPS" HEAD SCREWS.

COMPILED FOR
THE RUDDER
BY ROB'T. M. STEWARD

(1) GAUGE MAY BE REDUCED ONE SIZE FOR DECKING.
(2) TEST ON SAMPLES OF MATERIALS BEING USED.
(3) OTHER FASTENINGS SHOULD HAVE EQUAL CROSS-SECTION.

Fastening schedule

FASTENING SCHEDULE

USE FOR GUIDANCE ONLY. EXACT SIZES ARE AT OPTION OF BUILDER

MEMBERS	SIZE	TYPE OF FASTENING	MATERIAL	REMARKS
PLANKING TO FRAMES	1 3/4" NO. 12	FLAT HEAD WOOD SCREWS	EVERDUR	FURNISHED BY OWNER. 1/FR./PLANK
" " "	3"x.148" DIA.	RIVETS WITH FLAT BURS	COPPER (WIRE NAILS)	ALTERNATE WITH EVERDUR SCREWS 1/FR./PLANK
LEAD KEEL TO WOOD KEEL	15 5/8 DIA.	RODS WITH NUTS	MONEL	1/8" MONEL LARGE PLATE WASHERS
FLOORS TO WOOD KEEL	3/8" DIA.	RODS WITH NUTS	MONEL	NOTCH FLOORS 20-23 FOR CABIN SOLE
FLOORS TO FRAMES	1/4" DIA	CARRIAGE BOLTS	MONEL	
FRAMES TO BEAMS	3"x.148 DIA.	RIVET	COPPER (WIRE NAIL)	
TEAK DECK TO BEAMS	2" NO. 14	FLAT HEAD WOOD SCREWS	STAINLESS STEEL	
BULKHEADS TO FRAMES	1/4" DIA.	CARRIAGE BOLTS	MONEL	SPACED 6"
KEEL TO STEM	3/8" DIA.	CARRIAGE BOLTS	MONEL	
KEEL TO DEAD WOOD	1/2 ~~3/8~~ DIA.	RODS WITH NUTS	MONEL	SET AT DIFFERENT ANGLES
HORN TIMBER TO DEADW'D.	3/8" DIA.	RODS WITH NUTS	MONEL	
ENG. BEDS TO FLOORS	1/4" DIA	CARRIAGE BOLTS	MONEL	
DECK TIE RODS	3/16" DIA	RODS WITH NUTS	~~BRASS~~ MONEL	SPACED NEAR EVERY OTHER BEAM ON SIDE DECKS.
INTERIOR JOINER WORK	TO SUIT	TO SUIT	BRASS	
CHAIN PLATES TO HULL	3/8" DIA.	CARRIAGE BOLTS	MONEL	SEE DWG. 1
FRAMES TO CLAMP	1/4" DIA.	CARRIAGE BOLTS	MONEL	
BEAMS TO CLAMP	1/4" DIA.	CARRIAGE BOLTS	MONEL	
HOUSE SIDE TO HEADER	3/16" DIA.	RODS WITH NUTS	~~BRASS~~ MONEL	1 ROD EACH SIDE OF PORTS, 1 BETWEEN. BACK SCREW BETWEEN.
BILGE STRINGER TO FRS.	4"x.203" DIA.	RIVETS WITH FLAT BURS	COPPER (WIRE NAILS)	THRU PLANKING, FRAME & BILGE STRINGER.

FASTENING SCHEDULE
25'-5" W.L. ONE DESIGN CRUISING SLOOP
FRANCIS S. KINNEY & CO.
YACHT DESIGNERS
HUNTINGTON N.Y.
DEC. 2, '60 DESIGN 19, DWG. 8

HERRESHOFF'S RULES FOR WOODEN YACHTS

NATHANAEL G. HERRESHOFF, 1927

Even to this day, yachtsmen speak with awe of the excellence of Herreshoff boats. For a long time they were the best of the best, both in design and construction. I know from personal experience, having owned one of their Fishers Island 31's. She is now forty-three years old, is still very fast, and has a hull as sound as a nut.

The late Nathaniel G. Herreshoff, known as the "Wizard of Bristol," wrote down his rules for the construction of wooden yachts in 1927. Although they are more complicated than Nevins' rules, they will produce a lighter boat. In fact, one should not dare build any wooden boat of lighter construction than they allow lest she break up.

General Propositions

Frame Spaces: To be dependent on the displacement of the yacht or boat when at load conditions.   FUNDAMENTAL FACTOR   (I)

Planking: Also Decking, Keel, Clamps, Ceiling, and all other fore and aft members. To be dependent on the displacement of the yacht modified by the ratio of depth to length of hull.   FUNDAMENTAL FACTOR   (II)

Stem Siding: Also Timbers, Floor Timbers, including Plank Floors, etc. To be dependent on the displacement of the yacht.   FUNDAMENTAL FACTOR (III)

Deck Beams: Molded ways to be dependent on the displacement of the yacht modified by the breadth of beam.   FUNDAMENTAL FACTOR (IV)

Sided ways to be dependent on the displacement of the yacht.

FUNDAMENTAL FACTOR (III)

House Deck Beams: Molded ways to be dependent on the displacement of the yacht modified by the length of the longest house beam.

FUNDAMENTAL FACTOR   (V)

These Fundamental Factors depend upon special formulas developed at Bristol, and involve the practice of the Herreshoff Manufacturing Company during the years from 1878 to 1918. These formulas have been reduced to tabular form, and the resulting tables for finding these factors, directly from the principal dimensions of the yacht, are given on page 245.

Notation and Symbols Used

L.W.L. or l.w.l. Length of water line at load conditions, corresponding to L.W.L. as fixed for Universal Rule by New York Yacht Club in 1913 (same as D.W.L.).

O.a.l. or o.a. Extreme length of hull as measured for Universal Rule—between plumb lines.

L. L.W.L. plus ⅓ of overhangs or $\dfrac{2 \text{ L.W.L.} + \text{O.a.l.}}{3}$

B. Extreme breadth of hull, without moldings, taken at 55% of L.W.L. from the fore end of the water line. (Generally called "beam.")

Q.b.l. Quarter beam length as used in Universal Rule.

b. Breadth of hull taken at L.W.L. at 55% of L.W.L. from the fore end of the water line.

d_w or d. Extreme draft of water.

d_h. Depth of hull from top of deck beams to rabbet line taken at 55% of L.W.L. from the fore end of the water line.

b.c.g. Depth of outside ballast from top face to centre of gravity taken at 55% of L.W.L. from the fore end of the water line.

b_b. Breadth at top of outside ballast taken at 55% of L.W.L. from the fore end of the water line.

D. Displacement in cubic feet when in load condition. Corresponding to D in Universal Rule.

S. or S.a. Sail area in square feet. Corresponding to Sail area (S.A.) in Universal Rule.

All data dimensions in feet and decimals

RULES FOR THE USE OF THE TABLES

1. Enter the Table with $\sqrt[3]{D}$ and find at once the values of (I) and (III).
2. Enter the Table with L/d_h and find at once the value of a. Multiply this by (III) to find the value of (II).   Formula: (II) = a × (III).
3. Enter the Table with $\sqrt[4]{D \times B}$ (the square root of the square root) and under (III) find at once the value of (IV).
4. Enter the Table with $\sqrt[4]{D \times \text{length of longest house beam}}$ (the square root of the square root) and under (III) find at once the value of (V).

GENERAL RULES AND SPECIFICATIONS

Frame Spaces

The distance between the centers of frames in inches is to be equal to the Factor (I).

Keel

In standard construction, white oak or teak, in as long lengths as possible.

When it is necessary to be in two or more pieces or where connecting to stem or after overhang timber and deadwood, the scarf or lap joint must extend at least 2½ frame spaces, and be well bolted with Navy or Tobin bronze through bolts having head and nut, the nuts being exposed in the inside when possible.

Yachts having the main keel cast in lead and included in the outside ballast, the lead is to be in depth not less than 1½ times the depth required for oak or teak and the casting is to be stiffened by containing not less than 5% or more than 7½% of antimony.

Keels for inside ballasted yachts or power yachts and launches are to be in siding not less than siding of stem and overhang timber, or less than .35 (II). Molded way or depth to be not less than .8 (II); except near ends of vessel it may be reduced to .5 (II).

Tables of the Fundamental Factors

used in connection with

HERRESHOFF'S RULES FOR THE CONSTRUCTION OF WOODEN YACHTS

Enter with	(I)	(III) and (IV) (inches)	a	Enter with	(I)	(III) and (IV) (inches)	a	Enter with	(I)	(III) and (IV) (inches)	a	Enter with	(I)	(III) and (IV) (inches)	a
3.0	5.91	3.35	1.14	6.0	11.03	7.18	1.24	9.0	15.89	11.21	1.31	12.0	20.59	15.38	1.36
.1	6.09	3.47	1.15	.1	11.20	7.31	1.25	.1	16.05	11.35	1.31	.1	20.75	15.53	1.36
.2	6.27	3.59	1.15	.2	11.36	7.44	1.25	.2	16.21	11.49	1.31	.2	20.90	15.67	1.36
.3	6.44	3.72	1.15	.3	11.53	7.57	1.25	.3	16.37	11.62	1.31	.3	21.05	15.81	1.36
.4	6.62	3.84	1.16	.4	11.69	7.70	1.25	.4	16.53	11.76	1.32	.4	21.21	15.95	1.36
.5	6.79	3.97	1.16	.5	11.86	7.84	1.26	.5	16.69	11.90	1.32	.5	21.36	16.09	1.36
.6	6.97	4.09	1.17	.6	12.02	7.97	1.26	.6	16.85	12.04	1.32	.6	21.52	16.23	1.36
.7	7.14	4.22	1.17	.7	12.19	8.10	1.26	.7	17.00	12.17	1.32	.7	21.67	16.38	1.37
.8	7.31	4.34	1.18	.8	12.35	8.24	1.26	.8	17.16	12.31	1.32	.8	21.82	16.52	1.37
3.9	7.49	4.47	1.18	6.9	12.51	8.37	1.27	9.9	17.32	12.45	1.33	12.9	21.98	16.66	1.37
4.0	7.66	4.60	1.18	7.0	12.68	8.50	1.27	10.0	17.48	12.59	1.33	13.0	22.13	16.80	1.37
.1	7.83	4.72	1.19	.1	12.84	8.64	1.27	.1	17.63	12.73	1.33	.1	22.28	16.94	1.37
.2	8.00	4.85	1.19	.2	13.00	8.77	1.27	.2	17.79	12.87	1.33	.2	22.43	17.08	1.37
.3	8.17	4.97	1.19	.3	13.17	8.90	1.28	.3	17.95	13.01	1.33	.3	22.59	17.23	1.37
.4	8.35	5.10	1.20	.4	13.33	9.04	1.28	.4	18.10	13.14	1.33	.4	22.74	17.37	1.37
.5	8.52	5.23	1.20	.5	13.49	9.17	1.28	.5	18.26	13.28	1.33	.5	22.89	17.51	1.37
.6	8.69	5.36	1.20	.6	13.65	9.31	1.28	.6	18.42	13.42	1.34	.6	23.05	17.66	1.38
.7	8.86	5.49	1.21	.7	13.81	9.44	1.28	.7	18.57	13.56	1.34	.7	23.20	17.80	1.38
.8	9.03	5.61	1.21	.8	13.97	9.58	1.29	.8	18.73	13.70	1.34	.8	23.35	17.94	1.38
4.9	9.20	5.74	1.21	7.9	14.13	9.71	1.29	10.9	18.88	13.84	1.34	13.9	23.50	18.08	1.38
5.0	9.36	5.87	1.22	8.0	14.30	9.85	1.29	11.0	19.04	13.98	1.34	14.0	23.65	18.23	1.38
.1	9.53	6.00	1.22	.1	14.46	9.98	1.29	.1	19.20	14.12	1.34	.1	23.81	18.37	1.38
.2	9.70	6.13	1.22	.2	14.62	10.12	1.29	.2	19.35	14.26	1.34	.2	23.96	18.51	1.38
.3	9.87	6.26	1.22	.3	14.78	10.26	1.30	.3	19.51	14.40	1.34	.3	24.11	18.66	1.38
.4	10.04	6.39	1.23	.4	14.94	10.39	1.30	.4	19.66	14.54	1.35	.4	24.26	18.80	1.38
.5	10.20	6.52	1.23	.5	15.10	10.53	1.30	.5	19.82	14.68	1.35	.5	24.41	18.94	1.39
.6	10.37	6.65	1.23	.6	15.26	10.66	1.30	.6	19.97	14.82	1.35	.6	24.57	19.09	1.39
.7	10.54	6.78	1.24	.7	15.42	10.80	1.30	.7	20.13	14.96	1.35	.7	24.72	19.23	1.39
.8	10.70	6.91	1.24	.8	15.58	10.94	1.30	.8	20.28	15.10	1.35	.8	24.87	19.38	1.39
5.9	10.87	7.04	1.24	8.9	15.74	11.07	1.31	11.9	20.44	15.24	1.35	14.9	25.12	19.52	1.39

Keels in rowboats and centerboard sailing yachts to be not less than .35 (II) in depth and not less than .55 (II) plus centerboard slot in width, the ends gradually tapering to match siding of stem and sternpost. In case of centerboard yachts having main keel of lead, the lower pieces of centerboard casing (centerboard logs) and arms to bolt timbers to (floor timbers) are to be cast as part of the keel. The top of lead to be above top of floor timbers to give a clear caulking seam. Planking rabbet to be cast into lead.

Keels in sailing yachts as developed by the Universal Rule, having outside ballast bolted on, to be of flat plank type with planking rabbet worked into edges.

When one piece of proper size is not obtainable, make keel in two pieces butted together amidships and bolted to a deadwood piece underneath—to be steamed and bent to form. The deadwood where butt is made is to be in depth not less than the keel pieces. Butt to be square-ended and made midway between two consecutive floor timbers and fastened with bronze through-bolts, with nuts above a bronze plate covering the joint. Or make the keel in three pieces: the middle one running from forward of the outside ballast to the intersection with the sternpost and laying directly on top of the outside lead casting; the forward section of keel to be scarfed on top of middle section, with its aft end molded deep enough to make scarf, and then running to stem piece, which is scarfed on; the after section to run over deadwood and to transom, with transom knee lying on top.

The middle section of keel may be dispensed with if the outside lead is properly designed with rabbet for garboard planking and satisfactory connection is made with the forward and after overhang pieces and after deadwood. The last plan is preferable in yachts that are hauled out of water for long periods in dry atmosphere.

Stem Piece

Of white oak or teak as standard woods; but in small classes, of not over 150 cubic feet displacement (row and power boats), hackmatac or other tough and lasting wood may be used. Siding to be .5 (III) and molded way over .7 (III) as required. In yachts of over 100 cubic feet displacement, the back rabbet is to be wide enough for double fastening of wood ends of planking.

The stem piece is to lap the keel at least 2½ frame spaces and to be well bolted with not less than 4 through-bolts set up with nuts. There must always be a breast hook piece, well bolted to sheer strakes and clamps and having a good fore-and-aft bolt through stemhead.

Transom

To be white oak or teak plank in yachts of over 500 cubic feet displacement; in smaller ones may be of lighter wood, as mahogany, butternut, etc. To be steamed and bent to form if curved, and to be reinforced at the edges with white oak in larger, and hackmatac in smaller, yachts. Transom to be rabbeted at edge and reinforcement, making back rabbet to receive fastenings of ends of planks.

To be quarter knees and center line knee on to keel, and framing timbers, if necessary. In small yachts, rowboats, etc., without corner reinforcing, transom plank to be not less than .18 (II) and wood-ends of planking exposed.

Timbers or Frames

To be of best quality of white oak selected for ability to bend to required form when steamed. There is comparatively little white oak that has the proper qualities for first-class timbers, but when obtained there is no other wood equal to it for the purpose.

Timbers must be bent over traps or molds and the larger sizes strapped to prevent splitting. They should be square in section, so best side can be selected for bending. This is important. The size to be .2 (III) at head, and in unballasted power boats and yachts and small open boats size to be uniform for full length.

In sailing yachts that are ballasted, timbers are to increase in size below head as follows:

Inside ballasted yachts are to be .22 (III) square and from 7.2 (III) below head are to taper to size at head .2 (III). Taper equal .1 in 36. = $\frac{1}{32}''$ per ft. nearly.

Center-board and moderate draft yachts with ballast close to keel, timbers .23 (III) square and from 7.2 (III) below head are to taper to size at head. Taper .1 in 24. = $\frac{3}{64}''$ per ft. nearly.

Deep draft yachts with ballast well below hull, timbers .24 (III) square and from 7.2 (III) below head to taper to size at head. Taper .1 in 18. = $\frac{1}{16}''$ per ft. nearly.

In any case where the curvature of the bilge is too quick for timbers to bend safely without splitting or upsetting grain, it is best to split the timbers down with a fine saw into equal parts as far as bend extends, and have all planking fastening go through both parts.

In power yachts increase the siding of timbers that come in machinery section, 50% to 75%.

Floor Timbers

To be of white oak or equivalent in strength and lasting qualities. The arms should be long enough to lap the timbers from 6 to 9 times the size of timbers. Thickness of plank floors not less than .185 (III) and not less than 3 times diameter of keel bolts. Knee or crook floors are to be sided not less than .28 (III) with depth in throat not less than .32 (III) and arm ends not less than size of timbers.

There should be not less than 3 timber bolts each side, of diameter $\frac{1}{6}$ to $\frac{1}{8}$ size of timber, passing through timber and floor timber and set up with nuts. Bronze in smaller sizes, but over $\frac{5}{16}''$, good galvanized iron or steel may be used.

Keel bolts should always be bronze if they come in contact with lead ballast. If not, sizes over $\frac{3}{8}''$ may be good galvanized iron or steel. Have two keel bolts whenever possible, in diameter not less than $\frac{1}{5}$ to $\frac{1}{6}$ size of timber, but if only room for one bolt into keel to be larger, depending on character of keel and deadrise of hull section.

When floor timber bolts support outside lead ballast they are to be increased in size. Their diameter in inches is to be not less than the square root of weight of outside lead in tons divided by number of bolts supporting lead,

$$\sqrt{\frac{\text{Tons lead}}{\text{no. bolts}}}$$

If it is desirable to use bolts of different diameters, proper compensation should be made so the total bolt area is not reduced and when bolts are independent of floor timber bolts, their size is to be equivalent in size to the sectional area of adjacent floor timber bolts, as determined above.

Floor timbers over outside ballast are to be increased in size so their thickness is not less than three times diameter of bolts passing through them and length and depth sufficient to receive four timber bolts, each side.

Lead Bolts and Straps

Their diameter to be determined by the size and number of floor timber bolts as explained above. Always have them carefully distributed and as near each edge as possible, and have nuts at their upper end so they can be tightened up when necessary. One or more bolts at each end should pass way through lead. All others may be screwed into the lead and the threads that go into the lead should be similar to those on wood screws and lag screws. The bolts should penetrate the lead 8 diameters and the length threaded 7 diameters. The pitch of threads should be about $\frac{1}{5}$ diameter and depth 1/10 diameter.

All outside lead on wood yachts should have straps extending vertically to connect lead directly with timbers and planking. These straps are to be let in flush and to lap on lead about 5 times their breadth and on to the timbers and above the keel and deadwood about 8 times their breadth.

Tobin bronze appears to be the best material. There are to be 5 to 8 straps each side placed on consecutive timbers in the middle part and on alternate timbers near ends of lead. Their size to be determined by multiplying weight of outside lead in tons by ratio (depth of lead to center of gravity divided by breadth on top), *if over one* and if not, by one. Divide by one and eight-tenths times whole number of straps, which will give sectional area in square inches of each strap.

$$\frac{\text{b.c.g.}}{b_b} \times \frac{\text{Tons}}{1.8 \text{ number}} \text{ or } \frac{\text{Tons}}{1.8 \text{ number}}.$$

The breadth to be 4 times and thickness $\frac{1}{4}$ the square root of area.

Diameter of screws and bolts to be $\frac{1}{9}$ breadth of strap and there are to be not less than 8 brass wood screws into lead and not less than 9 bronze through-bolts with nuts through planking and timbers. Countersinking for heads of screws and bolts should not be over $1\frac{3}{4}$ diameter of bolts and the heads worked down flush after being set up.

Outside Planking

The thickness to be not less than .105 (II).

White cedar is the best wood for all small craft under 75 to 100 cu. ft. displacement.

In sizes from 75 to 200 or 250 cu. ft. a somewhat firmer wood is preferable, as Port Orford cedar, Mexican mahogany or Douglas fir. Larger yachts should have planking of woods of still harder texture as Georgia pine, western oak of good quality, teak or mahogany of hard texture.

Small lap streaked boats should have the laps well fastened with copper clinch nails or copper through fastening with bars.

Single planking with square seams should be well and closely fitted and caulked with cotton in small and intermediate sizes. The large sizes with hard wood planking, okum caulking may be used.

When double planked, it is found most practicable to have both layers parallel and the seams about equally lapped. The layers are to be well cemented together. Shellac is found best, but when there is plenty of time (2 or 3 months for setting) white lead is as good, or better in large work. The inner layer should be $\frac{3}{8}$ to $\frac{1}{2}$ of total thickness and softer or lighter wood may be used, as cedar or cypress with Mexican mahogany or Douglas fir outside. Have the layers well screw-fastened from inside between the timbers. It is always best to have garboard and sheer strakes single thickness and a good practice is to have a few strakes above the garboards also single.

The edges to receive double planking should be rabbeted to make a lap joint with one of the layers.

Sheer strakes should be of a hard wood that will well hold drive or screw fastening as white oak, teak, mahogany of hard texture, etc., and to be well seasoned. The molded form is desirable in smaller yachts and the thickness through swell about $1\frac{1}{4}$ times thickness of planking. Extra thickness in larger yachts than thickness of planking is also desirable—to have more wood for the vertical fastening of planksheer and rail.

Diagonal Strapping

In small yachts, under 100 cubic feet displacement, it is not necessary. In larger ones strap as follows:

Single planked, 100 to 175 cu. ft. displ. Double " 175 to 300 " " "	}	2 straps
Single planked, 175 to 300 cu. ft. displ. Double " 300 to 500 " " "	}	3 straps
Single planked, 300 to 500 cu. ft. displ. Double " 500 to 900 " " "	}	5 straps
Single planked, 500 to 900 cu. ft. displ. Double " 900 to 1500 " " "	}	5 diagonal and body strap
Single planked over 900 cu. ft. displ.		7 diagonal and body strap

Yachts over 1,200 cubic feet displacement had better be of composite build. The straps are to be arranged as shown in the diagrams below.

Diagonal strapping

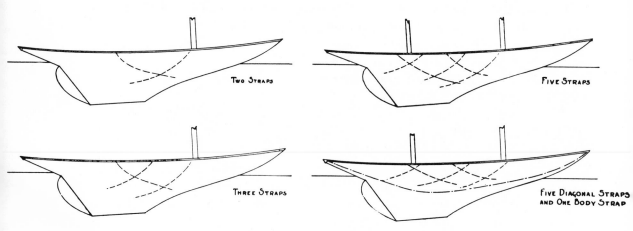

When body straps are used, the diagonal straps are to be fastened to them.

Light draft sailing yachts and power yachts of any considerable size, say over 300 cubic feet displacement, should be diagonally strapped or stiffened in some way. In hulls of from 300 to 500 cubic feet displacement a very good way is to have arched stringers intersected by short bilge stringers of oak or yellow pine, thus

The arched stringers if in two or more lengths to be well secured at the butts, and the bilge stringers well secured to the arch stringers at their ends. All to be well fastened to the inside of the timbers. Larger yachts to have the regular system of diagonal strapping laid on to the outside of the timbers before planking. Their arrangement depends so much on the character of hull and distribution of weights, it is difficult to formulate a rule, but generally, drooping of ends and sagging at position of machinery have to be looked out for.

In the sailing yachts that have body bands, they should be well secured to the stem near its head and run aft under the lower part of body amidships, finally terminating at the quarters where they should be well secured. The lower end of all diagonal straps should terminate at these bands and be well secured to them.

Arranged this way straps do not go into the bilge-water and therefore are not subjected to intense corrosion.

The size of straps to be about the same as determined for lead straps, or possibly a little wider and thinner, and body bands about the same thickness but 50% to 75% wider. Screw fastening at each edge into planking and also into timbers. Tobin bronze is standard but in larger sized yachts galvanized steel banding is usual.

Clamps

Clamps for supporting deck beams and making a longitudinal tie should be continuous from breast hook to quarter knees, and if in more than one length avoid if possible having any butt near amidships. The best practice is to have a long length amidship and butted to two shorter ones at ends. Connection to be made by a short filling piece between the clamp and sheer strake between adjacent timbers (the butt being midway of a frame space) and a long butt piece on the inside of clamp covering 5 frame spaces, and well through fastened. This inside piece may be of wood same as clamp or of galvanized steel angle. Bevel clamps at outside so top surface is level and correctly fays to the deck beams, which are to have a level seating. Their size before beveling should be .24 (II) each way and the inner lower corner may be chamfered away about .05 (II) excepting under butt pieces.

In the smaller classes, spruce or other stiff light wood may be used but in larger ones woods of harder texture, as Douglas fir, Georgia pine or oak, and in as long lengths as possible.

In yachts having long cabin trunks, or houses, that cut off the deck beams, it is desirable to have a secondary clamp inside the primary, and well bolted to it.

In many yachts having high topsides and flush decks clamps may be omitted, and the deck beams supported by metallic drop knees or brackets, bolted to deck beam and timber, both being placed in the same plane. If this construction be used longitudinal strength shall then be made up by having a molded or thicker sheer strake and a heavier planksheer or waterway.

Breast Hook and Quarter Knees

There should always be a breast hook to connect the stem, sheer strakes and decking securely together. In the modern sailing yacht it becomes a chunk of wood to receive bolts and fastening, but it should be selected with care for soundness and durability, and it must be well seasoned. There should be a long fore and aft bolt passing through stem and set up with a nut inside. The forward end of clamps should also be bolted to under side of breast hook.

Quarter knees must be fitted to securely connect the sheer strakes, clamps, and transom, and also a ledge piece to receive wood ends of deck. Take particular care that the quarter knees and other pieces in the vicinity are of thoroughly seasoned wood that is not subject to dry rot.

Deck Beams

The most·desirable wood is white oak or yellow-bark oak, in the larger sizes. Yellow-bark oak, white ash or chestnut in intermediate sizes, and white ash, chestnut or butternut in smaller. It is recommended they be placed on large side of every frame space, the timbers being on the small, or side towards ends of vessel, excepting at frames where there are hanging knees or when there is no clamp, but knee brackets, then they should be in same plane as timber.

The molded size to be .28 (IV). Camber for both top and bottom sides should be the same, for all beams, and between $\frac{1}{3}''$ and $\frac{1}{2}''$ per foot of beam of vessel, or between $\frac{B}{36}$ and $\frac{B}{24}$. The radius of curvature between 9B and 6B. Make the depth of end of all beams .20 (IV), and the under side on level line until intersected by molded or cambered part, as below.

The regular size for siding of deck beams to be .17 (III). Beams each side of mast, and each side of hatches with not more than two beams cut, and at position of belt frames, to be sided .23 (III). At hatches cutting more than two beams, and at breaks of deck, to be sided .30 (III).

Half beams with inboard end supported by hatch coaming or cabin house side may be molded .20 (IV) and sided .17 (III), and there are to be wedge shaped shims between under sides and clamps.

Deck Diagonal Strapping

In yachts over 175 and under 350 cubic feet displacement have one pair running from gunwale to gunwale and crossing near mast partners. Yachts between 300 and 700 cubic feet displacement 2 pairs, and over 700 three or more pairs—all placed where they can best run from gunwale to gunwale and not be cut by hatchways or other deck openings. The angle with center line between 30° and 45°. The size to be about the same as for planking straps. They may be cut into deck beam flush or fairing pieces, thickness of straps placed on top of beams laid in white lead. To be fastened into deck beams and also into deck between beams, with brass screws.

Margin Plank or Planksheer

To run continuously from stemhead over sheerstrakes and deckbeam ends, to and around transom and return on other side. To be worked in long lengths as possible with butts on buttblocks between timbers, and shifted two or more frame spaces from butts of sheerstrakes and clamps. The thickness to be not less than main deck and more is better if deck is bright for holystoning. Breadth to be .38 (II). To be screw fastened into sheerstrake and beam ends. If deck planks are to be laid straight, make breadth .42 (II) to allow nibbing in ends of decking.

Best woods are teak, white oak, mahogany of hard texture, in larger; and mahogany, Georgia pine or Douglas fir, in small yachts.

Main Deck

The best wood is clear white pine free from sap and shakes. If a deck is to be canvas covered, which is always recommended in decks less than $1\frac{1}{4}''$ thick, other light woods are good, as Washington spruce, Port Orford cedar, white cedar, etc.

The best practice is to lay with square seams of thoroughly dry stock and to be tightly caulked with cotton. Bare decks to have seams filled with marine glue after caulking. When canvas covered, seams puttied flush.

In the heavier decks a good practice is to get the stock out square so to be able to select the best side to be up, which must always show edge of grain. Such a deck has one fastening to each beam. For two fastenings, breadth should be from $1\frac{3}{4}$ to $2\frac{1}{2}$ times thickness .185 (II) to .260 (II). Standard thickness to be .105 (II), and if canvas covered, thickness may be reduced to .1 (II)—.05''. If teak is substituted for white pine in the larger sizes, thickness to be .075 (II). It is generally desirable to lay the deck parallel to the margin plank, with ends nibbed into a king plank when approaching center line.

Cabin Trunks, or Houses

If sides are of plank of soft wood, thickness to be .110 (II), and if mahogany, .1 (II), or if teak, .095 (II). The sides should be edge bolted at spacing not over 2 frame spaces.

The house deck beams should be secured to house sides either by a white oak lining strip in width $1\frac{3}{4}$ times molded size of beams and thickness .1 (II). The beams to be dove-tailed into it. Or by metal brackets or clips, securely fastened.

If the sides are framed and with glass or wood panels, frame to be either mahogany or teak .12 (II) in thickness, and glass not less than $\frac{7}{32}''$ thick or .018 (II), and with wood panels, .06 (II).

House deck beams may be dove-tailed into upper rail of framed side provided it is increased in thickness to .175 (II) and not cut through, but leaving not less than .70 (II) of wood at end of beam.

The molded depth of house or trunk deck beams to be .28 (V): where the factor (V) is taken from Table III by entering with $\sqrt[4]{D}$ × length of longest beam. (Square root of the square root); but not less than $\frac{2}{3}$ molded depth of main deck beams. The spacing,—siding of beams and thickness of deck, to be in proportion to corresponding scantling of main deck as the square root of the ratio of length of house to the mean length of hull (L), but not less than $\frac{2}{3}$ of corresponding dimensions of main deck, and to be of equivalent grade of wood. Beams each side of mast hatches, etc., are to be increased as in main deck beams.

Camber to be between 1/24 and 1/36 of length of longest house beam.

House deck to be laid in same manner as main deck, and same allowance of thickness for canvas to be made.

When the house deck extends forward of a mast it must be diagonally strapped as thoroughly as the main deck.

Mast Partners and Steps

At the position of each mast, bitts, capstan, mooring cleats, etc., the deck should be reinforced between deck beams by a well seasoned hardwood plank running thwartships,—in thickness .125 (II) and length equal to $2\frac{1}{2}$ frame spaces, for mast, bitts and main capstan, and not less than $1\frac{1}{2}$ frame spaces for other major deck fittings. Each side of a mast or bitt hole should be edge bolted, passing through adjacent deck beams and set up with nuts.

Mast steps should be of hard wood—white oak is best—and well supported against the intense thrust of the mast. They should rest on 3 or 4 floor timbers of extra size, and in the larger sizes of racing yachts, extra timbers and intermediate timbers or straps connecting with chainplates and passing down under mast step is desirable.

Inside Ceiling

Every wood framed yacht should be ceiled from the cabin sole to within a frame space length of the deck beams, or higher, and for at least $\frac{3}{4}$ length ($\frac{3}{4}$L) in middle part, but to extend as much farther as is necessary to reach by any sleeping berth. The thickness of ceiling to be .20″ + .025 (II). To be laid in reasonably long lengths, seams close and to be well fastened to timbers. Use cedar in smaller sizes and harder woods in larger, ranging up to Douglas fir or Georgia pine in the largest.

Bilge Stringers

Are not necessary in any yacht that is well ceiled as directed. In cases where a yacht is liable to lay aground and over on her bilge, it is well to have outside protection in the form of one or two or three thick bilge strakes of planking for the middle $\frac{1}{3}$ length, or a bilge keel in lieu of it.

Hanging Knees and Belt Frames

In larger sizes of sailing yachts—over 500 cubic feet displacement with outside ballast—they should be strengthened by belt frames and hanging knees. They can generally be placed at frame spaces that will not interfere with berth spaces, and at partitions, and not closer than $6\frac{1}{2}$ to 8 feet apart. Have two on each side on yachts between 500 and 900 cubic feet displacement and 3 or 4 each side on yachts over 900 cubic feet displacement. The belt timber to be .23 (III) square of best white oak, steamed and bent to place. These timbers should be fitted inside the ceiling and *not* cut it, and hanging knees should connect them to the deck beams of same siding as belt frames: have through fastenings of size for lead straps, with heads bunged into outside planking and passing through timber, ceiling, and belt timber, with nuts inside and not over 1 (III) apart.

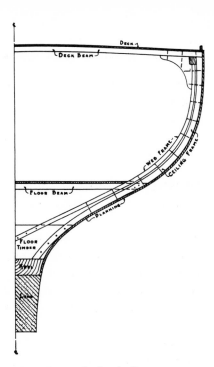

Wooden construction section by Herreshoff.

The lower end of belt frames to be well fastened to face of plank floors, as are the main timbers.

Cabin Floor, or Sole

Should be laid on oak beams, spaced same as main timbers and substantially secured to them, and to be stanchioned to floor timbers where necessary to prevent vibration. Floor may be cedar in small boats, ranging up to Douglas fir and Georgia pine in the largest. The thickness to be $.20'' + .035$ (II). Beams to be sided $.2'' + 0.55$ (II) and depth $2\frac{1}{2}$ times siding.

Rudder Stocks

Tobin bronze is standard material for all wood constructed yachts. The diameter in inches for sailing yachts to be not less than .155 times breadth of yacht in feet, (.155B) and also not less than the fourth root of 2/100 times distance of center of area of rudder blade from axis, times area of blade, times mean length of vessel, all in feet. $(\sqrt[4]{.02 \times v \times a \times L})$

The connection of rudder blade to stock to be by two bronze castings with double arms in the general form as shown. To be fitted and keyed tight to stock, and held to blade by two or three copper rivets.

Proportions:
If the diameter of the stock A is 1:
  then the other dimensions should be
  B = 1¾   C = 1   D = 1⅛
  E = 4   G = ⅜   K = ¼
  F = ¼ or ⅟₃₂ if 3 bolts.
  H and H′ as required for
    the thickness of the blade.
  K is the size of key.

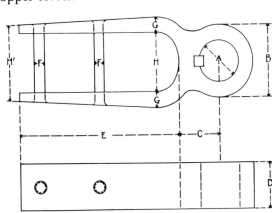

It is difficult to make a close rule for stocks to rudders of power vessels. As a rough rule: When blades are supported by a step or pintles. Diameter in inches not less than .18 (III), and not less than .85 (dia. of propeller shaft).

If blade is pendant, then stock to be not less than .225 (III) and not less than 1.25 (dia. of propeller shaft) and if twin screw, 1.5 (dia. of shafts).

Planking and Deck Fastenings

Brass wood screws are usually used and give good results generally, although occasionally there is trouble from electrolysis, and a different composition than that usually used in wood screws that is not subject to it would be better. For the special purpose, screws that are threaded but six-tenths of length, so the body part will extend into timber to give better sheering resistance, is better. Care should be taken to bore correct sizes for screw end—body and bung, and special bitts that will bore the three sizes at once are desirable. The sizes of screws under No. 10—it is generally more practical to putty or wax the heads instead of bunging, and in that case $\frac{1}{8}$ inch longer screws can be used and not counter-bored, but the head set in a short distance.

Table of Sizes of Screws for Planking and Deck Fastenings

Planking Thickness	Approximate Diameter	Screw Gauge Number	Length	Diameter of Bung
$\frac{3}{8}''$	$\frac{9}{64}''$	6	$\frac{3}{4}''$	$\frac{5}{16}''$
$\frac{7}{16}''$	$\frac{5}{32}''$	7	$\frac{7}{8}''$	$\frac{5}{16}''$
$\frac{1}{2}''$	$\frac{11}{64}''$	8	$1''$	$\frac{3}{8}''$
$\frac{9}{16}''$	$\frac{3}{16}''$	9	$1\frac{1}{8}''$	$\frac{3}{8}''$
$\frac{5}{8}''$	$\frac{3}{16}''$	10	$1\frac{1}{4}''$	$\frac{7}{16}''$
$\frac{3}{4}''$	$\frac{7}{32}''$	12	$1\frac{1}{2}''$	$\frac{7}{16}''$
$\frac{7}{8}''$	$\frac{1}{4}''$	14	$1\frac{3}{4}''$	$\frac{1}{2}''$
$1''$	$\frac{17}{64}''$	16	$2''$	$\frac{9}{16}''$
$1\frac{1}{8}''$	$\frac{19}{64}''$	18	$2\frac{1}{4}''$	$\frac{5}{8}''$
$1\frac{1}{4}''$	$\frac{5}{16}''$	20	$2\frac{1}{2}''$	$\frac{11}{16}''$
$1\frac{1}{2}''$	$\frac{11}{32}''$	22	$2\frac{3}{4}''$	$\frac{11}{16}''$ or $\frac{3}{4}''$
$1\frac{3}{4}''$	$\frac{3}{8}''$	24	$3''$	$\frac{3}{4}''$ or $\frac{13}{16}''$
$2''$	$\frac{13}{32}''$	26	$3\frac{1}{2}''$	$\frac{13}{16}''$

For double planked yachts use table sizes for inner plank fastening to timbers and same gauge but length as required for fastening between timbers. For outer plank use sizes for total thickness of both inner and outer planking.

Table of Dimensions in Terms of the Fundamental Factors

INCHES AND DECIMALS

	Deep Keel	Moderate Draft, Center-Board: Outside Ballast	Inside Ballast Sailing Yachts: Power-Boats
FRAME SPACES:	(I)	(I)	(I)
KEEL:			
Depth, or thickness at ends:	.28 (II)	.35 (II)	.80 (II)
Width:		.55 (II)	.55 (II)
		+ c. b. slot	+ c. b. slot
STEM PIECE:			
Sided:	.50 (III)	.50 (III)	.50 (III)
Molded:	.70 (III)	.70 (III)	.70 (III)
TRANSOM:			
Thickness:	.095 (II)	.095 (II)	.095 (II)
Reinforcing thickness:	.18 (II)	.18 (II)	.18 (II)
TIMBERS:			
At head (square)	.20 (III)	.20 (III)	.20 (III)
Maximum (square)	.24 (III)	.23 (III)	.22 (III)
Length of taper:	7.20 (III)	7.20 (III)	7.20 (III)
Taper (per foot)	$\frac{1}{16}''$	$\frac{3}{64}''$	$\frac{1}{32}''$
FLOOR TIMBERS:			
Plank Floors: thick	.185 (III)	.185 (III)	.185 (III)
Crook Floors: thick	.28 (III)	.28 (III)	.28 (III)
deep	.32 (III)	.32 (III)	.32 (III)
OUTSIDE PLANKING:			
Thickness:	.105 (II)	.105 (II)	.105 (II)
CLAMPS:			
Before beveling:	.24 (II)	.24 (II)	.24 (II)
Chamfer (not over):	.05 (II)	.05 (II)	.05 (II)
DECK BEAMS:			
Molded: maximum:	.28 (IV)	.28 (IV)	.28 (IV)
at ends:	.20 (IV)	.20 (IV)	.20 (IV)
Sided: regular	.17 (III)	.17 (III)	.17 (III)
at mast & small hatches:	.23 (III)	.23 (III)	.23 (III)
at large hatches:	.30 (III)	.30 (III)	.30 (III)
Half Beams:			
Molded:	.20 (IV)	.20 (IV)	.20 (IV)
Sided:	.17 (III)	.17 (III)	.17 (III)
PLANKSHEER:			
Thickness:	same as deck	same as deck	same as deck
Breadth:			
Curved deck:	.38 (II)	.38 (II)	.38 (II)
Straight deck:	.42 (II)	.42 (II)	.42 (II)
MAIN DECK:			
Thickness: Pine:	.105 (II)	.105 (II)	.105 (II)
Teak:	.075 (II)	.075 (II)	.075 (II)
Canvas:	.100 (II)	.100 (II)	.100 (II)
	—.05''	—.05''	—.05''

	Deep Keel	Moderate Draft, Centre-Board: Outside Ballast	Inside Ballast Sailing Yachts: Power-Boats
CABIN TRUNKS:			
Solid Plank:			
Soft wood:	.110 (II)	.110 (II)	.100 (II)
Mahogany:	.100 (II)	.100 (II)	.100 (II)
Teak:	.095 (II)	.095 (II)	.095 (II)
Glass or paneled:			
Frame (Mahogany or Teak):	.120 (II)	.120 (II)	.120 (II)
Panels	.060 (II)	.060 (II)	.060 (II)
Deck Beams:			
Molded depth:	.28 (V)	.28 (V)	.28 (V)
MAST PARTNERS AND DECK FITTINGS:			
Thickness:	.125 (II)	.125 (II)	.125 (II)
INSIDE CEILING:			
Thickness:	.025 (II) +.20″	.025 (II) +.20″	.025 (II) +.20″
BELT TIMBER:			
Square:	.23 (III)	.23 (III)	
CABIN FLOOR, OR SOLE:			
Thickness:	.035 (II) +.20″	.035 (II) +.20″	.035 (II) +.20″
Beams:			
Sided:	.055 (II) +.20″	.055 (II) +.20″	.055 (II) +.20″
Depth:	2.5 × siding	2.5 × siding	2.5 × siding

Example

The method of using these Rules and Tables is shown in the following example of finding the required scantlings of a 30-foot deep keel yacht.

1. DIMENSIONS OF YACHT.

Length over all:	42′ 3″	O.a.l.
Load water-line length:	30′ 0″	L.W.L.
Beam:	9′ 2″	B.
Depth of hull:	6′ 0″	d_h
Depth of outside lead:	2′ 5″	b.c.g.
Breadth of outside lead:	1′ 1″	b_b
Weight of outside lead:	5 tons	
Displacement	275 cu. ft.	D.

2. CALCULATION OF FUNDAMENTAL FACTORS.

a. From the above dimensions find (to nearest tenth).

$$L = \frac{42.25 + 60.00}{3} = 34.1$$

$$L/d_h = \frac{34.1}{6} = 5.7$$

$$D \times B = 275 \times 9.18 = 2525$$

From tables of square and cube roots, take out at once:

D $\quad$ = $\quad$ 275 $\quad$ $\sqrt[3]{D}$ $\quad$ = $\quad$ 6.5

D $\times$ B $\quad$ = $\quad$ 2525 $\quad$ $\sqrt[3]{D \times B}$ $\quad$ = $\quad$ 50.3

$\sqrt[3]{D \times B}$ $\quad$ = $\quad$ 50.3 $\quad$ $\sqrt{\sqrt[3]{D \times B}}$ $\quad$ = $\quad$ 7.1

b. From the Tables of Fundamental Factors:

Enter with 6.5 and find: $\quad\quad$ (I) $\quad$ = $\quad$ 11.86

$\quad\quad\quad\quad\quad\quad\quad\quad\quad\quad$ (III) $\quad$ = $\quad$ 7.84

Enter with 5.7 and find: $\quad\quad\quad$ a $\quad$ = $\quad$ 1.24

$\quad$ Thence: 1.24 $\times$ 7.84 $\quad$ = $\quad$ (II) $\quad$ = $\quad$ 9.72

Enter with 7.1 and find: $\quad$ (IV) $\quad$ = $\quad$ 8.64

3. Calculation of Scantlings and Dimensions.

FRAME SPACES:

$\quad$ Equal to (I), or to 11.86 inches:

$\quad$ Use 11¾″ or 12″

KEEL:

$\quad$ Thickness equals .28 (II) $\quad$ = $\quad$ 28 (9.72) $\quad$ = $\quad$ 2.72 inches

$\quad$ Use white oak plank, 2¾″

STEM PIECE:

$\quad$ Sided: $\quad\quad\quad\quad\quad\quad\quad$ .50 (III) $\quad$ = $\quad$ .50 (7.84) $\quad$ = $\quad$ 3.92 inches

$\quad$ Molded: not less: $\quad\quad\quad$ .70 (III) $\quad$ = $\quad$ .70 (7.84) $\quad$ = $\quad$ 5.49 inches

$\quad$ Use white oak: $\quad\quad\quad\quad$ 3⅛″ by 5½″ or more.

TRANSOM:

$\quad$ Thickness: $\quad\quad\quad\quad\quad$ .095 (II) $\quad$ = .095 (9.72) $\quad$ = $\quad$ 0.92 inches

$\quad$ Reinforcing: $\quad\quad\quad\quad$ .180 (II) $\quad$ = .180 (9.72) $\quad$ = $\quad$ 1.49 inches

$\quad$ Use oak or hackmatac:

$\quad$ Thickness: $\quad$ $\tfrac{15}{16}$″

$\quad$ Reinforcing: $\quad$ 1½″

TIMBERS:

$\quad$ At head: $\quad\quad\quad\quad\quad\quad$ .20 (III) $\quad$ = $\quad$ .20 (7.84) $\quad$ = $\quad$ 1.57 inches

$\quad$ Maximum: $\quad\quad\quad\quad\quad$ .24 (III) $\quad$ = $\quad$ .24 (7.84) $\quad$ = $\quad$ 1.88 inches

$\quad$ Length of taper: $\quad\quad$ 7.20 (III) $\quad$ = 7.2 (7.84) $\quad$ = 56.45 inches

$\quad$ Use selected white oak:

$\quad\quad$ 1$\tfrac{9}{16}$″ square at head: increasing for 56½″ to 1⅞″ square.

FLOOR TIMBERS:

$\quad$ Plank:

$\quad$ Thickness: $\quad\quad\quad\quad\quad$ .185 (III) $\quad$ = .185 (7.84) $\quad$ = 1.45 inches

$\quad$ Use oak plank: $\quad\quad\quad\quad$ 1⅜″ and for floor timbers over outside lead, thickness not less than 3 times size of bolts or 1⅞″

OUTSIDE PLANKING:

$\quad$ Thickness: $\quad\quad\quad\quad\quad$ .105 (II) $\quad$ = .105 (9.72) $\quad$ = 1.02 inches

$\quad$ Suggest lower third, Georgia pine and remainder double thickness:—Mexican mahogany $\tfrac{9}{16}$″ outside; White cedar or cypress $\tfrac{7}{16}$″ inside.

CLAMPS:

Before beveling:	.24 (II)	=	.24 (9.72)	=	2.33 inches
Chamfer:	.05 (II)	=	.05 (9.72)	=	0.48 inches

Use Douglas fir or Georgia pine:

$2\frac{3}{8}''$ square before beveling: chamfer not over $\frac{1}{2}''$

DECK BEAMS:

Molded:	.28 (IV)	=	.28 (8.64)	=	2.42 inches
At ends:	.20 (IV)	=	.20 (8.64)	=	1.73 inches
Sided: regular:	.17 (III)	=	.17 (7.84)	=	1.33 inches
at mast:	.23 (III)	=	.23 (7.84)	=	1.80 inches
large:	.30 (III)	=	.30 (7.84)	=	2.35 inches

Use white or yellow bark oak:

Molded maximum $2\frac{7}{16}''$: depth at ends $1\frac{3}{4}''$

Regular beams to be sided $1\frac{3}{8}''$

Two beams at mast partners, two at hatch, and one at aft end of cockpit to be sided $1\frac{3}{4}''$

Beam at forward end of companion to be sided $2\frac{3}{8}''$

Half-beams:

Molded:	.20 (IV)	=	.20 (8.64)	=	1.73 inches
Sided:	.17 (III)	=	.17 (7.84)	=	1.33 inches

Half-beams at sides of hatch, main companion way, and cockpit to be molded $1\frac{3}{4}''$; sided $1\frac{3}{8}''$

PLANKSHEER:

Breadth:	.38 (II)	=	.38 (9.72)	=	3.69 inches

Use long mahogany or Georgia pine if deck is bright; Georgia pine or Douglas fir if canvas covered: Breadth to be $3\frac{3}{4}''$

MAIN DECK:

Thickness: pine	.105 (II)	=	.105 (9.72)	=	1.02 inches

White pine, if bright and $1''$ thick:

White pine, Port Orford cedar, or Washington spruce if canvassed, and $\frac{15}{16}''$ thick.

Breadth of plank:	.22 (II)	=	.22 (9.72)	=	2.13 inches

Use $2\frac{1}{8}''$ or $2\frac{1}{4}''$

CEILING:

Thickness:	.025 (II)	.025 (9.72)		
	+ .20''	+ .20''	=	0.44 inches

Use $\frac{7}{16}''$

CABIN FLOOR:

Thickness:	.035 (II)	.035 (9.72)		
	+ .20''	+ .20''	=	0.54 inches

Use white pine or Douglas fir, $\frac{9}{16}''$ thick

Beams: thick	.055 (II)	.055 (9.72)		
	+ .20''	+ .20''	=	0.73 inches

To be $\frac{3}{4}''$ thick and $1\frac{7}{8}''$ deep.

LEAD BOLTS:

There should be 12. Diameter $= \sqrt{5 \text{ tons} \div 12} = 0.65$ inches. Hence make 5 pair of side bolts $\frac{5}{8}''$ diameter, and 2 centre end bolts going way through $\frac{3}{4}''$ diameter. Side bolts may be lag-screw type, threaded about $4\frac{1}{2}''$ and screwed into lead about $5''$; with machine screw and nuts at head end and set down tightly on packed washers on top of keel.

LEAD STRAPS:

There should be 5 on each side. Then sectional area in square inches is Tons $\div 1.8 \times$ number, or 5/18, which is .278 sq. in. The square root of this is .527: hence, Breadth of strap is $4 \times (.527) = 2.11$ inches: use $2\frac{1}{4}''$
Thickness is $.25 \times (.527) = 0.13$ inches: use $\frac{1}{8}''$

Screws and bolts $\frac{1}{4}''$ diameter. Straps to lap on lead not less than $11''$ and on timbers above keel not less than $17''$. For length add depth of deadwood, keel, and 11 and 17.

DIAGONAL STRAPS:

To be 2 on each side of size of lead straps and in position covering mast and greatest section, as shown in diagram.

RUDDER STOCK:

Tobin bronze, not less than .155B in diameter, or .155 (9.2) = 1.42 inches. Use $1\frac{7}{16}''$, or $1\frac{1}{2}''$ Tobin bronze shafting.

Fiberglass Construction. During the year 1959, it is estimated that 130,000 boats were built of fiberglass reinforced plastics. Today it is estimated that there are half a million fiberglass boats in use.

The outstanding advantages of boats built of fiberglass over boats built of the other well-known materials are:

1. Greatly reduced maintenance.
2. Resistance to corrosion and dry rot.
3. Monolithic (one-piece) construction.

Time has not yet told how long fiberglass boats will last, compared to wood or steel, but we do know that this material tends to become harder and more brittle as it gets older. This is its great disadvantage.

Fiberglass reinforced plastic is a combination of high-strength glass fibers bonded together with relatively low-strength resin. The glass fibers may be distributed, as a woven cloth, in two directions; as a mat of chopped fibers, in all directions; as continuous strands or rovings, in one direction; or as combinations of all of these.

Sandwiches are made utilizing a core of balsa wood, or foamed plastics (polyurethane is one; polystyrene is another), or light weight plastic spheres imbedded in resin, or honeycombed waterproof paper. These cores may be considered as the filling—and reinforced fiberglass as the bread—of the sandwich, delicious to the designer who has a craving for a light, strong material with which to construct his creations. Honeycomb shapes are also available in aluminum, cotton duck, and fiberglass laminates. The core material must never be solid hard wood which tends to swell and crack the laminate.

Molded-in stiffeners, with cores such as are mentioned above or cores of paper or aluminum tubing, take the place of separate structural members, such as beams and frames. This is almost the perfect monolithic construction and is to naval architecture what reinforced concrete is to other architecture.

Instead of the many members required in other types of construction—the stem, keel, horn timber, floors, frames, hundreds of planks, beams, stringers, etc., etc.—all of which have to be carefully fitted together and securely fastened, there are few major components. Fiberglass boats are sometimes built of only two pieces—the hull and the deck. A major problem seems to be how to make a good connection between the one-piece hull and the one-piece deck.

A joint must be easily made by the fabricators. Quality control in fiberglass construction is all-important, and a joint that the builder can make well will often be stronger than a joint that appears stronger on paper but can not be easily made and inspected.

Resins fall into two groups, polyesters and epoxy. The polyesters are subdivided into: rigid (stiff, very strong, but brittle; used for boats less than 16' over-all); semirigid (more resilient; preferred for boats above 16'); flexible (too elastic for use alone in boat construction); fast curing (better suited to pressure molding);

and fire-resistant (whose physical properties are not as great as the ordinary polyester resins, which unfortunately will burn).

One method of increasing the fire resistance of fiberglass boats and yet maintaining the strength required is to combine the two types of polyesters, using the ordinary high-strength polyester for the core and sealing its surface with outer plies of a self-extinguishing type.

Epoxy resins are syrup-like liquids which, like polyesters, can be cured into hard solids. They stick to almost anything, and have higher physical properties than the polyesters. The shrinkage during cure is considerably smaller than that of polyesters.

Fiberglass boats can not go for long without being painted, in spite of some claims, and in spite of fillers and pigments added to the molding resins. Ultraviolet rays in sunlight are considered to be the chief cause of weather deterioration and nature takes its course, regardless. If the boat is kept in the water, the bottom will soon foul up with slime, grass, and barnacles, unless it is painted with antifouling paint. The topsides will soon become dirty because fiberglass quickly collects dirt. So the only way to give a fiberglass boat a pleasing appearance is to paint it. Epoxy paints are used. They should be applied with a roller or a spray gun, instead of a brush.

Manufacturers of fiberglass and resins are more than willing to assist builders. Because of the large amount of technical data now available on resins, it is possible for a builder to obtain the highest quality laminates. The handling of resins, catalysts, accelerators, and stabilizers must be in strict accordance with the manufacturer's recommendations. The time interval between mixing and application is important because overage polyester should not be used. Temperature affects the chemical action. Shrinkage of the resin and temperature changes occurring during curing cause residual stresses. These stresses can affect the loading strength, fatigue strength, and resistance to weathering and crazing.

Franz Maas Method for "One off" Fiberglass Boats of Sandwich Construction
1. Makes station molds as in wooden construction for stations and half stations.
2. Mounts them upside down, then fasten ribbands closer together than for steam-bent frame construction.
3. Lays Airex foam sheets over this mold, obtaining necessary curvature by heat. This foam is polyvinyl chloride (PVC) developed by Airex Ltd. of Switzerland. It is the best plastic foam developed so far, being strong in sheer and compression and of closed cell structure, so it does not absorb liquids.
4. Ties the Airex foam to the ribbands with nylon lacing.
5. Lays wet fiberglass over the foam so that it is well bonded to the foam.

6. Adds more layers of fiberglass to this, increasing thickness at places where it is needed. This then becomes the outer layer or shell of the sandwich construction.
7. Cuts nylon lacing inside around the ribbands, and lifts hull off, turning the hull over.
8. Lays wet fiberglass over the inside of the foam, so that it is well bonded to it. This then becomes the inner shell of the sandwich.
9. Sets in bulkheads, attaching them to inner shell with fiberglass.
10. Makes deck beams of wood. Lays plywood decks over, covered with teak or fiberglass.
11. Finishes interior joinery, installation of machinery, piping, wiring and deck fittings.

Molding Methods. The cost of the mold is the main item of expense. Spreading this cost over 25 boats or more allows fiberglass construction to be competitive with wood.

The contact method is the most widely used. This method is simply the laying up of a number of plies of resin-impregnated fiberglass to the required thickness, on an open mold (either male or female) of the desired hull form, and allowing the laminate to cure at room or higher temperatures. It is easier to lay up the plies over a male mold, although an uneven outer surface results. Since a smooth outer surface is desirable in boats, the female mold is generally preferred.

A spray gun, capable of simultaneously depositing chopped-strand fiberglass and catalyzed resin on the mold, has recently been developed, thus reducing labor and speeding production.

Other molding methods are: the vacuum bag method; the autoclave method, using steam for pressure and heat; and the matched die method, using both male and female molds.

The orientation of the plies of reinforcement is most important. Generally, mat reinforced laminates are considered to have equal strength and elastic properties in every direction (like metals). Cloth and woven laminates are considered to have different strengths and elastic properties in different directions (like the physical properties of wood with and across the grain). So the direction of the load should determine the direction of the glass fibers. This is particularly true for tensile strength, where the fibers should follow the same direction as the load strain. If you were to pull a piece of loosely-woven cloth on the bias, it would stretch; the same applies to fiberglass cloth. So the maximum number of fibers should be arranged to run fore and aft.

The impact resistance of fiberglass reinforced plastics is very high. Bulletproof vests and lightweight armor plate are made of it.

Its resistance to vibration is still a matter of trial and error. The addition of extra stiffeners in way of the vibrating area seems to be the easiest solution.

The following laminates are recommended, based on current practice:

1. Round-bottomed boats less than 12′ long, for low speed service:
   1-ply 10-oz. cloth on the outboard side.
   1-ply 1½-oz. mat.
   1-ply 14–17-oz. woven roving.
2. Round-bottomed boats 12′ to 18′ long, for low speed service:
   1-ply 10-oz. cloth on the outboard side.
   1-ply 2-oz. mat.
   1-ply 24–27-oz. woven roving.

Additional plies of woven roving should be added for large, open sailboats un-stiffened by a deck; also, for boats intended for rougher service. The greatest reinforcing is required in a high speed planing power boat with a V bottom. The sides of such a boat of course may be thinner than the bottom, unless the boat is intended for a service where frequent dockings are required—such as a club launch or high speed ferry, in which case the sides should be at least as thick as the bottom.

Decks and bulkheads, being flat surfaces or nearly so, do not lend themselves to fiberglass construction which has no reinforcing. They should be stiffened, by using the sandwich method of construction or by molded-in stiffeners. If this is not economical, the builder should use plywood, with stiffeners or beams, as in wooden construction.

Use of good details in fiberglass construction is important in producing a successful design. No sharp corners can be permitted; all right-angle joints must be well rounded, otherwise cracking will occur. The illustrations shown should be helpful to designers and builders. (Figure 40)

A Typical Specification might read like this:

Fiberglass Construction—The hull shall be made with fiberglass layup having good multi-directional properties.

Hull Structural thicknesses are based on layups having wet properties (after 30-days' immersion in water as follows):

A minimum modulus in any direction of 1.0×10^6, a minimum tensile strength in any direction of 12,000 p.s.i., and a maximum density of 105 lbs. per cu. ft.

The glass content shall not be less than 30%. The Builder shall advise the Architect of the actual glass content he obtains, and on this basis, the Architect reserves the right to modify the layup so as to be suitable in strength and weight to the Builder's techniques.

The hull layup shall consist of gelcoat, then boat mat, followed by alternate layers of woven roving and mat.

Lesser thicknesses of laminate will be considered, if an equivalent strength and stiffness will result. Complete layup data and properties as proven by tests shall be submitted to the Architect.

The method of color impregnation shall be approved by the Architect.

Layup for decks shall be solid glass similar to the hull with suitable stiffening members on the underside. A light teak overlay will then be fastened in way of transverse stiffeners and the teak is to be bonded to the glass with a space filling adhesive such as epoxy.

Designers and builders interested in working in fiberglass should refer to a book which covers the subject thoroughly, entitled *Marine Design Manual for Fiberglass Reinforced Plastics*, by engineers of Gibbs & Cox Inc. (McGraw-Hill Book Co., 1960.)

(opposite page) Fiberglass details of a 25 ft. D. W. L. sloop.

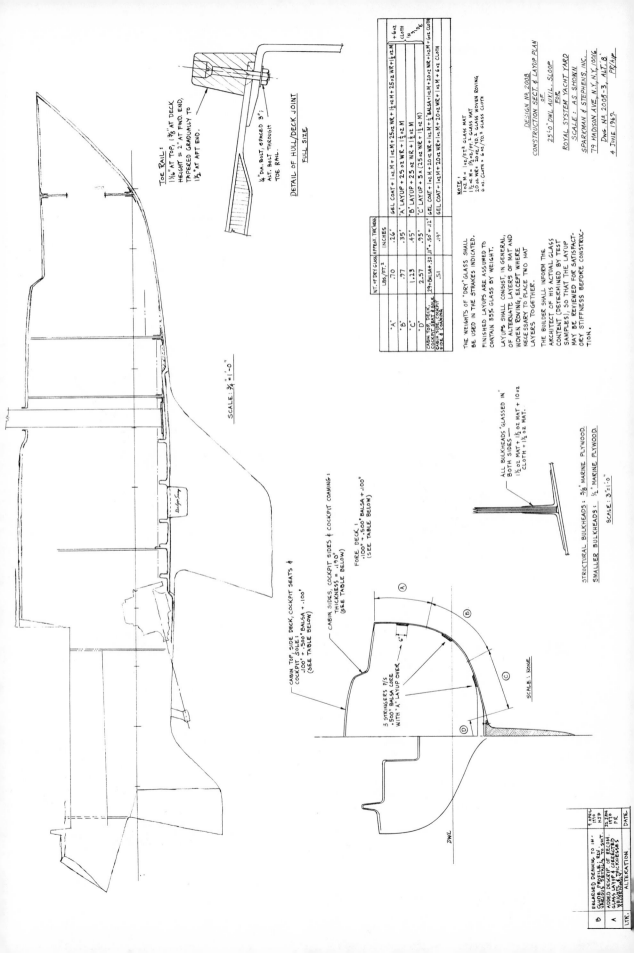

Figure 40. Fiberglass construction details

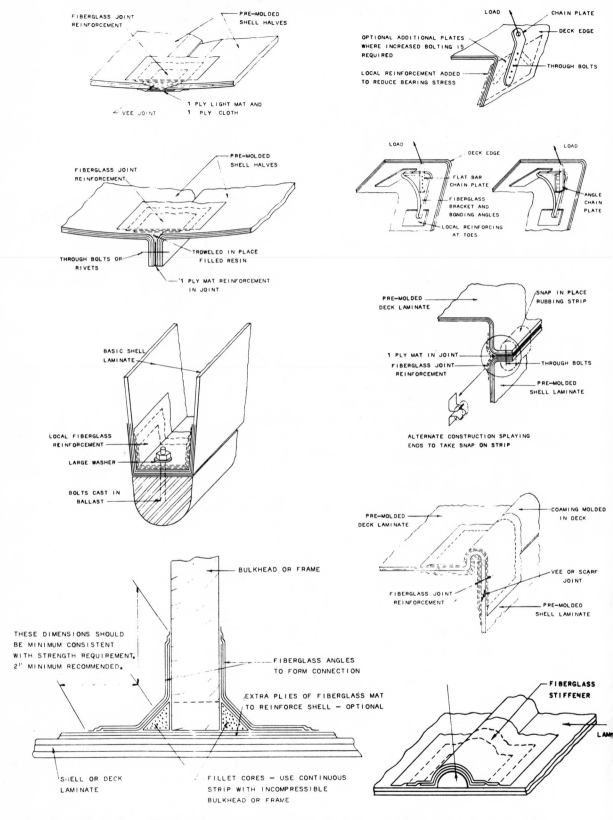

From *Marine Design Manual for Fiberglass Reinforced Plastics*, by Engineers of Gibbs & Cox, Inc. Copyright, 1960. McGraw-Hill Book Company. Used by permission.

Welded Steel Construction. It is surprising how small a boat can be built of welded steel nowadays. The Dutch are probably the leaders as builders of small steel boats. There are thousands of small work boats, tug boats, ferries, launches, barges, and yachts built by this method.

Welding is easy to master as a skill, so that today almost every town and hamlet has a welding shop, if only to repair damage to automobiles. Steel is plentiful and cheap and is available in all sizes, shapes, and thicknesses. When you combine these two facts, it is a wonder that more yachts are not built of welded steel.

There is only one Classification Society that has published a set of rules for the proper sizes of scantlings for small steel boats. This is Lloyd's. The book is *Rules and Regulations for the Construction and Classification of Steel Yachts*, obtainable from Lloyd's Register of Shipping, 17 Battery Place, New York 4, N.Y. The American Bureau of Shipping (A.B.S.) will approve or disapprove a designer's plans, but the nearest applicable publication they have is for inland steel barges and the smallest size listed is 75'. So it is pretty much up to the judgment of the designer, in the final analysis, as he strives to achieve not only adequate strength but economy of material; the latter is particularly important because steel is heavy, and it costs money to buy weight and push weight through the water.

Riveted construction has been completely superseded by welding. The lapping joint necessary for riveting must not be used in welded work because it makes for extra weight and pockets of rust. Tee bars make the best frames and beams but are difficult to obtain. Flat bars are most frequently used as frames and beams. When angle bars with unequal faces are welded to plating in an inverted position, as frames or beams with the end of the long face welded to the plating, they are smaller than flat bars similarly used and are stiff enough to stand unsupported during construction. Builders like this feature because it saves time.

Steel pipe should be used liberally for members of the ship's structure, such as stem, keel shoe, chines, guards, stanchions, stern shaft tube, rudder port, edging for coamings, edging for openings, edging for sun visors, etc., etc.

The proper sequence of welding is of the utmost importance, to minimize shrinkage and distortion. The many bumps and hollows, giving a washboard appearance to welded steel vessels, are a direct result of this lack of a proper sequence in welding. The framework and backbone should be welded together first, then the shell plating and deck plating tacked lightly to frames and beams, but only lightly. The seams of shell and deck plating should then be welded simultaneously. Weld the seams first, then the butts. This gives the plates a chance to shrink before they are held in restraint. If the deck is welded last, the shrinkage will lift the bow and stern of the vessel, throwing the propeller shaft out of line. Likewise, the port and starboard sides should be welded symmetrically, to keep the vessel straight. Finally, weld the frames to the shell and the beams to the deck.

Excessive gaps must not be spanned by welding, nor filled with "slugs."

Spacing of intermittent welds (tacks), either staggered or chained, has been carefully worked out. It would be well for a designer or builder to consult the A.B.S. rules on welding. Locked-up stresses that occur when a large vessel is welded together are like tying her into a knot. Sometimes ships break in half for this reason. The break usually starts at the corners of large deck openings, such as cargo hatches. Round those corners to relieve the strain!

As a rule of thumb, the welding bead should be the same size as the thinnest member. Thus, if a $\frac{3}{16}''$ flat bar were to be welded to a $\frac{1}{8}''$ shell plate, the welding bead should be $\frac{1}{8}''$, no more.

The strength of a welded joint may be considered to be 100% of the strength of the steel.

One of the advantages of steel construction is the fact that tanks may be welded as an integral part of the hull. Thus, the shell plating of the boat is used as one side of the tank, floors or bulkheads as other sides. As you can imagine, this saves a tremendous amount of space.

Rusting is the big disadvantage with steel. Both wrought iron and certain high-strength steels, such as "Cor-Ten" steel, rust less than common mild steel. Sandblasting before painting, and spraying with hot zinc also effectively reduce rusting.

Weight is the other disadvantage of steel construction, but by watching this carefully, the designer can keep his boat light enough for practical purposes, in all except the smallest craft.

Many people feel that the tremendous strength, the added room inside, the simplicity and ease of construction are advantages of steel which more than outweigh rusting and extra weight.

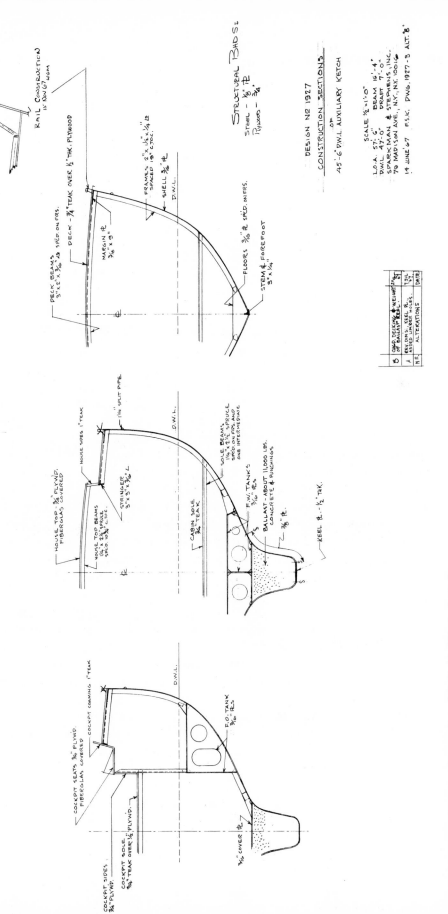

Steel construction sections of a 45 ft. D. W. L. ketch.

Aluminum Construction. "One third the weight but twice the cost of steel"—that's what they say of aluminum construction for boatbuilding. Comparative weights for metals are as follows:

Plate Thickness	Aluminum	Steel	Bronze	Monel
	(lbs./sq. ft.)	(lbs./sq. ft.)	(lbs./sq. ft.)	(lbs./sq. ft.)
1/16″	.90	2.50	2.80	2.80
1/8″	1.76	5.1	5.55	5.76
3/16″	2.64	7.65	8.35	8.64
1/4″	3.52	10.2	11.1	11.38
5/16″	4.53	12.8	13.8	14.49
3/8″	5.44	15.3	16.65	17.39

Some people think aluminum corrodes badly in salt water, that aluminum boats are noisy, and that they are too expensive to build.

Tremendous strides have been made in the manufacture of corrosion-resisting aluminum alloy, suitable for use in salt water, and in the invention of new welding processes. Nowadays one can say that all objections to aluminum construction have been overcome, except perhaps that of the extra expense. But this extra initial cost may be paid by the savings in maintenance over the years. In the case of work boats, the increased profits from extra cargo capacity and higher speed may make lightweight aluminum construction worth while financially.

Painting aluminum is a tricky business. No lead base paint or copper bottom paint should be applied next to the aluminum. The surface should be cleaned, then primed with two coats of zinc chromate. After that, lead base paints may be applied. Plastics can be bonded to aluminum to give color and texture.

Designers and builders must prevent galvanic corrosion of aluminum by insulating different metals from it. Bronze, so often thought of as tops, particularly in the marine field, is one of the worst metals to have touching aluminum. Stainless steel is the least harmful. (See Chapter XI, Galvanic Series of Metals) Insulation material should be Micarta, neoprene, Alumalastic, or equal. Where through fastenings of metal other than aluminum are required, insulation may be obtained by the use of Micarta bushings and washers. Rubber stern bearings solve the problem of insulation between shaft and aluminum hull. Of course the best solution is to have the castings made of aluminum instead of bronze.

Wood also should be insulated from aluminum. Be careful of wood that has been treated with copper.

Living aboard an aluminum boat, one finds that there is no noise, except perhaps the bell-like sound of a wire halyard slapping an aluminum mast. A good way to deaden this is to fill the inside of the mast with Styrofoam sawdust, which weighs practically nothing.

Small outboard aluminum boats are sprayed with some form of mastic to deaden the sound, as in undercoating on automobiles.

In welded construction for both steel and aluminum, shell plates need not be rectangular. One builder has pioneered in using triangular plates. Why? Because the sharp corner of a triangle is easier to manipulate around a compound curved· surface than is the unyielding shape of a rectangle.

Aluminum is a good conductor of heat, as we know from the use of aluminum pots and pans for cooking. But it isn't true that aluminum boats get hot in the broiling sun. Actually, a wooden deck would be far hotter than the surrounding aluminum. Living aboard an aluminum boat is a very pleasant experience. The feeling of strength is very reassuring. One should, however, prepare for cold weather. It seems colder inside an aluminum boat, but with a warm fire in a little stove, this can be overcome.

Aluminum welding is a highly skilled art. It requires more training and closer supervision than steel welding. Warping and distortion occur as in steel welding, and for this reason, particular attention should be paid to the proper sequence of welding.

The strength of aluminum welding is only 60% of the material, whereas the strength of steel welding is 100% of the material. So it is better to overlap joints, as though riveting, and thus increase the amount of welding in aluminum construction, although this is not done on shell plates.

Some designers prefer to use a thicker shell plating, with frames spaced further apart, than they would in the case of steel construction. This reduces distortion, because there is less welding.

Small boats built of thin-gauge aluminum must still be riveted. Before riveting, all faying or joining surfaces should be covered by a neoprene tape to prevent leaks.

Many small boats, such as canoes, are made by stretching the thin aluminum sheet over a form which gives it a compound curve. Most shells are made in two pieces. The two halves, port and starboard, are riveted to the keel, with thwarts, frames, gunwale, and decks riveted also.

To my mind, one of the outstanding vessels utilizing aluminum to great advantage is the steamer UNITED STATES. Although she is similar in her principal dimensions to the big Cunarders QUEEN MARY and QUEEN ELIZABETH, she is some 27,000 tons lighter because her designers used aluminum wherever it was possible. The Cunarders weigh approximately 80,000 tons; the UNITED STATES weighs about 53,000 tons. What a saving!

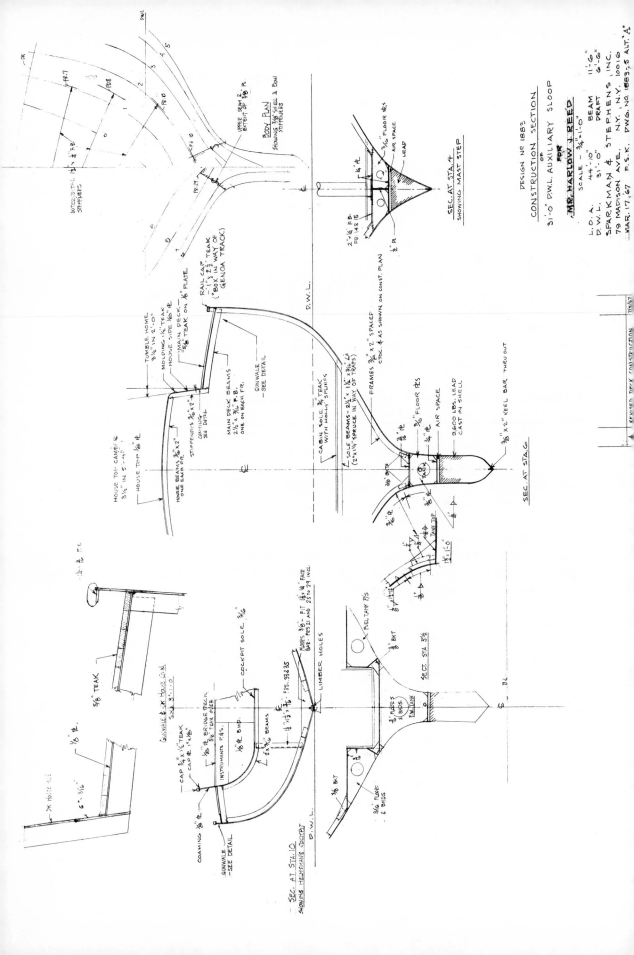

DESIGN Nº 1883
CONSTRUCTION SECTION
OF
31'-0" D.W.L. AUXILIARY SLOOP
FOR
"MR. HARLOW J. REED"

SCALE - ¾"=1'-0"

L.O.A.	44'-10"	BEAM	11'-6"
D.W.L.	31'-0"	DRAFT	6'-6"

SPARKMAN & STEPHENS, INC.
79 MADISON AVE.   N.Y., N.Y. 10016
MAR. 17, 67   F.S.K.   DWG. NO. 1883.5 ALT. "A"

BODY PLAN
SHOWING ⅜ SHELL & BOW STIFFENERS

SEC. AT STA. 4
SHOWING MAST STEP

SEC. AT STA. 6

SEC. AT STA. 10
SHOWING HELMSMAN'S COCKPIT

GUNWALE & ⅜ HOUSE C/N.
SCALE 3"=1'-0"

Ferro Cement Construction. In 1848 a Frenchman by the name of Joseph Louis Lambot thought of the idea of combining iron with concrete to give the combination tensile strength. The marriage of these two materials is a happy one. Compressive strength is obtained from concrete, tensile strength from iron, and both have the same coefficient of expansion, so this marriage does not break up. Monsieur Lambot constructed two row boats then, which have lasted for 124 years until the present time. He thought of this new material, ferro cement, as a substitute for wood.

To go back further in history, it was the Romans who first invented concrete, and used it with great success building foundations, walls, aqueducts, break waters, many of which are still well preserved.

This was a mixture of cement with an aggregate of sand, gravel and water.

Cement in a crude form of burnt lime mixed with water was used as far back as 3000 B.C.

Ferro cement for boat-building material consists of several layers of wire mesh reinforcing in combination with steel rods all thinly but thoroughly covered in a rich mortar.

Ferro cement can be flexible and capable of resisting considerable impact without cracking. A blow that would completely open up an ordinary wooden hull would shatter ferro cement only in a localized way and resist the passage of water.

This material lends itself particularly well to fishing vessels because of the low investment possible. The Chinese have a factory that turns out ferro cement sampans, which cost one-third less than wooden ones. In New Zealand a wide range of ferro cement boats are being built, including hundreds of fishing boats and yachts.

The proponents of this method of construction claim that the cost of building large craft is less than in any other material. For another thing, they claim that it is easier for an amateur to build a boat of ferro cement, because the skill demanded is considerably less than that required to build a wooden boat, in which hundreds of individual pieces have to be carefully fitted and fastened together. I should say this is probably true, except for that one critical operation—the mixing and plastering of the mortar. Here the amateur should hire a gang of professional plasterers, who will have to work skillfully and swiftly to finish the hull in one operation without stopping.

As far as weight is concerned ferro cement weighs 160 pounds per cu. ft. ($10\#$/sq. ft. at $\frac{3}{4}''$), whereas steel is 490 ($10.2\#$/sq. ft. at $\frac{1}{4}''$), aluminum is 168 ($10.8\#$/sq. ft. at $\frac{3}{4}''$), fiberglass is 96 ($10\#$/sq. ft. at $1\frac{1}{4}''$) and mahogany is 36 ($10.5\#$/sp. ft. at $3\frac{1}{2}''$). Of course what we are really concerned with is the weight of the complete structure of the hull, not just the shell. So by using thick mahogany planking, although it is lightest of all, the weight of oak frames, oak floor timbers,

(opposite page) Aluminum construction details of a 31 ft. D. W. L. sloop.

bilge stringer and oak backbone (stem, gripe, keel, horntimber) must be added to find the total weight of the complete hull. This can be compared to a metal hull using thin but heavy (in the case of steel) shell plating. To this must be added the thin (but heavy) flat bar or angle frames, floors, keel, etc., to obtain the complete hull-structure weight.

Compared against these weights the ferro cement hull of the same size will have a shell thickness of, say ¾″ but will not have any frames. Small boats of ferro cement are heavier than wood, steel or aluminum. But large boats of ferro cement are comparable in weight to fiberglass, lighter than steel or wood, but not lighter than aluminum. It seems that the dividing size is about 60-feet overall, all structural members being taken into consideration.

It is interesting to learn how flexible a plank made of ferro cement is. Such a plank supported at both ends and weighted in the middle will bend rather like wood. When eventually the weight is taken off, it will again resume its original shape.

In New Zealand it has been found that the weight of the steel reinforcing is between 27 and 37 pounds per cu. ft. with enough layers of mesh used to insure that there is no unreinforced space greater than about ⅜″ in the entire hull.

Shell thickness used there have worked out to be ⅝″ for boats up to 30 feet and ¾″ for boats over 30 feet and thicker nearing 50 feet. Frames of ¾″ mild steel pipe are used for boats up to 50 feet. Stringers of high tensile steel rods have been found best, because when bent around fore and aft they do so in fair curves without kinking.

Eight layers of ½″ diamond-shaped 19-gauge galvanized chicken wire (wired together) with steel rod frames and stringers seems to work well for reinforcing. As a substitute for chicken wire, expanded metal, which is cheaper than welded or twisted mesh, may be used. Because of its greater thickness fewer layers are required. Be sure that the mesh is capable of being formed to the desired compound curves, otherwise flat sections may result. Galvanizing is recommended because of reduced rusting, and has been found to be stronger under test. Aluminum should not be used in place of steel, because it expands about three times more than concrete.

When wiring together the mesh and the rods, be sure the free ends of this wiring are on the inside of the hull, and do not project beyond the mortar, otherwise rust spots will show. It has been found that welding the rods together is not as good as connecting them by wiring, because of distortion.

The upkeep of ferro cement boats is on a par with fiberglass. Paint work has to be maintained for antifouling protection of the bottom at least once a year. For the appearance of the rest of the boat the topsides, deck and deck house, painting should be done as required. The appearance of crazing has no significance strength-wise and can be covered by paint.

Unfortunately, it has been found that fuel oils have a tendency to seep through concrete, so fuel tanks should be made of metal.

As far as the type of mortar necessary, rich mortar with only a sand aggregate should be used. This is made of mixing Portland cement, dry sand, and fresh water in the ratio by weight of 1 part cement, 2 parts sand, 0.4 parts water added cautiously. This provides the best combination for the least shrinkage.

Portland cement is made from mixing clay and limestone, or chalk, ground up and burnt in a rotary kiln at high temperature. The clinker thus produced is ground to a fine powder and then ground again with a small amount of gypsum.

The number of days that it takes for concrete to cure varies from 45 days at 40° to 18 days at 80°, with 28 days being the normal time for 60°. At freezing temperature the expansion of water exerts enough force to break the bond between cement and sand and renders the concrete useless. At temperatures near boiling very rapid hardening takes place. Ordinary concrete should be kept moist for at least the first seven days, early strength cement concrete for the first three days. Under cold conditions these times should be doubled. Steam curing reduces shrinkage by up to 50% over dry air cured mortar. A steam cured hull can be worked on after twenty-four hours. Low pressure may be used under a plastic cover.

For boat building the mortar must be a dry mix just workable with water content kept to a minimum, so that when given the standard slump test, the mortar will not slump more than $2\frac{1}{2}''$. This type increases strength and reduces shrinkage. Be careful of moist sand, and allow for the water in it when adding water during the mixing. Dry sand weighs 90 to 105 pounds per cubic foot, while wet sand weighs 120. Cement weighs 183 pounds a cubic foot. Unless batches have a uniform water content one is liable to get different shrinkages as the water dries out. Sea water should not be used because it tends to encourage rust.

The mortar must be thoroughly worked through the mesh and around the frames and stringers to avoid air pockets.

It is necessary that the whole hull be plastered in one day because the final plastering is irrevocable. At least eight to ten professional hand plasterers are required to finish a 30- to 35-foot boat in a day. Decks, cabins and bulkheads can be left for another time, if necessary.

The practice in New Zealand has been to coat the outside of the hull with an epoxy resin, as this provides an additional water barrier. But good rich mortar is astonishingly impervious to water.

In the event that an occasional rust spot develops from a wire because it is too close to the surface, it can be eliminated by boring into the spot lightly with a counter-sinking drill and filling the hole with epoxy filler.

Ferro cement construction offers the advantage of lower investment costs to the fishing industry, and the ease of "do-it-yourself" building for the amateur yacht builder in the years ahead. It is both the most durable and the most economical of all boat-building materials, but yachts less than 60 feet overall built of it are apt to perform somewhat poorly, as they are so heavy.

The example on page 279 shows the construction sections of a 61′ displacement-type Power Cruiser designed by Robert B. Harris of ferro cement.

Comparative weights—shell and framing

Wood for this size	6.22#/sq. ft.
Steel for this size	9.27#/sq. ft.
Ferro cement	9.37#/sq. ft.

Shell .826″ thick

Displacement—99,999 lbs.

**(opposite page) Ferro cement construction sections of a
61 ft. motor cruiser by Robert B. Harris.**

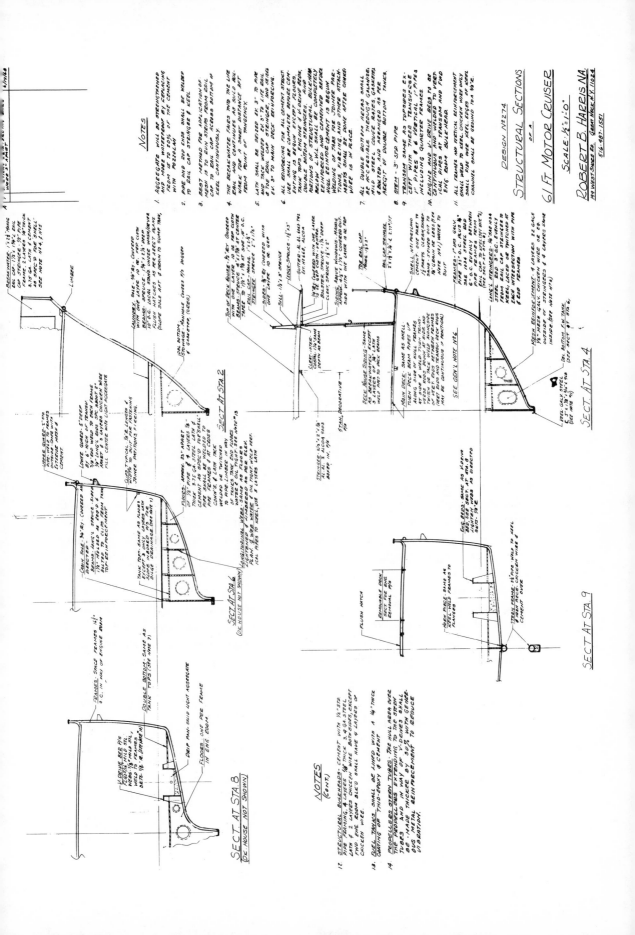

CHAPTER XXIII

A MANUAL OF CALCULATIONS

The long and tedious addition of all the weights of all the items that constitute the make-up of a boat is the real meat of ship calculations. Each item weighs so much and has its center of gravity in a vertical location and a longitudinal location. For convenience, let us use the base line from which to measure heights, and Station 0 from which to measure longitudinal distances. By multiplying each weight by its vertical distance from the base line we get its vertical moment. Then, adding all the vertical moments and adding all the weights, if we divide the total moments by the total weights, we will have the vertical center of gravity (V.C.G.) of the boat. The longitudinal moments and the longitudinal center of gravity (L.C.G.) are calculated similarly.

Moments, or weights times distances, should be clearly understood from the beginning, because they are used to locate all the various centers, which each designer must do. The seesaw in Figure 41 gives a picture of how moments work. Let's say the skipper weighs 200 pounds and sits 4 feet from the fulcrum (the moment on that side is 200 × 4 = 800 foot-pounds). His daughter weighs 80 pounds and sits 10 feet from the pivot (80 × 10 = 800 foot-pounds, the moment on the daughter's side). Because both moments are equal, the seesaw is in balance. Any one of those four quantities could be unknown, and you could solve the equation to find it. Thus, how far from the pivot point would the daughter have to sit to make the seesaw balance?

Figure 41.
The principle of moments

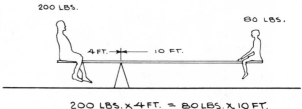

200 LBS. × 4 FT. = 80 LBS. × 10 FT.

800 FT. LBS. = 800 FT. LBS.

280

$$80X = 200 \times 4$$
$$X = 800 \div 80$$
$$X = 10$$

Substitute in this simple example the weight of a dinghy of 200 pounds, whose longitudinal center of gravity is 4 inches forward of its center of flotation (down by the head at her mooring). Where should the 80-pound child sit to make the dinghy sail on her lines? Use the center of flotation as the fulcrum or pivot on a seesaw. Answer: 10 inches aft of the center of flotation ($200 \times 4 = 80 \times 10$).

Displacement is the volume of water displaced by the floating boat, the weight of the displaced fluid being equal to that of the displacing boat. Our friend Archimedes discovered this 2200 years ago.

Choose a figure for displacement before drawing the lines based on other similar boats. (See Figure 42) Common practice is to divide the water line into 10 equal spaces, with Station 0 at the forward intersection of the profile and the designed water line (D.W.L.), and Station 10 at the corresponding after intersection. With this setup we can use Simpson's Rule which, while being the most accurate method of figuring displacement, requires an even number of stations.

It is easy for the designer to divide the D.W.L. into 10 equal spaces by simply moving the decimal point. Not so for the less mathematically-inclined builder. The apparently odd D.W.L. length of 25′ 5″ in the example of the sloop, given in this book, was deliberately chosen to give a station spacing easy for the builder to lay out, using the normal divisions—on his 6′ folding rule—of feet, inches and sixteenths of an inch. Using the tables of decimals of a foot for inches, at the back of this book, the designer can spot the proper numbers easily divisible by 10. Thus, 25′ 5″ = 25.4167′, so dividing by 10 the station space would be 2.5417′ which = 2′ 6½″ (easy for the builder to lay out). Now supposing a designer had chosen 26′ 0″ for the water-line length. This divided by 10 would be 2.60′ which would give a builder a station spacing of 2′ 7⁷⁄₃₂″, or a hair less, which is rather awkward.

To Find Displacement

1. Measure the area of each station or section below the D.W.L., by running the planimeter in a clockwise direction around the line. It is good practice to go around three times and take the average reading (throwing out any wild reading). The figure will be in square inches and it will be the area of only half the full section, since you don't draw both sides of the boat.
2. Multiply the planimeter reading by one of Simpson's multipliers, which are 1, 4, 2, 4, 2, 4, 2, 4, 2, 4, 1 laid out according to stations in the example below. This will give you a function of an area.
3. Add all the functions of areas.
4. Put this figure into *Simpson's formula:*
   $2 \times 1/3 \times$ sum of functions of ½ areas $\times$ (inverted scale)^2 $\times$ the common

Figure 42. Displacement of vessels 10′ to 120′ L.W.L.

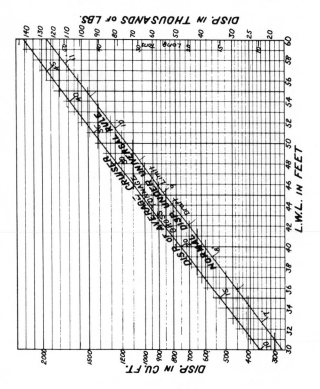

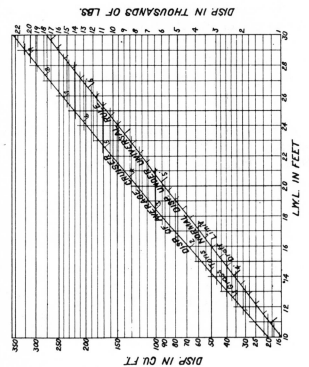

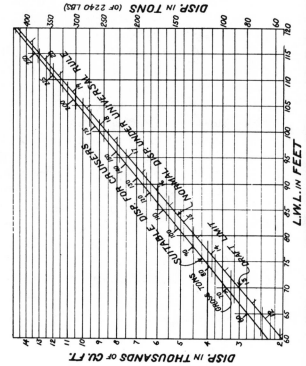

WATER CONVERSION FACTORS

UNIT		SALT WATER	FRESH WATER
1 CU. FT.	=	64 LBS.	62.2 LBS.
1 CU. FT.	=	7.48 GALS.	7.48 GALS.
1 GAL.	=	8.56 LBS.	8.32 LBS.
1 TON	=	262 GALS.	269 GALS.
1 LONG TON	=	2,240 LBS.	2,240 LBS.
1 LONG TON	=	35 CU. FT.	36 CU. FT.

interval $\times$ 64 = displacement in pounds for salt water. (For fresh water use 62.2 instead of 64.)

In the example of the 25' 5" D.W.L. sloop, the scale of the drawing is $\frac{3}{4}$" = 1' 0"; so the inverted scale is 4/3 and squared it is 16/9. (If the scale had been $\frac{3}{8}$", we would use 64/9. If the scale had been $\frac{1}{2}$", we would use 4, etc.) The common interval, or station spacing, is 2.54' and 64 is the weight of one cubic foot of salt water; 2 is for both sides of the hull; $\frac{1}{3}$ is part of Simpson's Rule.

Simpson's First or One-Third Rule, as it is called, is a formula that enables us to determine the areas of curvilinear figures very accurately. It was invented in 1730, by James Stirling, a Scottish mathematician, and has yet to be improved upon. The formula itself is given in the preceding paragraph on displacement. An example of how to set up a table of ship calculations, using Simpson's Rule, follows shortly.

The Trapezoidal Rule is a simple method for estimating the area of a curvilinear figure. The results obtained are not as accurate as those found by using Simpson's Rule. The procedure is as follows:

1. Divide the figure into any number of parallel strips by equally spaced parallel lines.

2. Measure the length of each of the parallel lines.

3. Obtain an estimate of the area by adding together the lengths of the parallels, taking the first and last at $\frac{1}{2}$ value, and multiplying by the common interval.

Longitudinal Center of Buoyancy (L.C.B.) is the longitudinal center of gravity of the displaced water and is determined by the shape of the underwater portion of the hull. A distance 54 to 59% of the D.W.L. aft of Station 0 seems to be the best location for the L.C.B., for good performance to windward. The calculation for finding the L.C.B. is quite simple and can be easily included in the work sheet for finding displacement. Add another column for lever arms 0, 1, 2, 3, 4, 5, 6, 7, 8, 9, 10, and multiply each function previously obtained for section areas by its lever arm, to get moments. Add all these moments, and divide by the sum of functions of $\frac{1}{2}$ areas.

Prismatic Coefficient (P.C.) is a fancy term for expressing how fine or how full the shape of a hull is. In more precise language, it is the ratio between the volume of displacement and a solid having a constant section the shape of the largest section multiplied by the water-line length.

The best sailboats today have prismatic coefficients between .55 and .49. Great importance is attached to this coefficient, because if it is larger than .55, the boat will be pretty much of a tub; and if it is less than .49, she will be so fine that she will suck up a horrible quarter wave.

Powerboats have prismatic coefficients which vary from .52 to .70, depending on their speed-length ratios (speed in knots $\div$ square root of D.W.L., or $V \div \sqrt{L}$). Thus, displacement-type vessels are fine ended, while fast planing craft are quite full.

There is great advantage, in terms of lower resistance, in designing to the proper value of the prismatic coefficient in craft for which a definite cruising speed should be established. The following table shows the relationship between the speed-length ratio and the most favorable prismatic coefficient for powerboats .

Speed-Length Ratio	*Optimum Prismatic Coefficient*
1.0	.52
1.1	.54
1.2	.58
1.3	.62
1.4	.64
1.5	.66
1.6	.68
1.7	.69
1.8	.69
1.9	.70
2.0	.70

To calculate the prismatic coefficient, take the volume of displacement in cubic feet, divide it by the volume of the prism in cubic feet, formed by the section having the greatest area times the designed water-line length. To find the area of the greatest section, plot a curve of the planimeter readings for Station 4, 5, 6, 7. The high point of the curve will be at about Station 5½ or 5¾ and will give a figure larger than that for Station 6. And to change this figure—the largest planimeter reading—to square feet, multiply it by 2 (for both sides) times the inverted scale squared (which would be 16/9 if the scale of ¾″ = 1′ 0″ were used). To sum up then—

$$\text{P.C.} = \frac{\text{Disp. in Cu. Ft.}}{\text{Vol. of Prism in Cu. Ft.}}$$

$$\text{P.C.} = \frac{\text{Disp. in Cu. Ft.}}{\text{Greatest Planimeter Reading from Curve} \times 2 \times \text{Inv. Scale}^2 \times \text{D.W.L. in Ft.}}$$

Some designers use the hull only, or canoe body, omitting the fin or keel in their calculations for prismatic coefficient. It seems to me that the whole boat has to go through the water—not just the hull without the keel—so the full shape of the boat should be used.

The thing to do to find displacement, L.C.B. and P.C. is to set up a table which will give these three calculations at the same time. Set it up in this way, using *Simpson's Rule:*

Disp., L.C.B., P.C., from faired lines.   **Date** ....

Sta.	Planimeter Reading	×	Simpson's Multipliers	=	Functions of ½ Areas	×	Arms	=	Functs. of Moments About Sta. 0
0			1				0		
1			4				1		
2			2				2		
3			4				3		
4			2				4		
5			4				5		
	Greatest from curve								
6			2				6		
7			4				7		
8			2				8		
9			4				9		
10			1				10		
					Sum				Sum

Disp. in Cu. Ft. = $2 \times \frac{1}{3} \times$ Sum of Functs. of ½ Areas $\times$ Inv. Scale^2 $\times$ Sta. Spcg. in Ft.

Disp. in lbs. = Disp. in Cu. Ft. $\times$ 64

$$\frac{\text{L.C.B. in Stas. or \% of}}{\text{D.W.L. aft of Sta. 0}} = \frac{\text{Sum of Functs. of Moms. Abt. Sta. 0}}{\text{Sum of Functs. of ½ Areas}}$$

$$\text{P.C.} = \frac{\text{Disp. in Cu. Ft.}}{\text{Greatest Plan. Reading from Curve} \times 2 \times \text{Inv. Scale}^2 \times \text{D.W.L. in Ft.}}$$

Pounds per Inch Immersion (Lbs./in. Imm.) It is often necessary to find how much a boat will sink if known weights are placed on board or how much she will rise if weights are removed. Or conversely, if she is deep when measured, how much greater her displacement will be. To find the number of pounds it takes to sink a boat one inch, use the Nomographic Chart (Figure 43). These figures are obtained by finding the area of the water plane, dividing by 12 and multiplying by 64, which gives the weight of a layer of water one inch thick and the shape of the D.W.L. To do this with greater accuracy than the chart, set up as follows:

Sta.	½ Breadth at D.W.L. in Ft.	×	Simpson's Multipliers	=	Functions
0			1		
1			4		
2			2		
3			4		
4			2		
5			4		
6			2		
7			4		
8			2		
9			4		
10			1		
					Sum

$$\text{Lbs./in. Imm.} = \frac{2 \times \frac{1}{3} \times \text{Sum of Functs.} \times \text{Sta. Spcg.}}{12} \times 64$$

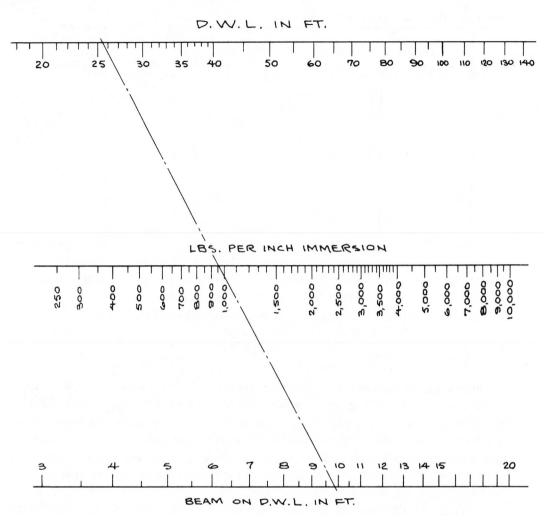

Figure 43. Nomograph for pounds per inch immersion in salt water

So, if she floats one inch below her designed water line, her displacement will be so many pounds greater.

Wetted Surface is the area of the underwater hull surface and should include the rudder and centerboards. It is important to use the ratio of sail area to wetted area as a relationship of power to resistance, in comparing different designs. (See Figure 44) To find the wetted surface, we measure off the girths of each station, by using a tick strip of paper and pivoting it on the pencil point every half inch or so, following the curves of the section to be measured from center line to designed

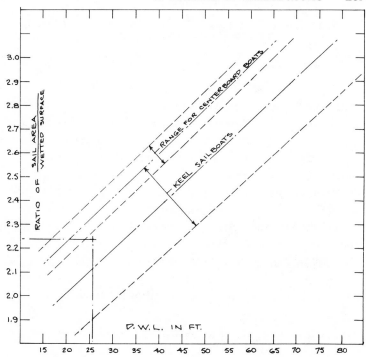

Figure 44. Ratio of sail area to wetted surface

water line. By measuring along the tick strip, the curved line is straightened out to its full length, and the girth measurement is obtained. Set up wetted surface calculation as follows:

Sta.	½ Girth in Ft.	× Simpson's Multipliers	=	Functions
0		1		
1		4		
2		2		
3		4		
4		2		
5		4		
6		2		
7		4		
8		2		
9		4		
10		1		
				Sum

Because of the curvature of the hull, the station spacing will not be great enough, and a factor should be added. Call it the "bilge factor," and obtain it by measuring the length of the 45° diagonal and dividing it by the designed water-line length. (Say it comes out to 1.026.)

Wetted Surface of Hull = 2 × ⅓ × Sum of Functs. × Sta. Spcg. × B. F. =   Sq. Ft.
Rudder   Area One Side × 2   =   Sq. Ft.
_____
                                                            Total   Sq. Ft.

Now pick a good sail area ÷ wetted area ratio by comparing with other boats. (See Chart Figure 44) The sail area should be this ratio times the wetted surface.

Of course, we must check this for stability, and if the design is found to be tender, then by adding a little more beam, the favorable ratio of sail area to wetted area can be maintained, and the boat stiffened or given more power to carry sail without increasing the wetted area excessively. This would be preferable to reducing the sail area and holding the same beam. "Plenty of beam never hurt a boat" is a good rule to remember.

Weight Estimate. After the proper sizes have been selected for the members of the ship's structure, based on scantling rules—such as Nevins', Herreshoff's, Lloyd's, or American Bureau of Shipping—and modified by the designer's experience and judgment, a weight estimate should be prepared. Figure 45 gives weights of materials per square foot, for different thicknesses.

Figure 45. Weights of materials (See also pp. 189, 272, 322, 324, 330, 331)

WEIGHTS
IN LBS. PER SQ. FT. FOR THESE THICKNESSES (WOODS AT 12% MOISTURE CONTENT)

BOAT BUILDING MATERIAL	LBS/CU.FT	2½"	2¼"	2"	1⅞"	1¾"	1⅝"	1½"	1⅜"	1¼"	1⅛"	1"	⅞"	¾"	⅝"	½"	⅜"	¼"
STYROFOAM	1.3	0.27		0.22		0.19		0.16		0.14		0.11		0.08		0.05		
FIBERGLASS INSULATION	3.5	0.73		0.58		0.51		0.44		0.36		0.29		0.22		0.15		
AIRFOAM RUBBER	6.6	6"THK=3.33		4½"=2.49		3"=1.66			2"=1.10			1"=0.55						
CORK BOARD	16	3.33		2.66		2.33		2.00		1.66		1.33	1.17	1.00	0.83	0.67	0.50	0.33
WHITE CEDAR	23	4.80	4.31	3.82	3.59	3.36	3.12	2.88	2.63	2.40	2.15	1.92	1.68	1.44	1.20	0.96	0.72	0.48
WHITE PINE	26	5.41	4.87	4.33	4.06	3.79	3.52	3.25	2.98	2.71	2.44	2.17	1.90	1.63	1.36	1.08	0.81	0.54
SPRUCE	27	5.62	5.04	4.50	4.22	3.94	3.65	3.38	3.09	2.81	2.53	2.25	1.97	1.69	1.41	1.12	0.84	0.56
REDWOOD	28	5.84	5.25	4.66	4.37	4.08	3.79	3.50	3.21	2.91	2.62	2.33	2.04	1.80	1.45	1.16	0.87	0.58
PORT ORFORD CEDAR	30	6.25	5.62	5.00	4.69	4.37	4.06	3.75	3.44	3.12	2.82	2.50	2.19	1.87	1.56	1.25	0.94	0.62
ALASKAN YELLOW CEDAR	31	6.46	5.81	5.17	4.85	4.52	4.20	3.88	3.55	3.24	2.91	2.58	2.26	1.94	1.61	1.29	0.97	0.65
DOUGLAS FIR, ORE. PINE	32	6.67	6.00	5.34	5.00	4.67	4.33	4.00	3.67	3.33	3.00	2.67	2.34	2.00	1.67	1.33	1.00	0.67
AFRICAN MAHOGANY	32																	
HONDURAS MAHOGANY	35	7.29	6.56	5.84	5.46	5.10	4.74	4.37	4.01	3.65	3.28	2.92	2.56	2.19	1.83	1.46	1.09	0.73
BUTTERNUT	35																	
PHILIPPINE MAHOGANY	36	7.50	6.75	6.00	5.62	5.25	4.87	4.50	4.12	3.75	3.37	3.00	2.62	2.25	1.87	1.50	1.12	0.75
FIR PLYWOOD	36																	
SPANISH CEDAR	37	7.70	6.95	6.16	5.78	5.40	5.00	4.62	4.24	3.85	3.47	3.08	2.70	2.31	1.93	1.54	1.15	0.77
CYPRESS	40	8.33	7.50	6.66	6.25	5.83	5.41	5.00	4.58	4.16	3.75	3.33	2.92	2.50	2.08	1.67	1.25	0.83
ELM	40																	
WALNUT	40																	
MEXICAN MAHOGANY	41	8.55	7.69	6.84	6.40	5.98	5.55	5.13	4.70	4.27	3.84	3.42	2.99	2.56	2.14	1.71	1.28	0.85
ASH	41																	
LONGLEAF YELLOW PINE	41																	
TEAK	45	9.37	8.44	7.50	7.03	6.56	6.10	5.62	5.16	4.69	4.22	3.75	3.28	2.80	2.34	1.87	1.41	0.93
BLACK LOCUST	49	10.20	9.20	8.17	7.65	7.15	6.63	6.13	5.61	5.10	4.60	4.08	3.58	3.06	2.55	2.04	1.53	1.02
HICKORY	53	11.05	9.94	8.84	8.28	7.73	7.17	6.63	6.07	5.52	4.97	4.42	3.87	3.32	2.76	2.21	1.66	1.10
WHITE OAK	53																	
GREEN HEART	62	12.90	11.60	10.30	9.70	9.05	8.40	7.75	7.10	6.45	5.80	5.16	4.52	3.87	3.23	2.58	1.93	1.29
FIBERGLASS – 30% GLASS, 70% RESIN	96											8.00	7.00	6.00	5.00	4.00	3.00	2.00
PLATE GLASS	161													10.10	8.40	6.71	5.04	3.36

Divide the entire estimate as you would the specifications—somewhat as follows: Hull Structure, Exterior Joiner Work, Interior Joinery, Fittings, Equipment, Machinery, Plumbing, Electrical, Spars and Rig, Soakage, Paint and Unknowns. The summary of these would be the light ship without ballast. To this, add half the fuel, half the fresh water, half the stores, half the light sails and gear, half the crew and their effects. The total of all of these would give you the half-load condition without ballast. Subtract this amount from the displacement, and the remainder can be used for ballast.

After the weight column, provide space for six more columns as follows: Vertical Lever Arm above Base in Ft., Vertical Moment, Aft Lever Arm from Station 0 in Stations, Aft Moment, Forward Lever Arm from Station 0 in Stations, Forward Moment. Then total moments divided by total weights equals the lever arm for the total weights. Never add or subtract lever arms—just moments.

Comparative Weights. To make a rough estimate of the weight of a new boat based on the known weights of an old boat multiply the known weights of the old boat by the length of the new boat ÷ the length of the old boat.

Example—We have a 47′ boat with hull weights of 8,000 pounds, interior joinery weights of 2,000 pounds, etc. What will the weights be for a new 52′ boat of the same type?

$$\text{Hull} \quad 8,000 \times \frac{52}{47} = 8,851 \text{ pounds}$$

$$\text{Interior Joinery} \quad 2,000 \times \frac{52}{47} = 2,212 \text{ pounds}$$

Location of Ballast. The L.C.B. found in the displacement calculations is used on sailboats as the center (the pivot point on a seesaw) about which moments are taken to locate the ballast. Set up the summary of all weights as follows:

Item	Weight	×	Vert. Arm Abv. Base	=	Vert. Mom.	×	Aft Arm from 0 in Stas.	=	Aft Mom.
Displacement			*Step 6*	?	*Step 5*	?	L.C.B.		
½ Load Ship without Ballast	—		*Step 1*	?			*Step 2*	?	—
Ballast	Remainder				*Step 3*	?	*Step 4*	?	Remainder

Now solve the equations below for the question marks above in the following sequence:

Step 1. $\dfrac{\text{Vert. Mom. ½ Load Ship Less Ball.}}{\text{Wt. ½ Load Ship Less Ball.}} = \text{Vert. Arm.}$

Step 2. $\dfrac{\text{Aft Mom. ½ Load Ship Less Ball.}}{\text{Wt. ½ Load Ship Less Ball.}} = \text{Aft Arm in Stas.}$

Step 3. Wt. of Ballast × Vert. Arm of Ball. = Vert. Mom.

Step 4. $\dfrac{\text{Aft Mom Bal.}}{\text{Bal.}}$ = Aft Arm or L.C.G. of Ballast.

Step 5. Vert. Mom. ½ Load Ship Less Bal. + Step 3 = Vert. Mom.

Step 6. $\dfrac{\text{Vert. Mom. Disp.}}{\text{Wt. of Disp.}}$ = Vert. Arm or V.C.G. Ship.

We have thus determined the amount of ballast, by subtracting the figure for "½ load ship without ballast" from the displacement. Check the ballast-displacement ratio thus—ballast ÷ displacement in lbs. = %—and compare it with other successful boats of the same type. Don't overemphasize this ratio, because what you are after is stability, and the incorporation of adequate beam and freeboard is a more effective means to this end.

We have located the L.C.G. of the ballast in its proper fore and aft position, in Step 4 above. We have also found the V.C.G. of the entire boat in Step 6 above.

Amount of Ballast. The Cruising Club rule penalizes a ballast-displacement ratio higher than 46%. Under the Universal rule, there is no limit, and the ratio goes as high as 71% on racing types such as Twelve Meters. Centerboard boats require less ballast, in proportion, than do keel boats, the range being from no ballast on small catboats to about 35% for ocean racers. A clever designer can utilize various useful items to keep the center of gravity low and take the place of part of the ballast. A metal centerboard of bronze or steel is useful in this respect; on a steel boat the bottom shell plating can be made considerably thicker; tanks can be located below the cabin sole, etc. Aluminum and fiberglass construction reduces the hull weights considerably, allowing a higher proportion of the total weight to be put down in the ballast.

Calculation of Ballast. Divide the hull into half stations in the area of the ballast, say 2, 2½, 3, 3½, 4, 4½, 5, 5½, 6, 6½. Using the trial-and-error method, fix a line for the top of the ballast, which will also be the bottom of the keel. Draw the ballast body plan, using the stations and half stations mentioned above, and running the planimeter around each. Use an average of three readings in the same manner as in finding displacement. Multiply by 2 for the full area and by the inverted scale squared to get square feet. Plot these full areas on a graph, using a horizontal scale similar to that used for the lines drawing—such as ¾″ = 1′ 0″, and a vertical scale (engineer's scale), such as 1″ = .50 sq. ft.

Then run the planimeter around this graph. Multiply its reading by the inverted horizontal scale (in this case we do not square it), and by the vertical scale, and by the weight per cubic foot of the ballast material used to find the total weight in pounds of ballast.

In the case of a centerboard boat, the areas for the centerboard slot can be found in the same manner and plotted as a deduction from the top of the curve on the graph. Since it is known where the L.C.G. of the ballast should be, you can judge pretty well by eye where the ballast should end, but it is a matter of try and try again, until you can cut out the area curve with scissors and balance it so that the balance point coincides with the desired center of gravity. Figure 46 shows the lead ballast drawing for our 25' 5" D.W.L. PIPE DREAM Cruising Sloop.

Set up the ballast calculation as follows (lines scaled at $\frac{3}{4}'' = 1' 0''$):

Sta.	*Planimeter Reading* $\frac{1}{2}$ *Area* *Ball. Sections*	*Inv. Scale^2* $\times$ *16/9*	$\times$ *2*	*= Full Area in Sq. Ft.*
2		"	"	
2½		"	"	
3		"	"	
3½		"	"	Plot these figures to make a curve of areas using vert. scale, say 1" = .50 sq. ft. Then run planimeter around it.
4		"	"	
4½		"	"	
5		"	"	
5½		"	"	
6		"	"	
6½		"	"	

Then: Plan. Reading Curve of A's. $\times$ Inv. Horiz. Scale (4/3) $\times$ Vert. Scale (.50) $\times$ 700 = Lbs. of Lead Ballast.

For cast iron, use 450 instead of 700, which is the weight per cubic foot.

By balancing cutout, L.C.G. lead = So many Stas.

Figure 46. Lead ballast for PIPE DREAM

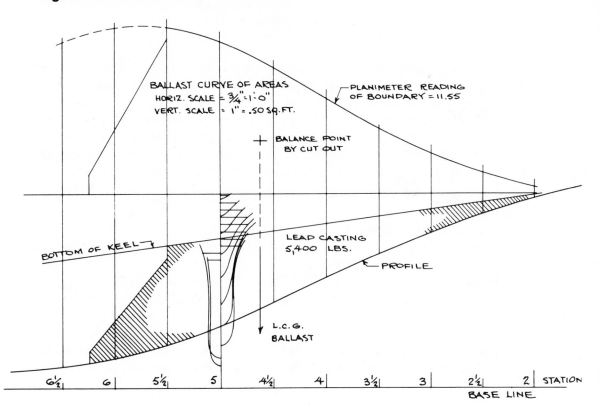

To Find the Vertical Center of Gravity of the Lead Ballast. Cut out the sections of the ballast (using an odd number of them). Balance each on an edge parallel to the base, and measure the distance from the base to this balance line, and then you have the vertical center of gravity of each section. Then set up the table as follows:

Stas. (odd number)	Planimeter Readings ½ areas	×	Simpson's Multipliers	=	Functs. ½ areas	×	Arms above base	=	Functs. of Moms.
2			1						
2½			4						
3			2						
3½			4						
4			2						
4½			4						
5			2						
5½			4						
6			1						
					Sum				Sum

$$\text{V.C.G. Ballast above base} = \frac{\text{Sum of Functs. of Moms.}}{\text{Sum of Functs. of } \tfrac{1}{2} \text{ areas}}$$

Stability

> A yacht is like a girl at that.
> She's feminine and swanky,
> You'll find the one that's broad and fat
> Is never mean and cranky.

Two methods are used by the leading designers in this country to determine whether a sailboat will be tender or stiff. One we shall call the Wind Pressure Coefficient (W.P.C.) Method, which for a given angle of heel, say 20°, comes up with a number between .6 and 1.8, which when compared with other boats tells us whether ours will be stiff or tender. The other we shall call the Dellenbaugh Angle Method, which uses a constant in the formula and comes up with an angle between, say, 10° and 22°, which then can be compared with other boats.

Wind Pressure Coefficient Method

Procedure:

1. Draw a full body plan.
2. Draw a heeled water line at 20° through the center line and the D.W.L.; call it W.L.–A. (See Figure 47)
3. Draw a heeled water line at 20° 4″ below W.L.–A; call it W.L.–B.
4. Planimeter each full section. Do all sections to W.L.–A and all sections to W.L.–B.
5. Trace each section, cut out with scissors, and balance to find the balance line on which lies the center of buoyancy for that section. Place the paper cutout on the edge of a triangle, so that the balance line will be parallel to

the heeled center line. The distance between the two lines will be the righting arm. (See Figure 48)

6. Set up as follows*:

Sta.	Planimeter Reading Full Sec.	×	S.M.	=	Funct. Areas	×	Righting Arm	=	Functs. of Moms.
0			1						
1			4						
2			2						
3			4						
4			2						
5			4						
6			2						
7			4						
8			2						
9			4						
10			1						
					Sum				Sum

Get displacement in normal way for W.L.–A; again for W.L.–B.

7. Righting Arm = Total Functs. of Moms. ÷ Total Functs. of Areas. Get this for W.L.–A; again for W.L.–B.

8. Make a graph, plotting displacement for W.L.–A and W.L.–B and righting arms A and B, to find required righting arm.

9. Correction to Righting Arm = Sine 20° × Dist. V.C.G. is below or above L.W.L. (Note: Sine 20° = .342) (See Figure 50)

10. Add correction, if V.C.G. is below L.W.L., or subtract correction, if V.C.G. is above L.W.L., to the required righting arm found in step 8. Result will be the actual righting arm.

11. Actual Righting Arm × Disp. in lbs. = Righting Moment.

12. Righting Moment = Heeling Moment.

    Heeling Moment = Sail Area × Vert. Dist. C.E. to C.L.P. (which is the Heeling Arm) × W.P.C. (See Figure 4, page 92)

    Thus: Righting Arm × Disp. = Sail Area × Heeling Arm × W.P.C.

    So: $$W.P.C. = \frac{\text{Righting Arm} \times \text{Disp.}}{\text{Sail Area} \times \text{Heeling Arm}}$$

Using 85% of the foretriangle in the sail area, the following boats have W.P.C.'s as shown for 20° heel and are useful for comparison:

21' 3" W.L.	Centerboarder	.95	
23' 0" W.L.	Keel Boat	.60	(tender)
27' 1" W.L.	Keel Boat	1.15	
27' 6" W.L.	Centerboarder	1.10	(tender)
29' 0" W.L.	Keel Boat	1.15	
30' 0" W.L.	Centerboarder	1.29	(Increased from 1.21 after tank tests)
32' 0" W.L.	Keel Boat	1.13	

* Note: See note on p.295 for alternate method for Steps 5 and 6, using integrator.

Figure 47. Full body plan, heeled to 20°

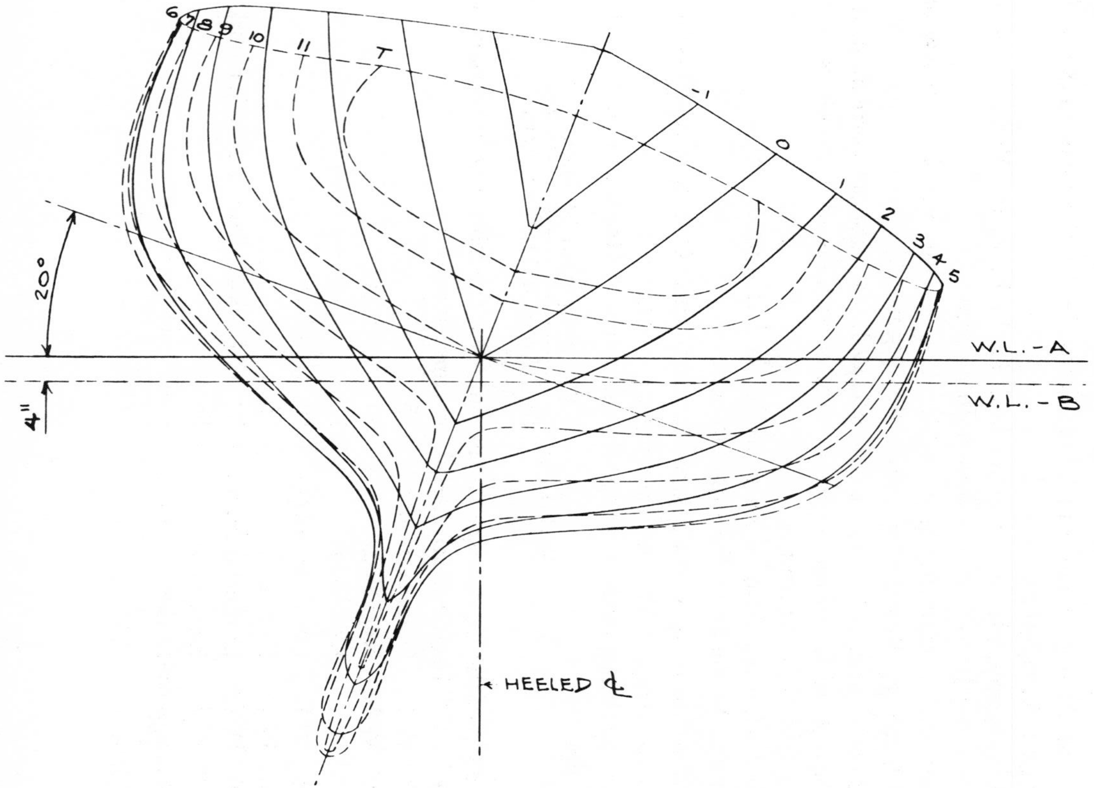

Figure 48. Sections cutout showing righting arm

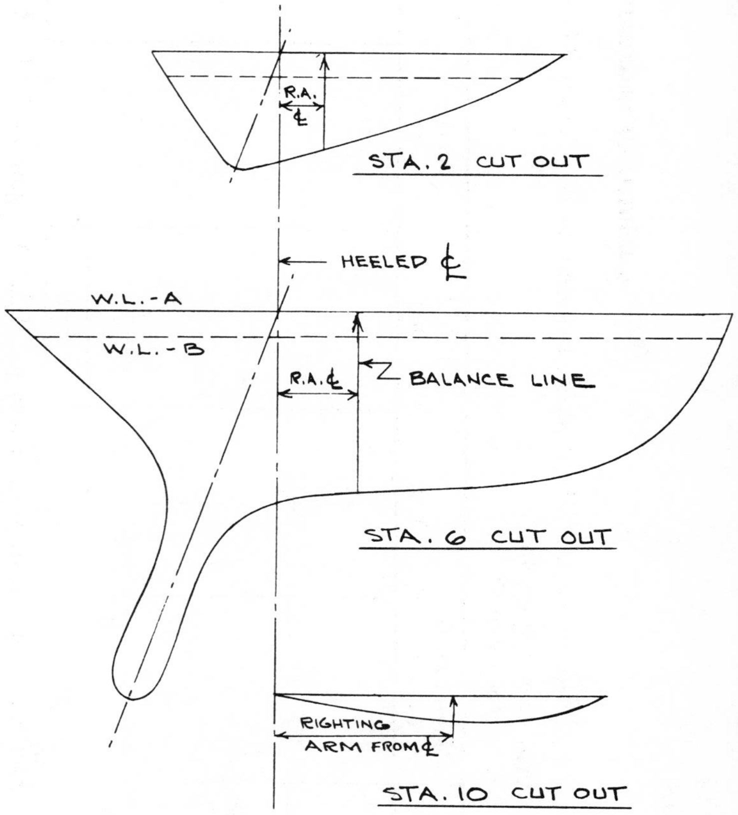

34′ 6″ W.L.   Centerboarder   1.37
34′ 6″ W.L.   Keel Boat   1.12
38′ 0″ W.L.   Keel Boat   1.59 (stiff)
55′ 0″ W.L.   Centerboarder   1.56
85′ 0″ W.L.   Keel Boat   1.75

Note that the centerboarders have W.P.C.'s about 10% higher than the keel boats. (See Figure 49)

**Figure 49.
Wind pressure
coefficient
at 20° heel.
The higher
the stiffer.**

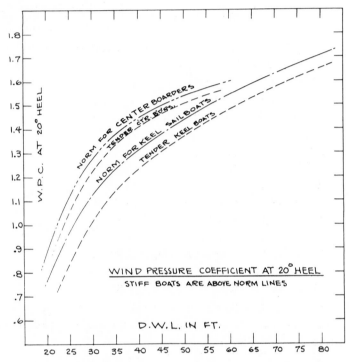

Consider our sketch (Figure 50) showing the heeled section; it is a simple matter to find the transverse metacentric height (GM), by projecting upward the line on which the center of buoyancy lies perpendicular to the 20° W.L., until it intersects the center line at M. We already have G. from our weight estimate (the V.C.G.). GM is then the distance in feet between these two points, G. and M.

Alternate method for Steps 5 and 6, using a mechanical integrator. Set up as follows:

20° Heel at W.L.—A (table shortened to save space)

Stas.	Area Dial			Mom. Dial		
	Reading, Full Sec.	× S.M.	= Funct. Areas	Reading	× S.M.	= Funct. Moms.
0, 10		1			1	
1, 3, 5, 7, 9		4			4	
2, 4, 6, 8		2			2	
			Sum			Sum

Disp. A in Cu. Ft. = ⅓ × Total Functs. Areas × Sta. Spcg. × Inv. Scale²
Mom. A = ⅓ × Total Functs. Moms. × Sta. Spcg. × Inv. Scale³
Righting Arm W.L.–A = Mom. A ÷ Disp. A in Cu. Ft.

The Dellenbaugh Angle Method gives us an angle as follows:

$$\frac{57.3 \times \text{Sail Area} \times \text{Heeling Arm} \times 1}{\text{GM} \times \text{Disp. in Lbs.}} = \text{Dellenbaugh Angle.}$$

$$\text{Righting Mom. @ } 1° = \frac{\text{GM} \times \text{Disp. in Lbs.}}{57.3}$$

$$\text{Dellenbaugh Angle} = \frac{\text{Sail Area} \times \text{Heeling Arm}}{\text{Righting Mom. @ } 1°}$$

Using 100% of the foretriangle in the sail area the following boats have Dellenbaugh heeling angles as follows:

18′ 6″ W.L.	Centerboarder	21°
21′ 3″ W.L.	Centerboarder	21.5°
25′ 0″ W.L.	Centerboarder	16.3° (stiff)
28′ 0″ W.L.	Keel	17.5°
32′ 0″ W.L.	Keel	17.5°
33′ 0″ W.L.	Keel	18.7° (tender)
36′ 0″ W.L.	Keel	18.5°
37′ 0″ W.L.	Centerboarder	15.7°
40′ 6″ W.L.	Keel	16.5°
47′ 0″ W.L.	Keel	14.5°
50′ 6″ W.L.	Centerboarder	7.8° (stiff)
52′ 6″ W.L.	Keel	13.5°
67′ 0″ W.L.	Keel	11.5°
80′ 0″ W.L.	Keel	10°

Note that centerboard boats have an angle approximately 10% less than the keel boats. (See Figure 51)

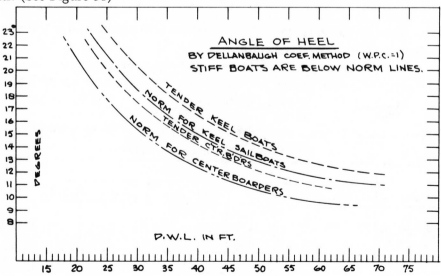

Figure 51. Angle of heel—Dellenbaugh angle. The lower the stiffer. Today (1972) new keel sailboats are 25% stiffer than shown on this chart.

Figure 50. Heeled section, showing righting arm and GM

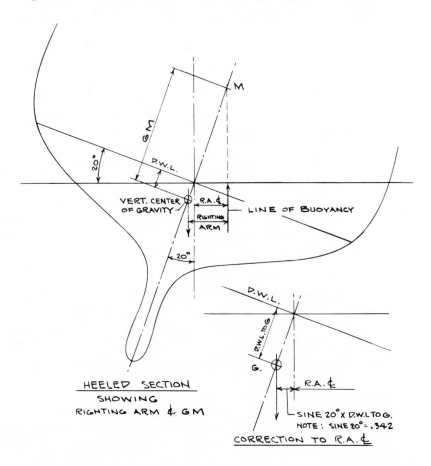

HEELED SECTION
SHOWING
RIGHTING ARM & GM

CORRECTION TO R.A. ₵

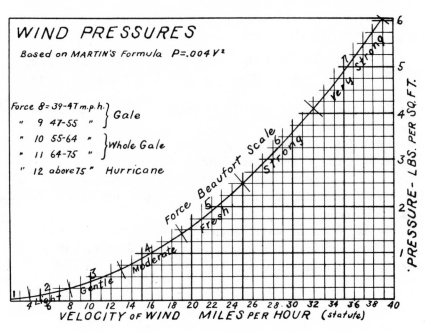

Typical stability curves. Note change in righting moment as center of gravity changes.

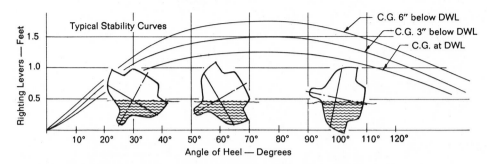

Inclining Experiment. To find the GM of an existing boat to check her stability or to rerig her, what is commonly called an inclining experiment is performed as follows:

1. On a calm day, determine the flotation of the boat, amount of liquid in the tanks, amount of inside ballast, stores and gear. Free the docking lines.

2. Rig a pendulum of string with a heavy nut as a weight at the bottom. Fasten it on the center line, say in the amidship hatch. To steady the pendulum, put a bucket of water on the cabin sole and hang the weight in it. Then place a horizontal batten across the two main cabin seats and tape a strip of paper on it so that the movement of the pendulum can be accurately recorded and measured.

3. Use people as moving weights, say as follows: one person for a boat up to 28 feet W.L.; 2 people up to 33 feet W.L.; 3 people up to 38 feet W.L.; 4 people up to 42 feet W.L.; 5 people up to 50 feet W.L.; etc. Mark the positions at which the people are to stand on deck at the center line and at the rail at the widest part of the boat on both sides.

4. Record pendulum movements on batten, with people in the above positions.

5. Find the GM from the following formula:

$$\text{Transv. GM} = \frac{\text{Wt. Moved} \times \text{Dist. Moved in Ft.} \times \text{Pendulum Length in Ft.}}{\text{Disp. in Lbs.} \times \text{Pendulum Movement in Ft.}}$$

With the GM thus obtained, use the Dellenbaugh Angle method to find how stable the boat will be, if a sailboat.

Period of Roll. GM may be found by timing the rolling of a vessel. It's like the swinging pendulum of a metronome with its weight adjusted to set the beat in music. Mark the time as the mast passes the vertical position. One complete roll (two ticks on a metronome) is from the vertical to one side, over to the other side and back to the vertical.

To induce violent rolling several men can stand with one foot on a dock, the other on the boat and shift their weight in time with the roll. Take the total time for say ten complete rolls and average it.

The formula is: $GM = (2R \div T)^2$, in which GM is transverse metacentric height, R is radius of gyration for which we can use a percentage of beam between .21B and .23B, T is time in seconds.

Stiff vessels have short periods of roll, tender vessels long periods. For example:

Sailing yachts (large GM) 4 to 8 seconds.

Ocean liners (small GM) 20 to 24 seconds.

Other craft roll between these extremes.

Transverse Metacenter (Transv. GM) It will be noted that the weight of a vessel acting vertically downward, through the center of gravity, and the buoyancy of the water acting vertically upward, through the center of buoyancy, form a couple called the "righting moment."

For power boats, a simple formula may be used to find the righting lever arm at small angles (up to 10°), because "M" remains approximately in a constant position.

Righting Arm = Transv. GM × Sine of Heel Angle.

Righting Mom. = Disp. in Lbs. × Transv. GM × Sine of Heel Angle.

Righting Mom. 30° = 30° × Disp. in Lbs. × GM ÷ 57.3.

Righting Mom. 1° = R.M. 30° ÷ 30°.

Table of Transv. GM for Different Types of Vessels

Harbor vessels, tugs	GM = 15–18″
Small power cruisers	GM = 2′–2′ 6″
Shallow-draft river boats	GM = 12′
Merchant steamers	GM = 1′–3′
Sailing Yachts	GM = 3′–4′ 6″

If G is below M the vessel is stable.

If G is above M the vessel is unstable.

If G and M coincide the vessel is in neutral equilibrium.

A vessel with a large GM comes to the upright position very suddenly, whereas a vessel with a small one comes to the upright position more slowly and is more comfortable in a seaway.

Steadying sails—so often seen on commercial fishing boats—bilge keels, activated antirolling fins and Frahm antirolling tanks are all useful in reducing the violent rolling motion of ships at sea.

Moment of Inertia (I) is the product of an area multiplied by its distance squared about an axis. Since this is something squared times something squared, the result is a power to the fourth. We use this to determine the size of mast and column sections, expressed in inches to the fourth, and to determine the stability of boats, by using the I of the water-line planes expressed in feet to the fourth.

Moment of Inertia of a Water Plane about the Center Line. The short method to find this is I = .04* × D.W.L. Length × D.W.L. Beam Cubed. The long method is more tedious but more accurate, as follows:

* The range is from .037 for fine to .043 for full D.W.L.'s.

Station	½ Ordinate Water Plane	Cubes of ½ Ords.	×	Simpson's Multipliers	=	Functs. of Cubes
0				1		
1				4		
2				2		
3				4		
etc.				etc.		
						Sum

The sum of the functions of cubes × ⅓ station spacing × ⅓ × 2 (for both sides) = Mom. of Inertia of the Water Plane about its Center Line.

Moment to Alter Trim One Inch. There is an approximate formula for the moment required to change the trim of a boat fore and aft a total of 1″. It is: C × A² ÷ B = Moment in foot-pounds. In this formula A = area of D.W.L. plane in square feet, B = beam of D.W.L. in feet, and C = a constant between .40 and .45.

Example: What is the moment to alter trim 1″ on a boat whose designed water line plane has an area of 150 square feet and a beam of 10 feet? Answer: .35 × 22,500 ÷ 10 = 787 foot-pounds. So if we move a weight of 787 pounds one foot say aft, the bow will rise ½″ and the stern will sink ½″. Interpolation is directly proportional.

It is generally sufficiently accurate to assume that one half the change of trim is forward and the other half is aft. Actually the center of flotation is not amidships but further aft, so that the change of trim at the bow will be greater than at the stern.

Longitudinal Center of Flotation is the centroid (C.G. of an area) of the waterplane at which a boat is floating. Say it is 55% aft of Sta. O, then she will be 55% of the total trim up by the bow, and 45% down by the stern.

D.W.L. IN FEET

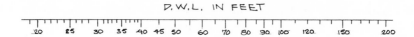

FT. LBS.—MOMENT TO CHANGE TRIM 1″ IN SALT WATER

BEAM OF D.W.L. IN FT.

NOMOGRAPH FOR MOMENT TO CHANGE TRIM 1″

To Find the Vertical Center of Buoyancy. Use the areas of the stations. Cut out the shape of each below the D.W.L., balance each on an edge parallel to the D.W.L. Its vertical center is thus obtained and measured above the base line. Lay out a table thus:

Stas.	Planimeter Readings ½ areas	×	Simpson's Multipliers	=	Functs. of ½ areas	×	Arms above Base	=	Functs. of Moms.
0			1						
1			4						
2			2						
3			4						
4			2						
5			4						
6			2						
7			4						
8			2						
9			4						
10			1						
					Sum				Sum

$$\text{V.C.B. above base} = \frac{\text{Sum of Functs. of Moms.}}{\text{Sum of Functs. of } \frac{1}{2} \text{ areas}}$$

To Find the Vertical Center of Gravity (having found GM from the inclining experiment, and vertical center of buoyancy from the lines, and BM from the moment of inertia of the waterplane), substitute the known quantities in the following formulas:

BM $= \dfrac{I}{V}$ or Mom. of Inertia of Water Plane about Center Line ÷ Disp. Cu. Ft.

I $= .04* \times$ D.W.L. Length $\times$ D.W.L. Beam Cubed.

M $=$ Metacenter.

B $=$ Dist. Vert. Center of Buoyancy above base found in preceding paragraph.

BM $=$ Dist. from B to M.

GM $=$ GM found from Inclining Experiment. Distance from G to M, or meta-centric height. Or found by GM $=$ BM $-$ (Dist. B to G).

G $=$ Dist. Vert. Center or Gravity above base $=$ (Dist. Vert. Center of Buoy-ancy Abv. Base $+$ BM) $-$ GM. Or found by weight estimate.

Radius of Gyration. This is equal to the square root of the quotient of the moment of inertia divided by the area of the section expressed thus:

$$R = \sqrt{\frac{I}{A}}$$

It is used in column or mast calculations. The unbraced length of the column divided by the radius of gyration is termed the "ratio of slenderness." You some-times hear it referred to as the "L over R" ratio.

* See footnote on page 299.

Section Modulus is the ratio of the moment of inertia ÷ the distance from the neutral axis to the extreme fiber, expressed in inches cubed since it is inches to the fourth power divided by inches.

This ratio is useful because by knowing the required section modulus, a designer may conveniently select the particular section he wishes to specify for beams.

The American Institute of Steel Construction gives a handy Section Modulus Table, listing sections of I-beams, channels, wide flange beams, and various miscellaneous beams, arranged in order of their economy of weight. Their book is titled *Steel Construction*.

Freeboard is the distance between the outboard edge of the deck and the water level. Next to beam, it is one of the most important factors contributing to safety. High freeboard in a design provides a greater range of stability, because the edge of the deck will not be heeled under the water until a much greater angle is reached. In sailboats this increases the power to carry sail. Another obvious advantage is the increased room inside the hull. And the deck will be drier, too.

But like everything else in this world, you pay for what you get, so here then is the disadvantage—increased wind resistance when sailing on the wind.

Free Surface. This phenomenon can easily be understood when the time comes to bail out a dinghy filled with rain water. Step aboard a craft in such a condition. The sudden rush of weight to the wrong side will amaze you. Imagine this effect magnified for a larger vessel.

The action of waves in a swimming pool on a large steamer is a good example of free surface. This sudden rush of weight to the wrong side is what happens inside a tank, whether it be full of fresh water, gasoline or fuel oil. To control free surface in a tank, it is necessary to install baffle plates, both transversely and longitudinally. Knowledge of this phenomenon by skippers of vessels damaged by the enemy in wartime was instrumental in deciding whether or not to give the command to abandon ship.

Some engineers can prove that the force increases forty to fifty times when free surface acts between two connected wing tanks. However, such is not the case in actual practice. The connecting pipe is relatively so small that by the time the liquid starts flowing from one tank to the other, the vessel has finished her roll in one direction and starts rolling the other way, thus reversing the flow. Nevertheless, good practice calls for a valve on any such cross connection. This principle is now used to reduce the violent motion of ships in a seaway. It is called the Frahm Stabilizing Method.

Frahm Antirolling Tanks. The Frahm antirolling tank system utilizes sea water in so-called "passive" tanks which are, in effect, connected wing tanks forming a "U" above the center of gravity. The weight of water (1 to 2% of the ship's displacement) is transferred, when the system is tuned to the frequency of the waves, so that most of this weight is on the high side at each roll, thus developing a restoring moment which reduces the rolling motion by 50%. In some installations, the cross duct was removed, and the bottoms of the tanks were kept open to the seas.

The passive tank system of stabilization relies on the natural rebound of water, or resonance. When designed so that the flow is in proper phase from one vertical leg of the "U" tube to the other, such flow is in frequency with the waves encountered. The period of transfer should be approximately equal to the natural period of roll of the ship to obtain the maximum stability.

So-called "active" tanks have been tried which used pumps to transfer the water. This was found to be complicated, expensive, and unnecessary. The passive tanks are therefore worth consideration because of their simplicity and low cost.

Trials. Boat speed trials must be run in deep water. In shallow water a sinking action holds a boat back even when running at slow speed. Choose a measured mile course with markers laid out on shore. Time the boat with a stop watch, steaming one way over the measured mile and then in the other direction over the same course. Average the speed for the round trip. Do not average the times, as this will lead to an erroneous result.

$$\text{Speed} = 3600 \div \text{Seconds to Run 1 Mile.}$$

If the measured mile course is a statute mile (5,280 feet), the speed obtained will be in miles per hour (M.P.H.). But if the course is a nautical mile (6,080 feet), the speed will be in knots. Changing knots into miles per hour is just a matter of multiplying by 1.152. To change M.P.H. to knots multiply by .868.

Make a chart plotting speed against engine revolutions and keep it on board for navigating. It will be vital when running through a fog.

Range is the total distance which a boat can cover under power using all available fuel.

Fuel Consumption. For rough estimates of pounds of fuel used per horsepower per hour (known as specific fuel consumption), use .6 pounds for gasoline and .4 pounds for diesel oil. These figures will vary depending on the engines.

Gasoline (1 gallon weighs 6.19 pounds). Example: The cruising horsepower of a power boat is 160, giving her a cruising speed of 12 knots. A range of 204 miles is required. How many gallons of gasoline are needed and what will this weigh? First find the time it will take to go 204 miles at 12 knots. 204 ÷ 12 = 17 hours. Next use the above fuel consumption formula, .6 × 160 × 17 = 1,632 pounds of gasoline needed, which is 1,632 ÷ 6.19 = 263 gallons of gasoline.

Diesel Oil (1 gallon weighs 7.13 pounds). Example: If we use the same figures of 160 horsepower, speed of 12 knots and required range of 204 miles taking 17 hours, but change the fuel to diesel oil, then the weight of fuel needed is .4 × 160 × 17 = 1,088 pounds of diesel oil, but this 1,088 ÷ 7.13 = 152 gallons of diesel oil, instead of 263 gallons of gasoline. In this example we can relate the range of a diesel powered boat to one powered by a gasoline engine. Roughly it would be 263 gallons ÷ 152 gallons or 1.73 times as far. Also there is a saving in the cost per gallon of diesel oil over gasoline. But the largest dividend in having a diesel engine is greater safety combined with less trouble than with a gasoline engine.

Electrical Loads. To find the proper size of storage batteries and generators required to supply electricity add up the watts for all electrical equipment aboard, estimating how much current will be used in port and underway. The time each item will be in daily use should be included in a column of watt hours. Use the following data:

Watts = Amperes × Volts
Amps. = Watts ÷ Volts
Watt Hrs. = Watts × Hours
Amp. Hrs. (A.H.) = Watt Hrs. ÷ Volts
1 Kilowatt (Kw) = 1,000 Watts

Set up a work sheet as follows:

Items	Total Watts	Generator Load		Battery Load	
		In Port	*Underway*	*Hours*	*Watts × Hrs.*
Starting					
Navig. Lts.					
Cabin Lts.					
Blower					
Bilge Pump					
Windlass					
Radio Tel.					
Etc.					
		Sum	Sum		Sum

Generator: Select a size to supply 25% more than sum of loads whichever is greater, in port or underway.

Batteries: Change sum of Watt Hrs. to Amp. Hrs. (A.H.). Select a size at least 25% greater.

Hrs. to charge batteries = Battery size (A.H.) ÷ Amps. of generator.

Wiring Size: See Booklet 302, National Fire Protection Assn., 60 Batterymarch St., Boston 10, Mass., from which the following table is given:

Wire Sizes for Amperes—Lengths

Total Current on Circuit in Amps.	Length of Wire in Feet from Source of Current to Most Distant Fixture										
	10	15	20	25	30	35	40	45	50	55	60
6 Volts Two Wire—10% Drop *Wire Sizes (A.W.G.)*											
5	14	14	14	12	12	12	10	10	10	10	8
10	14	12	10	10	8	8	8	8	6	6	6
15	12	10	8	8	8	6	6	6	4	4	4
20	10	8	8	6	6	6	4	4	4	4	3
25	10	8	6	6	4	4	4	4	3	3	2
12 Volts Two Wire—10% Drop *Wire Sizes (A.W.G.)*											
5	14	14	14	14	14	14	14	14	12	12	12
10	14	14	14	12	12	12	10	10	10	10	8
15	14	14	12	10	10	10	8	8	8	8	8
20	12	12	10	10	8	8	8	8	6	6	6
25	10	10	10	8	8	8	6	6	6	6	4

How To Calculate the Horsepower Needed to Run an Alternator.

Question: Let us say we would like to use a 100 amp. alternator on a boat to charge a 12-volt system. What is the horsepower drain on the engine?

Answer: It is the killowatts × 2.

So, since volts × amps. = watts, and watts ÷ 1000 = kilowatts, we have 12 × 100 ÷ 1000 = 1.2 KW.

1.2 × 2 = 2.4 H.P. required.

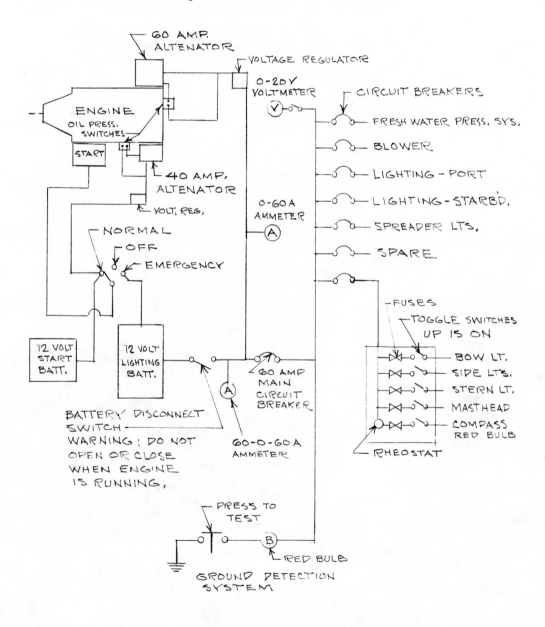

ELEMENTARY WIRING DIAGRAM
FOR
SANTA MARIA

CHAPTER XXIV

CALCULATIONS FOR
PIPE DREAM CRUISING SLOOP

DISPLACEMENT, LONGITUDINAL CENTER OF BUOYANCY AND PRISMATIC COEFFICIENT FROM FAIRED LINES

25' 5" D.W.L.		Sta. Spacing = 2.54'		Scale ¾" = 1' 0"	
Sta.	Planimeter Reading	Simpson's Multipliers	Functs.	Arms	Moments
0		1	—	0	—
1	.30	4	1.20	1	1.20
2	1.08	2	2.16	2	4.32
3	2.20	4	8.80	3	26.40
4	3.43	2	6.86	4	27.44
5	4.27	4	17.08	5	85.40
6	4.54	2	9.08	6	54.48
7	3.94	4	15.76	7	110.32
8	2.59	2	5.18	8	41.44
9	.91	4	3.64	9	32.76
10	—	1	—	10	—
			69.76		383.76

Displacement $= \frac{2}{3} \times 69.76 \times \frac{16}{9} \times 2.54 = 210$ cu. ft. $\times 64 = 13,450$ lbs.

Longitudinal Center of Buoyancy $= \frac{383.7}{69.76} = 5.50$ Stas.

Prismatic Coefficient $= \dfrac{210}{\frac{16}{9} \times 2 \times 4.54 \times 25.4} = \dfrac{210}{410} = .513$

Lbs. per Inch Immersion from chart = 950 lbs.

**(opposite page) PIPE DREAM Cruising Sloop SOUTHERLY
She is used as an example for calculations throughout this book.**

WETTED AREA

Sta.	½ Girth in Ft.	×	S.M.	=	Functs.
0	—		1		—
1	1.42		4		5.68
2	2.77		2		5.54
3	4.12		4		16.48
4	5.59		2		11.18
5	7.54		4		30.16
6	8.06		2		16.12
7	8.31		4		33.24
8	7.97		2		15.94
9	6.25		4		25.00
10	—		1		—
					159.34

Bilge factor 1.02

Wetted Area $= 159.34 \times \frac{2}{3} \times 2.54 \times 1.02 = 275$ sq. ft.

$\dfrac{\text{Sail Area}}{\text{Wetted Area}} = \dfrac{584}{275} = 2.12$ Note—on the low side. Increase sail if possible.

WEIGHT ESTIMATE FOR *PIPE DREAM* CRUISING SLOOP

		Above Base			About Sta. 0 in Stas.			
	Wt. in lbs.	Vert. Arm. in ft.	Vert. Mom.	Aft Arm.	Aft Mom.	Fwd. Arm.	Fwd. Mom.
Hull Structure								
1. *Backbone*—W. O. @ 53 lbs. cu. ft.								
Stern ⎫ Gripe ⎭ $13 \times .38 \times .45 \times 53 =$	118	6.0	708.–	.5	59.–	—	—
Keel $16 \times .23 \times .8 \times 53 =$	156	3.6	561.–	5.1	795.–		
Deadwd. (below keel) $4.5 \times 2.5 \times .42 \times 53 =$	250	1.7	425.–	7.1	1770.–		
Deadwd. (above keel) $1.8 \times 7 \times \frac{1}{2} \times .66 \times 53 =$	220	4.0	880.–	8.5	1870.–		
Horn Timber (Rudder aft) $5.5 \times .23 \times .62 \times 53 =$	42	6.5	273.–	10.5	440.–		
Transom Knee $2 \times .25 \times .25 \times 53 =$	7	7.7	54.–	11.6	81.–		
Transom Frame $9 \times .16 \times .33 \times 53 =$	25	8.2	205.–	11.8	295.–		

2. *Planking*—Afr. Mahog. ⅞″ @ 32 lbs. cu. ft. or 2.34 lbs. per sq. ft. in Stas. fr. −1

Sta.	½ Girth ft.	S. M.	Functs.	Vert. A.	Vert. Mom.	Aft A.	Aft Moms.
−1	2.3	1	2.30	9.2	21.20	0	0
0	4.4	4	17.60	8.1	142.50	1	17.60
1	5.7	2	11.40	7.3	83.20	2	22.80
2	6.6	4	26.40	6.7	177.00	3	79.20
3	7.1	2	14.20	6.2	88.00	4	56.80
4	7.5	4	30.00	6.0	180.00	5	150.00
5	8.0	2	16.00	5.8	92.80	6	96.00
6	8.1	4	32.40	5.6	181.50	7	226.80
7	8.3	2	16.60	5.6	93.00	8	132.80
8	8.0	4	32.00	5.9	189.00	9	288.00
9	6.6	2	13.20	6.4	84.50	10	132.00
10	5.7	4	22.80	7.0	160.00	11	251.00
11	4.7	1	4.70	7.5	35.30	12	56.50
			239.60		1,528.00		1,509.50

		Above Base		About Sta. 0 in Stas.			
	Wt. in lbs.	Vert. Arm. in ft.	Vert. Mom.	Aft Arm.	Aft Mom.	Fwd. Arm.	Fwd. Mom.
Planking wt. -1 to $11 = 239.6 \times \frac{2}{3} \times 2.54 \times$ 2.34 lbs. $=$	950	6.4	6,080.–	5.3	5,040.–		
V.C.G. $= \dfrac{1,528}{239.6} = 6.38.$ L.C.G. $= \dfrac{1,509}{239.6} =$							
6.3 stas. from -1 so 5.3 from sta. 0							
Total Area Planking $405 + 3.8 + 13.7 = 422.5$ sq. ft.						1.2	10.8
Planking fwd of Sta -1 $2 \times 2 \times 2/2 \times 2.34$ lbs. $=$	9	9.4	84.5	—	—		
Planking aft of Sta 11 $2 \times 4.5 \times 1.5 \times 2.34$ lbs. $=$	32	7.5	240.–	11.4	365.–		
Transom $6.3 \times 2.7 \times 2.34$ lbs. $=$	40	8.3	332.–	12.0	480.–		
Butt Blocks—Planking $-\frac{5}{8}$ W. O. say $30 \times .54 \times .54 \times 2.76 =$	25	6.4	160.–	5.3	133.–		
3. Framing $1\frac{3}{8}''$ x $1\frac{1}{2}''$ W. O. Spcd. $9''$							
Wt./lin. ft. $\dfrac{53 \text{ lbs.} \times 1.37 \times 1.5}{144} = .755$ lbs.							
Lin. ft. framing $= \dfrac{\text{Shell Area}}{\text{Fr. Spcg.}}$							
Shell Area $= \dfrac{950}{2.34} = 405$ sq. ft.							
$\dfrac{405}{.75} = 540$ Lin. ft. Sta. -1 to 11							
Wt. of Framing Sta. -1 to Sta. 11 $540 \times .755$ lbs. $=$	407	6.4	2,600.–	5.3	2,160.–		
" Frs. fwd Sta. -1 $3' \times .755$ lbs. $= 2.27$	2	9.4	18.8	—	—	1.2	2.4
" Frs. aft Sta. 11 $9.4' \times .755$ lbs. $= 7.1$	7	7.5	52.5	11.4	79.8		
4. Floor Timbers $1\frac{1}{8}''$ W. O. Spcd. $9''$ @ 4.97 lbs. per sq. ft.							
4 Floors fwd. of Sta. 0 $4 \times .58 \times .66 \times 4.97$ lbs. $=$	8	8.2	65.6	—	—	.8	6.4
9 Floors Sta. 0 to 3 $9 \times .41 \times 1.25 \times 4.97$ lbs. $=$	23	5.3	122.–	1.5	34.5		
Mast Step $\frac{1}{8}''$ Steel @ 5.1 lbs. per sq. ft.							
3 ft. I beam—vert pc $3 \times .25 \quad = .75$							
top and bot. $3 \times 2 \times .5 = 3.00$							
stl. floors $8 \times .25 \times 1 = 2.00$							
$\overline{\quad 5.75}$							
5.75 sq. ft. $\times 5.1$ lbs. $=$	30	4.2	126.–	3.5	105.–		
14 Floors Sta. 4 to 8 $14 \times .5 \times 1.4 \times 4.97$ lbs. $=$	49	3.8	186.–	6.0	294.–		
10 Floors Sta. 8 to Transom $10 \times .25 \times 2.3 \times 4.97 =$	29	6.5	188.–	10.0	290.–		
5. Rudder Blade—$1.4 \times 6 \times 2.6$ lbs. 22							
Rudder—Stock $1\frac{5}{8}''$ @ say 7 lbs. per sq. ft. $\times 5 =$ 35							
$1\frac{1}{2}''$ Tube—@ 2.7 lbs. per sq. ft. $2.7 \times 1.5 =$ 4							
Tiller Fitting say 7							
Straps and Castings say 10							
$\overline{\quad}$ $78 =$	78	3.5	273.–	9.1	710.–		
6. Engine Beds—$1\frac{1}{2}''$ W. O. $2 \times 2 \times .4 \times 6.6$ lbs. $\Big\} =$ brackets say 4×2	19	5.2	99.–	8.1	154.–		

	Wt. in lbs.	Above Base		About Sta. 0 in Stas.			
		Vert. Arm. in ft.	Vert. Mom.	Aft Arm.	Aft Mom.	Fwd. Arm.	Fwd. Mom.
7. Bilge Stringers $\frac{7}{8}''$ Fir—2 × .58 × 37 × 2.34 lbs. =	100	6.7	670.–	5.0	500.–		
8. Clamp $2\frac{5}{8}''$ × $2\frac{5}{8}''$ Fir 2 × .21 × .21 × 35 × 32 lbs. =	99	8.8	870.–	5.1	505.–		
9. Decks $\frac{1}{2}''$ Plywd with fiberglass 1.5 .2 1.7 lbs. per sq. ft.							
Main Deck Fwd. of House 9.2 × 8.5 × $\frac{1}{2}$ × 1.7 =	67	9.9	663.–	.6	40.–		
Main side decks 2 × 2 × 15 × 1.7 =	102	9.1	930.–	4.9	500.–		
Bridge Deck 1.75 × 10 × 1.7 =	30	9.0	270.–	8.1	243.–		
Side Dks. in way of cockpit 2 × 1.7 × 7.6 × 1.7 =	44	8.8	388.–	9.7	426.–		
Main Dk. at stern 2 × 6 × 1.7 =	21	9.2	193.–	11.5	241.–		

(1″ Teak 3.75 lbs. per sq. ft.

Teak Decks $264 \times \dfrac{3.75}{1.7}$ 585 lbs. or 321 lbs. more)

Deck Beams—$1\frac{1}{16}''$ × $2\frac{1}{8}''$ Spruce

Wt./lin. ft. $\dfrac{30 \text{ lbs.} \times 1.06 \times 2.12}{144}$ .325

Fore Dk. Beams Lengths   1.5′
2.4
3.2
3.8
4.5
5.1
5.7
6.2
6.7
7.2
7.7
8.1

	Wt. in lbs.	Vert. Arm. in ft.	Vert. Mom.	Aft Arm.	Aft Mom.	Fwd. Arm.	Fwd. Mom.
62.1′ × .325 lbs. =	20	9.8	196.–	.6	12.–		
Side Dk. Beams 2 × 19 × 2′ × .325 lbs. =	25	9.0	226.–	4.9	122.–		
Bridge Dk. " 3 × 10 × .325 lbs. =	10	8.9	89.–	8.1	81.–		
Side Dk. Beams—cockpit 2 × 9 × 1.7 × .325 lbs. =	10	8.7	87.–	9.7	97.–		
Stern Dk. Beams 3 × 6.5 × .325 lbs. =	7	9.1	63.7	11.5	80.6		
Deck Blocking $\frac{3}{4}''$ W. O. at Bow							
1.5 × 1 × $\frac{1}{2}$ × 3.32 lbs. =	3	10.2	30.6	—	—	1.3	3.9
Under Mooring cleats, 5 × .5 × 3.32 lbs. =	9	9.8	88.3	.2	1.8		
At stern, 5 × 6 × 3.32 =	10	9.2	92.–	11.8	118.–		
Under main sheet, 3 × .7 × .7 × 3.32 =	5	9.1	45.5	11.6	58.–		
Brackets on Beams $\frac{5}{8}''$ Plywd 2×2×2×$\frac{1}{2}$×1.87 =	8	8.6	68.8	3.8	30.4		
Total =	3,096	6.06	18,704.–	5.88	18,211.– −23.5		23.5
Paint and Fastenings 10% above =	309	6.06	1,870.–	5.88	18,187.5 1,815.–		

	Wt. in lbs.	Above Base		About Sta. 0 in Stas.			
		Vert. Arm. in ft.	Vert. Mom.	Aft Arm.	Aft Mom.	Fwd. Arm.	Fwd. Mom.
10. Soakage—say 15% total wetted planking, keel & deadwd.							
⅓ planking 310 keel 156 deadwd 250 716×.15 =	107	4.3	460.–	5.3	566.–		
Total Hull Structure, Fastenings, Paint and Soakage	3,512	6.08	21,034.–	5.85	20,568.–		
Deck Joinery—Cockpit sole 1¼″ teak—							
6.2 × 2.8 × 4.69 lbs./sq. ft. =	82	7.2	590.–	9.5	780.–		
Cockpit sole beams 8 × 3 × .325 lbs. =	8	7.1	56.8	9.5	76.–		
Cockpit seats ¾″ plywd. 2 × 1.5 × 7.5 × 2.4 lbs./sq. ft. =	54	8.4	454.–	9.8	530.–		
Cockpit seat beams 16 × 1.5 × .325 lbs. =	8	8.3	66.5	9.8	78.5		
Cockpit sides ½″ plywd. 2 × 1.5 × 6.5 × 1.5 lbs./sq. ft. =	29	7.7	224.–	9.7	281.–		
Aft cockpit seat ¾″ plywd. 2.5 × 1.5 × 2.4 =	9	8.5	76.5	11.0	99.–		
Aft end cockpit ½″ plywd. 1.4 × 2.5 × 1.5 =	6	7.8	46.8	10.8	65.–		
Cockpit coaming—sides ¾″ teak							
2 × 9.5 × .9 × 2.8 =	48	9.0	432.–	9.5	455.–		
" " aft end 4.7 × 1 × 2.8 =	13	9.0	117.–	11.4	148.–		
Tiller—say	3	8.0	24	9.4	28.2		
Cabin sides 1″ teak 2 × 1 × 15 × 3.75 lbs./sq. ft. =	112	9.6	1,075.–	4.9	550.–		
Fwd. end cabin 1″ teak .8 × 4.2 × 3.75 =	13	10.1	131.–	1.8	23.4		
Aft. end cabin Incl. drop slide 1.3 × 5.5 × 3.75 =	27	9.7	262.–	7.8	211.–		
House Top ½″ plywd [(5.7 × 15) − (3 × 2 × 2)] × 1.7 =	124	10.4	1,290.–	4.9	607.–		
House Top beams ¾″ × 2″ 17 × 5.5 × .3 =	28	10.3	288.–	4.9	137.–		
Fwd. Hatch top ⅝″ Plexigl. 2.2 × 2.2 × say 1.5 plus Hatch frame say 5 =	12	10.8	130.–	2.5	30.–		
Midship Hatch (ditto) =	12	10.8	130.–	5.1	61.2		
Companion Hatch ⅝″ Plywd. 2 × 2.3 × 1.87 plus runners say 3 plus							
Companion Hatch Cover ³⁄₁₆″ alum. 2×2.3×2.7 =	24	10.8	260.–	7.0	168.–		
Dorade Vents say @ 5 × 2 =	10	9.9	99.–	4.1	41.–		
Hand Rails say @ 5 × 2 =	10	10.4	104.–	5.0	50.–		
Dinghy Chocks say @ 2 × 4 =	8	10.6	85.–	5.5	44.–		
Toe Rail—sides teak 1¼ × 2¼″ 2 × 37 × .1 × .18 × 45 =	60	9.1	545.–	5.5	330.–		
Toe Rail at stern 5.7 × .2 × .17 × 45 lbs./cu. ft. =	9	9.4	84.5	12.1	109.–		
Winch Bases say @ 5 × 2 =	10	9.1	91.–	10.0	100.–		
Total Deck Joinery	719	9.29	6,662.–	6.96	5,002.–		

	Wt. in lbs.	Above Base		About Sta. 0 in Stas.			
		Vert. Arm. in ft.	Vert. Mom.	Aft Arm.	Aft Mom.	Fwd. Arm.	Fwd. Mom.
Interior Joinery—Bulkheads ⅝″ Plywd.							
Forepeak Bhd. 1.4 × 1.4 × 1.87 lbs./sq. ft. =	4	6.6	26.4	.6	2.4		
Fwd. Head Bhd. (5.5 × 2.5 2.6 × 2) × 1.87 =	36	7.5	270.−	3.3	119.−		
Longit. Head Bhd. & Door 3.5 × 6.1 × 1.87 =	40	7.4	296.−	3.8	152.−		
Aft Head Bhd. 5.5 × 2.7 3.1 × 2 × 1.87 =	39	7.5	292.−	4.5	175.−		
Lkr. Bhds opp. Head 3 × 3.1 × 2 × 1.87 =	35	7.5	262.−	3.9	136.−		
Ice Box top ⅝″ plywd + S.S							
2.6 × 2.2 × 3.0 = 17.							
Fwd. & after pcs. 2 × 2.5 × 2 × 3 = 30 } =	80	6.2	496.−	7.4	592.−		
Front & Bot. 5.5 × 2 × 3 = 33							
Aft Bhd. 10 × 2 + 1.2 × 3 × 1.87 =	44	7.3	322.−	8.4	370.−		
Engine Partition 3 × 3.5 × 1.87 =	20	6.0	120.−	7.7	154.−		
Lkr. near ice box 4.2 × 1.2 × 1.12 =	6	8.0	48.−	7.4	44.5		
Galley dresser top—⅝″ Plywd + S.S.							
1.7 × 4.5 × 3.8 =	29	7.4	214.−	8.0	232.−		
Lkr. near stove 3.5 × 1.2 × 1.12 =	5	8.1	40.5	8.0	40.−		
Stove base 2.3 × 6 × 3.0 =	41	6.0	246.−	7.4	304.−		
Bhd. fwd. of stove 2 × 3 × 1.87 =	11	6.5	71.5	6.9	76.−		
Berths—Tops of fwd berths ⅜″ plywd.							
2 × 6.5 × 2 × 1.12 =	29	6.5	189.−	2.0	58.−		
Sides of Fwd berths ⅜″ 2 × 1.7 × 4 × 1.12 =	15	5.6	84.−	2.5	37.5		
Drawers under Fwd berths say 2 × 7 =	14	6.0	84.−	2.7	37.8		
Seat in Fwd cabin ⅝″ 1.4 × 1.3 × 1.87 =	4	6.1	24.4	1.9	7.6		
Top of settee berth ⅜″ 2.2 × 6.5 × 1.12 =	16	5.2	83.1	5.6	89.5		
Side of settee berth ⅜″ 1.2 × 6.5 × 1.12 =	9	4.8	43.2	5.6	50.5		
Top of Ext. Transom ⅜″ 2.3 × 6.2 × 1.12 =	16	5.2	83.−	5.6	89.5		
Side of Ext. Transom ⅜″ 1.2 × 6.2 × 1.12 =	8	4.8	38.4	5.6	45.−		
Top of Port built in berth ⅜″ 2.2 × 6.2 × 1.12 =	15	6.0	90.−	5.6	84.−		
Side of Port built in berth ⅝″ 1 × 6.2 × 1.87 =	12	6.0	72.−	5.6	67.−		
Drawers under berth @ 6 lbs. (actual wt.) 3 × 6 =	18	5.9	106.−	5.6	101.−		
Mirror 1.5 × 1 × 3.36 =	5	9.7	48.5	3.2	16.−		
Head—sink dresser top ⅝″ 1.2 × 1.8 × 1.87 =	4	7.1	28.4	3.4	13.6		
Linen Lkr ⅜″ 3.2 × 4 × 1.12 =	14	8.3	116.−	3.8	53.2		
Companion Ladder—sides .5×5.2×2.25= 6 } =	13	6.5	84.5	7.3	95.−		
treads 4×1.3×.5×2.8 7							
Table—⅝″ mahog. 2.7 × 4 × 1.83 + legs say							
2 × 2 =	24	6.9	165.−	5.6	134.−		
Sound Proofing—Eng. 2″ Fiberglass ⅛″							
Masonite @ 1.3 lbs.							
4.5 × 2.5 × 1.3 15 } =	30	6.2	186.−	8.0	240.−		
2 × 2 × 3 × 1.3 15							
Cabin Sole ⅝″ Teak 14 × 2.5 × 2.34 =	82	4.5	370.−	4.8	392.−		
Total Interior Joinery	718	6.4	4,599.−	5.59	4,008.−		

	Wt. in lbs.	Above Base			About Sta. 0 in Stas.			
		Vert. Arm. in ft.	Vert. Mom.		Aft Arm.	Aft Mom.	Fwd. Arm.	Fwd. Mom.
Plumbing								
F. W. Tanks 1 Fwd. empty =	25	5.7	142.-		1.6	40.-		
2 midships @ 25 lbs. =	50	4.8	240.-		6.0	300.-		
F. W. Piping say	10	5.2	52.-		4.5	45.-		
Toilet 53 lbs. + Sea Cocks 12 lbs. + 4 lbs.								
Hose + loop 5 lbs. =	74	5.5	406.-		4.0	396.-		
Wash Basin & Pump 3 lbs. + 3.5 lbs. =	7	7.0	49.-		3.5	24.5		
Galley sink & pump + Sea Cock 6.5 + 3.5 + 4 =	14	7.1	99.4		8.0	112.-		
Bilge Pump 18.5 + Hose 7 + check V 3 =	28	8.0	224.-		8.2	230.-		
Toilet Rm. Fixtures say	5	7.3	36.5		3.8	19.-		
Total Plumbing	213	5.90	1,348.-		5.52	1,166.-		
Machinery								
Engine—Dry 326 + Oil & Water 64 =	390	5.5	2,140.-		8.2	3,200.-		
Cooling water piping & sea cock =	5	4.8	240.-		8.0	40.-		
Instrument Panel =	5	8.3	41.5		8.5	42.5		
Controls =	7	7.7	54.-		8.8	61.5		
Exhaust & Muffler 8 × 4.6 37 + 4.5 muff. =	42	7.0	294.-		10.0	420.-		
Propeller & Shafting 8 + 2 + 2 =	12	4.3	51.5		8.4	101.-		
Gasoline Tanks 25 lbs. + 25 lbs. =	50	6.5	325.-		9.0	450.-		
Gasoline Piping & Strainer =	5	6.0	30.-		8.5	42.5		
Drip Pan =	5	4.3	21.5		8.0	40.-		
Total Machinery	521	6.12	3,197.-		8.40	4,397.-		
Equipment								
Chocks & Cleats =	25	10	250.-		5.0	125.-		
Ventilators =	7	11.2	78.5		3.9	27.2		
Life Rail 14 × 1.7 × .91 = 21.6 + castings								
15 + wire 5 =	50	10.8	540.-		5.3	265.-		
Compass =	5	9.5	47.5		8.5	42.5		
Stove =	25	7.0	175.-		7.3	182.-		
Mattresses 4-6″ 4 × 3.33 × 2 × 6.5 = 173	205	6.1	1,250.-		4.0	820.-		
1-4½″ 1 × 2.49 × 2 × 6.5 = 32								
Anchor =	22	10.2	224.-		—	—	.7	15.4
Anchor Line =	5	6.7	33.5		.1	.5		
Fire Extinguishers =	5	9.4	47.-		7.5	37.5		
Life Preservers =	2	7.0	14.-		9.5	190.-		
Fog Horn =	1	8.0	8.0		6.8	6.8		
Docking Lines =	2	7.3	14.6		11.1	22.2		
Dinghy =	60	11.5	690.-		5.4	324.-		
Flag Staff								
Boat Hook =	3	10.3	30.9		5.0	15.-		
Fenders								
Lead Line =	5	9.2	46.-		7.5	37.5		
Tools =	10	5.2	52.-		8.0	80.-		
(Sails Hoisted—see Spars & Rig)						217.-		
Sails stowed—Genoa & Spinnaker say =	25	8.0	200.-		9.5	238.-		
Blankets & Linen =	20	6.1	122.-		4.0	80.-		
Total Equipment	477	8.0	3,823.-		5.19	2,493.2		15.4
						−15.4		
						2,477.8		

	Wt. in lbs.	Above Base		About Sta. 0	
		Vert. Arm. in ft.	Vert. Mom.	Aft Arm.	Aft Mom.
Electrical					
Batteries 2 @ 42 lbs. =	84	6.1	512.–	1.0	84.–
Wiring =	10	8.2	82.–	5.0	50.–
Switchboard & Master Switch =	5	8.3	41.5	8.4	42.–
Lights =	20	9.6	192.–	5.0	100.–
Total Electrical	119	6.92	827.5	2.32	276.–
Spars and Rig					
Mast Sides 1⅛″ Ends 1½″					
46′ × 8″ × 5½″					
Sides 2 × 46 × .58 × 2.82 = 150					
Ends 2 × 46 × .27 × 3.75 = 93					
Taper factor .85 243 × .85 =	206	27.0	5,550.–	3.8	782.–
Spreaders 2, Tangs 5, + standing rigging					
6 × 42 × .139 = 35 Total =	42	27.0	1,130.–	3.8	160.–
Turnbuckles @ 1 lb. =	8	10.2	81.6	4.5	36.–
Winches on Dk. 2 @ 15 lbs. =	30	7.3	219.–	10.0	300.–
Winches on Mast 1 @ 6 lbs., 1 @ 5 lbs. =	11	13.2	145.–	3.6	39.6
Jib Boom say =	7	12.3	86.–	1.0	7.–
Spinnaker Pole say =	12	10.3	124.–	4.8	57.5
Roller Reefing Fittings & Main Boom =	35	13.2	461.–	7.0	245.–
Running Rigging say =	15	12.0	180.–	6.0	90.–
Main sheet blocks =	4	11.3	45.2	11.0	44.–
Jib sheet blocks =	4	12.2	48.8	3.4	13.6
Sails Hoisted 584 sq. ft. × .09 lbs. =	53	24.2	1,280.–	4.1	217.–
Total Spars & Rig	427	21.9	9,350.–	4.67	1,991.–
Summary of All Weights.					
Total Hull Structure, with fastenings, paint, soakage	3,512	6.08	21,034	5.85	20,568
Total Deck Joinery	719	9.29	6,662	6.96	5,002
Total Interior Joinery	718	6.40	4,599	5.59	4,008
Total Plumbing	213	5.90	1,248	5.52	1,166
Total Machinery	521	6.12	3,197	8.40	4,397
Total Equipment	477	8.00	3,823	5.19	2,477
Total Electrical	119	6.92	827	2.32	276
Total Spars & Rig	427	21.90	9,350	4.67	1,991
Paint and unknowns	200	7.00	1,400	5.40	1,080
Light Boat without ballast	6,906	7.57	52,140	5.91	40,965
½ fuel, 14 gals. gas @ 6.19 =	87	6.5	565	9.0	783
½ water fwd. 7.5 gals. @ 8.32 =	63	5.7	359	1.6	101
½ water midship tanks 17.5 × 8.32 =	145	4.8	696	6.0	870
3 people @ 170 =	510	7.1	3,620	9.0	4,600
People's effects =	129	5.5	710	4.5	580
½ stores & ice	210	6.0	1,260	6.5	1,365
Half load condition without ballast	8,050	7.3	59,350	6.1	49,264
Remainder = Ballast (40% of total wt.)	5,400	2.75	14,850	4.57[a]	24,736
Total wt. or displacement	13,450	5.51[b]	74,200	5.50[c]	74,000

or .49′ below D.W.L.

NOTE: *a* = L.C.G. of ballast; *b* = V.C.G. of ship; *c* = L.C.B. of ship.
  For method see *Location of Ballast*, p. 289.

13,450	74,000	6.00
−8,050	49,264	5.51
5,400	24,736	.49 below D.W.L.

What happens when fwd F.W. tank is full. No people aboard?

Answer—L.C.G. ballast then would be 4.87 stas.
    So, locate L.C.G. ballast between 4.57 and 4.87 stás.,
    change angle of keel line—raise it fwd., lower aft.

3rd Trial—Lead Ballest for proper L.C.G.

Sta.	Reading	$\times 2 \times 16/9 =$	Full Areas in sq. ft.	
2	.02	32/9	.071	
2½	.04	"	.142	
3	.10	"	.355	
3½	.16	"	.569	
4	.24	"	.854	
4½	.30	"	1.07	Plot for area curve.
5	.36	"	1.28	
5½	.41	"	1.46	
6	.40	"	1.42	
6½	.36	"	1.28	

Horiz. Scale ¾″ = 1′ 0″   Vert. Scale 1″ = .50 sq. ft.
Reading—Curve of Areas 11.55
    11.55 × 4/3 × .50 × 700 lbs. = *5400 lbs. lead ballast.*

L.C.G. Lead by balancing cut out 11½″ fwd. of Sta. 5 which is 1′ 7″ aft of 4 or $\dfrac{1.58}{2.54}$ = .62 or 4.62 Stas.

O.K. Use it.
Required location   4.57 to 4.87 Stas.

Keel Bolts

Nevins—Bolts not less than 60,000 P.S.I.
No. of Bolts—Not less than 1 sq. inch of bolt sec. area for each 1500 lbs. of outside ballast.
    Ballast = 5400 lbs.
    $\dfrac{5400}{1500}$ = 3.6 sq. in. of bolt area req'd.

        15 bolts one each bay Frs. 12–27
        $\dfrac{3.6}{15}$ = .24 sq. in. each bolt or ⁹⁄₁₆ diam.

Net area under threads—½″ bolt = .126 sq. in. (from Steel Const. Manual)
                        ⅝″ bolt = .202
                        ¾″ bolt = .302
Use 15 ⅝″ Monel bolts (75,000 P.S.I.)

Stability Calculations

For WL–A

Sta.	Reading	Simpson's Multipliers	Full Functs.	By Balancing R. Arm Ft.	Functions of Rt. Moms.
0	—	1	—	—	
1	.72	4	2.88	.29	.83
2	2.63	2	5.26	.57	3.00
3	5.05	4	20.20	.89	18.00
4	7.70	2	15.40	.95	14.60
5	9.39	4	37.56	.95	35.60
6	10.20	2	20.40	1.00	20.40
7	9.05	4	36.20	1.08	39.10
8	6.67	2	13.34	1.16	15.50
9	3.20	4	12.80	1.50	19.20
10	.50	1	.50	2.25	1.12
			164.54		167.35

Displ. = ⅓ × 164.54 × 16/9 × 2.54 × 64 = 15,850 lbs. (See p. 281)

$$\text{Righting Arm } \frac{167.35}{164.54} = 1.018' \text{ for WL–A}$$

For WL–B

0	—	1	—	—	
1	.50	4	2.00	.16	.32
2	2.13	2	4.26	.51	2.17
3	4.38	4	17.52	.83	14.55
4	6.87	2	13.74	.91	12.50
5	8.53	4	34.12	.91	31.00
6	9.32	2	18.64	1.00	18.64
7	8.20	4	32.80	1.08	35.40
8	5.85	2	11.70	1.14	13.35
9	2.56	4	10.24	1.45	14.86
10	.15	1	.15	2.50	.37
			145.17		143.16

Displ. = ⅓ × 145.17 × 16/9 × 2.54 × 64 = 14,000 lbs.

$$\text{Righting Arm } \frac{143.16}{145.17} = .986' \text{ for WL–B}$$

Correction to R.A.—Centerline. Note: the sine of 20° = .342
    sine 20° × .49 = .342 × .49 = .1677
R.A. = .976 + .167 = 1.143′ Righting Arm
H.A. = 18.29 + 2.08 = 20.37′ Heeling Arm
Righting Mom. = 1.143 × 13,450 lbs. = 15,400 ft. lbs.
Sail Area—100% Fore Triangle = 584
        85% Fore Triangle = 548

W.P.C. $\dfrac{13,450 \times 1.14}{20.37 \times 548} = \dfrac{15,333}{11,150} = 1.37$ (see pg. 293)

    This would be a stiff boat. Shoot for W.P.C. = 1.15

Find GM $\dfrac{1.143}{.342} = 3.35'$ $\left(GM = \dfrac{RA}{\text{sine } 20°} \right)$

Dellenbough Angle = $\dfrac{57.3 \times 584 \times 20.37}{3.35 \times 13,450} = \dfrac{680,000}{45,000} = 15.1°$ (See pg. 297)

    Very stiff boat by this method.
    (Lorna Doone was 16.3°)

$\dfrac{\text{Sail Area}}{\text{Wetted Area}} = \dfrac{584}{275} = 2.12$ Too low, shoot for 2.3

275 × 2.3 = 630 sq. ft. sail area would be excellent,
    if she'll carry it.

Increase Sail Area—Raise top of mast 6″

Main Foot	17.9′				
Main Hoist	35.5′	Main	$35.5 \times 17.9 \times \frac{1}{2} = 318$		318
P_2	41.1′	Fore Triangle	$41.1 \times 6.9 \times \frac{1}{2} = 284 \times .85$		241
Base	13.8′				⎯
					559

Total Sail Area	602 sq. ft.
Formerly	−584
Increased by	18 sq. ft.

Sail Area to Wetted Area $\quad \dfrac{602}{275} \quad 2.19$

By Dellenbaugh Angle Method (using 100% F. Tri.) $\quad \dfrac{57.3 \times 602 \times 20.62}{3.35 \times 13.450} = \dfrac{713.000}{45,000} = 15.8°$ STIFF

By Wind Pressure Coef. (using 85% F. Tri.) $\quad \dfrac{13,450 \times 1.14}{20.62} \times 559 = 1.33$ STIFF

USE FOR EDGARTOWN RIG where breezes are strong

Raise top of mast 18″

Main Foot	17.9′	Main	$18.25 \times 17.9 =$	326	326
Main Hoist	36.5′	Fore Triangle	$21.05 \times 13.8 =$	$290 \times .85 =$	247
P_2	42.1′			⎯	⎯
Base	13.8′		*Total Sail Area*	616	573
			Formerly	−584	
			Increased by	32 sq. ft.	

Sail Area to Wetted Area $\quad \dfrac{616}{275} = 2.24$

$$\text{Aspect Ratio} \quad \dfrac{36.6}{17.9} = 2.02$$

$$\text{Tx} = \text{Md}$$
$$616\text{X} = 326 \times 11.33$$
$$\text{X} = 6.00′$$

$$\text{formerly} \quad \dfrac{35.0}{17.7} = 1.98$$

Dellenbaugh (100% F. Tri.) $\quad \dfrac{57.3 \times 616 \times 20.91}{3.35 \times 13,450} = \dfrac{739,000}{45,000} = 16.4°$

W.P.C. (85% F. Tri.) $\quad \dfrac{13,450 \times 1.14}{20.91 \times 573} = 1.27$

ON THE STIFF SIDE USE FOR PIPE DREAM

Figures for comparison

Endeavour	Dell. Angle = 20.0°	W.P.C. = 1.17
Demasiado	Dell. Angle = 16.1°	W.P.C. = 1.29

Raise top of mast 2 ft.

Main Foot	18.1′	Main	$9.05 \times 37.16 =$	336	336
Main Hoist	37.16′	Fore Triangle	$21 \times 13.5 =$	$283 \times .85 =$	240
J	42.0′			—	—
Base	13.5′	*Total Sail Area*		619 sq. ft.	576
				-584	

Increased by   35 sq. ft.

Sail Area to Wetted Area $\dfrac{619}{275} = 2.25$

Aspect Ratio $\dfrac{37.16}{18.1} = 2.05$

Dellenbaugh (100% F. Tri.) $\dfrac{57.3 \times 619 \times 21.08}{3.35 \times 13,450} = \dfrac{773,000}{45,000} = 17.2°$

O.K. by Dellenbaugh Angle Method

W.P.C. (using 85% F. Tri.) $= \dfrac{13,450}{21.08 \times 576} = 1.07$

Tender by W.P.C. method

Wood Mast Size (Short Method)

1. Rt. Mom. @ 30° from chart stiffest is say 23,000 ft. lbs. Beam at chain plates = 9.0′. ½ beam = 4.5′.
2. Mainmast Load $23,000 \times 2.78 \div 4.5 = 14,200$ lbs.
3. Mast Compression (P) $14,200 = 1.42 \times 10^4$
4. Panels
   Dk. to Spreaders L_T 21.3′ = 255″ $L_T^2 = 255^2$
   Dk. to Jibstay L_L 40.5′ = 486″ $L_L^2 = 486^2$
      $L_T^2 = 255^2 = 65,025 = 6.5 \times 10^4$
      $L_L^2 = 486^2 = 236,196 = 23.6 \times 10^4$
5. Moms. of Inertia $C \times L_T^2$ or $L_L^2 \times P$
   $I_{yy} = I_T = 6.78 \times 6.5 \times 1.42 = 62.5$ in^4
   $I_{xx} = I_L = 4.1 \times 23.6 \times 1.42 = 137.0$ in^4
6. From Oval Mast Chart   A = 8″   B = 5½″
   Fore and aft dimension should be 1.5 times athwartship,
      so $1.5 \times 5.5 = 8.25$ or 8¼″
   Max. Sec. then is 5½″ × 8¼″ Walls 20% thick = 1⅛″ P. & S.,
      1⅝″ fwd. & after walls.
   Top 55% max. (5½″ × 8¼″) or 3″ × 4⁹⁄₁₆″
   Start taper 65% from deck for masthead rig.

Tension on Shrouds (Long Method)

Ht. of mast abv. dk. 40′ 11″
Sail Area Main 326; Jib 550 (Reacher)
Assume a W.P.C. of 1 lb. per sq. ft.
$\dfrac{\text{Area Main}}{\text{Ht. of Mast}} \times 1$ lb. = Wind pressure per ft. on mast.
$\dfrac{326}{40.9} \times 1 = 8$ lbs. ft.

Bottom panel: 8 lbs. × 21.3′ = 170 lbs. Each end takes half.
$\dfrac{170}{2} = 85$

Top panel: 8 lbs. × 19.4 = 155 lbs. Half for each end 77.5 lbs.
Jib Stay: 1 lb. × 550 sq. ft. = 550 lbs.
Add each column starting at top. Bring fwd. total to each succeeding panel.

Upper shroud tension

Resolve $\dfrac{\text{X lbs.}}{19.3} = \dfrac{627.5}{3.5}$

$\qquad$ X lbs. $= \dfrac{627.5 \times 19.3}{3.5} = 3{,}460$ lbs. Tension Upper Shroud

For upper use $\%_{32}''$ wire, breaking strength $= 10{,}300$ lbs. from catalogue.

$\dfrac{10{,}300}{3{,}460} = 2.99$ Factor of safety. O.K. Use it to minimize stretch.

If $\%_{16}''$ is used $\quad \dfrac{12{,}500}{3{,}460} = 3.6$ Factor of safety. Too great.

Lower Shroud Tension

$\quad$ Resolve

$\dfrac{\text{X}}{23} = \dfrac{790}{4.8}$

$\quad$ X $= \dfrac{790 \times 23}{4.8}$

$\quad$ X $= 3{,}790$ lbs. Lower shroud tension

Use $\frac{1}{4}'' \dfrac{8{,}200}{3{,}790} = 2.16$ Factor of Safety O.K. Two required.

Tension on Shrouds (Short Method)

Lower: 62% Mast Compression $= .62 \times 14{,}200 = 8{,}800$ lbs. $= \frac{1}{4}''$
Uppers: 38% Mast Compression $= .38 \times 14{,}200 = 5{,}400$ lbs. $= \%_{32}''$
Increase uppers to minimize stretch.

Lower Shroud Tangs

$\frac{1}{4}''$ wire 8,200 lbs. breaking strength from catalogue.

1. $\text{X} = \dfrac{8{,}200}{85{,}000} \times .109 = .885''$ width of strap. Use $1\frac{1}{4}''$ tube bolt.
   Two wires $2 \times .885'' = 1.77 + 1.25 = 3.02''$ width at bolt

2. Bearing required in wood 2 wires $\dfrac{8{,}000}{5{,}000} \times 2 = 2.74$ sq. inches

3. Use tube bolt. Say $1\frac{1}{4}''$ O.D.
   Wall thickness $1\frac{1}{8}''$
   Bearing from bolt $1\frac{1}{8} \quad \times 1\frac{1}{4} \; =$
   $\qquad\qquad\qquad 1.125 \times 1.25 = 1.41$
   $2.74 - 1.41 = 1.33$ Remaining bearing for screws.

4. Use No. 16 screws
   Bearing each $\frac{1}{3} \times 1 \times .268'' = .087''$
   No. screws required $\dfrac{1.33}{.087} = 15.2$ say 16 screws.

Upper Shroud Tang

$\%_{32}''$ wire $= 10.300$ lbs. breaking str.
$\frac{1}{2}''$ pin. Use Stainless Steel 85,000 PSI tensile str.
Thickness say $.109''$ Find width at pin.
$\quad .109 \times \text{X} \times 85{,}000 = 10{,}300$
$\qquad\qquad \text{X} = \dfrac{10{,}300}{85{,}000 \times .109} = \dfrac{103}{92.8} = 1.11''$

$\quad$ (2 tangs used) $\dfrac{1.11}{2} = .55''$ width $+$ pin $.5 = 1.05''$

1. So width of each tang say $1\frac{1}{16}''$

2. Total bearing req'd in wood 10,000 lbs.
   (down pull by scale) Solid spruce
   bearing 5,000 P S I

   $\dfrac{10,000}{5,000}$ = 2 sq. inches bearing req'd.

   $\frac{1}{2}''$ bolt $2''$ deep = area $\frac{1}{2} \times 2$ =   1
   two $\frac{3}{8}''$ sheave bolts $\frac{3}{4}''$ deep $2 \times \frac{3}{8} \times \frac{3}{4}$ = $\frac{9}{16}$

                   Remainder for screws $\frac{7}{16}$ = .437 sq. in.

   Use $1\frac{1}{2}''$ No. 14 screws. Bearing each screw $\frac{1}{3} \times .242 \times 1.5$ = .12 sq. in.

3. No. screws required $\dfrac{.437}{.12}$ = 4

Size of Spreaders

Compression on spreaders

$$\frac{X}{10,300} = \frac{3.5}{19.3}$$

$19.3X = 3.5 \times 10,300$

$X = 1,860$ lbs.

Sec. from spreader chart lies between $1\frac{1}{8}'' \times 2\frac{13}{16}''$
      and $1\frac{1}{4}'' \times 3\frac{1}{8}''$

Make it say $1\frac{3}{16}'' \times 3''$ Max. Sec. A = $1\frac{3}{16}''$ B = $3''$

Outboard End   .4A $\times$ .6B   A = $\frac{1}{2}''$ B = $1\frac{13}{16}''$
Inboard End   .85A $\times$ .8B   A = $1''$ B = $2\frac{7}{16}''$
Outboard   .5 $\times$ 1.81 = .9 sq. in. area req'd.
Try $1\frac{1}{4}'' \times X$ $1\frac{1}{4}X$ =   .9

$$X = \frac{.9}{1.25} = .72''$$

So use $1\frac{1}{4}'' \times \frac{3}{4}''$ for outboard end.

Propeller Diameter & Pitch

Engine—Universal Atomic 4   1.67 : 1 reduction

R.P.M.	H.P.
600	2.5
800	4.5
1000	6.5
1500	11.2
2000	16
2500 ←	20.5 ← Use this
3000	25.5
3500	30

Hull speed $\sqrt{\text{LWL}} \times 1.25$ = 6.25 kn. = 7.2 M.P.H. (Knots $\times$ 1.15)

$\dfrac{2500}{1.67}$ = 1500 R.P.M. at prop. for this reduction gear.

Diam. from Chart = $14\frac{1}{4}''$ for 3 bl.
   for 2 bl. + 5% = $15''$

Pitch from Crouch's Chart. For 40% slip, 7.2 M.P.H. speed
   Pitch = $8''$

Using 50% slip, same speed. Pitch = $10''$
   Use $9''$ pitch.

Prop. = $15''$ diam. $\times$ $9''$ pitch. 2 bl. rt. hand
   bore for $\frac{7}{8}''$ shaft.

CHAPTER XXV

USEFUL DATA

Conversion Factors

Arranged alphabetically

To convert	Multiply by	To obtain
Centimeters	.03281	Feet
Centimeters	.3937	Inches
Cubic Feet	7.480	Gallons
Fathoms	6.0	Feet
Feet	30.48	Centimeters
Feet	.3048	Meters
Gallons	.133	Cubic Feet
Gallons	3.785	Liters
Horsepower	.7457	Kilowatts
Inches	2.540	Centimeters
Inches	25.40	Millimeters
Kilograms	2.2046	Pounds
Kilometers	.5396	Miles, Nautical
Kilometers	.6214	Miles, Statute
Kilowatts	1.341	Horsepower
Knots	1.1516	Miles Per Hour
Liters	.264	Gallons
Meters	3.2808	Feet
Meters	39.37	Inches
Miles Per Hour	.8684	Knots
Miles, Nautical	1.1516	Miles, Statute
Miles, Nautical	1.853	Kilometers
Miles, Statute	1.609	Kilometers
Miles, Statute	.8684	Miles, Nautical
Millimeters	.0394	Inches
Pounds	.4536	Kilograms
Sq. Centimeters	.001076	Sq. Feet
Sq. Centimeters	.1550	Sq. Inches
Sq. Feet	929.0	Sq. Centimeters
Sq. Feet	144.0	Sq. Inches
Sq. Inches	6.452	Sq. Centimeters
Sq. Inches	.006944	Sq. Feet
Tons, Long	2,240.0	Pounds
Tons, Short	2,000.0	Pounds

NOTES: For water conversion factors see page 282.
The easiest way to convert from inches and feet to millimeters and centimeters is visually by using a folding rule or tape marked with inches on one side or edge and millimeters on the other.

USEFUL FORMULAS FOR FINDING WEIGHTS

To find the weight per square foot of a given thickness:

$$\text{Wt./sq. ft. for thickness} = \frac{\text{Wt./cu. ft.}}{\text{Inverted thickness }'' \times 12}$$

To find the lineal feet of framing in a hull:

$$\text{Lin. ft. framing} = \frac{\text{Shell area in sq. ft.}}{\text{Fr. spacing in ft.}}$$

To find the weight per lineal ft. of framing:

$$\text{Wt./lin. ft.} = \frac{\text{Lbs./cu. ft.} \times \text{molding }'' \times \text{siding }''}{144}$$

Muscular Energy of Man

Nature of Work	Weight Moved	Work Done Ft. lbs. per Sec.
Pushing or pulling horizontally, oar, tiller.	26.4	52.8
Turning a crank.	17.6	44
Pushing or pulling vertically, pump.	13.2	33
Hoisting weight, single part line.	40	26.4
Lifting weights by hand.	44	24.6
Carrying weights on back.	143	18.6
Pushing loaded wheelbarrow up 1:12 incline.	132	8.6

The above table was compiled by Dr. F. W. Taylor, who observed that the maximum amount of shoveling may be accomplished by the use of a shovel taking up a load of 22 pounds. The rate is over the period of a working day.

It should be useful to have these figures as a basis for the design of manually operated winches, pumps, tillers, steering wheels, quadrants, the number of parts for a block and tackle—in short, all the devices on a boat that a man must operate with his own muscular energy.

CHAIN LOCKER VOLUME FOR SELF-STOWING CHAIN

$$\text{Vol. in Cu. Ft.} = \frac{\text{Fathoms of chain} \times \text{Chain size in inches}^2}{2} \times 1.7$$

Example. It is necessary to design a self-stowing chain locker for 40 fathoms of $\frac{7}{16}''$ chain. What volume is needed?

$$\text{Vol.} = \frac{40 \times \frac{7}{16}^2}{2} \times 1.7$$

$$\frac{40 \times .4375^2}{2} \times 1.7$$

$$20 \times .1914 \times 1.7 = 6.5 \text{ cu. ft. required}$$

COMPARISON OF WHEEL TO TILLER

It is interesting to learn the length of a tiller required to steer with the same force exerted on a wheel. Let us say that the sprocket size for chain is 2.2'' diameter* and we use a 12''-quadrant on the rudder stock, then for each wheel diameter given we will need this length tiller:

$$\text{For 24'' Wheel} \quad \frac{24'' \times 12''}{2.2''} = 131'' \text{ or } 10'–11'' \text{ tiller}$$

$$\text{For 28'' Wheel} \quad \frac{28'' \times 12''}{2.2''} = 153'' \text{ or } 12'–9'' \text{ tiller}$$

$$\text{For 32'' Wheel} \quad \frac{32'' \times 12''}{2.2''} = 174'' \text{ or } 14'–6'' \text{ tiller}$$

This shows how advantageous it is to have wheel steering versus tiller steering. Thus a designer can recommend to the owner of a tiller-steered boat with a bad weather helm that changing to a wheel can alleviate the problem, because less force is required to steer with a wheel.

* Pitch diam. of the most popular Edson sprocket.

SOUND LEVEL READINGS

Engine rooms on boats must be made as soundproof as possible. The following table compares the sound level readings taken aboard SEA STAR, a large motor sailer, with sound levels.

Noise Maker	*Decibels*
10 ft. away from rock drill	130
Discotheque	120
2000 ft. from jet taking off	105
Subway station with train entering	95
50 ft. from a moving heavy truck	90
Noisy kitchen in city	85
Cocktail party, crowded, in small room	80
50 ft. from a highway, heavy traffic	70
Stateroom next to engine room with engine running— SEA STAR	64
Quiet conversation	60
On deck, at anchor, one generator running—SEA STAR	55
In main salon with above condition—SEA STAR	40
Quiet rural night	30
Threshold of hearing	0

NOTE: Prolonged exposure to sound between 85 and 115 decibels will begin to cause hearing loss. Limited exposure to sound over 115 decibels will cause hearing loss.

Strength and Weight of BBB Chain

Size	*Working load in lbs.*	*Wt. in lbs. per ft.*
$3/16''$	800	.43
$1/4$	1,325	.76
$5/16$	1,950	1.13
$3/8$	2,750	1.64
$7/16$	3,625	2.22
$1/2$	4,750	2.85
$9/16$	5,875	3.55
$5/8$	7,250	4.25
$3/4$	10,250	6.15
$7/8$	12,000	8.40
1	15,500	10.68

HOW TO DESIGN A COMFORTABLE LADDER

The slope of a ladder and the spacing of the steps make a great deal of difference in the habitability of a boat. The ideal is to be able to descend a ladder with one's hands free to carry things.

The foreman in a yard where I was working taught me how to lay out such a ladder. It is this:

Step 1—Divide the vertical distance between deck and cabin sole into equal spaces less than 12″. From 9″ to 11″ is suitable. (This can be done graphically simply by using the same scale, say ¾″ = 1′ 0″ and pivoting "O" at the deck and swinging its bottom forward on a diagonal until a whole number, say "5" strikes the cabin sole.) Note that vertical ladders have their rungs spaced 12″, and a sloping ladder therefore must have its steps spaced closer together. There must be nothing unexpected in a ladder (hence the equal spacing) to prevent accidents at night and in bad weather.

Step 2—Layout the horizontal distance as follows: Top step projects forward 9″. Next lower step projects forward 5″. Each step thereafter also 5″. Each step should be at least 6″ deep, so that it projects back 1″ under the one above.

Step 3—Project the vertical equal divisions in Step 1 forward. Project the horizontal divisions of 9″, 5″, 5″, 5″, etc. of Step 2 down to meet them. Then where these intersections lie, they will line up to form the slope of the ladder.

Step 4—The width of the ladder can be as narrow as 15″, but 18″ will make it easier to sit on the top step. Don't forget to put hand holes in the side pieces near the top to hang onto in rough weather.

For an example of a companion ladder designed by using this method, see SANTA MARIA's Arrangement Plan in Chapter VII. Her ladder is mighty comfortable to ascend and descend.

HOW TO CONSTRUCT AN ELLIPSE

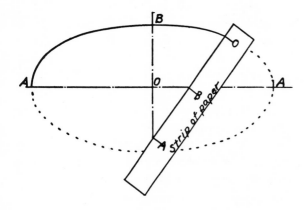

The designer has frequent occasion to construct an ellipse, as, for instance, in drawing port lights, manholes, developed propeller blades, etc. The diagram shows a simple method. Knowing the semi major axis $O\ A$ and semi minor axis $O\ B$, lay these distances off on a strip of paper. Then, keeping point B on the strip on the major axis and point A on the minor axis, dot a series of points opposite O on the strip.

KNOTS AND HITCHES

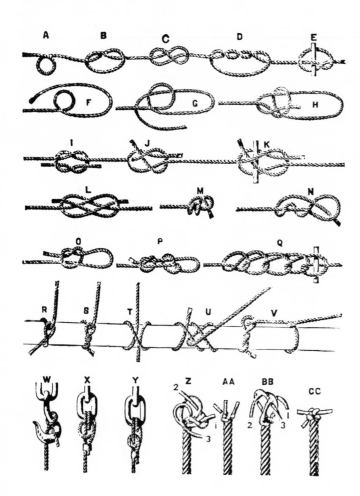

A.   Bight of a rope
B.   Simple or overhand knot
C.   Figure 8 knot
D.   Double knot
E.   Boat knot
F.   Bowline, first step
G.   Bowline, second step
H.   Bowline completed
I.   Square or reef knot
J.   Sheet bend or weaver's knot
K.   Sheet bend with a toggle
L.   Carrick bend
M.   Stevedore knot completed
N.   Beginning of stevedore knot
O.   Slip knot
P.   Flemish loop
Q.   Chain knot with toggle
R.   Half hitch
S.   Timber hitch
T.   Clove hitch
U.   Rolling hitch
V.   Timber hitch and half hitch
W.   Blackwall hitch
X.   Fisherman's bend
Y.   Round turn and half hitch
Z.   Wall knot commenced
AA. Wall knot completed
BB. Wall knot crown commenced
CC. Wall knot crown completed

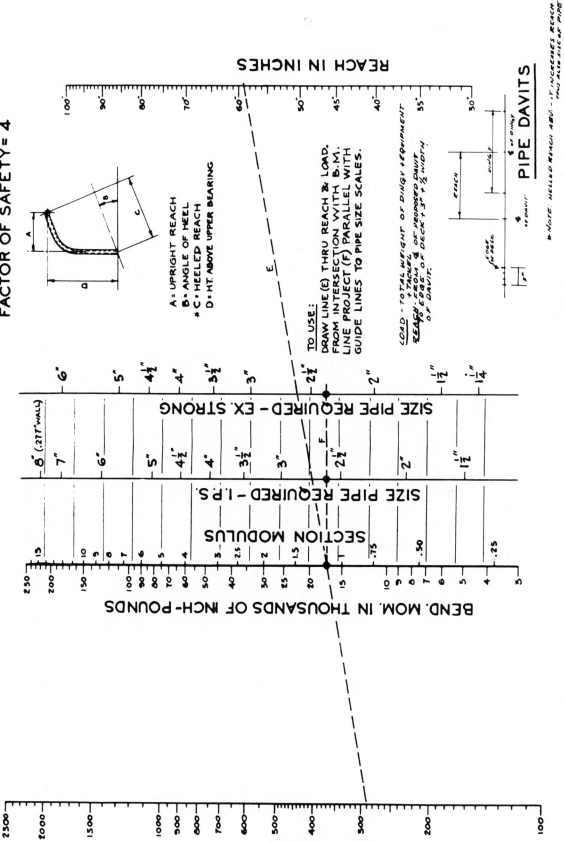

MATERIAL: 60,000 LBS.P.S.I. STEEL
FACTOR OF SAFETY = 4

REACH IN INCHES

A: UPRIGHT REACH
B: ANGLE OF HEEL
*C: HEELED REACH
D: HT. ABOVE UPPER BEARING

TO USE:
DRAW LINE (E) THRU REACH & LOAD.
FROM INTERSECTION WITH B.M.
LINE PROJECT (F) PARALLEL WITH
GUIDE LINES TO PIPE SIZE SCALES.

LOAD - TOTAL WEIGHT OF DINGY + EQUIPMENT
+ TACKEL
REACH - FROM ℄ OF PROPOSED DAVIT
TO EDGE OF DECK + 3" + ½ WIDTH
OF DAVIT.

SIZE PIPE REQUIRED - EX. STRONG

SIZE PIPE REQUIRED - I.P.S.

SECTION MODULUS

BEND. MOM. IN THOUSANDS OF INCH-POUNDS

LOAD IN POUNDS

PIPE DAVITS

* NOTE: HEELED REACH ABV.— IT INCREASES REACH
THU ALSO SIZE OF PIPE.

R.M. STEWARD 10-10-42

PIPE

DIMENSIONS							COUPLINGS			PROPERTIES		
Nom. Dia. In.	Outside Dia. In.	Inside Dia. In.	Thick-ness In.	Weight per Foot Lb. Plain Ends	Weight per Foot Lb. Thread & Cplg.	Threads per Inch	Outside Dia. In.	Length In.	Weight Lb.	I In.⁴	Sec. Mod. Z In.³	r In.
STANDARD												
1/8	.405	.269	.068	.24	.25	27	.562	7/8	.03	.001	.005	.12
1/4	.540	.364	.088	.42	.43	18	.685	1	.04	.003	.012	.16
3/8	.675	.493	.091	.57	.57	18	.848	1 1/8	.07	.007	.022	.21
1/2	.840	.622	.109	.85	.85	14	1.024	1 3/8	.12	.017	.041	.26
3/4	1.050	.824	.113	1.13	1.13	14	1.281	1 5/8	.21	.037	.071	.33
1	1.315	1.049	.133	1.68	1.68	11 1/2	1.576	1 7/8	.35	.087	.133	.42
1 1/4	1.660	1.380	.140	2.27	2.28	11 1/2	1.950	2 1/8	.55	.195	.235	.54
1 1/2	1.900	1.610	.145	2.72	2.73	11 1/2	2.218	2 3/8	.76	.310	.326	.62
2	2.375	2.067	.154	3.65	3.68	11 1/2	2.760	2 5/8	1.23	.666	.561	.79
2 1/2	2.875	2.469	.203	5.79	5.82	8	3.276	2 7/8	1.76	1.530	1.064	.95
3	3.500	3.068	.216	7.58	7.62	8	3.948	3 1/8	2.55	3.017	1.724	1.16
3 1/2	4.000	3.548	.226	9.11	9.20	8	4.591	3 5/8	4.33	4.788	2.394	1.34
4	4.500	4.026	.237	10.79	10.89	8	5.091	3 5/8	5.41	7.233	3.214	1.51
5	5.563	5.047	.258	14.62	14.81	8	6.296	4 1/8	9.16	15.16	5.451	1.88
6	6.625	6.065	.280	18.97	19.19	8	7.358	4 1/8	10.82	28.14	8.496	2.25
8	8.625	8.071	.277	24.70	25.00	8	9.420	4 5/8	15.84	63.35	14.69	2.95
8	8.625	7.981	.322	28.55	28.81	8	9.420	4 5/8	15.84	72.49	16.81	2.94
10	10.750	10.192	.279	31.20	32.00	8	11.721	6 1/8	33.92	125.9	23.42	3.70
10	10.750	10.136	.307	34.24	35.00	8	11.721	6 1/8	33.92	137.4	25.57	3.69
10	10.750	10.020	.365	40.48	41.13	8	11.721	6 1/8	33.92	160.7	29.90	3.67
12	12.750	12.090	.330	43.77	45.00	8	13.958	6 1/8	48.27	248.5	38.97	4.39
12	12.750	12.000	.375	49.56	50.71	8	13.958	6 1/8	48.27	279.3	42.82	4.38
EXTRA STRONG												
1/8	.405	.215	.095	.31	.32	27	.582	1 1/8	.05	.001	.006	.11
1/4	.540	.302	.119	.54	.54	18	.724	1 3/8	.07	.004	.014	.15
3/8	.675	.423	.126	.74	.75	18	.898	1 5/8	.13	.009	.026	.20
1/2	.840	.546	.147	1.09	1.10	14	1.085	1 7/8	.22	.020	.048	.25
3/4	1.050	.742	.154	1.47	1.49	14	1.316	2 1/8	.33	.045	.085	.32
1	1.315	.957	.179	2.17	2.20	11 1/2	1.575	2 3/8	.47	.106	.161	.41
1 1/4	1.660	1.278	.191	3.00	3.05	11 1/2	2.054	2 7/8	1.04	.242	.291	.52
1 1/2	1.900	1.500	.200	3.63	3.69	11 1/2	2.294	2 7/8	1.17	.391	.412	.61
2	2.375	1.939	.218	5.02	5.13	11 1/2	2.870	3 5/8	2.17	.868	.731	.77
2 1/2	2.875	2.323	.276	7.66	7.83	8	3.389	4 1/8	3.43	1.924	1.339	.92
3	3.500	2.900	.300	10.25	10.46	8	4.014	4 1/8	4.13	3.894	2.225	1.14
3 1/2	4.000	3.364	.318	12.51	12.82	8	4.628	4 5/8	6.29	6.280	3.140	1.31
4	4.500	3.826	.337	14.98	15.39	8	5.233	4 5/8	8.16	9.610	4.271	1.48
5	5.563	4.813	.375	20.78	21.42	8	6.420	5 1/8	12.87	20.67	7.431	1.84
6	6.625	5.761	.432	28.57	29.33	8	7.482	5 1/8	15.18	40.49	12.22	2.20
8	8.625	7.625	.500	43.39	44.72	8	9.596	6 1/8	26.63	105.7	24.51	2.88
10	10.750	9.750	.500	54.74	56.94	8	11.958	6 5/8	44.16	211.9	39.43	3.63
12	12.750	11.750	.500	65.42	68.02	8	13.958	6 5/8	51.99	361.5	56.71	4.34
DOUBLE EXTRA STRONG												
1/2	.840	.252	.294	1.71	1.73	14	1.085	1 7/8	.22	.024	.058	.22
3/4	1.050	.434	.308	2.44	2.46	14	1.316	2 1/8	.33	.058	.110	.28
1	1.315	.599	.358	3.66	3.68	11 1/2	1.575	2 3/8	.47	.140	.214	.36
1 1/4	1.660	.896	.382	5.21	5.27	11 1/2	2.054	2 7/8	1.04	.341	.411	.47
1 1/2	1.900	1.100	.400	6.41	6.47	11 1/2	2.294	2 7/8	1.17	.568	.598	.55
2	2.375	1.503	.436	9.03	9.14	11 1/2	2.870	3 5/8	2.17	1.311	1.104	.70
2 1/2	2.875	1.771	.552	13.70	13.87	8	3.389	4 1/8	3.43	2.871	1.997	.84
3	3.500	2.300	.600	18.58	18.79	8	4.014	4 1/8	4.13	5.992	3.424	1.05
3 1/2	4.000	2.728	.636	22.85	23.16	8	4.628	4 5/8	6.29	9.848	4.924	1.21
4	4.500	3.152	.674	27.54	27.95	8	5.233	4 5/8	8.16	15.28	6.793	1.37
5	5.563	4.063	.750	38.55	39.20	8	6.420	5 1/8	12.87	33.64	12.09	1.72
6	6.625	4.897	.864	53.16	53.92	8	7.482	5 1/8	15.18	66.33	20.02	2.06
8	8.625	6.875	.875	72.42	73.76	8	9.596	6 1/8	26.63	162.0	37.56	2.76

LARGE O. D. PIPE

Pipe 14″ and larger is sold by actual O. S. diameter and thickness.
Sizes 14″, 15″, and 16″ are available regularly in thicknesses varying by 1/16″ from 1/4″ to 1″, inclusive.

All pipe is furnished random length unless otherwise ordered, viz: 12 to 22 feet with privilege of furnishing 5 per cent in 6 to 12 feet lengths. Pipe railing is most economically detailed with slip joints and random lengths between couplings.

HOW TO FIND THE SQUARE ROOT OF A NUMBER

Point off or draw light lines dividing the number into periods of two places, beginning at the decimal point, adding ciphers as may be required.

Find the largest number whose square is less than the left-hand period, and write the square under the first period and the root at the right of the bracket. Subtract the square from the first period, and to the remainder annex the two figures of the next period for a dividend.

Double the number in the bracket, and see how many times it will go in the dividend exclusive of the right-hand figure. Place the figure representing the number of times as the second figure in the quotient, and annex it to the right of the partial divisor, thus forming the complete divisor. Multiply the complete divisor by the second figure in the quotient, and subtract the product from the dividend.

Example.   Find the square root of 5.243.

$$
\begin{array}{r|l}
5.'24'30 & 2.28 + \text{square root} \\
4 & \\
\hline
\end{array}
$$

$$
\begin{array}{r|r}
42 & 1\ 24 \\
 & \ \ 84 \\
\hline
448 & 4030 \\
 & 3584 \\
\hline
 & \ 446 \\
\end{array}
$$

HOW TO FIND THE CUBE ROOT OF A NUMBER

Point off or draw light lines dividing the number into periods of three figures each beginning at the right hand on units place.

Find the largest cube that does not exceed the left-hand period, and write its root as the first figure in the required root. Subtract the cube from the left-hand period, and to the remainder bring down the next period for a dividend.

Square the first figure of the root, and multiply it by 300. Divide the product into the dividend for a trial divisor, and write the quotient after the first figure of the root as a trial second figure. Complete the divisor by adding 30 times the product of the first and the second figure. Multiply this divisor by the second figure, and subtract the product from the remainder. Should the product be greater than the remainder, the last figure of the root and the complete divisor are too large, in which case try a smaller number for the last figure, and change the trial divisor accordingly.

Example.   Find the cube root of 39,904.125.

$$
\begin{array}{rl}
 & 39'904.'125 \mid 34.1 + \text{cube root} \\
 & 27 \\
3^2 \times 300 = 2700 & \\
3 \times 4 \times 30 = 360 \Big\} = 3076 & \mid 12\ 904 \\
4^2 = 16 & \mid 12\ 304 \\
 & \\
34^2 \times 300 = 346,800 & \\
34 \times 1 \times 30 = 1,020 \Big\} = 347,821 & \mid\ \ \ 600\ 125 \\
1^2 = 1 & \mid\ \ \ 347\ 821 \\
 & \ \ \ \ \ 252\ 304 \\
\end{array}
$$

WEIGHTS OF MATERIALS

Material	Pounds	Pounds per cu. ft.
Aluminum, cast		165
Aluminum, sheet		168
Asbestos		153
Babbitt metal		456
Beer, carton 6 cans, 12 fluid oz. each	5	
Brass, cast, rolled		534
Brick, common		120
Bronze (aluminum bronze)		481
Bronze (7.9–14% tin)		509
Bronze, Tobin (60% copper—39% zinc)		**525**
Cement, set (12 lbs./sq. ft. for 1″ thick)		183
Charcoal, bushel of	30	
Charcoal, piled		10–14
Clams, bushel of	100	
Coal, broken anthracite		47–58
Coca Cola, carton 6 bottles, 6 fluid oz. each	7	
Concrete (cement, stone, sand)		144
Copper, cast, rolled		556
Cotton, bale of U.S.		500
Earth, dry, loose		76
Earth, mud, packed		115
Gasoline, aviation (1 gal. = 6.12 lbs.)		45.8
Gasoline, boat (1 gal. = 6.19 lbs.)		46.3
Gin, one quart bottle of	3	
Gold		1,205
Granite		175
Gunmetal		528
Ice (cake 1′ x 2′ x 3.5′ = 300–310 lbs.)		44
Iron, cast, pig		450
Iron, wrought		485
Kerosene (1 gal. = 6.8 lbs.)		50.9
Lead, scrap		700
Lead, virgin		712
Leather		59

Material	Pounds	Pounds per cu. ft.
Lignum Vitae		83
Linoleum (1.5 lbs./sq. ft. for ¼″ thick)		
Linseed Oil		58
Manganese		475
Maple, chord of dry	2,862	
Mercury		849
Monel Metal		556
Nickel		565
Oil, diesel (1 gal. = 7.13 lbs.)		53.3
Oil, fuel (1 gal. = 8.09 lbs.)		60.6
Oil, lubricating (1 gal. = 7.69 lbs.)		57.5
Paper		58
Pitch		69
Phosphor bronze		537
Potatoes, bushel of	60	
Potatoes, piled		42
Rubber Tiling (2 lbs./sq. ft. for 5⁄16″ thick)		
Sand, dry, loose		90–105
Sand, wet		120
Shale, slate, piled		92
Snow, fresh fallen		8
Soda, carton 6 bottles, 7 fluid oz. each	6.5	
Steel, cast		493
Steel, stainless, rolled		492–510
Steel, structural, rolled		490
Tile, Terrazzo, Mastic (12 lbs./sq. ft. for 1″ thick)		
Water, fresh (at 39° F.)		62.4
Water, fresh (at 212° F.)		59.8
Water, sea		64
Wheat		48
Wheat, bushel of	60	
Whiskey, one quart bottle of	3	
White metal (Babbitt)		456
Woods (See page 288)		
Zinc, cast, rolled		440

WEIGHTS OF CARGOES

Cargo	Cubic ft. per ton (2,240 lbs.)	Cargo	Cubic ft. per ton (2,240 lbs.)
Bananas	90	Milk, condensed, in cases	45
Beer, bottled in cases	80	Nails, in kegs	21
Books	50	Olives, in barrels	67
Bottles, empty in crates	85	Oranges, in boxes	90
Bricks	22	Paint, in drums	16
Carpets, in rolls	80	Pineapples, canned, in boxes	60
Coal	43	Potatoes, in bags	55
Coconuts, in bulk	140	Rice, in bags	48
Coffee, in bags	61	Rope	135
Cotton, U.S., in bales	114	Rum, in bottles, cases	66
Earth, loose	27	Rum, in hogsheads	70
Fish, in boxes	95	Sand, fine	19
Fish, frozen	60	Sand, coarse	20
Food for ship's company:		Shellac	83
Dry stores, 2.9 lbs. per man per day		Soap, in boxes	46
Refrig. stores, 1.9 lbs. per man per day		Sponge	152
Vegetables, 1.7 lbs. per man per day		Stores (see "Food" above)	
Fuel oil	38–40	Tea, Chinese, in cases	57
Gunpowder	48	Tea, Indian, in cases	54
Hay, compressed	120	Tobacco, Brazilian, in bales	40
Herrings, in boxes	85	Tobacco, Turkish, in small bales	150
Ice	39	Turpentine, in barrels	60
Iron, pig	10	Water, fresh	36
Ivory	28	Water, sea	35
Lead, pig	8	Wheat, in bags	52
Lemons	85	Wheat, in bulk	48

FUNCTIONS OF NUMBERS

.50 / .99

No.	Square	Cube	Square Root	Cube Root	Logarithm	1000 × Reciprocal	No. = Diameter Circum	Area
50	2500	125000	0.7071	0.7937	1.69897	2000.000	1.5708	.19635
51	2601	132651	0.7141	0.7990	1.70757	1960.784	1.6022	.20428
52	2704	140608	0.7211	0.8041	1.71600	1923.077	1.6336	.21237
53	2809	148877	0.7280	0.8093	1.72428	1886.793	1.6650	.22062
54	2916	157464	0.7348	0.8143	1.73239	1851.852	1.6965	.22902
55	3025	166375	0.7416	0.8193	1.74036	1818.182	1.7279	.23758
56	3136	175616	0.7483	0.8243	1.74819	1785.714	1.7593	.24630
57	3249	185193	0.7550	0.8291	1.75587	1754.386	1.7907	.25518
58	3364	195112	0.7616	0.8340	1.76343	1724.138	1.8221	.26401
59	3481	205379	0.7681	0.8387	1.77085	1694.915	1.8535	.27340
60	3600	216000	0.7746	0.8434	1.77815	1666.667	1.8850	.28274
61	3721	226981	0.7810	0.8481	1.78533	1639.344	1.9164	.29225
62	3844	238328	0.7874	0.8527	1.79239	1612.903	1.9478	.30191
63	3969	250047	0.7937	0.8573	1.79934	1587.302	1.9792	.31173
64	4096	262144	0.8000	0.8618	1.80618	1562.500	2.0106	.32170
65	4225	274625	0.8062	0.8662	1.81291	1538.462	2.0420	.33183
66	4356	287496	0.8124	0.8707	1.81954	1515.152	2.0735	.34212
67	4489	300763	0.8185	0.8750	1.82607	1492.537	2.1049	.35257
68	4624	314432	0.8246	0.8794	1.83251	1470.588	2.1363	.36317
69	4761	328509	0.8307	0.8837	1.83885	1449.275	2.1677	.37393
70	4900	343000	0.8367	0.8879	1.84510	1428.571	2.1991	.38485
71	5041	357911	0.8426	0.8921	1.85126	1408.451	2.2305	.39592
72	5184	373248	0.8485	0.8963	1.85733	1388.889	2.2620	.40715
73	5329	389017	0.8544	0.9004	1.86332	1369.863	2.2934	.41854
74	5476	405224	0.8602	0.9045	1.86923	1351.351	2.3248	.43008
75	5625	421875	0.8660	0.9086	1.87506	1333.333	2.3562	.44179
76	5776	438976	0.8718	0.9126	1.88081	1315.790	2.3876	.45365
77	5929	456533	0.8775	0.9166	1.88649	1298.701	2.4190	.46566
78	6084	474552	0.8832	0.9205	1.89209	1282.051	2.4504	.47784
79	6241	493039	0.8888	0.9244	1.89763	1265.823	2.4819	.49017
80	6400	512000	0.8944	0.9283	1.90309	1250.000	2.5133	.50266
81	6561	531441	0.9000	0.9322	1.90849	1234.568	2.5447	.51530
82	6724	551368	0.9055	0.9360	1.91381	1219.512	2.5761	.52810
83	6889	571787	0.9110	0.9398	1.91908	1204.819	2.6075	.54106
84	7056	592704	0.9165	0.9435	1.92428	1190.476	2.6389	.55418
85	7225	614125	0.9220	0.9473	1.92942	1176.471	2.6704	.56745
86	7396	636056	0.9274	0.9510	1.93450	1162.791	2.7018	.58088
87	7569	658503	0.9327	0.9546	1.93952	1149.425	2.7332	.59447
88	7744	681472	0.9381	0.9583	1.94448	1136.364	2.7646	.60821
89	7921	704969	0.9434	0.9619	1.94939	1123.596	2.7960	.62211
90	8100	729000	0.9487	0.9655	1.95424	1111.111	2.8274	.63617
91	8281	753571	0.9539	0.9691	1.95904	1098.901	2.8589	.65039
92	8464	778688	0.9592	0.9726	1.96379	1086.957	2.8903	.66476
93	8649	804357	0.9644	0.9761	1.96848	1075.269	2.9217	.67929
94	8836	830584	0.9695	0.9796	1.97313	1063.830	2.9531	.69398
95	9025	857375	0.9747	0.9830	1.97772	1052.632	2.9845	.70882
96	9216	884736	0.9798	0.9865	1.98227	1041.667	3.0159	.72382
97	9409	912673	0.9849	0.9899	1.98677	1030.928	3.0473	.73898
98	9604	941192	0.9899	0.9933	1.99123	1020.408	3.0788	.75430
99	9801	970299	0.9950	0.9967	1.99564	1010.101	3.1102	.76077

FUNCTIONS OF NUMBERS

.01 / .49

No.	Square	Cube	Square Root	Cube Root	Logarithm	1000 × Reciprocal	No. = Diameter Circum	Area
.01	.0001	.000001	0.1000	0.2154	$\bar{2}$.00000	100000.000	.03142	.000079
.02	.0004	.000008	0.1414	0.2714	$\bar{2}$.30103	50000.000	.06283	.000314
.03	.0009	.000027	0.1732	0.3107	$\bar{2}$.47712	33333.333	.09425	.000707
.04	.0016	.000064	0.2000	0.3420	$\bar{2}$.60206	25000.000	.12566	.001257
.05	.0025	.000125	0.2236	0.3684	$\bar{2}$.69897	20000.000	.15708	.001964
.06	.0036	.000216	0.2449	0.3915	$\bar{2}$.77815	16666.667	.18850	.002827
.07	.0049	.000343	0.2646	0.4121	$\bar{2}$.84510	14285.714	.21991	.003849
.08	.0064	.000512	0.2828	0.4309	$\bar{2}$.90309	12500.000	.25133	.005027
.09	.0081	.000729	0.3000	0.4481	$\bar{2}$.95424	11111.111	.28274	.006362
.10	.0100	.001000	0.3162	0.4642	$\bar{1}$.00000	10000.000	.31416	.007854
.11	.0121	.001331	0.3317	0.4791	$\bar{1}$.04139	9090.909	.34558	.009503
.12	.0144	.001728	0.3464	0.4932	$\bar{1}$.07918	8333.333	.37699	.011310
.13	.0169	.002197	0.3606	0.5066	$\bar{1}$.11394	7692.308	.40841	.013273
.14	.0196	.002744	0.3742	0.5192	$\bar{1}$.14613	7142.857	.43982	.015394
.15	.0225	.003375	0.3873	0.5313	$\bar{1}$.17609	6666.667	.47124	.017672
.16	.0256	.004096	0.4000	0.5429	$\bar{1}$.20412	6250.000	.50265	.020106
.17	.0289	.004913	0.4123	0.5540	$\bar{1}$.23045	5882.353	.53407	.022698
.18	.0324	.005832	0.4243	0.5646	$\bar{1}$.25527	5555.556	.56549	.025447
.19	.0361	.006859	0.4359	0.5749	$\bar{1}$.27875	5263.158	.59690	.028353
.20	.0400	.008000	0.4472	0.5848	$\bar{1}$.30103	5000.000	.62832	.031416
.21	.0441	.009261	0.4583	0.5944	$\bar{1}$.32222	4761.905	.65973	.034636
.22	.0484	.010648	0.4690	0.6037	$\bar{1}$.34242	4545.455	.69115	.038013
.23	.0529	.012167	0.4796	0.6127	$\bar{1}$.36173	4347.826	.72257	.041548
.24	.0576	.013824	0.4899	0.6214	$\bar{1}$.38021	4166.667	.75398	.045239
.25	.0625	.015625	0.5000	0.6300	$\bar{1}$.39794	4000.000	.78540	.049087
.26	.0676	.017576	0.5099	0.6383	$\bar{1}$.41497	3846.154	.81681	.053093
.27	.0729	.019683	0.5196	0.6463	$\bar{1}$.43136	3703.704	.84823	.057256
.28	.0784	.021952	0.5292	0.6542	$\bar{1}$.44716	3571.429	.87965	.061575
.29	.0841	.024389	0.5385	0.6619	$\bar{1}$.46240	3448.276	.91106	.066052
.30	.0900	.027000	0.5477	0.6694	$\bar{1}$.47712	3333.333	.94248	.070686
.31	.0961	.029791	0.5568	0.6768	$\bar{1}$.49136	3225.807	.97389	.075477
.32	.1024	.032768	0.5657	0.6840	$\bar{1}$.50515	3125.000	1.00531	.080425
.33	.1089	.035937	0.5745	0.6910	$\bar{1}$.51851	3030.303	1.03673	.085530
.34	.1156	.039304	0.5831	0.6980	$\bar{1}$.53148	2941.177	1.06814	.090792
.35	.1225	.042875	0.5916	0.7047	$\bar{1}$.54407	2857.143	1.09956	.096211
.36	.1296	.046656	0.6000	0.7114	$\bar{1}$.55630	2777.778	1.13097	.101788
.37	.1369	.050653	0.6083	0.7179	$\bar{1}$.56820	2702.703	1.16239	.107521
.38	.1444	.054872	0.6164	0.7243	$\bar{1}$.57978	2631.579	1.19381	.113411
.39	.1521	.059319	0.6245	0.7306	$\bar{1}$.59106	2564.103	1.22522	.119459
.40	.1600	.064000	0.6325	0.7368	$\bar{1}$.60206	2500.000	1.25664	.125664
.41	.1681	.068921	0.6403	0.7429	$\bar{1}$.61278	2439.024	1.28805	.132025
.42	.1764	.074088	0.6481	0.7489	$\bar{1}$.62325	2380.952	1.31947	.138544
.43	.1849	.079507	0.6557	0.7548	$\bar{1}$.63347	2325.581	1.35088	.145220
.44	.1936	.085184	0.6633	0.7606	$\bar{1}$.64345	2272.727	1.38230	.152053
.45	.2025	.091125	0.6708	0.7663	$\bar{1}$.65321	2222.222	1.41372	.159043
.46	.2116	.097336	0.6782	0.7719	$\bar{1}$.66276	2173.913	1.44513	.166190
.47	.2209	.103823	0.6856	0.7775	$\bar{1}$.67210	2127.660	1.47655	.173494
.48	.2304	.110592	0.6928	0.7830	$\bar{1}$.68124	2083.333	1.50796	.180956
.49	.2401	.117649	0.7000	0.7884	$\bar{1}$.69020	2040.816	1.53938	.188574

FUNCTIONS OF NUMBERS

50 — 99

No. = Diameter

No.	Square	Cube	Square Root	Cube Root	Logarithm	1000 × Reciprocal	Circum.	Area
50	2500	125000	7.0711	3.6840	1.69897	20.0000	157.08	1963.50
51	2601	132651	7.1414	3.7084	1.70757	19.6078	160.22	2042.82
52	2704	140608	7.2111	3.7325	1.71600	19.2308	163.36	2123.72
53	2809	148877	7.2801	3.7563	1.72428	18.8679	166.50	2206.18
54	2916	157464	7.3485	3.7798	1.73239	18.5185	169.65	2290.22
55	3025	166375	7.4162	3.8030	1.74036	18.1818	172.79	2375.83
56	3136	175616	7.4833	3.8259	1.74819	17.8571	175.93	2463.01
57	3249	185193	7.5498	3.8485	1.75587	17.5439	179.07	2551.76
58	3364	195112	7.6158	3.8709	1.76343	17.2414	182.21	2642.08
59	3481	205379	7.6811	3.8930	1.77085	16.9492	185.35	2733.97
60	3600	216000	7.7460	3.9149	1.77815	16.6667	188.50	2827.43
61	3721	226981	7.8102	3.9365	1.78533	16.3934	191.64	2922.47
62	3844	238328	7.8740	3.9579	1.79239	16.1290	194.78	3019.07
63	3969	250047	7.9373	3.9791	1.79934	15.8730	197.92	3117.25
64	4096	262144	8.0000	4.0000	1.80618	15.6250	201.06	3216.99
65	4225	274625	8.0623	4.0207	1.81291	15.3846	204.20	3318.31
66	4356	287496	8.1240	4.0412	1.81954	15.1515	207.35	3421.19
67	4489	300763	8.1854	4.0615	1.82607	14.9254	210.49	3525.65
68	4624	314432	8.2462	4.0817	1.83251	14.7059	213.63	3631.68
69	4761	328509	8.3066	4.1016	1.83885	14.4928	216.77	3739.28
70	4900	343000	8.3666	4.1213	1.84510	14.2857	219.91	3848.45
71	5041	357911	8.4261	4.1408	1.85126	14.0845	223.05	3959.19
72	5184	373248	8.4853	4.1602	1.85733	13.8889	226.19	4071.50
73	5329	389017	8.5440	4.1793	1.86332	13.6986	229.34	4185.39
74	5476	405224	8.6023	4.1983	1.86923	13.5135	232.48	4300.84
75	5625	421875	8.6603	4.2172	1.87506	13.3333	235.62	4417.86
76	5776	438976	8.7178	4.2358	1.88081	13.1579	238.76	4536.46
77	5929	456533	8.7750	4.2543	1.88649	12.9870	241.90	4656.63
78	6084	474552	8.8318	4.2727	1.89209	12.8205	245.04	4778.36
79	6241	493039	8.8882	4.2908	1.89763	12.6582	248.19	4901.67
80	6400	512000	8.9443	4.3089	1.90309	12.5000	251.33	5026.55
81	6561	531441	9.0000	4.3267	1.90849	12.3457	254.47	5153.00
82	6724	551368	9.0554	4.3445	1.91381	12.1951	257.61	5281.02
83	6889	571787	9.1104	4.3621	1.91908	12.0482	260.75	5410.61
84	7056	592704	9.1652	4.3795	1.92428	11.9048	263.89	5541.77
85	7225	614125	9.2195	4.3968	1.92942	11.7647	267.04	5674.50
86	7396	636056	9.2736	4.4140	1.93450	11.6279	270.18	5808.80
87	7569	658503	9.3274	4.4310	1.93952	11.4943	273.32	5944.68
88	7744	681472	9.3808	4.4480	1.94448	11.3636	276.46	6082.12
89	7921	704969	9.4340	4.4647	1.94939	11.2360	279.60	6221.14
90	8100	729000	9.4868	4.4814	1.95424	11.1111	282.74	6361.73
91	8281	753571	9.5394	4.4979	1.95904	10.9890	285.88	6503.88
92	8464	778688	9.5917	4.5144	1.96379	10.8696	289.03	6647.61
93	8649	804357	9.6437	4.5307	1.96848	10.7527	292.17	6792.91
94	8836	830584	9.6954	4.5468	1.97313	10.6383	295.31	6939.78
95	9025	857375	9.7468	4.5629	1.97772	10.5263	298.45	7088.22
96	9216	884736	9.7980	4.5789	1.98227	10.4167	301.59	7238.23
97	9409	912673	9.8489	4.5947	1.98677	10.3093	304.73	7389.81
98	9604	941192	9.8995	4.6104	1.99123	10.2041	307.88	7542.96
99	9801	970299	9.9499	4.6261	1.99564	10.1010	311.02	7697.69

FUNCTIONS OF NUMBERS

1 — 49

No. = Diameter

No.	Square	Cube	Square Root	Cube Root	Logarithm	1000 × Reciprocal	Circum.	Area
1	1	1	1.0000	1.0000	0.00000	1000.000	3.142	0.7854
2	4	8	1.4142	1.2599	0.30103	500.000	6.283	3.1416
3	9	27	1.7321	1.4422	0.47712	333.333	9.425	7.0686
4	16	64	2.0000	1.5874	0.60206	250.000	12.566	12.5664
5	25	125	2.2361	1.7100	0.69897	200.000	15.708	19.6350
6	36	216	2.4495	1.8171	0.77815	166.667	18.850	28.2743
7	49	343	2.6458	1.9129	0.84510	142.857	21.991	38.4845
8	64	512	2.8284	2.0000	0.90309	125.000	25.133	50.2655
9	81	729	3.0000	2.0801	0.95424	111.111	28.274	63.6173
10	100	1000	3.1623	2.1544	1.00000	100.000	31.416	78.5398
11	121	1331	3.3166	2.2240	1.04139	90.9091	34.558	95.0332
12	144	1728	3.4641	2.2894	1.07918	83.3333	37.699	113.097
13	169	2197	3.6056	2.3513	1.11394	76.9231	40.841	132.732
14	196	2744	3.7417	2.4101	1.14613	71.4286	43.982	153.938
15	225	3375	3.8730	2.4662	1.17609	66.6667	47.124	176.715
16	256	4096	4.0000	2.5198	1.20412	62.5000	50.265	201.062
17	289	4913	4.1231	2.5713	1.23045	58.8235	53.407	226.980
18	324	5832	4.2426	2.6207	1.25527	55.5556	56.549	254.469
19	361	6859	4.3589	2.6684	1.27875	52.6316	59.690	283.529
20	400	8000	4.4721	2.7144	1.30103	50.0000	62.832	314.159
21	441	9261	4.5826	2.7589	1.32222	47.6190	65.973	346.361
22	484	10648	4.6904	2.8020	1.34242	45.4545	69.115	380.133
23	529	12167	4.7958	2.8439	1.36173	43.4783	72.257	415.476
24	576	13824	4.8990	2.8845	1.38021	41.6667	75.398	452.389
25	625	15625	5.0000	2.9240	1.39794	40.0000	78.540	490.874
26	676	17576	5.0990	2.9625	1.41497	38.4615	81.681	530.929
27	729	19683	5.1962	3.0000	1.43136	37.0370	84.823	572.555
28	784	21952	5.2915	3.0366	1.44716	35.7143	87.965	615.752
29	841	24389	5.3852	3.0723	1.46240	34.4828	91.106	660.520
30	900	27000	5.4772	3.1072	1.47712	33.3333	94.248	706.858
31	961	29791	5.5678	3.1414	1.49136	32.2581	97.389	754.768
32	1024	32768	5.6569	3.1748	1.50515	31.2500	100.531	804.248
33	1089	35937	5.7446	3.2075	1.51851	30.3030	103.673	855.299
34	1156	39304	5.8310	3.2396	1.53148	29.4118	106.814	907.920
35	1225	42875	5.9161	3.2711	1.54407	28.5714	109.956	962.113
36	1296	46656	6.0000	3.3019	1.55630	27.7778	113.097	1017.88
37	1369	50653	6.0828	3.3322	1.56820	27.0270	116.239	1075.21
38	1444	54872	6.1644	3.3620	1.57978	26.3158	119.381	1134.11
39	1521	59319	6.2450	3.3912	1.59106	25.6410	122.522	1194.59
40	1600	64000	6.3246	3.4200	1.60206	25.0000	125.66	1256.64
41	1681	68921	6.4031	3.4482	1.61278	24.3902	128.81	1320.25
42	1764	74088	6.4807	3.4760	1.62325	23.8095	131.95	1385.44
43	1849	79507	6.5574	3.5034	1.63347	23.2558	135.09	1452.20
44	1936	85184	6.6332	3.5303	1.64345	22.7273	138.23	1520.53
45	2025	91125	6.7082	3.5569	1.65321	22.2222	141.37	1590.43
46	2116	97336	6.7823	3.5830	1.66276	21.7391	144.51	1661.90
47	2209	103823	6.8557	3.6088	1.67210	21.2766	147.65	1734.94
48	2304	110592	6.9282	3.6342	1.68124	20.8333	150.80	1809.56
49	2401	117649	7.0000	3.6593	1.69020	20.4082	153.94	1885.74

FUNCTIONS OF NUMBERS

No.	Square	Cube	Square Root	Cube Root	Logarithm	1000 × Reciprocal	Circum.	Area (No. = Diameter)
150	22500	3375000	12.2474	5.3133	2.17609	6.66667	471.24	17671.5
151	22801	3442951	12.2882	5.3251	2.17898	6.62252	474.38	17907.9
152	23104	3511808	12.3288	5.3368	2.18184	6.57895	477.52	18145.8
153	23409	3581577	12.3693	5.3485	2.18469	6.53595	480.66	18385.4
154	23716	3652264	12.4097	5.3601	2.18752	6.49351	483.81	18626.5
155	24025	3723875	12.4499	5.3717	2.19033	6.45161	486.95	18869.2
156	24336	3796416	12.4900	5.3832	2.19312	6.41026	490.09	19113.4
157	24649	3869893	12.5300	5.3947	2.19590	6.36943	493.23	19359.3
158	24964	3944312	12.5698	5.4061	2.19866	6.32911	496.37	19606.7
159	25281	4019679	12.6095	5.4175	2.20140	6.28931	499.51	19855.7
160	25600	4096000	12.6491	5.4288	2.20412	6.25000	502.65	20106.2
161	25921	4173281	12.6886	5.4401	2.20683	6.21118	505.80	20358.3
162	26244	4251528	12.7279	5.4514	2.20952	6.17284	508.94	20612.0
163	26569	4330747	12.7671	5.4626	2.21219	6.13497	512.08	20867.2
164	26896	4410944	12.8062	5.4737	2.21484	6.09756	515.22	21124.1
165	27225	4492125	12.8452	5.4848	2.21748	6.06061	518.36	21382.5
166	27556	4574296	12.8841	5.4959	2.22011	6.02410	521.50	21642.4
167	27889	4657463	12.9228	5.5069	2.22272	5.98802	524.65	21904.0
168	28224	4741632	12.9615	5.5178	2.22531	5.95238	527.79	22167.1
169	28561	4826809	13.0000	5.5288	2.22789	5.91716	530.93	22431.8
170	28900	4913000	13.0384	5.5397	2.23045	5.88235	534.07	22698.0
171	29241	5000211	13.0767	5.5505	2.23300	5.84795	537.21	22965.8
172	29584	5088448	13.1149	5.5613	2.23553	5.81395	540.35	23235.2
173	29929	5177717	13.1529	5.5721	2.23805	5.78035	543.50	23506.2
174	30276	5268024	13.1909	5.5828	2.24055	5.74713	546.64	23778.7
175	30625	5359375	13.2288	5.5934	2.24304	5.71429	549.78	24052.8
176	30976	5451776	13.2665	5.6041	2.24551	5.68182	552.92	24328.5
177	31329	5545233	13.3041	5.6147	2.24797	5.64972	556.06	24605.7
178	31684	5639752	13.3417	5.6252	2.25042	5.61798	559.20	24884.6
179	32041	5735339	13.3791	5.6357	2.25285	5.58659	562.35	25164.9
180	32400	5832000	13.4164	5.6462	2.25527	5.55556	565.49	25446.9
181	32761	5929741	13.4536	5.6567	2.25768	5.52486	568.63	25730.4
182	33124	6028568	13.4907	5.6671	2.26007	5.49451	571.77	26015.5
183	33489	6128487	13.5277	5.6774	2.26245	5.46448	574.91	26302.2
184	33856	6229504	13.5647	5.6877	2.26482	5.43478	578.05	26590.4
185	34225	6331625	13.6015	5.6980	2.26717	5.40541	581.19	26880.3
186	34596	6434856	13.6382	5.7083	2.26951	5.37634	584.34	27171.6
187	34969	6539203	13.6748	5.7185	2.27184	5.34759	587.48	27464.6
188	35344	6644672	13.7113	5.7287	2.27416	5.31915	590.62	27759.1
189	35721	6751269	13.7477	5.7388	2.27646	5.29101	593.76	28055.2
190	36100	6859000	13.7840	5.7489	2.27875	5.26316	596.90	28352.9
191	36481	6967871	13.8203	5.7590	2.28103	5.23560	600.04	28652.1
192	36864	7077888	13.8564	5.7690	2.28330	5.20833	603.19	28952.9
193	37249	7189057	13.8924	5.7790	2.28556	5.18135	606.33	29255.3
194	37636	7301384	13.9284	5.7890	2.28780	5.15464	609.47	29559.2
195	38025	7414875	13.9642	5.7989	2.29003	5.12821	612.61	29864.8
196	38416	7529536	14.0000	5.8088	2.29226	5.10204	615.75	30171.9
197	38809	7645373	14.0357	5.8186	2.29447	5.07614	618.89	30480.5
198	39204	7762392	14.0712	5.8285	2.29667	5.05051	622.04	30790.7
199	39601	7880599	14.1067	5.8383	2.29885	5.02513	625.18	31102.6

FUNCTIONS OF NUMBERS

No.	Square	Cube	Square Root	Cube Root	Logarithm	1000 × Reciprocal	Circum.	Area (No. = Diameter)
100	10000	1000000	10.0000	4.6416	2.00000	10.0000	314.16	7853.98
101	10201	1030301	10.0499	4.6570	2.00432	9.90099	317.30	8011.85
102	10404	1061208	10.0995	4.6723	2.00860	9.80392	320.44	8171.28
103	10609	1092727	10.1489	4.6875	2.01284	9.70874	323.58	8332.29
104	10816	1124864	10.1980	4.7027	2.01703	9.61538	326.73	8494.87
105	11025	1157625	10.2470	4.7177	2.02119	9.52381	329.87	8659.01
106	11236	1191016	10.2956	4.7326	2.02531	9.43396	333.01	8824.73
107	11449	1225043	10.3441	4.7475	2.02938	9.34579	336.15	8992.02
108	11664	1259712	10.3923	4.7622	2.03342	9.25926	339.29	9160.88
109	11881	1295029	10.4403	4.7769	2.03743	9.17431	342.43	9331.32
110	12100	1331000	10.4881	4.7914	2.04139	9.09091	345.58	9503.32
111	12321	1367631	10.5357	4.8059	2.04532	9.00901	348.72	9676.89
112	12544	1404928	10.5830	4.8203	2.04922	8.92857	351.86	9852.03
113	12769	1442897	10.6301	4.8346	2.05308	8.84956	355.00	10028.7
114	12996	1481544	10.6771	4.8488	2.05690	8.77193	358.14	10207.0
115	13225	1520875	10.7238	4.8629	2.06070	8.69565	361.28	10386.9
116	13456	1560896	10.7703	4.8770	2.06446	8.62069	364.42	10568.3
117	13689	1601613	10.8167	4.8910	2.06819	8.54701	367.57	10751.3
118	13924	1643032	10.8628	4.9049	2.07188	8.47458	370.71	10935.9
119	14161	1685159	10.9087	4.9187	2.07555	8.40336	373.85	11122.0
120	14400	1728000	10.9545	4.9324	2.07918	8.33333	376.99	11309.7
121	14641	1771561	11.0000	4.9461	2.08279	8.26446	380.13	11499.0
122	14884	1815848	11.0454	4.9597	2.08636	8.19672	383.27	11689.9
123	15129	1860867	11.0905	4.9732	2.08991	8.13008	386.42	11882.3
124	15376	1906624	11.1355	4.9866	2.09342	8.06452	389.56	12076.3
125	15625	1953125	11.1803	5.0000	2.09691	8.00000	392.70	12271.8
126	15876	2000376	11.2250	5.0133	2.10037	7.93651	395.84	12469.0
127	16129	2048383	11.2694	5.0265	2.10380	7.87402	398.98	12667.7
128	16384	2097152	11.3137	5.0397	2.10721	7.81250	402.12	12868.0
129	16641	2146689	11.3578	5.0528	2.11059	7.75194	405.27	13069.8
130	16900	2197000	11.4018	5.0658	2.11394	7.69231	408.41	13273.2
131	17161	2248091	11.4455	5.0788	2.11727	7.63359	411.55	13478.2
132	17424	2299968	11.4891	5.0916	2.12057	7.57576	414.69	13684.8
133	17689	2352637	11.5326	5.1045	2.12385	7.51880	417.83	13892.9
134	17956	2406104	11.5758	5.1172	2.12710	7.46269	420.97	14102.6
135	18225	2460375	11.6190	5.1299	2.13033	7.40741	424.12	14313.9
136	18496	2515456	11.6619	5.1426	2.13354	7.35294	427.26	14526.7
137	18769	2571353	11.7047	5.1551	2.13672	7.29927	430.40	14741.1
138	19044	2628072	11.7473	5.1676	2.13988	7.24638	433.54	14957.1
139	19321	2685619	11.7898	5.1801	2.14301	7.19424	436.68	15174.7
140	19600	2744000	11.8322	5.1925	2.14613	7.14286	439.82	15393.8
141	19881	2803221	11.8743	5.2048	2.14922	7.09220	442.96	15614.5
142	20164	2863288	11.9164	5.2171	2.15229	7.04225	446.11	15836.8
143	20449	2924207	11.9583	5.2293	2.15534	6.99301	449.25	16060.6
144	20736	2985984	12.0000	5.2415	2.15836	6.94444	452.39	16286.0
145	21025	3048625	12.0416	5.2536	2.16137	6.89655	455.53	16513.0
146	21316	3112136	12.0830	5.2656	2.16435	6.84932	458.67	16741.5
147	21609	3176523	12.1244	5.2776	2.16732	6.80272	461.81	16971.7
148	21904	3241792	12.1655	5.2896	2.17026	6.75676	464.96	17203.4
149	22201	3307949	12.2066	5.3015	2.17319	6.71141	468.10	17436.6

FUNCTIONS OF NUMBERS   250 / 299

No.	Square	Cube	Square Root	Cube Root	Logarithm	1000 × Reciprocal	Circum.	Area
250	62500	15625000	15.8114	6.2996	2.39794	4.00000	785.40	49087.4
251	63001	15813251	15.8430	6.3080	2.39967	3.98406	788.54	49480.9
252	63504	16003008	15.8745	6.3164	2.40140	3.96825	791.68	49875.9
253	64009	16194277	15.9060	6.3247	2.40312	3.95257	794.82	50272.6
254	64516	16387064	15.9374	6.3330	2.40483	3.93701	797.96	50670.7
255	65025	16581375	15.9687	6.3413	2.40654	3.92157	801.11	51070.5
256	65536	16777216	16.0000	6.3496	2.40824	3.90625	804.25	51471.9
257	66049	16974593	16.0312	6.3579	2.40993	3.89105	807.39	51874.8
258	66564	17173512	16.0624	6.3661	2.41162	3.87597	810.53	52279.2
259	67081	17373979	16.0935	6.3743	2.41330	3.86100	813.67	52685.3
260	67600	17576000	16.1245	6.3825	2.41497	3.84615	816.81	53092.9
261	68121	17779581	16.1555	6.3907	2.41664	3.83142	819.96	53502.1
262	68644	17984728	16.1864	6.3988	2.41830	3.81679	823.10	53912.9
263	69169	18191447	16.2173	6.4070	2.41996	3.80228	826.24	54325.2
264	69696	18399744	16.2481	6.4151	2.42160	3.78788	829.38	54739.1
265	70225	18609625	16.2788	6.4232	2.42325	3.77358	832.52	55154.6
266	70756	18821096	16.3095	6.4312	2.42488	3.75940	835.66	55571.6
267	71289	19034163	16.3401	6.4393	2.42651	3.74532	838.81	55990.2
268	71824	19248832	16.3707	6.4473	2.42813	3.73134	841.95	56410.4
269	72361	19465109	16.4012	6.4553	2.42975	3.71747	845.09	56832.2
270	72900	19683000	16.4317	6.4633	2.43136	3.70370	848.23	57255.5
271	73441	19902511	16.4621	6.4713	2.43297	3.69004	851.37	57680.4
272	73984	20123648	16.4924	6.4792	2.43457	3.67647	854.51	58106.9
273	74529	20346417	16.5227	6.4872	2.43616	3.66300	857.65	58534.9
274	75076	20570824	16.5529	6.4951	2.43775	3.64964	860.80	58964.6
275	75625	20796875	16.5831	6.5030	2.43933	3.63636	863.94	59395.7
276	76176	21024576	16.6132	6.5108	2.44091	3.62319	867.08	59828.5
277	76729	21253933	16.6433	6.5187	2.44248	3.61011	870.22	60262.8
278	77284	21484952	16.6733	6.5265	2.44404	3.59712	873.36	60698.7
279	77841	21717639	16.7033	6.5343	2.44560	3.58423	876.50	61136.2
280	78400	21952000	16.7332	6.5421	2.44716	3.57143	879.65	61575.2
281	78961	22188041	16.7631	6.5499	2.44871	3.55872	882.79	62015.8
282	79524	22425768	16.7929	6.5577	2.45025	3.54610	885.93	62458.0
283	80089	22665187	16.8226	6.5654	2.45179	3.53357	889.07	62901.8
284	80656	22906304	16.8523	6.5731	2.45332	3.52113	892.21	63347.1
285	81225	23149125	16.8819	6.5808	2.45484	3.50877	895.35	63794.0
286	81796	23393656	16.9115	6.5885	2.45637	3.49650	898.50	64242.4
287	82369	23639903	16.9411	6.5962	2.45788	3.48432	901.64	64692.5
288	82944	23887872	16.9706	6.6039	2.45939	3.47222	904.78	65144.1
289	83521	24137569	17.0000	6.6115	2.46090	3.46021	907.92	65597.2
290	84100	24389000	17.0294	6.6191	2.46240	3.44828	911.06	66052.0
291	84681	24642171	17.0587	6.6267	2.46389	3.43643	914.20	66508.3
292	85264	24897088	17.0880	6.6343	2.46538	3.42466	917.35	66966.2
293	85849	25153757	17.1172	6.6419	2.46687	3.41297	920.49	67425.6
294	86436	25412184	17.1464	6.6494	2.46835	3.40136	923.63	67886.7
295	87025	25672375	17.1756	6.6569	2.46982	3.38983	926.77	68349.3
296	87616	25934336	17.2047	6.6644	2.47129	3.37838	929.91	68813.4
297	88209	26198073	17.2337	6.6719	2.47276	3.36700	933.05	69279.2
298	88804	26463592	17.2627	6.6794	2.47422	3.35570	936.19	69746.5
299	89401	26730899	17.2916	6.6869	2.47567	3.34448	939.34	70215.4

(Circum. and Area columns headed: No. = Diameter)

FUNCTIONS OF NUMBERS   200 / 249

No.	Square	Cube	Square Root	Cube Root	Logarithm	1000 × Reciprocal	Circum.	Area
200	40000	8000000	14.1421	5.8480	2.30103	5.00000	628.32	31415.9
201	40401	8120601	14.1774	5.8578	2.30320	4.97512	631.46	31730.9
202	40804	8242408	14.2127	5.8675	2.30535	4.95050	634.60	32047.4
203	41209	8365427	14.2478	5.8771	2.30750	4.92611	637.74	32365.5
204	41616	8489664	14.2829	5.8868	2.30963	4.90196	640.88	32685.1
205	42025	8615125	14.3178	5.8964	2.31175	4.87805	644.03	33006.4
206	42436	8741816	14.3527	5.9059	2.31387	4.85437	647.17	33329.2
207	42849	8869743	14.3875	5.9155	2.31597	4.83092	650.31	33653.5
208	43264	8998912	14.4222	5.9250	2.31806	4.80769	653.45	33979.5
209	43681	9129329	14.4568	5.9345	2.32015	4.78469	656.59	34307.0
210	44100	9261000	14.4914	5.9439	2.32222	4.76190	659.73	34636.1
211	44521	9393931	14.5258	5.9533	2.32428	4.73934	662.88	34966.7
212	44944	9528128	14.5602	5.9627	2.32634	4.71698	666.02	35298.9
213	45369	9663597	14.5945	5.9721	2.32838	4.69484	669.16	35632.7
214	45796	9800344	14.6287	5.9814	2.33041	4.67290	672.30	35968.1
215	46225	9938375	14.6629	5.9907	2.33244	4.65116	675.44	36305.0
216	46656	10077696	14.6969	6.0000	2.33445	4.62963	678.58	36643.5
217	47089	10218313	14.7309	6.0092	2.33646	4.60829	681.73	36983.6
218	47524	10360232	14.7648	6.0185	2.33846	4.58716	684.87	37325.3
219	47961	10503459	14.7986	6.0277	2.34044	4.56621	688.01	37668.5
220	48400	10648000	14.8324	6.0368	2.34242	4.54545	691.15	38013.3
221	48841	10793861	14.8661	6.0459	2.34439	4.52489	694.29	38359.6
222	49284	10941048	14.8997	6.0550	2.34635	4.50450	697.43	38707.6
223	49729	11089567	14.9332	6.0641	2.34830	4.48430	700.58	39057.1
224	50176	11239424	14.9666	6.0732	2.35025	4.46429	703.72	39408.1
225	50625	11390625	15.0000	6.0822	2.35218	4.44444	706.86	39760.8
226	51076	11543176	15.0333	6.0912	2.35411	4.42478	710.00	40115.0
227	51529	11697083	15.0665	6.1002	2.35603	4.40529	713.14	40470.8
228	51984	11852352	15.0997	6.1091	2.35793	4.38596	716.28	40828.1
229	52441	12008989	15.1327	6.1180	2.35984	4.36681	719.42	41187.1
230	52900	12167000	15.1658	6.1269	2.36173	4.34783	722.57	41547.6
231	53361	12326391	15.1987	6.1358	2.36361	4.32900	725.71	41909.6
232	53824	12487168	15.2315	6.1446	2.36549	4.31034	728.85	42273.3
233	54289	12649337	15.2643	6.1534	2.36736	4.29185	731.99	42638.5
234	54756	12812904	15.2971	6.1622	2.36922	4.27350	735.13	43005.3
235	55225	12977875	15.3297	6.1710	2.37107	4.25532	738.27	43373.6
236	55696	13144256	15.3623	6.1797	2.37291	4.23729	741.42	43743.5
237	56169	13312053	15.3948	6.1885	2.37475	4.21941	744.56	44115.0
238	56644	13481272	15.4272	6.1972	2.37658	4.20168	747.70	44488.1
239	57121	13651919	15.4596	6.2058	2.37840	4.18410	750.84	44862.7
240	57600	13824000	15.4919	6.2145	2.38021	4.16667	753.98	45238.9
241	58081	13997521	15.5242	6.2231	2.38202	4.14938	757.12	45616.7
242	58564	14172488	15.5563	6.2317	2.38382	4.13223	760.27	45996.1
243	59049	14348907	15.5885	6.2403	2.38561	4.11523	763.41	46377.0
244	59536	14526784	15.6205	6.2488	2.38739	4.09836	766.55	46759.5
245	60025	14706125	15.6525	6.2573	2.38917	4.08163	769.69	47143.5
246	60516	14886936	15.6844	6.2658	2.39094	4.06504	772.83	47529.2
247	61009	15069223	15.7162	6.2743	2.39270	4.04858	775.97	47916.4
248	61504	15252992	15.7480	6.2828	2.39445	4.03226	779.12	48305.1
249	62001	15438249	15.7797	6.2912	2.39620	4.01606	782.26	48695.5

(Circum. and Area columns headed: No. = Diameter)

FUNCTIONS OF NUMBERS

300–349

No.	Square	Cube	Square Root	Cube Root	Logarithm	1000 × Reciprocal	No. ÷ Diameter Circum.	Area
300	90000	27000000	17.3205	6.6943	2.47712	3.33333	942.48	70685.8
301	90601	27270901	17.3494	6.7018	2.47857	3.32226	945.62	71157.9
302	91204	27543608	17.3781	6.7092	2.48001	3.31126	948.76	71631.5
303	91809	27818127	17.4069	6.7166	2.48144	3.30033	951.90	72106.6
304	92416	28094464	17.4356	6.7240	2.48287	3.28947	955.04	72583.4
305	93025	28372625	17.4642	6.7313	2.48430	3.27869	958.19	73061.7
306	93636	28652616	17.4929	6.7387	2.48572	3.26797	961.33	73541.5
307	94249	28934443	17.5214	6.7460	2.48714	3.25733	964.47	74023.0
308	94864	29218112	17.5499	6.7533	2.48855	3.24675	967.61	74506.0
309	95481	29503629	17.5784	6.7606	2.48996	3.23625	970.75	74990.6
310	96100	29791000	17.6068	6.7679	2.49136	3.22581	973.89	75476.8
311	96721	30080231	17.6352	6.7752	2.49276	3.21543	977.04	75964.5
312	97344	30371328	17.6635	6.7824	2.49415	3.20513	980.18	76453.8
313	97969	30664297	17.6918	6.7897	2.49554	3.19489	983.32	76944.7
314	98596	30959144	17.7200	6.7969	2.49693	3.18471	986.46	77437.1
315	99225	31255875	17.7482	6.8041	2.49831	3.17460	989.60	77931.1
316	99856	31554496	17.7764	6.8113	2.49969	3.16456	992.74	78426.7
317	100489	31855013	17.8045	6.8185	2.50106	3.15457	995.88	78923.9
318	101124	32157432	17.8326	6.8256	2.50243	3.14465	999.03	79422.6
319	101761	32461759	17.8606	6.8328	2.50379	3.13480	1002.2	79922.9
320	102400	32768000	17.8885	6.8399	2.50515	3.12500	1005.3	80424.8
321	103041	33076161	17.9165	6.8470	2.50651	3.11526	1008.5	80928.2
322	103684	33386248	17.9444	6.8541	2.50786	3.10559	1011.6	81433.2
323	104329	33698267	17.9722	6.8612	2.50920	3.09598	1014.7	81939.8
324	104976	34012224	18.0000	6.8683	2.51055	3.08642	1017.9	82448.0
325	105625	34328125	18.0278	6.8753	2.51188	3.07692	1021.0	82957.7
326	106276	34645976	18.0555	6.8824	2.51322	3.06749	1024.2	83469.0
327	106929	34965783	18.0831	6.8894	2.51455	3.05810	1027.3	83981.8
328	107584	35287552	18.1108	6.8964	2.51587	3.04878	1030.4	84496.3
329	108241	35611289	18.1384	6.9034	2.51720	3.03951	1033.6	85012.3
330	108900	35937000	18.1659	6.9104	2.51851	3.03030	1036.7	85529.9
331	109561	36264691	18.1934	6.9174	2.51983	3.02115	1039.9	86049.0
332	110224	36594368	18.2209	6.9244	2.52114	3.01205	1043.0	86569.7
333	110889	36926037	18.2483	6.9313	2.52244	3.00300	1046.2	87092.0
334	111556	37259704	18.2757	6.9382	2.52375	2.99401	1049.3	87615.9
335	112225	37595375	18.3030	6.9451	2.52504	2.98507	1052.4	88141.3
336	112896	37933056	18.3303	6.9521	2.52634	2.97619	1055.6	88668.3
337	113569	38272753	18.3576	6.9589	2.52763	2.96736	1058.7	89196.9
338	114244	38614472	18.3848	6.9658	2.52892	2.95858	1061.9	89727.0
339	114921	38958219	18.4120	6.9727	2.53020	2.94985	1065.0	90258.7
340	115600	39304000	18.4391	6.9795	2.53148	2.94118	1068.1	90792.0
341	116281	39651821	18.4662	6.9864	2.53275	2.93255	1071.3	91326.9
342	116964	40001688	18.4932	6.9932	2.53403	2.92398	1074.4	91863.3
343	117649	40353607	18.5203	7.0000	2.53529	2.91545	1077.6	92401.3
344	118336	40707584	18.5472	7.0068	2.53656	2.90698	1080.7	92940.9
345	119025	41063625	18.5742	7.0136	2.53782	2.89855	1083.8	93482.0
346	119716	41421736	18.6011	7.0203	2.53908	2.89017	1087.0	94024.7
347	120409	41781923	18.6279	7.0271	2.54033	2.88184	1090.1	94569.0
348	121104	42144192	18.6548	7.0338	2.54158	2.87356	1093.3	95114.9
349	121801	42508549	18.6815	7.0406	2.54283	2.86533	1096.4	95662.3

350–399

No.	Square	Cube	Square Root	Cube Root	Logarithm	1000 × Reciprocal	No. = Diameter Circum.	Area
350	122500	42875000	18.7083	7.0473	2.54407	2.85714	1099.6	96211.3
351	123201	43243551	18.7350	7.0540	2.54531	2.84900	1102.7	96761.8
352	123904	43614208	18.7617	7.0607	2.54654	2.84091	1105.8	97314.0
353	124609	43986977	18.7883	7.0674	2.54777	2.83286	1109.0	97867.7
354	125316	44361864	18.8149	7.0740	2.54900	2.82486	1112.1	98423.0
355	126025	44738875	18.8414	7.0807	2.55023	2.81690	1115.3	98979.8
356	126736	45118016	18.8680	7.0873	2.55145	2.80899	1118.4	99538.2
357	127449	45499293	18.8944	7.0940	2.55267	2.80112	1121.5	100098
358	128164	45882712	18.9209	7.1006	2.55388	2.79330	1124.7	100660
359	128881	46268279	18.9473	7.1072	2.55509	2.78552	1127.8	101223
360	129600	46656000	18.9737	7.1138	2.55630	2.77778	1131.0	101788
361	130321	47045881	19.0000	7.1204	2.55751	2.77008	1134.1	102354
362	131044	47437928	19.0263	7.1269	2.55871	2.76243	1137.3	102922
363	131769	47832147	19.0526	7.1335	2.55991	2.75482	1140.4	103491
364	132496	48228544	19.0788	7.1400	2.56110	2.74725	1143.5	104062
365	133225	48627125	19.1050	7.1466	2.56229	2.73973	1146.7	104635
366	133956	49027896	19.1311	7.1531	2.56348	2.73224	1149.8	105209
367	134689	49430863	19.1572	7.1596	2.56467	2.72480	1153.0	105785
368	135424	49836032	19.1833	7.1661	2.56585	2.71739	1156.1	106362
369	136161	50243409	19.2094	7.1726	2.56703	2.71003	1159.2	106941
370	136900	50653000	19.2354	7.1791	2.56820	2.70270	1162.4	107521
371	137641	51064811	19.2614	7.1855	2.56937	2.69542	1165.5	108103
372	138384	51478848	19.2873	7.1920	2.57054	2.68817	1168.7	108687
373	139129	51895117	19.3132	7.1984	2.57171	2.68097	1171.9	109272
374	139876	52313624	19.3391	7.2048	2.57287	2.67380	1175.0	109858
375	140625	52734375	19.3649	7.2112	2.57403	2.66667	1178.1	110447
376	141376	53157376	19.3907	7.2177	2.57519	2.65957	1181.2	111036
377	142129	53582633	19.4165	7.2240	2.57634	2.65252	1184.4	111628
378	142884	54010152	19.4422	7.2304	2.57749	2.64550	1187.5	112221
379	143641	54439939	19.4679	7.2368	2.57864	2.63852	1190.7	112815
380	144400	54872000	19.4936	7.2432	2.57978	2.63158	1193.8	113411
381	145161	55306341	19.5192	7.2495	2.58093	2.62467	1196.9	114009
382	145924	55742968	19.5448	7.2558	2.58206	2.61780	1200.1	114608
383	146689	56181887	19.5704	7.2622	2.58320	2.61097	1203.2	115209
384	147456	56623104	19.5959	7.2685	2.58433	2.60417	1206.4	115812
385	148225	57066625	19.6214	7.2748	2.58546	2.59740	1209.5	116416
386	148996	57512456	19.6469	7.2811	2.58659	2.59067	1212.7	117021
387	149769	57960603	19.6723	7.2874	2.58771	2.58398	1215.8	117628
388	150544	58411072	19.6977	7.2936	2.58883	2.57732	1218.0	118237
389	151321	58863869	19.7231	7.2999	2.58995	2.57069	1222.1	118847
390	152100	59319000	19.7484	7.3061	2.59106	2.56410	1225.2	119459
391	152881	59776471	19.7737	7.3124	2.59218	2.55754	1228.4	120072
392	153664	60236288	19.7990	7.3186	2.59329	2.55102	1231.5	120687
393	154449	60698457	19.8242	7.3248	2.59439	2.54453	1234.6	121304
394	155236	61162984	19.8494	7.3310	2.59550	2.53807	1237.8	121922
395	156025	61629875	19.8746	7.3372	2.59660	2.53165	1240.9	122542
396	156816	62099136	19.8997	7.3434	2.59770	2.52525	1244.1	123163
397	157609	62570773	19.9249	7.3496	2.59879	2.51889	1247.2	123786
398	158404	63044792	19.9499	7.3558	2.59988	2.51256	1250.4	124410
399	159201	63521199	19.9750	7.3619	2.60097	2.50627	1253.5	125036

FUNCTIONS OF NUMBERS

450 – 499

No.	Square	Cube	Square Root	Cube Root	Logarithm	1000 × Reciprocal	Circum.	Area
450	202500	91125000	21.2132	7.6631	2.65321	2.22222	1413.7	159043
451	203401	91733851	21.2368	7.6688	2.65418	2.21729	1416.9	159751
452	204304	92345408	21.2603	7.6744	2.65514	2.21239	1420.0	160460
453	205209	92959677	21.2838	7.6801	2.65610	2.20751	1423.1	161171
454	206116	93576664	21.3073	7.6857	2.65706	2.20264	1426.3	161883
455	207025	94196375	21.3307	7.6914	2.65801	2.19780	1429.4	162597
456	207936	94818816	21.3542	7.6970	2.65896	2.19298	1432.6	163313
457	208849	95443993	21.3776	7.7026	2.65992	2.18818	1435.7	164030
458	209764	96071912	21.4009	7.7082	2.66087	2.18341	1438.8	164748
459	210681	96702579	21.4243	7.7138	2.66181	2.17865	1442.0	165468
460	211600	97336000	21.4476	7.7194	2.66276	2.17391	1445.1	166190
461	212521	97972181	21.4709	7.7250	2.66370	2.16920	1448.3	166914
462	213444	98611128	21.4942	7.7306	2.66464	2.16450	1451.4	167639
463	214369	99252847	21.5174	7.7362	2.66558	2.15983	1454.6	168365
464	215296	99897344	21.5407	7.7418	2.66652	2.15517	1457.7	169093
465	216225	100544625	21.5639	7.7473	2.66745	2.15054	1460.8	169823
466	217156	101194696	21.5870	7.7529	2.66839	2.14592	1464.0	170554
467	218089	101847563	21.6102	7.7584	2.66932	2.14133	1467.1	171287
468	219024	102503232	21.6333	7.7639	2.67025	2.13675	1470.3	172021
469	219961	103161709	21.6564	7.7695	2.67117	2.13220	1473.4	172757
470	220900	103823000	21.6795	7.7750	2.67210	2.12766	1476.5	173494
471	221841	104487111	21.7025	7.7805	2.67302	2.12314	1479.7	174234
472	222784	105154048	21.7256	7.7860	2.67394	2.11864	1482.8	174974
473	223729	105823817	21.7486	7.7915	2.67486	2.11416	1486.0	175716
474	224676	106496424	21.7715	7.7970	2.67578	2.10970	1489.1	176460
475	225625	107171875	21.7945	7.8025	2.67669	2.10526	1492.3	177205
476	226576	107850176	21.8174	7.8079	2.67761	2.10084	1495.4	177952
477	227529	108531333	21.8403	7.8134	2.67852	2.09644	1498.5	178701
478	228484	109215352	21.8632	7.8188	2.67943	2.09205	1501.7	179451
479	229441	109902239	21.8861	7.8243	2.68034	2.08768	1504.8	180203
480	230400	110592000	21.9089	7.8297	2.68124	2.08333	1508.0	180956
481	231361	111284641	21.9317	7.8352	2.68215	2.07900	1511.1	181711
482	232324	111980168	21.9545	7.8406	2.68305	2.07469	1514.2	182467
483	233289	112678587	21.9773	7.8460	2.68395	2.07039	1517.4	183225
484	234256	113379904	22.0000	7.8514	2.68485	2.06612	1520.5	183984
485	235225	114084125	22.0227	7.8568	2.68574	2.06186	1523.7	184745
486	236196	114791256	22.0454	7.8622	2.68664	2.05761	1526.8	185508
487	237169	115501303	22.0681	7.8676	2.68753	2.05339	1530.0	186272
488	238144	116214272	22.0907	7.8730	2.68842	2.04918	1533.1	187038
489	239121	116930169	22.1133	7.8784	2.68931	2.04499	1536.2	187805
490	240100	117649000	22.1359	7.8837	2.69020	2.04082	1539.4	188574
491	241081	118370771	22.1585	7.8891	2.69108	2.03666	1542.5	189345
492	242064	119095488	22.1811	7.8944	2.69197	2.03252	1545.7	190117
493	243049	119823157	22.2036	7.8998	2.69285	2.02840	1548.8	190890
494	244036	120553784	22.2261	7.9051	2.69373	2.02429	1551.9	191665
495	245025	121287375	22.2486	7.9105	2.69461	2.02020	1555.1	192442
496	246016	122023936	22.2711	7.9158	2.69548	2.01613	1558.2	193221
497	247009	122763473	22.2935	7.9211	2.69636	2.01207	1561.4	194000
498	248004	123505992	22.3159	7.9264	2.69723	2.00803	1564.5	194782
499	249001	124251499	22.3383	7.9317	2.69810	2.00401	1567.7	195565

FUNCTIONS OF NUMBERS

400 – 449

No.	Square	Cube	Square Root	Cube Root	Logarithm	1000 × Reciprocal	Circum.	Area
400	160000	64000000	20.0000	7.3681	2.60206	2.50000	1256.6	125664
401	160801	64481201	20.0250	7.3742	2.60314	2.49377	1259.8	126293
402	161604	64964808	20.0499	7.3803	2.60423	2.48756	1262.9	126923
403	162409	65450827	20.0749	7.3864	2.60531	2.48139	1266.1	127556
404	163216	65939264	20.0998	7.3925	2.60638	2.47525	1269.2	128190
405	164025	66430125	20.1246	7.3986	2.60746	2.46914	1272.3	128825
406	164836	66923416	20.1494	7.4047	2.60853	2.46305	1275.5	129462
407	165649	67419143	20.1742	7.4108	2.60959	2.45700	1278.6	130100
408	166464	67917312	20.1990	7.4169	2.61066	2.45098	1281.8	130741
409	167281	68417929	20.2237	7.4229	2.61172	2.44499	1284.9	131382
410	168100	68921000	20.2485	7.4290	2.61278	2.43902	1288.1	132025
411	168921	69426531	20.2731	7.4350	2.61384	2.43309	1291.2	132670
412	169744	69934528	20.2978	7.4410	2.61490	2.42718	1294.3	133317
413	170569	70444997	20.3224	7.4470	2.61595	2.42131	1297.5	133965
414	171396	70957944	20.3470	7.4530	2.61700	2.41546	1300.6	134614
415	172225	71473375	20.3715	7.4590	2.61805	2.40964	1303.8	135265
416	173056	71991296	20.3961	7.4650	2.61909	2.40385	1306.9	135918
417	173889	72511713	20.4206	7.4710	2.62014	2.39808	1310.0	136572
418	174724	73034632	20.4450	7.4770	2.62118	2.39234	1313.2	137228
419	175561	73560059	20.4695	7.4829	2.62221	2.38663	1316.3	137885
420	176400	74088000	20.4939	7.4889	2.62325	2.38095	1319.5	138544
421	177241	74618461	20.5183	7.4948	2.62428	2.37530	1322.6	139205
422	178084	75151448	20.5426	7.5007	2.62531	2.36967	1325.8	139867
423	178929	75686967	20.5670	7.5067	2.62634	2.36407	1328.9	140531
424	179776	76225024	20.5913	7.5126	2.62737	2.35849	1332.0	141196
425	180625	76765625	20.6155	7.5185	2.62839	2.35294	1335.4	141863
426	181476	77308776	20.6398	7.5244	2.62941	2.34742	1338.3	142531
427	182329	77854483	20.6640	7.5302	2.63043	2.34192	1341.5	143201
428	183184	78402752	20.6882	7.5361	2.63144	2.33645	1344.6	143872
429	184041	78953589	20.7123	7.5420	2.63246	2.33100	1347.7	144545
430	184900	79507000	20.7364	7.5478	2.63347	2.32558	1350.9	145220
431	185761	80062991	20.7605	7.5537	2.63448	2.32019	1354.0	145896
432	186624	80621568	20.7846	7.5595	2.63548	2.31481	1357.2	146574
433	187489	81182737	20.8087	7.5654	2.63649	2.30947	1360.3	147254
434	188356	81746504	20.8327	7.5712	2.63749	2.30415	1363.5	147934
435	189225	82312875	20.8567	7.5770	2.63849	2.29885	1366.6	148617
436	190096	82881856	20.8806	7.5828	2.63949	2.29358	1369.7	149301
437	190969	83453453	20.9045	7.5886	2.64048	2.28833	1372.9	149987
438	191844	84027672	20.9284	7.5944	2.64147	2.28311	1376.0	150674
439	192721	84604519	20.9523	7.6001	2.64246	2.27790	1379.2	151363
440	193600	85184000	20.9762	7.6059	2.64345	2.27273	1382.3	152053
441	194481	85766121	21.0000	7.6117	2.64444	2.26757	1385.4	152745
442	195364	86350888	21.0238	7.6174	2.64542	2.26244	1388.6	153439
443	196249	86938307	21.0476	7.6232	2.64640	2.25734	1391.7	154134
444	197136	87528384	21.0713	7.6289	2.64738	2.25225	1394.9	154830
445	198025	88121125	21.0950	7.6346	2.64836	2.24719	1398.0	155528
446	198916	88716536	21.1187	7.6403	2.64933	2.24215	1401.2	156228
447	199809	89314623	21.1424	7.6460	2.65031	2.23714	1404.3	156930
448	200704	89915392	21.1660	7.6517	2.65128	2.23214	1407.4	157633
449	201601	90518849	21.1896	7.6574	2.65225	2.22717	1410.6	158337

FUNCTIONS OF NUMBERS

550 – 599

No.	Square	Cube	Square Root	Cube Root	Logarithm	1000 × Reciprocal	Circum. (No. = Diameter)	Area
550	302500	166375000	23.4521	8.1932	2.74036	1.81818	1727.9	237583
551	303601	167284151	23.4734	8.1982	2.74115	1.81488	1731.0	238448
552	304704	168196608	23.4947	8.2031	2.74194	1.81159	1734.2	239314
553	305809	169112377	23.5160	8.2081	2.74273	1.80832	1737.3	240182
554	306916	170031464	23.5372	8.2130	2.74351	1.80505	1740.4	241051
555	308025	170953875	23.5584	8.2180	2.74429	1.80180	1743.6	241922
556	309136	171879616	23.5797	8.2229	2.74507	1.79856	1746.7	242795
557	310249	172808693	23.6008	8.2278	2.74586	1.79533	1749.9	243669
558	311364	173741112	23.6220	8.2327	2.74663	1.79211	1753.0	244545
559	312481	174676879	23.6432	8.2377	2.74741	1.78891	1756.2	245422
560	313600	175616000	23.6643	8.2426	2.74819	1.78571	1759.3	246301
561	314721	176558481	23.6854	8.2475	2.74896	1.78253	1762.4	247181
562	315844	177504328	23.7065	8.2524	2.74974	1.77936	1765.6	248063
563	316969	178453547	23.7276	8.2573	2.75051	1.77620	1768.7	248947
564	318096	179406144	23.7487	8.2621	2.75128	1.77305	1771.9	249832
565	319225	180362125	23.7697	8.2670	2.75205	1.76991	1775.0	250719
566	320356	181321496	23.7908	8.2719	2.75282	1.76678	1778.1	251607
567	321489	182284263	23.8118	8.2768	2.75358	1.76367	1781.3	252497
568	322624	183250432	23.8328	8.2816	2.75435	1.76056	1784.4	253388
569	323761	184220009	23.8537	8.2865	2.75511	1.75747	1787.6	254281
570	324900	185193000	23.8747	8.2913	2.75587	1.75439	1790.7	255176
571	326041	186169411	23.8956	8.2962	2.75664	1.75131	1793.8	256072
572	327184	187149248	23.9165	8.3010	2.75740	1.74825	1797.0	256970
573	328329	188132517	23.9374	8.3059	2.75815	1.74520	1800.1	257869
574	329476	189119224	23.9583	8.3107	2.75891	1.74216	1803.3	258770
575	330625	190109375	23.9792	8.3155	2.75967	1.73913	1806.4	259672
576	331776	191102976	24.0000	8.3203	2.76042	1.73611	1809.6	260576
577	332929	192100033	24.0208	8.3251	2.76118	1.73310	1812.7	261482
578	334084	193100552	24.0416	8.3300	2.76193	1.73010	1815.8	262389
579	335241	194104539	24.0624	8.3348	2.76268	1.72712	1819.0	263298
580	336400	195112000	24.0832	8.3396	2.76343	1.72414	1822.1	264208
581	337561	196122941	24.1039	8.3443	2.76418	1.72117	1825.3	265120
582	338724	197137368	24.1247	8.3491	2.76492	1.71821	1828.4	266033
583	339889	198155287	24.1454	8.3539	2.76567	1.71527	1831.6	266948
584	341056	199176704	24.1661	8.3587	2.76641	1.71233	1834.7	267865
585	342225	200201625	24.1868	8.3634	2.76716	1.70940	1837.8	268783
586	343396	201230056	24.2074	8.3682	2.76790	1.70648	1841.0	269703
587	344569	202262003	24.2281	8.3730	2.76864	1.70358	1844.1	270624
588	345744	203297472	24.2487	8.3777	2.76938	1.70068	1847.3	271547
589	346921	204336469	24.2693	8.3825	2.77012	1.69779	1850.4	272471
590	348100	205379000	24.2899	8.3872	2.77085	1.69492	1853.5	273397
591	349281	206425071	24.3105	8.3919	2.77159	1.69205	1856.7	274325
592	350464	207474688	24.3311	8.3967	2.77232	1.68919	1859.8	275254
593	351649	208527857	24.3516	8.4014	2.77305	1.68634	1863.0	276184
594	352836	209584584	24.3721	8.4061	2.77379	1.68350	1866.1	277117
595	354025	210644875	24.3926	8.4108	2.77452	1.68067	1869.2	278051
596	355216	211708736	24.4131	8.4155	2.77525	1.67785	1872.4	278986
597	356409	212776173	24.4336	8.4202	2.77597	1.67504	1875.5	279923
598	357604	213847192	24.4540	8.4249	2.77670	1.67224	1878.7	280862
599	358801	214921799	24.4745	8.4296	2.77743	1.66945	1881.8	281802

FUNCTIONS OF NUMBERS

500 – 549

No.	Square	Cube	Square Root	Cube Root	Logarithm	1000 × Reciprocal	Circum. (No. = Diameter)	Area
500	250000	125000000	22.3607	7.9370	2.69897	2.00000	1570.8	196350
501	251001	125751501	22.3830	7.9423	2.69984	1.99601	1573.9	197136
502	252004	126506008	22.4054	7.9476	2.70070	1.99203	1577.1	197923
503	253009	127263527	22.4277	7.9528	2.70157	1.98807	1580.2	198713
504	254016	128024064	22.4499	7.9581	2.70243	1.98413	1583.4	199504
505	255025	128787625	22.4722	7.9634	2.70329	1.98020	1586.5	200296
506	256036	129554216	22.4944	7.9686	2.70415	1.97628	1589.6	201090
507	257049	130323843	22.5167	7.9739	2.70501	1.97239	1592.8	201886
508	258064	131096512	22.5389	7.9791	2.70586	1.96850	1595.9	202683
509	259081	131872229	22.5610	7.9843	2.70672	1.96464	1599.1	203482
510	260100	132651000	22.5832	7.9896	2.70757	1.96078	1602.2	204282
511	261121	133432831	22.6053	7.9948	2.70842	1.95695	1605.4	205084
512	262144	134217728	22.6274	8.0000	2.70927	1.95312	1608.5	205887
513	263169	135005697	22.6495	8.0052	2.71012	1.94932	1611.6	206692
514	264196	135796744	22.6716	8.0104	2.71096	1.94553	1614.8	207499
515	265225	136590875	22.6936	8.0156	2.71181	1.94175	1617.9	208307
516	266256	137388096	22.7156	8.0208	2.71265	1.93798	1621.1	209117
517	267289	138188413	22.7376	8.0260	2.71349	1.93424	1624.2	209928
518	268324	138991832	22.7596	8.0311	2.71433	1.93050	1627.3	210741
519	269361	139798359	22.7816	8.0363	2.71517	1.92678	1630.5	211556
520	270400	140608000	22.8035	8.0415	2.71600	1.92308	1633.6	212372
521	271441	141420761	22.8254	8.0466	2.71684	1.91939	1636.8	213189
522	272484	142236648	22.8473	8.0517	2.71767	1.91571	1639.9	214008
523	273529	143055667	22.8692	8.0569	2.71850	1.91205	1643.1	214829
524	274576	143877824	22.8910	8.0620	2.71933	1.90840	1646.2	215651
525	275625	144703125	22.9129	8.0671	2.72016	1.90476	1649.3	216475
526	276676	145531576	22.9347	8.0723	2.72099	1.90114	1652.5	217301
527	277729	146363183	22.9565	8.0774	2.72181	1.89753	1655.6	218128
528	278784	147197952	22.9783	8.0825	2.72263	1.89394	1658.8	218956
529	279841	148035889	23.0000	8.0876	2.72346	1.89036	1661.9	219787
530	280900	148877000	23.0217	8.0927	2.72428	1.88679	1665.0	220618
531	281961	149721291	23.0434	8.0978	2.72509	1.88324	1668.2	221452
532	283024	150568768	23.0651	8.1028	2.72591	1.87970	1671.3	222287
533	284089	151419437	23.0868	8.1079	2.72673	1.87617	1674.5	223123
534	285156	152273304	23.1084	8.1130	2.72754	1.87266	1677.6	223961
535	286225	153130375	23.1301	8.1180	2.72835	1.86916	1680.8	224801
536	287296	153990656	23.1517	8.1231	2.72916	1.86567	1683.9	225642
537	288369	154854153	23.1733	8.1281	2.72997	1.86220	1687.0	226484
538	289444	155720872	23.1948	8.1332	2.73078	1.85874	1690.2	227329
539	290521	156590819	23.2164	8.1382	2.73159	1.85529	1693.3	228175
540	291600	157464000	23.2379	8.1433	2.73239	1.85185	1696.5	229022
541	292681	158340421	23.2594	8.1483	2.73320	1.84843	1699.6	229871
542	293764	159220088	23.2809	8.1533	2.73400	1.84502	1702.7	230722
543	294849	160103007	23.3024	8.1583	2.73480	1.84162	1705.9	231574
544	295936	160989184	23.3238	8.1633	2.73560	1.83824	1709.0	232428
545	297025	161878625	23.3452	8.1683	2.73640	1.83486	1712.2	233283
546	298116	162771336	23.3666	8.1733	2.73719	1.83150	1715.3	234140
547	299209	163667323	23.3880	8.1783	2.73799	1.82815	1718.5	234998
548	300304	164566592	23.4094	8.1833	2.73878	1.82482	1721.6	235858
549	301401	165469149	23.4307	8.1882	2.73957	1.82149	1724.7	236720

FUNCTIONS OF NUMBERS

650 – 699

No.	Square	Cube	Square Root	Cube Root	Logarithm	1000 × Reciprocal	No. = Diameter Circum.	Area
650	422500	274625000	25.4951	8.6624	2.81291	1.53846	2042.0	331831
651	423801	275894451	25.5147	8.6668	2.81358	1.53610	2045.2	332853
652	425104	277167808	25.5343	8.6713	2.81425	1.53374	2048.3	333876
653	426409	278445077	25.5539	8.6757	2.81491	1.53139	2051.5	334901
654	427716	279726264	25.5734	8.6801	2.81558	1.52905	2054.6	335927
655	429025	281011375	25.5930	8.6845	2.81624	1.52679	2057.7	336955
656	430336	282300416	25.6125	8.6890	2.81690	1.52439	2060.9	337985
657	431649	283593393	25.6320	8.6934	2.81757	1.52207	2064.0	339016
658	432964	284890312	25.6515	8.6978	2.81823	1.51976	2067.2	340049
659	434281	286191179	25.6710	8.7022	2.81889	1.51745	2070.3	341084
660	435600	287496000	25.6905	8.7066	2.81954	1.51515	2073.5	342119
661	436921	288804781	25.7099	8.7110	2.82020	1.51286	2076.6	343157
662	438244	290117528	25.7294	8.7154	2.82086	1.51057	2079.7	344196
663	439569	291434247	25.7488	8.7198	2.82151	1.50830	2082.9	345237
664	440896	292754944	25.7682	8.7241	2.82217	1.50602	2086.0	346279
665	442225	294079625	25.7876	8.7285	2.82282	1.50376	2089.2	347323
666	443556	295408296	25.8070	8.7329	2.82347	1.50150	2092.3	348368
667	444889	296740963	25.8263	8.7373	2.82413	1.49925	2095.4	349415
668	446224	298077632	25.8457	8.7416	2.82478	1.49701	2098.6	350464
669	447561	299418309	25.8650	8.7460	2.82543	1.49477	2101.7	351514
670	448900	300763000	25.8844	8.7503	2.82607	1.49254	2104.9	352565
671	450241	302111711	25.9037	8.7547	2.82672	1.49031	2108.0	353618
672	451584	303464448	25.9230	8.7590	2.82737	1.48810	2111.2	354673
673	452929	304821217	25.9422	8.7634	2.82802	1.48588	2114.3	355730
674	454276	306182024	25.9615	8.7677	2.82866	1.48368	2117.4	356788
675	455625	307546875	25.9808	8.7721	2.82930	1.48148	2120.6	357847
676	456976	308915776	26.0000	8.7764	2.82995	1.47929	2123.7	358908
677	458329	310288733	26.0192	8.7807	2.83059	1.47710	2126.9	359971
678	459684	311665752	26.0384	8.7850	2.83123	1.47493	2130.0	361035
679	461041	313046839	26.0576	8.7893	2.83187	1.47275	2133.1	362101
680	462400	314432000	26.0768	8.7937	2.83251	1.47059	2136.3	363168
681	463761	315821241	26.0960	8.7980	2.83315	1.46843	2139.4	364237
682	465124	317214568	26.1151	8.8023	2.83378	1.46628	2142.6	365308
683	466489	318611987	26.1343	8.8066	2.83442	1.46413	2145.7	366380
684	467856	320013504	26.1534	8.8109	2.83506	1.46199	2148.8	367453
685	469225	321419125	26.1725	8.8152	2.83569	1.45985	2152.0	368528
686	470596	322828856	26.1916	8.8194	2.83632	1.45773	2155.1	369605
687	471969	324242703	26.2107	8.8237	2.83696	1.45560	2158.3	370684
688	473344	325660672	26.2298	8.8280	2.83759	1.45349	2161.4	371764
689	474721	327082769	26.2488	8.8323	2.83822	1.45138	2164.6	372845
690	476100	328509000	26.2679	8.8366	2.83885	1.44928	2167.7	373928
691	477481	329939371	26.2869	8.8408	2.83948	1.44718	2170.8	375013
692	478864	331373888	26.3059	8.8451	2.84011	1.44509	2174.0	376099
693	480249	332812557	26.3249	8.8493	2.84073	1.44300	2177.1	377187
694	481636	334255384	26.3439	8.8536	2.84136	1.44092	2180.3	378276
695	483025	335702375	26.3629	8.8578	2.84198	1.43885	2183.4	379367
696	484416	337153536	26.3818	8.8621	2.84261	1.43678	2186.5	380459
697	485809	338608873	26.4008	8.8663	2.84323	1.43472	2189.7	381553
698	487204	340068392	26.4197	8.8706	2.84386	1.43266	2192.8	382649
699	488601	341532099	26.4386	8.8748	2.84448	1.43062	2196.0	383746

FUNCTIONS OF NUMBERS

600 – 649

No.	Square	Cube	Square Root	Cube Root	Logarithm	1000 × Reciprocal	No. = Diameter Circum.	Area
600	360000	216000000	24.4949	8.4343	2.77815	1.66667	1885.0	282743
601	361201	217081801	24.5153	8.4390	2.77887	1.66389	1888.1	283687
602	362404	218167208	24.5357	8.4437	2.77960	1.66113	1891.4	284631
603	363609	219256227	24.5561	8.4484	2.78032	1.65837	1894.4	285578
604	364816	220348864	24.5764	8.4530	2.78104	1.65563	1897.5	286526
605	366025	221445125	24.5967	8.4577	2.78176	1.65289	1900.7	287475
606	367236	222545016	24.6171	8.4623	2.78247	1.65017	1903.8	288426
607	368449	223648543	24.6374	8.4670	2.78319	1.64745	1906.9	289379
608	369664	224755712	24.6577	8.4716	2.78390	1.64474	1910.1	290333
609	370881	225866529	24.6779	8.4763	2.78462	1.64204	1913.2	291289
610	372100	226981000	24.6982	8.4809	2.78533	1.63934	1916.4	292247
611	373321	228099131	24.7184	8.4856	2.78604	1.63666	1919.5	293206
612	374544	229220928	24.7386	8.4902	2.78675	1.63399	1922.7	294166
613	375769	230346397	24.7588	8.4948	2.78746	1.63132	1925.8	295128
614	376996	231475544	24.7790	8.4994	2.78817	1.62866	1928.9	296092
615	378225	232608375	24.7992	8.5040	2.78888	1.62602	1932.1	297057
616	379456	233744896	24.8193	8.5086	2.78958	1.62338	1935.2	298024
617	380689	234885113	24.8395	8.5132	2.79029	1.62075	1938.4	298992
618	381924	236029032	24.8596	8.5178	2.79099	1.61812	1941.5	299962
619	383161	237176659	24.8797	8.5224	2.79169	1.61551	1944.6	300934
620	384400	238328000	24.8998	8.5270	2.79239	1.61290	1947.8	301907
621	385641	239483061	24.9199	8.5316	2.79309	1.61031	1950.9	302882
622	386884	240641848	24.9399	8.5362	2.79379	1.60772	1954.1	303858
623	388129	241804367	24.9600	8.5408	2.79449	1.60514	1957.2	304836
624	389376	242970624	24.9800	8.5453	2.79518	1.60256	1960.4	305815
625	390625	244140625	25.0000	8.5499	2.79588	1.60000	1963.5	306796
626	391876	245314376	25.0200	8.5544	2.79657	1.59744	1966.6	307779
627	393129	246491883	25.0400	8.5590	2.79727	1.59490	1969.8	308763
628	394384	247673152	25.0599	8.5635	2.79796	1.59236	1972.9	309748
629	395641	248858189	25.0799	8.5681	2.79865	1.58983	1976.1	310736
630	396900	250047000	25.0998	8.5726	2.79934	1.58730	1979.2	311725
631	398161	251239591	25.1197	8.5772	2.80003	1.58479	1982.3	312715
632	399424	252435968	25.1396	8.5817	2.80072	1.58228	1985.5	313707
633	400689	253636137	25.1595	8.5862	2.80140	1.57978	1988.6	313707
634	401956	254840104	25.1794	8.5907	2.80209	1.57729	1991.8	315696
635	403225	256047875	25.1992	8.5952	2.80277	1.57480	1994.9	316692
636	404496	257259456	25.2190	8.5997	2.80346	1.57233	1998.1	317690
637	405769	258474853	25.2389	8.6043	2.80414	1.56986	2001.2	318690
638	407044	259694072	25.2587	8.6088	2.80482	1.56740	2004.2	319692
639	408321	260917119	25.2784	8.6132	2.80550	1.56495	2007.5	320696
640	409600	262144000	25.2982	8.6177	2.80618	1.56250	2010.6	321699
641	410881	263374721	25.3180	8.6222	2.80686	1.56006	2013.8	322705
642	412164	264609288	25.3377	8.6267	2.80754	1.55763	2016.9	323713
643	413449	265847707	25.3574	8.6312	2.80821	1.55521	2020.0	324722
644	414736	267089984	25.3772	8.6357	2.80889	1.55280	2023.2	325733
645	416025	268336125	25.3969	8.6401	2.80956	1.55039	2026.3	326745
646	417316	269586136	25.4165	8.6446	2.81023	1.54799	2029.5	327759
647	418609	270840023	25.4362	8.6490	2.81090	1.54560	2032.6	328775
648	419904	272097792	25.4558	8.6535	2.81158	1.54321	2035.8	329792
649	421201	273359449	25.4755	8.6579	2.81224	1.54083	2038.9	330810

FUNCTIONS OF NUMBERS

750 – 799

No.	Square	Cube	Square Root	Cube Root	Logarithm	1000 × Reciprocal	Circum.	Area
							No. = Diameter	
750	562500	421875000	27.3861	9.0856	2.87506	1.33333	2356.2	441786
751	564001	423564751	27.4044	9.0896	2.87564	1.33156	2359.3	442965
752	565504	425259008	27.4226	9.0937	2.87622	1.32979	2362.5	444146
753	567009	426957777	27.4408	9.0977	2.87680	1.32802	2365.6	445328
754	568516	428661064	27.4591	9.1017	2.87737	1.32626	2368.8	446511
755	570025	430368875	27.4773	9.1057	2.87795	1.32450	2371.9	447697
756	571536	432081216	27.4955	9.1098	2.87852	1.32275	2375.0	448883
757	573049	433798093	27.5136	9.1138	2.87910	1.32100	2378.2	450072
758	574564	435519512	27.5318	9.1178	2.87967	1.31926	2381.3	451262
759	576081	437245479	27.5500	9.1218	2.88024	1.31752	2384.3	452453
760	577600	438976000	27.5681	9.1258	2.88081	1.31579	2387.6	453646
761	579121	440711081	27.5862	9.1298	2.88138	1.31406	2390.8	454841
762	580644	442450728	27.6043	9.1338	2.88196	1.31234	2393.9	456037
763	582169	444194947	27.6225	9.1378	2.88252	1.31062	2397.0	457234
764	583696	445943744	27.6405	9.1418	2.88309	1.30890	2400.2	458434
765	585225	447697125	27.6586	9.1458	2.88366	1.30719	2403.3	459635
766	586756	449455096	27.6767	9.1498	2.88423	1.30548	2406.5	460837
767	588289	451217663	27.6948	9.1537	2.88480	1.30378	2409.6	462041
768	589824	452984832	27.7128	9.1577	2.88536	1.30208	2412.7	463247
769	591361	454756609	27.7308	9.1617	2.88593	1.30039	2415.9	464454
770	592900	456533000	27.7489	9.1657	2.88649	1.29870	2419.0	465663
771	594441	458314011	27.7669	9.1696	2.88705	1.29702	2422.2	466873
772	595984	460099648	27.7849	9.1736	2.88762	1.29534	2425.3	468085
773	597529	461889917	27.8029	9.1775	2.88818	1.29366	2428.5	469298
774	599076	463684824	27.8209	9.1815	2.88874	1.29199	2431.6	470513
775	600625	465484375	27.8388	9.1855	2.88930	1.29032	2434.7	471730
776	602176	467288576	27.8568	9.1894	2.88986	1.28866	2437.9	472948
777	603729	469097433	27.8747	9.1933	2.89042	1.28700	2441.0	474168
778	605284	470910952	27.8927	9.1973	2.89098	1.28535	2444.2	475389
779	606841	472729139	27.9106	9.2012	2.89154	1.28370	2447.3	476612
780	608400	474552000	27.9285	9.2052	2.89209	1.28205	2450.4	477836
781	609961	476379541	27.9464	9.2091	2.89265	1.28041	2453.6	479062
782	611524	478211768	27.9643	9.2130	2.89321	1.27877	2456.7	480290
783	613089	480048687	27.9821	9.2170	2.89376	1.27714	2459.9	481519
784	614656	481890304	28.0000	9.2209	2.89432	1.27551	2463.0	482750
785	616225	483736625	28.0179	9.2248	2.89487	1.27389	2466.2	483982
786	617796	485587656	28.0357	9.2287	2.89542	1.27226	2469.3	485216
787	619369	487443403	28.0535	9.2326	2.89597	1.27065	2472.4	486451
788	620944	489303872	28.0713	9.2365	2.89653	1.26904	2475.6	487688
789	622521	491169069	28.0891	9.2404	2.89708	1.26743	2478.7	488927
790	624100	493039000	28.1069	9.2443	2.89763	1.26582	2481.9	490167
791	625681	494913671	28.1247	9.2482	2.89818	1.26422	2485.0	491409
792	627264	496793088	28.1425	9.2521	2.89873	1.26263	2488.1	492652
793	628849	498677257	28.1603	9.2560	2.89927	1.26103	2491.3	493897
794	630436	500566184	28.1780	9.2599	2.89982	1.25945	2494.4	495143
795	632025	502459875	28.1957	9.2638	2.90037	1.25786	2497.6	496391
796	633616	504358336	28.2135	9.2677	2.90091	1.25628	2500.7	497641
797	635209	506261573	28.2312	9.2716	2.90146	1.25471	2503.8	498892
798	636804	508169592	28.2489	9.2754	2.90200	1.25313	2507.0	500145
799	638401	510082399	28.2666	9.2793	2.90255	1.25156	2510.1	501399

FUNCTIONS OF NUMBERS

700 – 749

No.	Square	Cube	Square Root	Cube Root	Logarithm	1000 × Reciprocal	Circum.	Area
							No. = Diameter	
700	490000	343000000	26.4575	8.8790	2.84510	1.42857	2199.1	384845
701	491401	344472101	26.4764	8.8833	2.84572	1.42653	2202.3	385945
702	492804	345948408	26.4953	8.8875	2.84634	1.42450	2205.4	387047
703	494209	347428927	26.5141	8.8917	2.84696	1.42248	2208.5	388151
704	495616	348913664	26.5330	8.8959	2.84757	1.42045	2211.7	389256
705	497025	350402625	26.5518	8.9001	2.84819	1.41844	2214.8	390363
706	498436	351895816	26.5707	8.9043	2.84880	1.41643	2218.0	391471
707	499849	353393243	26.5895	8.9085	2.84942	1.41443	2221.1	392580
708	501264	354894912	26.6083	8.9127	2.85003	1.41243	2224.2	393692
709	502681	356400829	26.6271	8.9169	2.85065	1.41044	2227.4	394805
710	504100	357911000	26.6458	8.9211	2.85126	1.40845	2230.5	395919
711	505521	359425431	26.6646	8.9253	2.85187	1.40647	2233.7	397035
712	506944	360944128	26.6833	8.9295	2.85248	1.40449	2236.8	398153
713	508369	362467097	26.7021	8.9337	2.85309	1.40252	2240.0	399272
714	509796	363994344	26.7208	8.9378	2.85370	1.40056	2243.1	400393
715	511225	365525875	26.7395	8.9420	2.85431	1.39860	2246.2	401515
716	512656	367061696	26.7582	8.9462	2.85491	1.39665	2249.4	402639
717	514089	368601813	26.7769	8.9503	2.85552	1.39470	2252.5	403765
718	515524	370146232	26.7955	8.9545	2.85612	1.39276	2255.7	404892
719	516961	371694959	26.8142	8.9587	2.85673	1.39082	2258.8	406020
720	518400	373248000	26.8328	8.9628	2.85733	1.38889	2261.9	407150
721	519841	374805361	26.8514	8.9670	2.85794	1.38696	2265.1	408282
722	521284	376367048	26.8701	8.9711	2.85854	1.38504	2268.2	409415
723	522729	377933067	26.8887	8.9752	2.85914	1.38313	2271.4	410550
724	524176	379503424	26.9072	8.9794	2.85974	1.38122	2274.5	411687
725	525625	381078125	26.9258	8.9835	2.86034	1.37931	2277.7	412825
726	527076	382657176	26.9444	8.9876	2.86094	1.37741	2280.8	413965
727	528529	384240583	26.9629	8.9918	2.86153	1.37552	2283.9	415106
728	529984	385828352	26.9815	8.9959	2.86213	1.37363	2287.0	416248
729	531441	387420489	27.0000	9.0000	2.86273	1.37174	2290.2	417393
730	532900	389017000	27.0185	9.0041	2.86332	1.36986	2293.4	418539
731	534361	390617891	27.0370	9.0082	2.86392	1.36799	2296.5	419686
732	535824	392223168	27.0555	9.0123	2.86451	1.36612	2299.6	420835
733	537289	393832837	27.0740	9.0164	2.86510	1.36426	2302.8	421986
734	538756	395446904	27.0924	9.0205	2.86570	1.36240	2305.9	423138
735	540225	397065375	27.1109	9.0246	2.86629	1.36054	2309.1	424293
736	541696	398688256	27.1293	9.0287	2.86688	1.35870	2312.2	425447
737	543169	400315553	27.1477	9.0328	2.86747	1.35685	2315.4	426604
738	544644	401947272	27.1662	9.0369	2.86806	1.35501	2318.5	427762
739	546121	403583419	27.1846	9.0410	2.86864	1.35318	2321.6	428922
740	547600	405224000	27.2029	9.0450	2.86923	1.35135	2324.8	430084
741	549081	406869021	27.2213	9.0491	2.86982	1.34953	2327.9	431247
742	550564	408518488	27.2397	9.0532	2.87040	1.34771	2331.0	432412
743	552049	410172407	27.2580	9.0572	2.87099	1.34590	2334.2	433578
744	553536	411830784	27.2764	9.0613	2.87157	1.34409	2337.3	434746
745	555025	413493625	27.2947	9.0654	2.87216	1.34228	2340.5	435916
746	556516	415160936	27.3130	9.0694	2.87274	1.34048	2343.6	437087
747	558009	416832723	27.3313	9.0735	2.87332	1.33869	2346.8	438259
748	559504	418508992	27.3496	9.0775	2.87390	1.33690	2349.9	439433
749	561001	420189749	27.3679	9.0816	2.87448	1.33511	2353.1	440609

FUNCTIONS OF NUMBERS — 850–899

No.	Square	Cube	Square Root	Cube Root	Logarithm	1000 × Reciprocal	No. = Diameter Circum.	Area
850	722500	614125000	29.1548	9.4727	2.92942	1.17647	2670.4	567450
851	724201	616295051	29.1719	9.4764	2.92993	1.17509	2673.5	568786
852	725904	618470208	29.1890	9.4801	2.93044	1.17371	2676.6	570124
853	727609	620650477	29.2062	9.4838	2.93095	1.17233	2679.8	571463
854	729316	622835864	29.2233	9.4875	2.93146	1.17096	2682.9	572803
855	731025	625026375	29.2404	9.4912	2.93197	1.16959	2686.1	574146
856	732736	627222016	29.2575	9.4949	2.93247	1.16822	2689.2	575490
857	734449	629422793	29.2746	9.4986	2.93298	1.16686	2692.3	576835
858	736164	631628712	29.2916	9.5023	2.93349	1.16550	2695.5	578182
859	737881	633839779	29.3087	9.5060	2.93399	1.16414	2698.6	579530
860	739600	636056000	29.3258	9.5097	2.93450	1.16279	2701.8	580880
861	741321	638277381	29.3428	9.5134	2.93500	1.16144	2704.9	582232
862	743044	640503928	29.3598	9.5171	2.93551	1.16009	2708.1	583585
863	744769	642735647	29.3769	9.5207	2.93601	1.15875	2711.2	584940
864	746496	644972544	29.3939	9.5244	2.93651	1.15741	2714.3	586297
865	748225	647214625	29.4109	9.5281	2.93702	1.15607	2717.5	587655
866	749956	649461896	29.4279	9.5317	2.93752	1.15473	2720.6	589014
867	751689	651714363	29.4449	9.5354	2.93802	1.15340	2723.8	590375
868	753424	653972032	29.4618	9.5391	2.93852	1.15207	2726.9	591738
869	755161	656234909	29.4788	9.5427	2.93902	1.15075	2730.0	593102
870	756900	658503000	29.4958	9.5464	2.93952	1.14943	2733.2	594468
871	758641	660776311	29.5127	9.5501	2.94002	1.14811	2736.3	595835
872	760384	663054848	29.5296	9.5537	2.94052	1.14679	2739.4	597204
873	762129	665338617	29.5466	9.5574	2.94101	1.14548	2742.6	598575
874	763876	667627624	29.5635	9.5610	2.94151	1.14416	2745.8	599947
875	765625	669921875	29.5804	9.5647	2.94201	1.14286	2748.9	601320
876	767376	672221376	29.5973	9.5683	2.94250	1.14155	2752.0	602696
877	769129	674526133	29.6142	9.5719	2.94300	1.14025	2755.2	604073
878	770884	676836152	29.6311	9.5756	2.94349	1.13895	2758.3	605451
879	772641	679151439	29.6479	9.5792	2.94399	1.13766	2761.5	606831
880	774400	681472000	29.6648	9.5828	2.94448	1.13636	2764.6	608212
881	776161	683797841	29.6816	9.5865	2.94498	1.13507	2767.7	609595
882	777924	686128968	29.6985	9.5901	2.94547	1.13379	2770.9	610980
883	779689	688465387	29.7153	9.5937	2.94596	1.13250	2774.0	612366
884	781456	690807104	29.7321	9.5973	2.94645	1.13122	2777.2	613754
885	783225	693154125	29.7489	9.6010	2.94694	1.12994	2780.3	615143
886	784996	695506456	29.7658	9.6046	2.94743	1.12867	2783.5	616534
887	786769	697864103	29.7825	9.6082	2.94792	1.12740	2786.6	617927
888	788544	700227072	29.7993	9.6118	2.94841	1.12613	2789.7	619321
889	790321	702595369	29.8161	9.6154	2.94890	1.12486	2792.9	620717
890	792100	704969000	29.8329	9.6190	2.94939	1.12360	2796.0	622114
891	793881	707347971	29.8496	9.6226	2.94988	1.12233	2799.2	623513
892	795664	709732288	29.8664	9.6262	2.95036	1.12108	2802.3	624913
893	797449	712121957	29.8831	9.6298	2.95085	1.11982	2805.4	626315
894	799236	714516984	29.8998	9.6334	2.95134	1.11857	2808.6	627718
895	801025	716917375	29.9166	9.6370	2.95182	1.11732	2811.7	629124
896	802816	719323136	29.9333	9.6406	2.95231	1.11607	2814.9	630530
897	804609	721734273	29.9500	9.6442	2.95279	1.11483	2818.0	631938
898	806404	724150792	29.9666	9.6477	2.95328	1.11359	2821.2	633348
899	808201	726572699	29.9833	9.6513	2.95376	1.11235	2824.3	634760

FUNCTIONS OF NUMBERS — 800–849

No.	Square	Cube	Square Root	Cube Root	Logarithm	1000 × Reciprocal	No. = Diameter Circum.	Area
800	640000	512000000	28.2843	9.2832	2.90309	1.25000	2513.3	502655
801	641601	513922401	28.3019	9.2870	2.90363	1.24844	2516.4	503912
802	643204	515849608	28.3196	9.2909	2.90417	1.24688	2519.6	505171
803	644809	517781627	28.3373	9.2948	2.90472	1.24533	2522.7	506432
804	646416	519718464	28.3549	9.2986	2.90526	1.24378	2525.8	507694
805	648025	521660125	28.3725	9.3025	2.90580	1.24224	2529.0	508958
806	649636	523606616	28.3901	9.3063	2.90634	1.24069	2532.1	510223
807	651249	525557943	28.4077	9.3102	2.90687	1.23916	2535.3	511490
808	652864	527514112	28.4253	9.3140	2.90741	1.23762	2538.4	512758
809	654481	529475129	28.4429	9.3179	2.90795	1.23609	2541.5	514028
810	656100	531441000	28.4605	9.3217	2.90849	1.23457	2544.7	515300
811	657721	533411731	28.4781	9.3255	2.90902	1.23305	2547.8	516573
812	659344	535387328	28.4956	9.3294	2.90956	1.23153	2551.0	517848
813	660969	537367797	28.5132	9.3332	2.91009	1.23001	2554.1	519124
814	662596	539353144	28.5307	9.3370	2.91062	1.22850	2557.3	520402
815	664225	541343375	28.5482	9.3408	2.91116	1.22699	2560.4	521681
816	665856	543338496	28.5657	9.3447	2.91169	1.22549	2563.5	522962
817	667489	545338513	28.5832	9.3485	2.91222	1.22399	2566.7	524245
818	669124	547343432	28.6007	9.3523	2.91275	1.22249	2569.8	525529
819	670761	549353259	28.6182	9.3561	2.91328	1.22100	2573.0	526814
820	672400	551368000	28.6356	9.3599	2.91381	1.21951	2576.1	528102
821	674041	553387661	28.6531	9.3637	2.91434	1.21803	2579.2	529391
822	675684	555412248	28.6705	9.3675	2.91487	1.21655	2582.4	530681
823	677329	557441767	28.6880	9.3713	2.91540	1.21507	2585.5	531973
824	678976	559476224	28.7054	9.3751	2.91593	1.21359	2588.7	533267
825	680625	561515625	28.7228	9.3789	2.91645	1.21212	2591.8	534562
826	682276	563559976	28.7402	9.3827	2.91698	1.21065	2595.0	535858
827	683929	565609283	28.7576	9.3865	2.91751	1.20919	2598.1	537157
828	685584	567663552	28.7750	9.3902	2.91803	1.20773	2601.2	538456
829	687241	569722789	28.7924	9.3940	2.91855	1.20627	2604.4	539758
830	688900	571787000	28.8097	9.3978	2.91908	1.20482	2607.5	541061
831	690561	573856191	28.8271	9.4016	2.91960	1.20337	2610.7	542365
832	692224	575930368	28.8444	9.4053	2.92012	1.20192	2613.8	543671
833	693889	578009537	28.8617	9.4091	2.92065	1.20048	2616.9	544979
834	695556	580093704	28.8791	9.4129	2.92117	1.19904	2620.1	546288
835	697225	582182875	28.8964	9.4166	2.92169	1.19760	2623.2	547599
836	698896	584277056	28.9137	9.4204	2.92221	1.19617	2626.4	548912
837	700569	586376253	28.9310	9.4241	2.92273	1.19474	2629.5	550226
838	702244	588480472	28.9482	9.4279	2.92324	1.19332	2632.7	551541
839	703921	590589719	28.9655	9.4316	2.92376	1.19190	2635.8	552858
840	705600	592704000	28.9828	9.4354	2.92428	1.19048	2638.9	554177
841	707281	594823321	29.0000	9.4391	2.92480	1.18906	2642.1	555497
842	708964	596947688	29.0172	9.4429	2.92531	1.18765	2645.2	556819
843	710649	599077107	29.0345	9.4466	2.92583	1.18624	2648.4	558142
844	712336	601211584	29.0517	9.4503	2.92634	1.18483	2651.5	559467
845	714025	603351125	29.0689	9.4541	2.92686	1.18343	2654.6	560794
846	715716	605495736	29.0861	9.4578	2.92737	1.18203	2657.8	562122
847	717409	607645423	29.1033	9.4615	2.92788	1.18064	2660.9	563452
848	719104	609800192	29.1204	9.4652	2.92840	1.17925	2664.1	564783
849	720801	611960049	29.1376	9.4690	2.92891	1.17786	2667.2	566116

FUNCTIONS OF NUMBERS

950 – 999

No.	Square	Cube	Square Root	Cube Root	Logarithm	1000 × Reciprocal	No. = Diameter Circum.	No. = Diameter Area
950	902500	857375000	30.8221	9.8305	2.97772	1.05263	2984.5	708822
951	904401	860085351	30.8383	9.8339	2.97818	1.05152	2987.7	710315
952	906304	862801408	30.8545	9.8374	2.97864	1.05042	2990.8	711809
953	908209	865523177	30.8707	9.8408	2.97909	1.04932	2993.9	713306
954	910116	868250664	30.8869	9.8443	2.97955	1.04822	2997.1	714803
955	912025	870983875	30.9031	9.8477	2.98000	1.04712	3000.2	716303
956	913936	873722816	30.9192	9.8511	2.98046	1.04603	3003.4	717804
957	915849	876467493	30.9354	9.8546	2.98091	1.04493	3006.6	719306
958	917764	879217912	30.9516	9.8580	2.98137	1.04384	3009.6	720810
959	919681	881974079	30.9677	9.8614	2.98182	1.04275	3012.8	722316
960	921600	884736000	30.9839	9.8648	2.98227	1.04167	3015.9	723823
961	923521	887503681	31.0000	9.8683	2.98272	1.04058	3019.1	725332
962	925444	890277128	31.0161	9.8717	2.98318	1.03950	3022.2	726842
963	927369	893056347	31.0322	9.8751	2.98363	1.03842	3025.4	728354
964	929296	895841344	31.0483	9.8785	2.98408	1.03734	3028.5	729867
965	931225	898632125	31.0644	9.8819	2.98453	1.03627	3031.6	731382
966	933156	901428696	31.0805	9.8854	2.98498	1.03520	3034.8	732899
967	935089	904231063	31.0966	9.8888	2.98543	1.03413	3037.9	734417
968	937024	907039232	31.1127	9.8922	2.98588	1.03306	3041.1	735937
969	938961	909853209	31.1288	9.8956	2.98632	1.03199	3044.2	737458
970	940900	912673000	31.1448	9.8990	2.98677	1.03093	3047.3	738981
971	942841	915498611	31.1609	9.9024	2.98722	1.02987	3050.5	740506
972	944784	918330048	31.1769	9.9058	2.98767	1.02881	3053.6	742032
973	946729	921167317	31.1929	9.9092	2.98811	1.02775	3056.8	743559
974	948676	924010424	31.2090	9.9126	2.98856	1.02669	3059.9	745088
975	950625	926859375	31.2250	9.9160	2.98900	1.02564	3063.1	746619
976	952576	929714176	31.2410	9.9194	2.98945	1.02459	3066.2	748151
977	954529	932574833	31.2570	9.9227	2.98989	1.02354	3069.3	749685
978	956484	935441352	31.2730	9.9261	2.99034	1.02249	3072.5	751221
979	958441	938313739	31.2890	9.9295	2.99078	1.02145	3075.6	752758
980	960400	941192000	31.3050	9.9329	2.99123	1.02041	3078.8	754296
981	962361	944076141	31.3209	9.9363	2.99167	1.01937	3081.9	755837
982	964324	946966168	31.3369	9.9396	2.99211	1.01833	3085.0	757378
983	966289	949862087	31.3528	9.9430	2.99255	1.01729	3088.2	758922
984	968256	952763904	31.3688	9.9464	2.99300	1.01626	3091.3	760466
985	970225	955671625	31.3847	9.9497	2.99344	1.01523	3094.5	762013
986	972196	958585256	31.4006	9.9531	2.99388	1.01420	3097.6	763561
987	974169	961504803	31.4166	9.9565	2.99432	1.01317	3100.8	765111
988	976144	964430272	31.4325	9.9598	2.99476	1.01215	3103.9	766662
989	978121	967361669	31.4484	9.9632	2.99520	1.01112	3107.0	768214
990	980100	970299000	31.4643	9.9666	2.99564	1.01010	3110.2	769769
991	982081	973242271	31.4802	9.9699	2.99607	1.00908	3113.3	771325
992	984064	976191488	31.4960	9.9733	2.99651	1.00806	3116.5	772882
993	986049	979146657	31.5119	9.9766	2.99695	1.00705	3119.6	774441
994	988036	982107784	31.5278	9.9800	2.99739	1.00604	3122.7	776002
995	990025	985074875	31.5436	9.9833	2.99782	1.00503	3125.9	777564
996	992016	988047936	31.5595	9.9866	2.99826	1.00402	3129.0	779128
997	994009	991026973	31.5753	9.9900	2.99870	1.00301	3132.2	780693
998	996004	994011992	31.5911	9.9933	2.99913	1.00200	3135.3	782260
999	998001	997002999	31.6070	9.9967	2.99957	1.00100	3138.5	783828

FUNCTIONS OF NUMBERS

900 – 949

No.	Square	Cube	Square Root	Cube Root	Logarithm	1000 × Reciprocal	No. = Diameter Circum.	No. = Diameter Area
900	810000	729000000	30.0000	9.6549	2.95424	1.11111	2827.4	636173
901	811801	731432701	30.0167	9.6585	2.95472	1.10988	2830.6	637587
902	813604	733870808	30.0333	9.6620	2.95521	1.10865	2833.7	639003
903	815409	736314327	30.0500	9.6656	2.95569	1.10742	2836.9	640421
904	817216	738763264	30.0666	9.6692	2.95617	1.10619	2840.0	641840
905	819025	741217625	30.0832	9.6727	2.95665	1.10497	2843.1	643261
906	820836	743677416	30.0998	9.6763	2.95713	1.10375	2846.3	644683
907	822649	746142643	30.1164	9.6799	2.95761	1.10254	2849.4	646107
908	824464	748613312	30.1330	9.6834	2.95809	1.10132	2852.6	647533
909	826281	751089429	30.1496	9.6870	2.95856	1.10011	2855.7	648960
910	828100	753571000	30.1662	9.6905	2.95904	1.09890	2858.8	650388
911	829921	756058031	30.1828	9.6941	2.95952	1.09769	2862.0	651818
912	831744	758550528	30.1993	9.6976	2.95999	1.09649	2865.1	653250
913	833569	761048497	30.2159	9.7012	2.96047	1.09529	2868.3	654684
914	835396	763551944	30.2324	9.7047	2.96095	1.09409	2871.4	656118
915	837225	766060875	30.2490	9.7082	2.96142	1.09290	2874.6	657555
916	839056	768575296	30.2655	9.7118	2.96190	1.09170	2877.7	658993
917	840889	771095213	30.2820	9.7153	2.96237	1.09051	2880.8	660433
918	842724	773620632	30.2985	9.7188	2.96284	1.08932	2884.0	661874
919	844561	776151559	30.3150	9.7224	2.96332	1.08814	2887.1	663317
920	846400	778688000	30.3315	9.7259	2.96379	1.08696	2890.3	664761
921	848241	781229961	30.3480	9.7294	2.96426	1.08578	2893.4	666207
922	850084	783777448	30.3645	9.7329	2.96473	1.08460	2896.5	667654
923	851929	786330467	30.3809	9.7364	2.96520	1.08342	2899.7	669103
924	853776	788889024	30.3974	9.7400	2.96567	1.08225	2902.8	670554
925	855625	791453125	30.4138	9.7435	2.96614	1.08108	2906.0	672006
926	857476	794022776	30.4302	9.7470	2.96661	1.07991	2909.1	673460
927	859329	796597983	30.4467	9.7505	2.96708	1.07875	2912.3	674915
928	861184	799178752	30.4631	9.7540	2.96755	1.07759	2915.4	676372
929	863041	801765089	30.4795	9.7575	2.96802	1.07643	2918.5	677831
930	864900	804357000	30.4959	9.7610	2.96848	1.07527	2921.7	679291
931	866761	806954491	30.5123	9.7645	2.96895	1.07411	2924.8	680752
932	868624	809557568	30.5287	9.7680	2.96942	1.07296	2928.0	682216
933	870489	812166237	30.5450	9.7715	2.96988	1.07181	2931.1	683680
934	872356	814780504	30.5614	9.7750	2.97035	1.07066	2934.2	685147
935	874225	817400375	30.5778	9.7785	2.97081	1.06952	2937.4	686615
936	876096	820025856	30.5941	9.7819	2.97128	1.06838	2940.5	688084
937	877969	822656953	30.6105	9.7854	2.97174	1.06724	2943.7	689555
938	879844	825293672	30.6268	9.7889	2.97220	1.06610	2946.8	691028
939	881721	827936019	30.6431	9.7924	2.97267	1.06496	2950.0	692502
940	883600	830584000	30.6594	9.7959	2.97313	1.06383	2953.1	693978
941	885481	833237621	30.6757	9.7993	2.97359	1.06270	2956.2	695455
942	887364	835896888	30.6920	9.8028	2.97405	1.06157	2959.4	696934
943	889249	838561807	30.7083	9.8063	2.97451	1.06045	2962.5	698415
944	891136	841232384	30.7246	9.8097	2.97497	1.05932	2965.7	699897
945	893025	843908625	30.7409	9.8132	2.97543	1.05820	2968.8	701380
946	894916	846590536	30.7571	9.8167	2.97589	1.05708	2971.9	702865
947	896809	849278123	30.7734	9.8201	2.97635	1.05597	2975.1	704352
948	898704	851971392	30.7896	9.8236	2.97681	1.05485	2978.2	705840
949	900601	854670349	30.8058	9.8270	2.97727	1.05374	2981.4	707330

DECIMALS OF AN INCH
FOR EACH 64TH OF AN INCH

WITH MILLIMETER EQUIVALENTS

Fraction	¹⁄₆₄ths	Decimal	Millimeters (approx.)	Fraction	¹⁄₆₄ths	Decimal	Millimeters (approx.)
....	1	.015625	0.397	....	33	.515625	13.097
¹⁄₃₂	2	.03125	0.794	¹⁷⁄₃₂	34	.53125	13.494
....	3	.046875	1.191	....	35	.546875	13.891
¹⁄₁₆	4	.0625	1.588	⁹⁄₁₆	36	.5625	14.288
....	5	.078125	1.984	....	37	.578125	14.684
³⁄₃₂	6	.09375	2.381	¹⁹⁄₃₂	38	.59375	15.081
....	7	.109375	2.778	....	39	.609375	15.478
¹⁄₈	8	.125	3.175	⁵⁄₈	40	.625	15.875
....	9	.140625	3.572	....	41	.640625	16.272
⁵⁄₃₂	10	.15625	3.969	²¹⁄₃₂	42	.65625	16.669
....	11	.171875	4.366	....	43	.671875	17.066
³⁄₁₆	12	.1875	4.763	¹¹⁄₁₆	44	.6875	17.463
....	13	.203125	5.159	....	45	.703125	17.859
⁷⁄₃₂	14	.21875	5.556	²³⁄₃₂	46	.71875	18.256
....	15	.234375	5.953	....	47	.734375	18.653
¹⁄₄	16	.250	6.350	³⁄₄	48	.750	19.050
....	17	.265625	6.747	....	49	.765625	19.447
⁹⁄₃₂	18	.28125	7.144	²⁵⁄₃₂	50	.78125	19.844
....	19	.296875	7.541	....	51	.796875	20.241
⁵⁄₁₆	20	.3125	7.938	¹³⁄₁₆	52	.8125	20.638
....	21	.328125	8.334	....	53	.828125	21.034
¹¹⁄₃₂	22	.34375	8.731	²⁷⁄₃₂	54	.84375	21.431
....	23	.359375	9.128	....	55	.859375	21.828
³⁄₈	24	.375	9.525	⁷⁄₈	56	.875	22.225
....	25	.390625	9.922	....	57	.890625	22.622
¹³⁄₃₂	26	.40625	10.319	²⁹⁄₃₂	58	.90625	23.019
....	27	.421875	10.716	....	59	.921875	23.416
⁷⁄₁₆	28	.4375	11.113	¹⁵⁄₁₆	60	.9375	23.813
....	29	.453125	11.509	....	61	.953125	24.209
¹⁵⁄₃₂	30	.46875	11.906	³¹⁄₃₂	62	.96875	24.606
....	31	.484375	12.303	....	63	.984375	25.003
¹⁄₂	32	.500	12.700	1	64	1.000	25.400

DECIMALS OF A FOOT FOR

Inch	0″	1″	2″	3″	4″	5″
0	0	.0833	.1667	.2500	.3333	.4167
1/32	.0026	.0859	.1693	.2526	.3359	.4193
1/16	.0052	.0885	.1719	.2552	.3385	.4219
3/32	.0078	.0911	.1745	.2578	.3411	.4245
1/8	.0104	.0938	.1771	.2604	.3438	.4271
5/32	.0130	.0964	.1797	.2630	.3464	.4297
3/16	.0156	.0990	.1823	.2656	.3490	.4323
7/32	.0182	.1016	.1849	.2682	.3516	.4349
1/4	.0208	.1042	.1875	.2708	.3542	.4375
9/32	.0234	.1068	.1901	.2734	.3568	.4401
5/16	.0260	.1094	.1927	.2760	.3594	.4427
11/32	.0286	.1120	.1953	.2786	.3620	.4453
3/8	.0313	.1146	.1979	.2812	.3646	.4479
13/32	.0339	.1172	.2005	.2839	.3672	.4505
7/16	.0365	.1198	.2031	.2865	.3698	.4531
15/32	.0391	.1224	.2057	.2891	.3724	.4557
1/2	.0417	.1250	.2083	.2917	.3750	.4583
17/32	.0443	.1276	.2109	.2943	.3776	.4609
9/16	.0469	.1302	.2135	.2969	.3802	.4635
19/32	.0495	.1328	.2161	.2995	.3828	.4661
5/8	.0521	.1354	.2188	.3021	.3854	.4688
21/32	.0547	.1380	.2214	.3047	.3880	.4714
11/16	.0573	.1406	.2240	.3073	.3906	.4740
23/32	.0599	.1432	.2266	.3099	.3932	.4766
3/4	.0625	.1458	.2292	.3125	.3958	.4792
25/32	.0651	.1484	.2318	.3151	.3984	.4818
13/16	.0677	.1510	.2344	.3177	.4010	.4844
27/32	.0703	.1536	.2370	.3203	.4036	.4870
7/8	.0729	.1563	.2396	.3229	.4063	.4896
29/32	.0755	.1589	.2422	.3255	.4089	.4922
15/16	.0781	.1615	.2448	.3281	.4115	.4948
31/32	.0807	.1641	.2474	.3307	.4141	.4974

EACH 32ND OF AN INCH

6"	7"	8"	9"	10"	11"
.5000	.5833	.6667	.7500	.8333	.9167
.5026	.5859	.6693	.7526	.8359	.9193
.5052	.5885	.6719	.7552	.8385	.9219
.5078	.5911	.6745	.7578	.8411	.9245
.5104	.5938	.6771	.7604	.8438	.9271
.5130	.5964	.6797	.7630	.8464	.9297
.5156	.5990	.6823	.7656	.8490	.9323
.5182	.6016	.6849	.7682	.8516	.9349
.5208	.6042	.6875	.7708	.8542	.9375
.5234	.6068	.6901	.7734	.8568	.9401
.5260	.6094	.6927	.7760	.8594	.9427
.5286	.6120	.6953	.7786	.8620	.9453
.5313	.6146	.6979	.7813	.8646	.9479
.5339	.6172	.7005	.7839	.8672	.9505
.5365	.6198	.7031	.7865	.8698	.9531
.5391	.6224	.7057	.7891	.8724	.9557
.5417	.6250	.7083	.7917	.8750	.9583
.5443	.6276	.7109	.7943	.8776	.9609
.5469	.6302	.7135	.7969	.8802	.9635
.5495	.6328	.7161	.7995	.8828	.9661
.5521	.6354	.7188	.8021	.8854	.9688
.5547	.6380	.7214	.8047	.8880	.9714
.5573	.6406	.7240	.8073	.8906	.9740
.5599	.6432	.7266	.8099	.8932	.9766
.5625	.6458	.7292	.8125	.8958	.9792
.5651	.6484	.7318	.8151	.8984	.9818
.5677	.6510	.7344	.8177	.9010	.9844
.5703	.6536	.7370	.8203	.9036	.9870
.5729	.6563	.7396	.8229	.9063	.9896
.5755	.6589	.7422	.8255	.9089	.9922
.5781	.6615	.7448	.8281	.9115	.9948
.5807	.6641	.7474	.8307	.9141	.9974

INDEX